# Python for Finance Cookbook

Over 50 recipes for applying modern Python libraries to financial data analysis

**Eryk Lewinson**

**BIRMINGHAM - MUMBAI**

# Python for Finance Cookbook

Copyright © 2020 Packt Publishing

**Commissioning Editor:** Sunith Shetty
**Acquisition Editor:** Joshua Nadar
**Content Development Editor:** Nathanya Dias
**Senior Editor:** Ayaan Hoda
**Technical Editor:** Utkarsha S. Kadam
**Copy Editor:** Safis Editing
**Project Coordinator:** Aishwarya Mohan
**Proofreader:** Safis Editing
**Indexer:** Priyanka Dhadke
**Production Designer:** Shraddha Falebhai

First published: January 2020

Production reference: 1300120

Published by Packt Publishing Ltd.
Livery Place
35 Livery Street
Birmingham
B3 2PB, UK.

ISBN 978-1-78961-851-8

www.packt.com

*To my father. Your love for books was truly inspiring. You will always remain in our hearts*

# Contributors

## About the author

**Eryk Lewinson** received his master's degree in quantitative finance from Erasmus University Rotterdam (EUR). In his professional career, he gained experience in the practical application of data science methods while working for two "Big 4" companies and a Dutch FinTech scale-up. In his work, he focuses on using machine learning to provide business value to his company. In his spare time, he enjoys writing about topics related to data science, playing video games, and traveling with his girlfriend.

*Writing this book was quite a journey for me and I learned a lot during it, both in terms of knowledge and about myself. However, it was not easy, as life showed a considerable number of obstacles. Thankfully, with the help of the people closest to me, I managed to overcome them. I would like to thank my family for always being there for me, my brother for his patience and constructive feedback at random times of the day and night, my girlfriend for her undeterred support and making me believe in myself. I also greatly appreciate all the kind words of encouragement from my friends and colleagues. Without all of you, completing this book would not have been possible. Thank you.*

# About the reviewers

**Ratanlal Mahanta** is currently working as a Managing Partner at bittQsrv, a global quantitative research company offering quant models for its investors. He has several years' experience in the modeling and simulation of quantitative trading. Ratanlal holds a master's degree in science in computational finance, and his research areas include quant trading, optimal execution, and high-frequency trading. He has over 9 years' work experience in the finance industry, and is gifted at solving difficult problems that lie at the intersection of the market, technology, research, and design.

**Jiri Pik** is an artificial intelligence architect and strategist who works with major investment banks, hedge funds, and other players. He has architected and delivered breakthrough trading, portfolio, and risk management systems, as well as decision support systems, across numerous industries.

Jiri's consulting firm, Jiri Pik – RocketEdge, provides its clients with certified expertise, judgment, and execution at the drop of a hat.

# Packt is searching for authors like you

If you're interested in becoming an author for Packt, please visit `authors.packtpub.com` and apply today. We have worked with thousands of developers and tech professionals, just like you, to help them share their insight with the global tech community. You can make a general application, apply for a specific hot topic that we are recruiting an author for, or submit your own idea.

# Table of Contents

# Preface

This book begins by exploring various ways of downloading financial data and preparing it for modeling. We check the basic statistical properties of asset prices and returns, and investigate the existence of so-called **stylized facts**. We then calculate popular indicators used in technical analysis (such as Bollinger Bands, **Moving Average Convergence Divergence (MACD)**, and **Relative Strength Index (RSI)**) and backtest automatic trading strategies built on their basis.

The next section introduces time series analysis and explores popular models such as exponential smoothing, **AutoRegressive Integrated Moving Average (ARIMA)**, and **Generalized Autoregressive Conditional Heteroskedasticity (GARCH)** (including multivariate specifications). We also introduce you to factor models, including the famous **Capital Asset Pricing Model (CAPM)** and the Fama-French three-factor model. We end this section by demonstrating different ways to optimize asset allocation, and we use Monte Carlo simulations for tasks such as calculating the price of American options or estimating the **Value at Risk (VaR)**.

In the last part of the book, we carry out an entire data science project in the financial domain. We approach credit card fraud/default problems using advanced classifiers such as random forest, XGBoost, LightGBM, stacked models, and many more. We also tune the hyperparameters of the models (including Bayesian optimization) and handle class imbalance. We conclude the book by demonstrating how deep learning (using PyTorch) can solve numerous financial problems.

## Who this book is for

This book is for financial analysts, data analysts/scientists, and Python developers who want to learn how to implement a broad range of tasks in the financial domain. This book should also be helpful to data scientists who want to devise intelligent financial strategies in order to perform efficient financial analytics. Working knowledge of the Python programming language is mandatory.

# What this book covers

Chapter 1, *Financial Data and Preprocessing*, explores how financial data is different from other types of data commonly used in machine learning tasks. You will be able to use the functions provided to download financial data from a number of sources (such as Yahoo Finance and Quandl) and preprocess it for further analysis. Finally, you will learn how to investigate whether the data follows the stylized facts of asset returns.

Chapter 2, *Technical Analysis in Python*, demonstrates some fundamental basics of technical analysis as well as how to quickly create elegant dashboards in Python. You will be able to draw some insights into patterns emerging from a selection of the most commonly used metrics (such as MACD and RSI).

Chapter 3, *Time Series Modeling*, introduces the basics of time series modeling (including time series decomposition and statistical stationarity). Then, we look at two of the most widely used approaches of time series modeling—exponential smoothing methods and ARIMA class models. Lastly, we present a novel approach to modeling a time series using the additive model from Facebook's Prophet library.

Chapter 4, *Multi-Factor Models*, shows you how to estimate various factor models in Python. We start with the simplest one-factor model and then explain how to estimate more advanced three-, four-, and five-factor models.

Chapter 5, *Modeling Volatility with GARCH Class Models*, introduces you to the concept of volatility forecasting using (G)ARCH class models, how to choose the best-fitting model, and how to interpret your results.

Chapter 6, *Monte Carlo Simulations in Finance*, introduces you to the concept of Monte Carlo simulations and how to use them for simulating stock prices, the valuation of European/American options, and for calculating the VaR.

Chapter 7, *Asset Allocation in Python*, introduces the concept of Modern Portfolio Theory and shows you how to obtain the Efficient Frontier in Python. Then, we look at how to identify specific portfolios, such as minimum variance or the maximum Sharpe ratio. We also show you how to evaluate the performance of such portfolios.

Chapter 8, *Identifying Credit Default with Machine Learning*, presents a case of using machine learning for predicting credit default. You will get to know the state-of-the-art classification algorithms, learn how to tune the hyperparameters of the models, and handle problems with imbalanced data.

Chapter 9, *Advanced Machine Learning Models in Finance*, introduces you to a selection of advanced classifiers (including stacking multiple models). Additionally, we look at how to deal with class imbalance, use Bayesian optimization for hyperparameter tuning, and retrieve feature importance from a model.

Chapter 10, *Deep Learning in Finance*, demonstrates how to use deep learning techniques for working with time series and tabular data. The networks will be trained using PyTorch (with possible GPU acceleration).

# To get the most out of this book

For this book, we assume that you have the following:

- A good understanding of programming in Python and machine/deep learning models
- Knowledge of how to use popular libraries, such as NumPy, pandas, and matplotlib
- Knowledge of basic statistics and quantitative finance

In this book, we attempt to give you a high-level overview of various techniques; however, we will focus on the practical applications of these methods. For a deeper dive into the theoretical foundations, we provide references for further reading.

The best way to learn anything is by doing. That is why we highly encourage you to experiment with the code samples provided (the code can be found in the accompanying GitHub repository), apply the techniques to different datasets, and explore possible extensions.

The code for this book was successfully run on a MacBook; however, it should work on any operating system. Additionally, you can always use online services such as Google Colab.

At the very beginning of each notebook (available on the book's GitHub repository), we run a few cells that import and set up plotting with matplotlib. We will not mention this later on, as this would be repetitive, so at any time, assume that matplotlib is imported.

In the first cell, we first set up the backend of matplotlib to inline:

```
%matplotlib inline
%config InlineBackend.figure_format = 'retina'
```

By doing so, each plotted figure will appear below the cell that generated it and the plot will also be visible in the Notebook should it be exported to another format (such as PDF or

HTML). The second line is used for MacBooks and displays the plot in higher resolution for Retina displays.

The second cell appears as follows:

```
import matplotlib.pyplot as plt
import warnings

plt.style.use('seaborn')
plt.rcParams['figure.figsize'] = [16, 9]
plt.rcParams['figure.dpi'] = 300
warnings.simplefilter(action='ignore', category=FutureWarning)
```

In this cell, we import `matplotlib` and warnings, set up the style of the plots to `'seaborn'` (this is a personal preference), as well as default plot settings, such as figure size and resolution. We also disable (ignore) some warnings. In some chapters, we might modify these settings for better readability of the figures (especially in black and white).

# Download the example code files

You can download the example code files for this book from your account at `www.packt.com`. If you purchased this book elsewhere, you can visit `www.packtpub.com/support` and register to have the files emailed directly to you.

You can download the code files by following these steps:

1. Log in or register at `www.packt.com`.
2. Select the **Support** tab.
3. Click on **Code Downloads**.
4. Enter the name of the book in the **Search** box and follow the onscreen instructions.

Once the file is downloaded, please make sure that you unzip or extract the folder using the latest version of:

- WinRAR/7-Zip for Windows
- Zipeg/iZip/UnRarX for Mac
- 7-Zip/PeaZip for Linux

The code bundle for the book is also hosted on GitHub at `https://github.com/PacktPublishing/Book-Name`. In case there's an update to the code, it will be updated on the existing GitHub repository.

We also have other code bundles from our rich catalog of books and videos available at `https://github.com/PacktPublishing/`. Check them out!

# Download the color images

We also provide a PDF file that has color images of the screenshots/diagrams used in this book. You can download it here: `https://static.packtcdn.com/downloads/9781789618518_ColorImages.pdf`.

# Conventions used

There are a number of text conventions used throughout this book.

`CodeInText`: Indicates code words in text, database table names, folder names, filenames, file extensions, pathnames, dummy URLs, user input, and Twitter handles. Here is an example: "Finally, we took the natural logarithm of the divided values by using `np.log`."

A block of code is set as follows:

```
df_yahoo = yf.download('AAPL',
                       start='2000-01-01',
                       end='2010-12-31',
                       progress=False)
```

**Bold**: Indicates a new term, an important word, or words that you see on screen. For example, words in menus or dialog boxes appear in the text like this. Here is an example: "A single candlestick (typically corresponding to one day, but a higher frequency is possible) combines the **open, high, low, and close prices (OHLC)**."

 Warnings or important notes appear like this.

 Tips and tricks appear like this.

# Sections

In this book, you will find several headings that appear frequently (*Getting ready, How to do it..., How it works..., There's more...,* and *See also*).

To give clear instructions on how to complete a recipe, use these sections as follows:

# Getting ready

This section tells you what to expect in the recipe and describes how to set up any software or any preliminary settings required for the recipe.

# How to do it...

This section contains the steps required to follow the recipe.

# How it works...

This section usually consists of a detailed explanation of what happened in the previous section.

# There's more...

This section consists of additional information about the recipe in order to make you more knowledgeable about the recipe.

# See also

This section provides helpful links to other useful information for the recipe.

# Get in touch

Feedback from our readers is always welcome.

**General feedback**: If you have questions about any aspect of this book, mention the book title in the subject of your message and email us at `customercare@packtpub.com`.

**Errata**: Although we have taken every care to ensure the accuracy of our content, mistakes do happen. If you have found a mistake in this book, we would be grateful if you would report this to us. Please visit www.packtpub.com/support/errata, selecting your book, clicking on the Errata Submission Form link, and entering the details.

**Piracy**: If you come across any illegal copies of our works in any form on the internet, we would be grateful if you would provide us with the location address or website name. Please contact us at copyright@packt.com with a link to the material.

**If you are interested in becoming an author**: If there is a topic that you have expertise in and you are interested in either writing or contributing to a book, please visit authors.packtpub.com.

# Reviews

Please leave a review. Once you have read and used this book, why not leave a review on the site that you purchased it from? Potential readers can then see and use your unbiased opinion to make purchase decisions, we at Packt can understand what you think about our products, and our authors can see your feedback on their book. Thank you!

For more information about Packt, please visit packt.com.

# 1
# Financial Data and Preprocessing

The first chapter of this book is dedicated to a very important (if not the most important) part of any data science/quantitative finance project—gathering and working with data. In line with the "garbage in, garbage out" maxim, we should strive to have data of the highest possible quality, and correctly preprocess it for later use with statistical and machine learning algorithms. The reason for this is simple—the results of our analyses highly depend on the input data, and no sophisticated model will be able to compensate for that.

In this chapter, we cover the entire process of gathering financial data and preprocessing it into the form that is most commonly used in real-life projects. We begin by presenting a few possible sources of high-quality data, show how to convert prices into returns (which have properties desired by statistical algorithms), and investigate how to rescale asset returns (for example, from daily to monthly or yearly). Lastly, we learn how to investigate whether our data follows certain patterns (called stylized facts) commonly observed in financial assets.

One thing to bear in mind while reading this chapter is that data differs among sources, so the prices we see, for example, at Yahoo Finance and Quandl will most likely differ, as the respective sites also get their data from different sources and might use other methods to adjust the prices for corporate actions. The best practice is to find a source we trust the most concerning a particular type of data (based on, for example, opinion on the internet) and then use it for downloading data.

In this chapter, we cover the following recipes:

- Getting data from Yahoo Finance
- Getting data from Quandl
- Getting data from Intrinio
- Converting prices to returns

- Changing frequency
- Visualizing time series data
- Identifying outliers
- Investigating stylized facts of asset returns

 The content presented in the book is valid for educational purposes only—we show how to apply different statistical/data science techniques to problems in the financial domain, such as stock price prediction and asset allocation. By no means should the information in the book be considered investment advice. Financial markets are very volatile and you should invest only at your own risk!

# Getting data from Yahoo Finance

One of the most popular sources of free financial data is Yahoo Finance. It contains not only historical and current stock prices in different frequencies (daily, weekly, monthly), but also calculated metrics, such as the beta (a measure of the volatility of an individual asset in comparison to the volatility of the entire market) and many more. In this recipe, we focus on retrieving historical stock prices.

For a long period of time, the go-to tool for downloading data from Yahoo Finance was the `pandas-datareader` library. The goal of the library was to extract data from a variety of sources and store it in the form of a `pandas` DataFrame. However, after some changes to the Yahoo Finance API, this functionality was deprecated. It is still good to be familiar with this library, as it facilitates downloading data from sources such as FRED (Federal Reserve Economic Data), the Fama/French Data Library or the World Bank, which might come in handy for different kinds of analyses (some of them are presented in the following chapters).

As of now, the easiest and fastest way of downloading historical stock prices is to use the `yfinance` library (formerly known as `fix_yahoo_finance`), which can be used on top of `pandas-datareader` or as a standalone library for downloading stock prices from Yahoo Finance. We focus on the latter use case.

For the sake of this example, we are interested in Apple's stock prices from the years 2000-2010.

# How to do it...

Execute the following steps to download data from Yahoo Finance.

1. Import the libraries:

```
import pandas as pd
import yfinance as yf
```

2. Download the data:

```
df_yahoo = yf.download('AAPL',
                       start='2000-01-01',
                       end='2010-12-31',
                       progress=False)
```

We can inspect the downloaded data:

| ⬍ | Open ⬍ | High ⬍ | Low ⬍ | Close ⬍ | Adj Close ⬍ | Volume ⬍ |
|---|---|---|---|---|---|---|
| Date ⬍ | ⬍ | ⬍ | ⬍ | ⬍ | ⬍ | ⬍ |
| 1999-12-31 | 3.604911 | 3.674107 | 3.553571 | 3.671875 | 3.194901 | 40952800 |
| 2000-01-03 | 3.745536 | 4.017857 | 3.631696 | 3.997768 | 3.478462 | 133949200 |
| 2000-01-04 | 3.866071 | 3.950893 | 3.613839 | 3.660714 | 3.185191 | 128094400 |
| 2000-01-05 | 3.705357 | 3.948661 | 3.678571 | 3.714286 | 3.231803 | 194580400 |
| 2000-01-06 | 3.790179 | 3.821429 | 3.392857 | 3.392857 | 2.952128 | 191993200 |

The result of the request is a DataFrame (2,767 rows) containing daily **Open, High, Low,** and **Close (OHLC)** prices, as well as the adjusted close price and volume.

# How it works...

The download function is very intuitive; in the most basic case, we just need to provide the ticker (symbol), and it will try to download all data since 1950.

In the preceding example, we downloaded data from a specific range (2000-2010).

# There's more...

Some additional features of the `download` function:

- We can pass a list of multiple tickers, such as `['AAPL', 'MSFT']`.
- We can set `auto_adjust=True` to download only the adjusted prices.
- We can additionally download dividends and stock splits by setting `actions='inline'`.
- Setting `progress=False` disables the progress bar.

Another popular library for downloading data from Yahoo Finance is `yahoofinancials`.

# Getting data from Quandl

Quandl is a provider of alternative data products for investment professionals, and offers an easy way to download data, also via a Python library.

A good starting place for financial data would be the WIKI Prices database, which contains stock prices, dividends, and splits for 3,000 US publicly traded companies. The drawback of this database is that as of April, 2018, it is no longer supported (meaning there is no recent data). However, for purposes of getting historical data or learning how to access the databases, it is more than enough.

We use the same example that we used in the previous recipe – we download Apple's stock prices for the years 2000-2010.

# Getting ready

Before downloading the data, we need to create an account at Quandl (`https://www.quandl.com`) and then we can find our personal API key in our profile (`https://www.quandl.com/account/profile`). We can search for data of interest using the search functionality (`https://www.quandl.com/search`).

# How to do it...

Execute the following steps to download data from Quandl.

1. Import the libraries:

```
import pandas as pd
import quandl
```

2. Authenticate using the personal API key:

```
QUANDL_KEY = '{key}'
quandl.ApiConfig.api_key = QUANDL_KEY
```

You need to replace {key} with your own API key.

3. Download the data:

```
df_quandl = quandl.get(dataset='WIKI/AAPL',
                       start_date='2000-01-01',
                       end_date='2010-12-31')
```

We can inspect the downloaded data:

| | Open ⬍ | High ⬍ | Low ⬍ | Close ⬍ | Volume ⬍ | Ex-Dividend ⬍ | Split Ratio ⬍ | Adj. Open ⬍ | Adj. High ⬍ | Adj. Low ⬍ | Adj. Close ⬍ | Adj. Volume ⬍ |
|---|---|---|---|---|---|---|---|---|---|---|---|---|
| Date ⬍ | ⬍ | ⬍ | ⬍ | ⬍ | ⬍ | ⬍ | ⬍ | ⬍ | ⬍ | ⬍ | ⬍ | ⬍ |
| 2000-01-03 | 104.87 | 112.50 | 101.69 | 111.94 | 4783900.0 | 0.0 | 1.0 | 3.369314 | 3.614454 | 3.267146 | 3.596463 | 133949200.0 |
| 2000-01-04 | 108.25 | 110.62 | 101.19 | 102.50 | 4574800.0 | 0.0 | 1.0 | 3.477908 | 3.554053 | 3.251081 | 3.293170 | 128094400.0 |
| 2000-01-05 | 103.75 | 110.56 | 103.00 | 104.00 | 6949300.0 | 0.0 | 1.0 | 3.333330 | 3.552125 | 3.309234 | 3.341362 | 194580400.0 |
| 2000-01-06 | 106.12 | 107.00 | 95.00 | 95.00 | 6856900.0 | 0.0 | 1.0 | 3.409475 | 3.437748 | 3.052206 | 3.052206 | 191993200.0 |
| 2000-01-07 | 96.50 | 101.00 | 95.50 | 99.50 | 4113700.0 | 0.0 | 1.0 | 3.100399 | 3.244977 | 3.068270 | 3.196784 | 115183600.0 |

The result of the request is a DataFrame (2,767 rows) containing the daily OHLC prices, the adjusted prices, dividends, and potential stock splits.

# How it works...

The first step after importing the required libraries was authentication using the API key (paste it instead of {key}). When providing the dataset argument, we used the following structure: DATASET/TICKER.

# There's more...

Some additional features of the `get` function are:

- We can specify multiple datasets at once using a list such as `['WIKI/AAPL', 'WIKI/MSFT']`.
- The `collapse` parameter can be used to define the frequency (available options: daily, weekly, monthly, quarterly, or annually).

# See also

Additional resources are available here:

- `https://github.com/quandl/quandl-python/blob/master/FOR_DEVELOPERS.md`—You can read the *Detailed Method Guide* to discover more functionalities offered by the library, such as inspecting the list of databases and their contents in Python.

# Getting data from Intrinio

Another source of financial data is Intrinio, which offers access to its free (with limits) database. An additional feature is that we can also download already calculated technical indicators such as the **Moving Average Convergence Divergence** (**MACD**) and many more.

 Please see `https://github.com/intrinio/python-sdk` for the full list of available indicators to download.

The database is not only restricted to stock prices, but we follow with the preceding example of downloading Apple's stock prices for the years 2000-2010.

# Getting ready

Before downloading the data, we need to register at `https://intrinio.com` to obtain the API key.

# How to do it...

Execute the following steps to download data from Intrinio.

1. Import the libraries:

```
import intrinio_sdk
import pandas as pd
```

2. Authenticate using the personal API key, and select the API:

```
intrinio_sdk.ApiClient().configuration.api_key['api_key'] = '{key}'
security_api = intrinio_sdk.SecurityApi()
```

You need to replace `{key}` with your own API key.

3. Request the data:

```
r = security_api.get_security_stock_prices(identifier='AAPL',
                                           start_date='2000-01-01',
                                           end_date='2010-12-31',
                                           frequency='daily',
                                           page_size=10000)
```

4. Convert the results into a DataFrame:

```
response_list = [x.to_dict() for x in r.stock_prices]
df_intrinio = pd.DataFrame(response_list).sort_values('date')
df_intrinio.set_index('date', inplace=True)
```

The output looks like this:

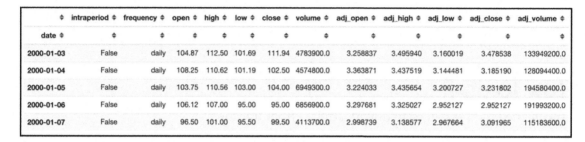

| date | intraperiod | frequency | open | high | low | close | volume | adj_open | adj_high | adj_low | adj_close | adj_volume |
|---|---|---|---|---|---|---|---|---|---|---|---|---|
| 2000-01-03 | False | daily | 104.87 | 112.50 | 101.69 | 111.94 | 4783900.0 | 3.258837 | 3.495940 | 3.160019 | 3.478538 | 133949200.0 |
| 2000-01-04 | False | daily | 108.25 | 110.62 | 101.19 | 102.50 | 4574800.0 | 3.363871 | 3.437519 | 3.144481 | 3.185190 | 128094400.0 |
| 2000-01-05 | False | daily | 103.75 | 110.56 | 103.00 | 104.00 | 6949300.0 | 3.224033 | 3.435654 | 3.200727 | 3.231802 | 194580400.0 |
| 2000-01-06 | False | daily | 106.12 | 107.00 | 95.00 | 95.00 | 6856900.0 | 3.297681 | 3.325027 | 2.952127 | 2.952127 | 191993200.0 |
| 2000-01-07 | False | daily | 96.50 | 101.00 | 95.50 | 99.50 | 4113700.0 | 2.998739 | 3.138577 | 2.967664 | 3.091965 | 115183600.0 |

The resulting DataFrame (2,771 rows) contains the OHLC prices and volume, as well as their adjusted counterparts.

# How it works...

The first step after importing the required libraries was to authenticate using the API key (paste it instead of {key}). Then, we selected the API we wanted to use for the recipe – in the case of stock prices, it was `SecurityApi`.

To download the data, we used the `get_security_stock_prices` method of the `SecurityApi` class. The parameters we can specify are as follows:

- `identifier`: Stock ticker or another acceptable identifier.
- `start_date`/`end_date`: This is self-explanatory.
- `frequency`: Which data frequency is of interest to us (available choices: daily, weekly, monthly, quarterly, or yearly).
- `page_size`: Defines the number of observations to return on one page; we set it to a high number to collect all data in one request with no need for the `next_page` token.

The API returns a JSON-like object, which we then transformed into a DataFrame and set the date as an index using the `set_index` method of a `pandas` DataFrame.

# There's more...

In this chapter, we have covered a few sources of financial data. Some additional, potentially interesting data sources are:

- `iexfinance`: A library that can be used to download data from IEX Cloud
- `tiingo`: A library that can be used to download data from Tiingo
- `alpha_vantage`: A library that is a wrapper for the Alpha Vantage API

# Converting prices to returns

Asset prices are usually non-stationary, that is, their statistics, such as mean and variance (mathematical moments) change over time. This could also mean observing some trends or seasonality in the price series (see `Chapter 3`, *Time Series Modeling*). By transforming the prices into returns, we attempt to make the time series stationary, which is the desired property in statistical modeling.

There are two types of returns:

- **Simple returns:** They aggregate over assets; the simple return of a portfolio is the weighted sum of the returns of the individual assets in the portfolio. Simple returns are defined as:

$$R_t = (P_t - P_{t-1})/P_{t-1} = P_t/P_{t-1} - 1$$

- **Log returns:** They aggregate over time; it is easier to understand with the help of an example—the log return for a given month is the sum of the log returns of the days within that month. Log returns are defined as:

$$r_t = log(P_t/P_{t-1}) = log(P_t) - log(P_{t-1})$$

$P_t$ is the price of an asset in time $t$. In the preceding case, we do not consider dividends, which obviously impact the returns and require a small modification of the formulas.

The best practice while working with stock prices is to use adjusted values, as they account for possible corporate actions, such as stock splits.

The difference between simple and log returns for daily/intraday data will be very small, however, the general rule is that log returns are smaller in value than simple returns.

In this recipe, we show how to calculate both types of returns using Apple's stock prices.

# How to do it...

Execute the following steps to download the stock prices and calculate simple/log returns.

1. Import the libraries:

```
import pandas as pd
import numpy as np
import yfinance as yf
```

2. Download the data and keep the adjusted close prices only:

```
df = yf.download('AAPL',
                 start='2000-01-01',
                 end='2010-12-31',
                 progress=False)

df = df.loc[:, ['Adj Close']]
df.rename(columns={'Adj Close':'adj_close'}, inplace=True)
```

3. Calculate the simple and log returns using the adjusted close prices:

```
df['simple_rtn'] = df.adj_close.pct_change()
df['log_rtn'] = np.log(df.adj_close/df.adj_close.shift(1))
```

The resulting DataFrame looks as follows:

| Date | adj_close | simple_rtn | log_rtn |
|---|---|---|---|
| 1999-12-31 | 3.194901 | NaN | NaN |
| 2000-01-03 | 3.478462 | 0.088754 | 0.085034 |
| 2000-01-04 | 3.185191 | -0.084311 | -0.088078 |
| 2000-01-05 | 3.231803 | 0.014634 | 0.014528 |
| 2000-01-06 | 2.952128 | -0.086538 | -0.090514 |

The first row will always contain a **not a number (NaN)** value, as there is no previous price to use for calculating the returns.

# How it works...

In *Step 2*, we downloaded price data from Yahoo Finance, and only kept the adjusted close price for the returns calculation.

To calculate the simple returns, we used the `pct_change` method of `pandas` Series/DataFrame, which calculates the percentage change between the current and prior element (we can specify the number of lags, but for this specific case, the default value of 1 suffices).

To calculate the log returns, we followed the formula given in the introduction to this recipe. When dividing each element of the series by its lagged value, we used the `shift` method with a value of 1 to access the prior element. In the end, we took the natural logarithm of the divided values by using `np.log`.

# There's more...

We will also discuss how to account for inflation in the returns series. To do so, we continue with the example used in this recipe.

We first download the monthly **Consumer Price Index** (**CPI**) values from Quandl and calculate the percentage change (simple return) in the index. We can then merge the inflation data with Apple's stock returns, and account for inflation by using the following formula:

$$R_t^r = \frac{1 + R_t}{1 + \pi_t} - 1$$

Here, $R_t$ is a time $t$ simple return and $\pi_t$ is the inflation rate.

Execute the following steps to account for inflation in the returns series.

1. Import libraries and authenticate:

```
import pandas as pd
import quandl

QUANDL_KEY = '{key}'
quandl.ApiConfig.api_key = QUANDL_KEY
```

2. Create a DataFrame with all possible dates, and left join the prices to it:

```
df_all_dates = pd.DataFrame(index=pd.date_range(start='1999-12-31',
                                                 end='2010-12-31'))
df = df_all_dates.join(df[['adj_close']], how='left') \
                 .fillna(method='ffill') \
                 .asfreq('M')
```

We used a left join, which is a type of join (used for merging DataFrames) that returns all rows from the left table and the matched rows from the right table while leaving the unmatched rows empty. In case the last day of the month was not a trading day, we used the last known price of that month (fillna(method='ffill')). Lastly, we selected the end-of-month rows only by applying asfreq('M').

3. Download the inflation data from Quandl:

```
df_cpi = quandl.get(dataset='RATEINF/CPI_USA',
                    start_date='1999-12-01',
                    end_date='2010-12-31')
df_cpi.rename(columns={'Value':'cpi'}, inplace=True)
```

4. Merge the inflation data to the prices:

```
df_merged = df.join(df_cpi, how='left')
```

5. Calculate the simple returns and inflation rate:

```
df_merged['simple_rtn'] = df_merged.adj_close.pct_change()
df_merged['inflation_rate'] = df_merged.cpi.pct_change()
```

6. Adjust the returns for inflation:

```
df_merged['real_rtn'] = (df_merged.simple_rtn + 1) /
(df_merged.inflation_rate + 1) - 1
```

The output looks as follows:

| ⬦ | adj_close ⬦ | cpi ⬦ | simple_rtn ⬦ | inflation_rate ⬦ | real_rtn ⬦ |
|---|---|---|---|---|---|
| **1999-12-31** | 3.194901 | 168.3 | NaN | NaN | NaN |
| **2000-01-31** | 3.224035 | 168.8 | 0.009119 | 0.002971 | 0.006130 |
| **2000-02-29** | 3.561976 | 169.8 | 0.104819 | 0.005924 | 0.098313 |
| **2000-03-31** | 4.220376 | 171.2 | 0.184841 | 0.008245 | 0.175152 |
| **2000-04-30** | 3.855247 | 171.3 | -0.086516 | 0.000584 | -0.087049 |

The DataFrame contains all the intermediate results, and the `real_rtn` column contains the inflation-adjusted returns.

# Changing frequency

The general rule of thumb for changing frequency can be broken down into the following:

- Multiply/divide the log returns by the number of time periods.
- Multiply/divide the volatility by the square root of the number of time periods.

In this recipe, we present an example of how to calculate the monthly realized volatilities for Apple using daily returns and then annualize the values.

The formula for realized volatility is as follows:

$$RV = \sqrt{\sum_{i=1}^{T} r_t^2}$$

Realized volatility is frequently used for daily volatility using the intraday returns.

The steps we need to take are as follows:

- Download the data and calculate the log returns.
- Calculate the realized volatility over the months.
- Annualize the values by multiplying by $\sqrt{12}$, as we are converting from monthly values.

# Getting ready

We assume you have followed the instructions from earlier recipes and have a DataFrame called df with a single log_rtn column and timestamps as the index.

# How to do it...

Execute the following steps to calculate and annualize the monthly realized volatility.

1. Import the libraries:

```
import pandas as pd
```

2. Define the function for calculating the realized volatility:

```
def realized_volatility(x):
    return np.sqrt(np.sum(x**2))
```

3. Calculate the monthly realized volatility:

```
df_rv = df.groupby(pd.Grouper(freq='M')).apply(realized_volatility)
df_rv.rename(columns={'log_rtn': 'rv'}, inplace=True)
```

4. Annualize the values:

```
df_rv.rv = df_rv.rv * np.sqrt(12)
```

5. Plot the results:

```
fig, ax = plt.subplots(2, 1, sharex=True)
ax[0].plot(df)
ax[1].plot(df_rv)
```

Executing the preceding code results in the following plots:

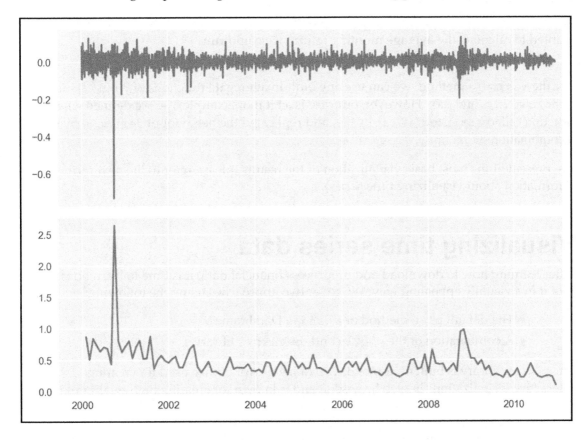

We can see that the spikes in the realized volatility coincide with some extreme returns (which might be outliers).

# How it works...

Normally, we could use the `resample` method of a `pandas` DataFrame. Supposing we wanted to calculate the average monthly return, we could run `df.log_rtn.resample('M').mean()`.

For the `resample` method, we can use any built-in aggregate functions of `pandas`, such as `mean`, `sum`, `min`, and `max`. However, our case is a bit more complex, so we defined a helper function called `realized_volatility`, and replicated the behavior of `resample` by using a combination of `groupby`, `Grouper`, and `apply`.

We presented the most basic visualization of the results (please refer to the next recipe for information about visualizing time series).

# Visualizing time series data

After learning how to download and preprocess financial data, it is time to learn how to plot it in a visually appealing way. We cover two approaches using the following:

- The default `plot` method of a `pandas` DataFrame
- A combination of the `plotly` and `cufflinks` libraries

The `plotly` library is built on top of `d3.js` (a JavaScript library used for creating interactive visualizations in web browsers) and is known for creating high-quality plots with a significant degree of interactivity (inspecting values of observations, viewing tooltips of a given point, zooming in, and so on). Plotly is also the company responsible for developing this library and provides hosting for our visualizations. We can create an infinite number of offline visualizations and up to 25 free ones to share online (with a limited number of views per day).

The `cufflinks` library also makes the process easier, as it enables us to create the `plotly` visualizations directly on top of `pandas` DataFrames.

In this recipe, we plot Microsoft's stock prices (all-time) and returns. For details on how to download and preprocess the data, please refer to the earlier recipes.

# Getting ready

For this recipe, we assume we already have a DataFrame called df with three columns (adj_close, simple_rtn, and log_rtn) and dates set as the index. Please refer to the notebook on the GitHub repository for details on downloading data for this recipe.

# How to do it...

In this section, we introduce how to plot time series data. We start by using the default plot method of a pandas DataFrame/Series, and then present the interactive alternative offered by the combination of plotly and cufflinks.

## The plot method of pandas

Execute the following code to plot Microsoft's stock prices together with the simple and log returns.

```
fig, ax = plt.subplots(3, 1, figsize=(24, 20), sharex=True)

df.adj_close.plot(ax=ax[0])
ax[0].set(title = 'MSFT time series',
          ylabel = 'Stock price ($)')
df.simple_rtn.plot(ax=ax[1])
ax[1].set(ylabel = 'Simple returns (%)')

df.log_rtn.plot(ax=ax[2])
ax[2].set(xlabel = 'Date',
          ylabel = 'Log returns (%)')
```

Executing the preceding code results in the following plot:

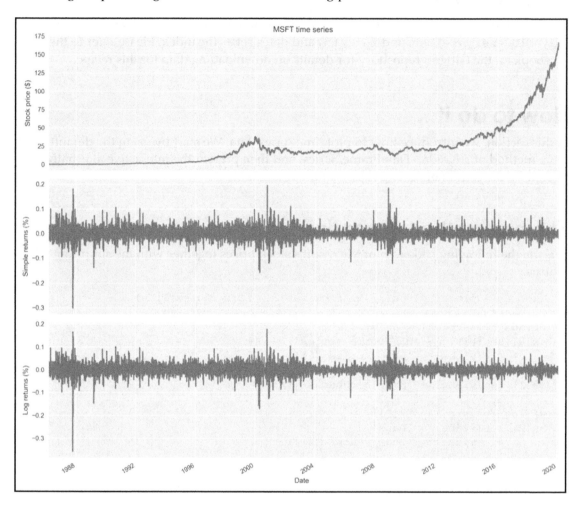

The resulting plot contains three axes. Each one of them presents a different series: raw prices, simple returns, and log returns. Inspecting the plot in such a setting enables us to see the periods of heightened volatility and what was happening at the same time with the price of Microsoft's stock. Additionally, we see how similar simple and log returns are.

# plotly and cufflinks

Execute the following code to plot Microsoft's stock prices together with the simple and log returns.

1. Import the libraries and handle the settings:

```
import cufflinks as cf
from plotly.offline import iplot, init_notebook_mode

# set up configuration (run it once)
#cf.set_config_file(world_readable=True, theme='pearl',
#                   offline=True)

init_notebook_mode()
```

2. Create the plot:

```
df.iplot(subplots=True, shape=(3,1), shared_xaxes=True,
         title='MSFT time series')
```

We can observe the time series in the following plot:

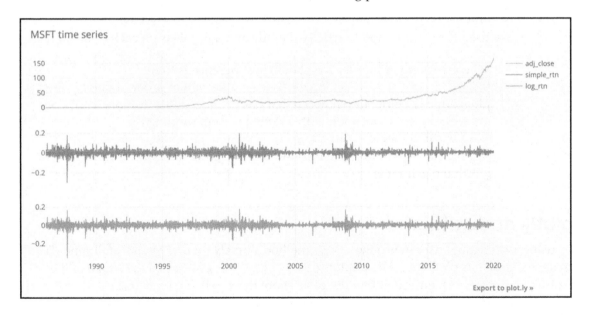

The main advantage of using `plotly` with `cufflinks` is the interactivity of the preceding chart, which is unfortunately only demonstrable in the Notebook (please refer to the accompanying GitHub repository).

# How it works...

In the next section, we go over the details of the two selected methods of plotting time series in Python.

## The plot method of pandas

Our goal was to visualize all three series on the same plot (sharing the *x*-axis) to enable a quick visual comparison. To achieve this, we had to complete the following steps:

- We created a subplot, which we then populated with individual plots. We specified that we wanted three plots vertically (by indicating `plt.subplots(3, 1)`). We also specified the figure size by setting the `figsize` parameter.
- We added the individual plots using the `plot` method on a single Series (column) and specifying the axis on which we wanted to place the plot.
- We used the `set` method to specify the title and axis labels on each of the plots.

When working in Jupyter Notebook, best practice is to run the `%matplotlib inline` magic (once per kernel) in order to display the plots directly below the code cell that has produced it. Additionally, if you are working on a MacBook with a Retina screen, running the extra IPython magic `%config InlineBackend.figure_format ='retina'` will double the resolution of the plots we make. Definitely worth the extra line!

## plotly and cufflinks

By using `cufflinks`, we can use the `iplot` method directly on a `pandas` DataFrame. To create the previous plot, we used subplots (`subplots=True`), specified the shape of the figure (`shape=(3,1)`), indicated that the plots share the x-axis (`shared_xaxes=True`), and added the title (`title='MSFT time series'`). By default, the selected type of plot is a line chart (`kind='line'`).

One note about using `plotly` in Jupyter—in order to share a notebook with the option to view the plot (without running the script again), you should use `nbviewer` or render the notebook as an HTML file and share it then.

The extra line of code `cf.set_config_file(world_readable=True, theme='pearl', offline=True)` sets up the configuration (such as the current theme or the offline mode) and should be used only once. It can be used again to reconfigure.

# There's more...

There are many more ways to create plots in Python. We list some of the libraries:

- `matplotlib`
- `seaborn`
- `plotly`
- `plotly_express`
- `altair`
- `plotnine`

We have decided to present the two selected for their simplicity, however, a specific use case might require using some of the previously mentioned libraries as they offer more freedom when creating the visualization. We should also mention that the `plot` method of a `pandas` DataFrame actually uses `matplotlib` for plotting, but the `pandas` API makes the process easier.

# See also

Additional resources are available here:

- `cufflinks` **documentation:** `https://plot.ly/python/v3/ipython-notebooks/cufflinks/`
- **nbviewer:** `https://nbviewer.jupyter.org/`

# Identifying outliers

While working with any kind of data, we often encounter observations that are significantly different from the majority, that is, outliers. They can be a result of a wrong tick (price), something major happening on the financial markets, an error in the data processing pipeline, and so on. Many machine learning algorithms and statistical approaches can be influenced by outliers, leading to incorrect/biased results. That is why we should handle the outliers before creating any models.

In this recipe, we look into detecting outliers using the 3σ approach.

# Getting ready

We continue from the *Converting prices to returns* recipe and have a DataFrame with Apple's stock price history and returns.

# How to do it...

Execute the following steps to detect outliers using the 3σ approach, and mark them on a plot.

1. Calculate the rolling mean and standard deviation:

```
df_rolling = df[['simple_rtn']].rolling(window=21) \
                        .agg(['mean', 'std'])
df_rolling.columns = df_rolling.columns.droplevel()
```

2. Join the rolling metrics to the original data:

```
df_outliers = df.join(df_rolling)
```

3. Define a function for detecting outliers:

```
def indentify_outliers(row, n_sigmas=3):
    x = row['simple_rtn']
    mu = row['mean']
    sigma = row['std']
    if (x > mu + 3 * sigma) | (x < mu - 3 * sigma):
        return 1
    else:
        return 0
```

4. Identify the outliers and extract their values for later use:

```
df_outliers['outlier'] = df_outliers.apply(indentify_outliers,
                                            axis=1)
outliers = df_outliers.loc[df_outliers['outlier'] == 1,
                            ['simple_rtn']]
```

5. Plot the results:

```
fig, ax = plt.subplots()

ax.plot(df_outliers.index, df_outliers.simple_rtn,
        color='blue', label='Normal')
ax.scatter(outliers.index, outliers.simple_rtn,
            color='red', label='Anomaly')
ax.set_title("Apple's stock returns")
ax.legend(loc='lower right')
```

Executing the code results in the following plot:

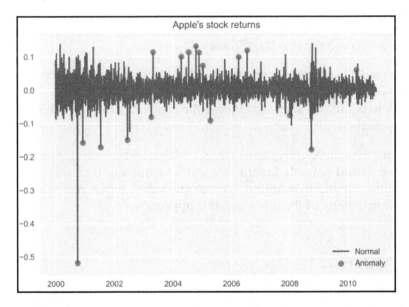

In the plot, we can observe outliers marked with a red dot. One thing to notice is that when there are two large returns in the vicinity, the algorithm identifies the first one as an outlier and the second one as a regular observation. This might be due to the fact that the first outlier enters the rolling window and affects the moving average/standard deviation.

We should also be aware of the so-called **ghost effect/feature**. When a single outlier enters the rolling window, it inflates the values of the rolling statistics for as long as it is in the window.

# How it works...

In the 3σ approach, for each time point, we calculated the moving average (μ) and standard deviation (σ) using the last 21 days (not including that day). We used 21 as this is the average number of trading days in a month, and we work with daily data. However, we can choose different values, and then the moving average will react faster/slower to changes. We can also use (exponentially) weighted moving average if we find it more meaningful in our particular case.

The condition for a given observation x to be qualified as an outlier is $x > μ + 3σ$ or $x < μ - 3σ$.

In the first step, we calculated the rolling metrics using the `rolling` method of a `pandas` DataFrame. We specified the window's size and the metrics we would like to calculate. In the second step, we joined the two DataFrames.

In *Step 3*, we defined a function that returns 1 if the observation is considered an outlier, according to the 3σ rule (we parametrized the number of standard deviations), and 0 otherwise. Then, in the fourth step, we applied the function to all rows in the DataFrame using the `apply` method.

In the last step, we visualized the returns series and marked the outliers using a red dot. In real-life cases, we should not only identify the outliers, but also treat them, for example, by capping them at the maximum/minimum acceptable value, replacing them by interpolated values, or by following any of the other possible approaches.

# There's more...

There are many different methods of identifying outliers in a time series, for example, using Isolation Forest, Hampel Filter, Support Vector Machines, and z-score (which is similar to the presented approach).

# Investigating stylized facts of asset returns

**Stylized facts** are statistical properties that appear to be present in many empirical asset returns (across time and markets). It is important to be aware of them because when we are building models that are supposed to represent asset price dynamics, the models must be able to capture/replicate these properties.

In the following recipes, we investigate the five stylized facts using an example of daily S&P 500 returns from the years 1985 to 2018.

## Getting ready

We download the S&P 500 prices from Yahoo Finance (following the approach in the *Getting data from Yahoo Finance* recipe) and calculate returns as in the *Converting prices to returns* recipe.

We use the following code to import all the required libraries:

```
import pandas as pd
import numpy as np
import yfinance as yf
import seaborn as sns
import scipy.stats as scs
import statsmodels.api as sm
import statsmodels.tsa.api as smt
```

## How to do it...

In this section, we investigate, one by one, five stylized facts in the S&P 500 series.

# Non-Gaussian distribution of returns

Run the following steps to investigate the existence of this first fact by plotting the histogram of returns and a Q-Q plot.

1. Calculate the normal **Probability Density Function (PDF)** using the mean and standard deviation of the observed returns:

```
r_range = np.linspace(min(df.log_rtn), max(df.log_rtn), num=1000)
mu = df.log_rtn.mean()
sigma = df.log_rtn.std()
norm_pdf = scs.norm.pdf(r_range, loc=mu, scale=sigma)
```

2. Plot the histogram and the Q-Q plot:

```
fig, ax = plt.subplots(1, 2, figsize=(16, 8))

# histogram
sns.distplot(df.log_rtn, kde=False, norm_hist=True, ax=ax[0])
ax[0].set_title('Distribution of MSFT returns', fontsize=16)
ax[0].plot(r_range, norm_pdf, 'g', lw=2,
           label=f'N({mu:.2f}, {sigma**2:.4f})')
ax[0].legend(loc='upper left');

# Q-Q plot
qq = sm.qqplot(df.log_rtn.values, line='s', ax=ax[1])
ax[1].set_title('Q-Q plot', fontsize = 16)
```

Executing the preceding code results in the following plot:

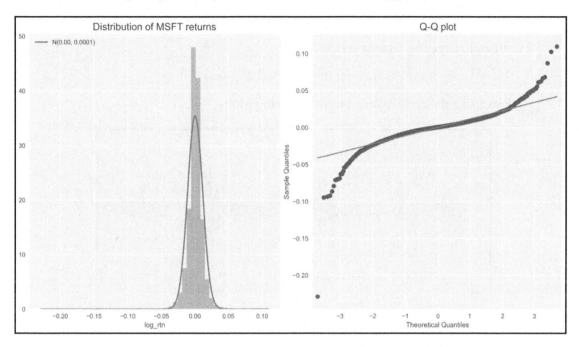

We can use the histogram (showing the shape of the distribution) and the Q-Q plot to assess the normality of the log returns. Additionally, we can print the summary statistics (please refer to the GitHub repository for the code):

```
---------- Descriptive Statistics ----------
Range of dates: 1985-01-02 - 2018-12-28
Number of observations: 8569
Mean: 0.0003
Median: 0.0006
Min: -0.2290
Max: 0.1096
Standard Deviation: 0.0113
Skewness: -1.2624
Kurtosis: 28.0111
Jarque-Bera statistic: 282076.61 with p-value: 0.00
```

By looking at the metrics such as the mean, standard deviation, skewness, and kurtosis we can infer that they deviate from what we would expect under normality. Additionally, the Jarque-Bera normality test gives us reason to reject the null hypothesis stating that the distribution is normal at the 99% confidence level.

# Volatility clustering

Run the following code to investigate this second fact by plotting the log returns series.

1.  Visualize the log returns series:

    ```
    df.log_rtn.plot(title='Daily MSFT returns')
    ```

    Executing the code results in the following plot:

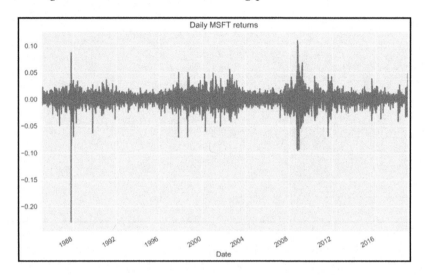

    We can observe clear clusters of volatility—periods of higher positive and negative returns.

# Absence of autocorrelation in returns

Investigate this third fact about the absence of autocorrelation in returns.

1.  Define the parameters for creating the autocorrelation plots:

    ```
    N_LAGS = 50
    SIGNIFICANCE_LEVEL = 0.05
    ```

2. Run the following code to create the **autocorrelation function (ACF)** plot of log returns:

```
acf = smt.graphics.plot_acf(df.log_rtn,
                            lags=N_LAGS,
                            alpha=SIGNIFICANCE_LEVEL)
```

Executing the preceding code results in the following plot:

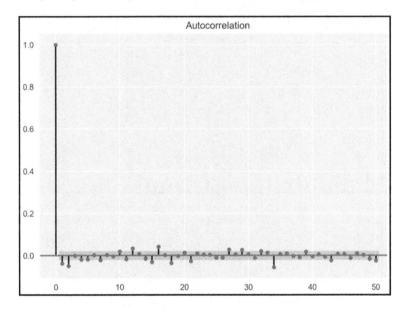

Only a few values lie outside the confidence interval (we do not look at lag 0) and can be considered statistically significant. We can assume that we have verified that there is no autocorrelation in the log returns series.

# Small and decreasing autocorrelation in squared/absolute returns

Investigate this fourth fact by creating the ACF plots of squared and absolute returns.

1. Create the ACF plots:

```
fig, ax = plt.subplots(2, 1, figsize=(12, 10))

smt.graphics.plot_acf(df.log_rtn ** 2, lags=N_LAGS,
                      alpha=SIGNIFICANCE_LEVEL, ax = ax[0])
```

```
ax[0].set(title='Autocorrelation Plots',
          ylabel='Squared Returns')

smt.graphics.plot_acf(np.abs(df.log_rtn), lags=N_LAGS,
                      alpha=SIGNIFICANCE_LEVEL, ax = ax[1])
ax[1].set(ylabel='Absolute Returns',
          xlabel='Lag')
```

Executing the preceding code results in the following plots:

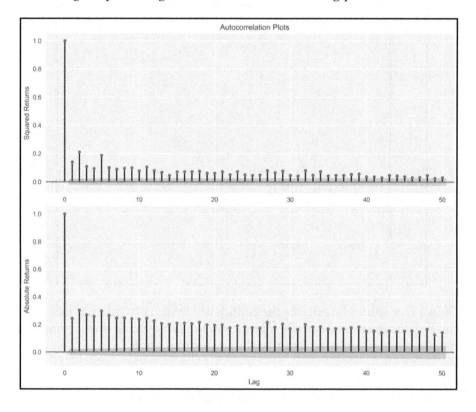

We can observe the small and decreasing values of autocorrelation for the squared and absolute returns, which are in line with the fourth stylized fact.

# Leverage effect

For the fifth fact, run the following steps to investigate the existence of the leverage effect.

1. Calculate volatility measures as rolling standard deviations:

```
df['moving_std_252'] = df[['log_rtn']].rolling(window=252).std()
df['moving_std_21'] = df[['log_rtn']].rolling(window=21).std()
```

2. Plot all the series for comparison:

```
fig, ax = plt.subplots(3, 1, figsize=(18, 15),
                       sharex=True)

df.adj_close.plot(ax=ax[0])
ax[0].set(title='MSFT time series',
          ylabel='Stock price ($)')

df.log_rtn.plot(ax=ax[1])
ax[1].set(ylabel='Log returns (%)')

df.moving_std_252.plot(ax=ax[2], color='r',
                       label='Moving Volatility 252d')
df.moving_std_21.plot(ax=ax[2], color='g',
                      label='Moving Volatility 21d')
ax[2].set(ylabel='Moving Volatility',
          xlabel='Date')
ax[2].legend()
```

We can now investigate the leverage effect by visually comparing the price series to the (rolling) volatility metric:

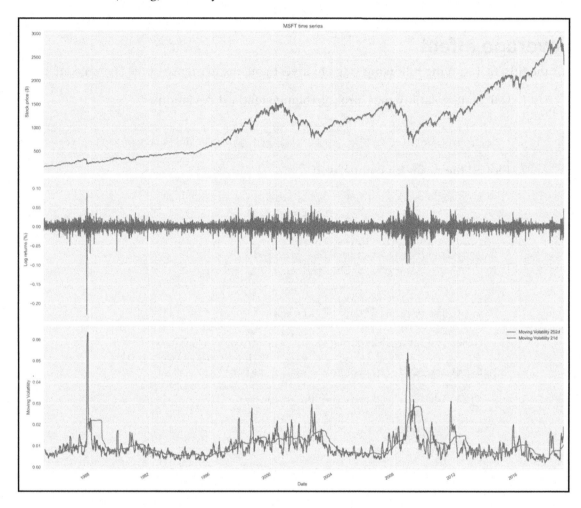

This fact states that most measures of an asset's volatility are negatively correlated with its returns, and we can indeed observe a pattern of increased volatility when the prices go down and decreased volatility when they are rising.

# How it works...

In this section, we describe the approaches we used to investigate the existence of the stylized facts in the S&P 500 log return series.

# Fact 1

The name of the fact (Non-Gaussian distribution of returns) is pretty much self-explanatory. It was observed in the literature that (daily) asset returns exhibit the following:

- **Negative skewness (third moment)**: Large negative returns occur more frequently than large positive ones.
- **Excess kurtosis (fourth moment)**: Large (and small) returns occur more often than expected.

 The `pandas` implementation of kurtosis is the one that literature refers to as excess kurtosis or Fisher's kurtosis. Using this metric, the excess kurtosis of a Gaussian distribution is 0, while the standard kurtosis is 3. This is not to be confused with the name of the stylized fact's excess kurtosis, which simply means kurtosis higher than that of normal distribution.

We break down investigating this fact into three parts.

**Histogram of returns**

The first step of investigating this fact was to plot a histogram visualizing the distribution of returns. To do so, we used `sns.distplot` while setting `kde=False` (which does not use the Gaussian kernel density estimate) and `norm_hist=True` (this plot shows density instead of the count).

To see the difference between our histogram and Gaussian distribution, we superimposed a line representing the PDF of the Gaussian distribution with the mean and standard deviation coming from the considered return series.

First, we specified the range over which we calculated the PDF by using `np.linspace` (we set the number of points to 1,000, generally the more points the smoother the line) and then calculated the PDF using `scs.norm.pdf`. The default arguments correspond to the standard normal distribution, that is, with zero mean and unit variance. That is why we specified the `loc` and `scale` arguments as the sample mean and standard deviation, respectively.

To verify the existence of the previously mentioned patterns, we should look at the following:

- **Negative skewness**: The left tail of the distribution is longer, while the mass of the distribution is concentrated on the right side of the distribution.
- **Excess kurtosis**: Fat-tailed and peaked distribution.

The second point is easier to observe on our plot, as there is a clear peak over the PDF and we see more mass in the tails.

### Q-Q plot

After inspecting the histogram, we looked at the Q-Q (quantile-quantile) plot, on which we compared two distributions (theoretical and observed) by plotting their quantiles against each other. In our case, the theoretical distribution is Gaussian (Normal) and the observed one comes from the S&P 500 returns.

To obtain the plot, we used the `sm.qqplot` function. If the empirical distribution is Normal, then the vast majority of the points will lie on the red line. However, we see that this is not the case, as points on the left side of the plot are more negative (that is, lower empirical quantiles are smaller) than expected in the case of the Gaussian distribution, as indicated by the line. This means that the left tail of the returns distribution is heavier than that of the Gaussian distribution. Analogical conclusions can be drawn about the right tail, which is heavier than under normality.

### Descriptive statistics

The last part involves looking at some statistics. We calculated them using the appropriate methods of `pandas` Series/DataFrames. We immediately see that the returns exhibit negative skewness and excess kurtosis. We also ran the Jarque-Bera test (`scs.jarque_bera`) to verify that returns do not follow a Gaussian distribution. With a p-value of zero, we reject the null hypothesis that sample data has skewness and kurtosis matching those of a Gaussian distribution.

# Fact 2

The first thing we should be aware of when investigating stylized facts is the volatility clustering—periods of high returns alternating with periods of low returns, suggesting that volatility is not constant. To quickly investigate this fact, we plot the returns using the `plot` method of a `pandas` DataFrame.

# Fact 3

Autocorrelation (also known as **serial correlation**) measures how similar is a given time series to the lagged version of itself, over successive time intervals.

To investigate whether there is significant autocorrelation in returns, we created the autocorrelation plot using `plot_acf` from the `statsmodels` library. We inspected 50 lags and used the default `alpha=0.05`, which means that we also plotted the 95% confidence interval. Values outside of this interval can be considered statistically significant.

# Fact 4

To verify this fact, we also used the `plot_acf` function from the `statsmodels` library; however, this time we applied it to the squared and absolute returns.

# Fact 5

This fact states that most measures of asset volatility are negatively correlated with their returns. To investigate it, we used the moving standard deviation (calculated using the `rolling` method of a `pandas` DataFrame) as a measure of historical volatility. We used windows of 21 and 252 days, which correspond to one month and one year of trading data.

# There's more...

We present another method of investigating the leverage effect (fact 5). To do so, we use the VIX (CBOE Volatility Index), which is a popular metric of the stock market's expectation regarding volatility. The measure is implied by option prices on the S&P 500 index. We take the following steps:

1. Download and preprocess the prices of the S&P 500 and VIX:

```
df = yf.download(['^GSPC', '^VIX'],
                 start='1985-01-01',
                 end='2018-12-31',
                 progress=False)
df = df[['Adj Close']]
df.columns = df.columns.droplevel(0)
df = df.rename(columns={'^GSPC': 'sp500', '^VIX': 'vix'})
```

2. Calculate the log returns (we can just as well use percentage change-simple returns):

```
df['log_rtn'] = np.log(df.sp500 / df.sp500.shift(1))
df['vol_rtn'] = np.log(df.vix / df.vix.shift(1))
df.dropna(how='any', axis=0, inplace=True)
```

3. Plot a scatterplot with the returns on the axes and fit a regression line to identify the trend:

```
corr_coeff = df.log_rtn.corr(df.vol_rtn)

ax = sns.regplot(x='log_rtn', y='vol_rtn', data=df,
                 line_kws={'color': 'red'})
ax.set(title=f'S&P 500 vs. VIX ($\\rho$ = {corr_coeff:.2f})',
       ylabel='VIX log returns',
       xlabel='S&P 500 log returns')
```

We additionally calculated the correlation coefficient between the two series and included it in the title:

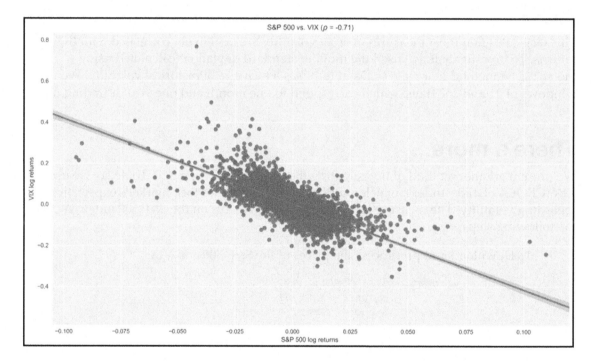

We can see that both the negative slope of the regression line and a strong negative correlation between the two series confirm the existence of the leverage effect in the return series.

# See also

For more information, refer to the following:

- Cont, R. (2001). Empirical properties of asset returns: stylized facts and statistical issues.

# Technical Analysis in Python

2

In this chapter, we will cover the basics of **technical analysis (TA)** in Python. In short, TA is a methodology for determining (forecasting) the future direction of asset prices and identifying investment opportunities, based on studying past market data, especially the prices themselves and the traded volume.

We begin by introducing a simple way of visualizing stock prices using the candlestick chart. Then, we show how to calculate selected indicators (with hints on how to calculate others using selected Python libraries) used for TA. Using established Python libraries, we show how easy it is to backtest trading strategies built on the basis of TA indicators. In this way, we can evaluate the performance of these strategies in a real-life context (even including commission fees and so on).

At the end of the chapter, we also demonstrate how to create an interactive dashboard in Jupyter Notebook, which enables us to add and inspect the predefined TA indicators on the fly.

We present the following recipes in this chapter:

- Creating a candlestick chart
- Backtesting a strategy based on simple moving average
- Calculating Bollinger Bands and testing a buy/sell strategy
- Calculating the relative strength index and testing a long/short strategy
- Building an interactive dashboard for TA

# Creating a candlestick chart

A candlestick chart is a type of financial graph, used to describe a given security's price movements. A single candlestick (typically corresponding to one day, but a higher frequency is possible) combines the **open, high, low, and close prices (OHLC)**. The elements of a bullish candlestick (where the close price in a given time period is higher than the open price) are presented in the following image (for a bearish one, we should swap the positions of the open and close prices):

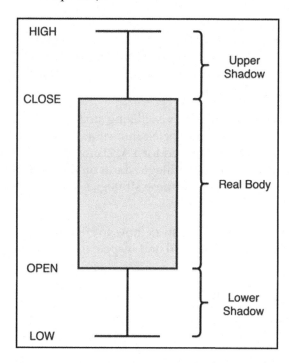

In comparison to the plots introduced in the previous chapter, candlestick charts convey much more information than a simple line plot of the adjusted close price. That is why they are often used in real trading platforms, and traders use them for identifying patterns and making trading decisions.

In this recipe, we also add moving average lines (which are one of the most basic technical indicators), as well as bar charts representing volume.

# Getting ready

In this recipe, we download Twitter's (adjusted) stock prices for the year 2018. We use Yahoo Finance to download the data, as described in the *Getting data from Yahoo Finance* recipe, found in `Chapter 1`, *Financial Data and Preprocessing*. Follow these steps:

1. Import the libraries:

```
import pandas as pd
import yfinance as yf
```

2. Download the adjusted prices:

```
df_twtr = yf.download('TWTR',
                      start='2018-01-01',
                      end='2018-12-31',
                      progress=False,
                      auto_adjust=True)
```

For creating the plot, we use the `plotly` and `cufflinks` libraries. For more details, please refer to the *Visualizing time series data* recipe, found in `Chapter 1`, *Financial Data and Preprocessing*.

# How to do it...

Execute the following steps to create an interactive candlestick chart.

1. Import the libraries:

```
import cufflinks as cf
from plotly.offline import iplot, init_notebook_mode

init_notebook_mode()
```

2. Create the candlestick chart, using Twitter's stock prices:

```
qf = cf.QuantFig(df_twtr, title="Twitter's Stock Price",
                 legend='top', name='TWTR')
```

3. Add volume and moving averages to the figure:

```
qf.add_volume()
qf.add_sma(periods=20, column='Close', color='red')
qf.add_ema(periods=20, color='green')
```

4. Display the plot:

```
qf.iplot()
```

We can observe the following plot (it is interactive in the notebook):

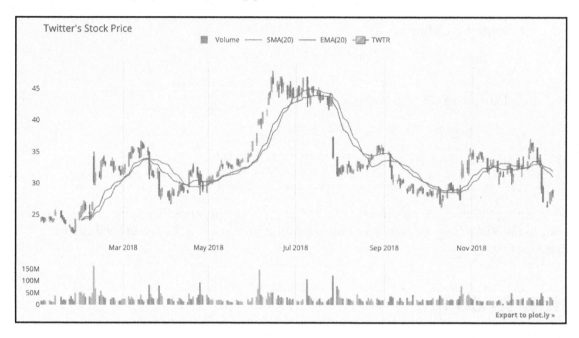

In the plot, we can see that the **exponential moving average (EMA)** adapts to the changes in prices much faster than the **SMA**. Some discontinuities in the chart are caused by the fact that we are using daily data, and there is no data for weekends/bank holidays.

# How it works...

In *Step 2*, we created a `QuantFig` object by passing a DataFrame containing the input data, as well as some arguments for the title and legend's position. We could have created a simple candlestick chart by running the `iplot` method of `QuantFig` immediately afterward.

However, in *Step 3*, we also added two moving average lines by using the `add_sma`/`add_ema` methods. We decided to consider 20 periods (days, in this case). By default, the averages are calculated using the `close` column, however, we can change this by providing the `column` argument.

The difference between the two moving averages is that the exponential one puts more weight on recent prices. By doing so, it is more responsive to new information and reacts faster to any changes in the general trend.

## See also

For more information on the available methods (different indicators and settings), please refer to the source code available at the GitHub repository of `cufflinks`, at `https://github.com/santosjorge/cufflinks/blob/master/cufflinks/quant_figure.py`.

# Backtesting a strategy based on simple moving average

The general idea behind backtesting is to evaluate the performance of a trading strategy—built using some heuristics or technical indicators—by applying it to historical data.

In this recipe, we introduce one of the available frameworks for backtesting in Python: `backtrader`. Key features of this framework include:

- A vast amount of available technical indicators (`backtrader` also provides a wrapper around the popular `TA-Lib` library) and performance measures
- Ease of building and applying new indicators
- Multiple data sources available (including Yahoo Finance, Quandl)
- Simulating many aspects of real brokers, such as different types of orders (market, limit, stop), slippage (the difference between the intended and actual execution prices of an order), commission, going long/short, and so on
- A one-line call for a plot, with all results

For this recipe, we consider a basic strategy based on the SMA. The key points of the strategy are as follows:

- When the close price becomes higher than the 20-day SMA, buy one share.

- When the close price becomes lower than the 20-day SMA and we have a share, sell it.
- We can only have a maximum of one share at any given time.
- No short selling is allowed.

We run the backtesting of this strategy, using Apple's stock prices from the year 2018.

# How to do it...

In this example, we present two possible approaches: building a trading strategy, using a signal (bt.Signal) or defining a full strategy (bt.Strategy). Both yield the same results, however, the lengthier one, using bt.Strategy, provides more logging of what is actually happening in the background. This makes it easier to debug and keep track of all operations (the level of detail included in the logging depends on our needs).

## Signal

Execute the following steps to create a backtest, using the bt.Signal class.

1. Import the libraries:

```
from datetime import datetime
import backtrader as bt
```

2. Define a class representing the trading strategy:

```
class SmaSignal(bt.Signal):
    params = (('period', 20), )
    def __init__(self):
        self.lines.signal = self.data -
bt.ind.SMA(period=self.p.period)
```

3. Download data from Yahoo Finance:

```
data = bt.feeds.YahooFinanceData(dataname='AAPL',
                                 fromdate=datetime(2018, 1, 1),
                                 todate=datetime(2018, 12, 31))
```

4. Set up the backtest:

```
cerebro = bt.Cerebro(stdstats = False)

cerebro.adddata(data)
```

```
cerebro.broker.setcash(1000.0)
cerebro.add_signal(bt.SIGNAL_LONG, SmaSignal)
cerebro.addobserver(bt.observers.BuySell)
cerebro.addobserver(bt.observers.Value)
```

5. Run the backtest:

```
print(f'Starting Portfolio Value: {cerebro.broker.getvalue():.2f}')
cerebro.run()
print(f'Final Portfolio Value: {cerebro.broker.getvalue():.2f}')
```

6. Plot the results:

```
cerebro.plot(iplot=True, volume=False)
```

The plot is divided into three parts: the evolution of the portfolio's value, the price of the asset (together with the buy/sell signals), and—lastly—the technical indicator of our choosing, as shown in the following plot:

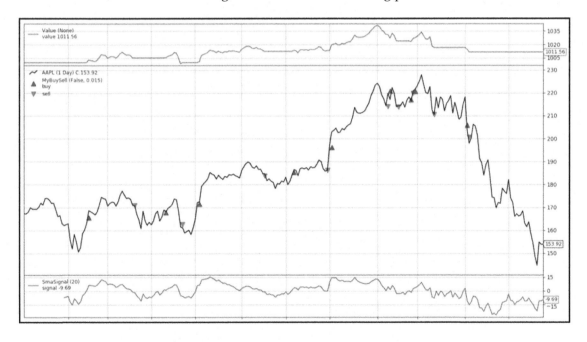

From the preceding plot, we can see that, in the end, the trading strategy made money: the terminal value of the portfolio is $1011.56.

# Strategy

To make the code more readable, we first present the general outline of the class (trading strategy) and then define separate pieces in the following code blocks.

1. The template of the strategy is presented below:

```python
class SmaStrategy(bt.Strategy):
    params = (('ma_period', 20), )

    def __init__(self):
        # some code
    def log(self, txt):
        # some code

    def notify_order(self, order):
        # some code

    def notify_trade(self, trade):
        # some code

    def next(self):
        # some code
```

The __init__ block is defined as:

```python
def __init__(self):
        self.data_close = self.datas[0].close

        self.order = None
        self.price = None
        self.comm = None

        self.sma = bt.ind.SMA(self.datas[0],
                        period=self.params.ma_period)
```

The log block is defined as:

```python
def log(self, txt):
        dt = self.datas[0].datetime.date(0).isoformat()
        print(f'{dt}, {txt}')
```

The `notify_order` **block is defined as:**

```
def notify_order(self, order):
        if order.status in [order.Submitted, order.Accepted]:
            return

        if order.status in [order.Completed]:
            if order.isbuy():
                self.log(f'BUY EXECUTED --- Price:
{order.executed.price:.2f}, Cost: {order.executed.value:.2f},
Commission: {order.executed.comm:.2f}')
                self.price = order.executed.price
                self.comm = order.executed.comm
            else:
                self.log(f'SELL EXECUTED --- Price:
{order.executed.price:.2f}, Cost: {order.executed.value:.2f},
Commission: {order.executed.comm:.2f}')

            self.bar_executed = len(self)

        elif order.status in [order.Canceled, order.Margin,
                                order.Rejected]:
            self.log('Order Failed')

        self.order = None
```

The `notify_trade` **block is defined as:**

```
def notify_trade(self, trade):
        if not trade.isclosed:
            return

        self.log(f'OPERATION RESULT --- Gross: {trade.pnl:.2f},
    Net: {trade.pnlcomm:.2f}')
```

The `next` **block is defined as:**

```
def next(self):
        if self.order:
            return

        if not self.position:
            if self.data_close[0] > self.sma[0]:
                self.log(f'BUY CREATED --- Price:
{self.data_close[0]:.2f}')
                self.order = self.buy()
        else:
            if self.data_close[0] < self.sma[0]:
```

```
                         self.log(f'SELL CREATED --- Price:
{self.data_close[0]:.2f}')
                         self.order = self.sell()
```

 The code for `data` is the same as in the signal strategy, so it is not included here, to avoid repetition.

2. Set up the backtest:

```
cerebro = bt.Cerebro(stdstats = False)

cerebro.adddata(data)
cerebro.broker.setcash(1000.0)
cerebro.addstrategy(SmaStrategy)
cerebro.addobserver(bt.observers.BuySell)
cerebro.addobserver(bt.observers.Value)
```

3. Run the backtest:

```
print(f'Starting Portfolio Value: {cerebro.broker.getvalue():.2f}')
cerebro.run()
print(f'Final Portfolio Value: {cerebro.broker.getvalue():.2f}')
```

4. Plot the results:

```
cerebro.plot(iplot=True, volume=False)
```

The resulting graph is presented below:

From the preceding graph, we see that the strategy managed to make $11.56 over the year. Additionally, we present a piece of the log:

```
Starting Portfolio Value: 1000.00
2018-02-14, BUY CREATED --- Price: 164.23
2018-02-15, BUY EXECUTED --- Price: 166.60, Cost: 166.60, Commission: 0.00
2018-03-19, SELL CREATED --- Price: 172.01
2018-03-20, SELL EXECUTED --- Price: 171.95, Cost: 166.60, Commission: 0.00
2018-03-20, OPERATION RESULT --- Gross: 5.35, Net: 5.35
2018-04-10, BUY CREATED --- Price: 170.00
2018-04-11, BUY EXECUTED --- Price: 169.00, Cost: 169.00, Commission: 0.00
2018-04-20, SELL CREATED --- Price: 162.61
2018-04-23, SELL EXECUTED --- Price: 163.70, Cost: 169.00, Commission: 0.00
2018-04-23, OPERATION RESULT --- Gross: -5.30, Net: -5.30
```

The log contains information about all the created and executed trades, as well as the operation results, in case it was a sell.

# How it works...

The key idea of working with `backtrader` is that there is the main brain—`Cerebro`—and by using different methods, we provided it with historical data, the designed trading strategy, additional metrics we wanted to calculate (for example, **Portfolio Value** over the investment horizon, or the overall **Sharpe ratio**), information about commissions/slippage, and so on. These were the common elements between the two approaches. The part that differed was the definition of the strategy. We start by describing the common elements of the `backtrader` framework while assuming a trading strategy already exists, and we then explain the details of the particular strategies.

## Common elements

We started with downloading price data from Yahoo Finance, with the help of the `bt.feeds.YahooFinanceData()` function. What followed was a series of operations connected to `Cerebro`, as described here:

1. Creating the instance of `bt.Cerebro` and setting `stdstats = False`, in order to suppress a lot of default elements of the plot. Doing so avoided cluttering the output, and then we manually picked the interesting elements (observers and indicators).
2. Adding data, using the `adddata` method.
3. Setting up the amount of available money, using the `broker.setcash` method.
4. Adding the signal/strategy, using the `add_signal`/`addstrategy` methods.
5. Adding Observers, using `addobserver`. We selected two Observers: `BuySell`, to display the buy/sell decisions on the plot (denoted by blue and red triangles), and `Value`, for tracking how the portfolio value changed over time.

 You can also add data from a CSV file, a `pandas` DataFrame, Quandl, and other sources. For a list of available options, please refer to `bt.feeds`.

The last step involved running the backtest with `cerebro.run()` and displaying the resulting plot with `cerebro.plot()`. In the latter step, we disabled displaying the volume bar charts, to avoid cluttering the graph.

# Signal

The signal was built as a class, inheriting from `bt.Signal`. The signal was represented as a number—in this case, the difference between the current data point (`self.data`) and the moving average (`bt.ind.SMA`). If the signal is positive, it is an indication to go long (buy). A negative one indicates short (selling). The value of 0 means there is no signal.

The next step was to add the signal to `Cerebro`, using the `add_signal` method. When doing so, we also had to specify what kind of signal we were adding.

The following is a description of the available signal types:

- **LONGSHORT**: This takes into account both long and short indications from the signal.
- **LONG**: Positive signals indicate going long; negative ones are used to close the long position.
- **SHORT**: Negative signals indicate shorting; positive ones are used to close the short position.
- **LONGEXIT**: A negative signal is used to exit a long position.
- **SHORTEXIT**: A positive signal is used to exit a short position.

However, exiting positions can be more complex (enabling users to build more sophisticated strategies), as described here:

- **LONG**: If there is a `LONGEXIT` signal, it is used to exit the long position, instead of the default behavior mentioned previously. If there is a `SHORT` signal and no `LONGEXIT` signal, the `SHORT` signal is used to close the long position before opening a short one.
- **SHORT**: If there is a `SHORTEXIT` signal, it is used to exit the short position, instead of the default behavior mentioned previously. If there is a `LONG` signal and no `SHORTEXIT` signal, the `LONG` signal is used to close the short position before opening a long one.

As you might have already realized, the signal is calculated for every time point (as visualized in the bottom of the plot), which effectively creates a continuous stream of positions to be opened/closed (the signal value of 0 is not very likely to happen). That is why backtrader, by default, disables accumulation (the constant opening of new positions, even when we have one already opened) and concurrency (generating new orders without hearing back from the broker whether the previously submitted ones were executed successfully).

# Strategy

The strategy was built as a class, inheriting from bt.Strategy. Inside the class, we defined the following methods (we were actually overwriting them to make them tailor-made for our needs):

- __init__: Here, we defined the objects that we would like to keep track of, for example, close price, order, buy price, commission, indicators such as SMA, and so on.
- log: This is defined for logging purposes.
- notify_order: This is defined for reporting the status of the order (position). In general, on day *t*, the indicator can suggest opening/closing a position based on the close price (assuming we are working with daily data). Then, the (market) order will be carried out on the next day (using day *t* + 1's open price). However, there is no guarantee that the order will be executed, as it can be canceled, or we might have insufficient cash. This behavior is also true for strategies built with signals. It also removes any pending order, by setting self.order = None.
- notify_trade: This is defined for reporting the results of trades (after the positions are closed).
- next: This is the place containing the trading strategy's logic. First, we check whether there is an order already pending, and do nothing if there is. The second check is to see whether we already have a position (enforced by our strategy; not a must), and, if we do not, we check whether the close price is higher than the moving average. A positive outcome results in an entry to the log, and the placing of a buy order self.order = self.buy(). This is also the place where we can choose the stake (number of assets we want to buy). A default outcome in self.buy(size=1).

Here are some general notes:

- `Cerebro` should only be used once. If we want to run another backtest, we should create a new instance, not add something to it after prior calculations.
- The strategy built on `bt.Signal` inherits from `bt.Signal`, and uses only one signal. However, we can combine multiple signals, based on different conditions, when we use `bt.SignalStrategy` instead.
- When we do not specify otherwise, all trades are carried out on one unit of the asset.
- `backtrader` automatically handles the warm-up period. In this case, no trade can be carried out until there are enough data points to calculate the 20-day SMA. When considering multiple indicators at once, `backtrader` automatically selects the longest necessary period.

# There's more...

It is worth mentioning that `backtrader` has parameter optimization capabilities, which we present in the code that follows. The code is a modified version of the strategy from this recipe, in which we optimize the number of days in the SMA.

The following list provides details of modifications to the code (we only show the relevant ones, as the bulk of the code is identical to that using `bt.Strategy`):

- We add an extra attribute called `stop` to the class definition—it returns the Terminal portfolio value for each parameter:

```
def stop(self):
        self.log(f'(ma_period = {self.params.ma_period:2d}) ---
Terminal Value: {self.broker.getvalue():.2f}')
```

- Instead of using `cerebro.addstrategy()`, we use `cerebro.optstrategy()`, and provide the strategy name and parameter values:

```
cerebro.optstrategy(SmaStrategy, ma_period=range(10, 31))
```

- We increase the number of CPU cores when running the backtesting:
  `cerebro.run(maxcpus=4)`

We present the results in the following summary (the order of parameters is not preserved, as the testing was carried out on four cores):

```
2018-12-28, (ma_period = 10) --- Terminal Value: 1006.25
2018-12-28, (ma_period = 13) --- Terminal Value: 992.28
2018-12-28, (ma_period = 11) --- Terminal Value: 1004.34
2018-12-28, (ma_period = 12) --- Terminal Value: 1005.81
2018-12-28, (ma_period = 14) --- Terminal Value: 977.05
2018-12-28, (ma_period = 15) --- Terminal Value: 981.33
2018-12-28, (ma_period = 17) --- Terminal Value: 992.73
2018-12-28, (ma_period = 16) --- Terminal Value: 979.72
2018-12-28, (ma_period = 19) --- Terminal Value: 1005.23
2018-12-28, (ma_period = 18) --- Terminal Value: 994.77
2018-12-28, (ma_period = 20) --- Terminal Value: 1011.62
2018-12-28, (ma_period = 21) --- Terminal Value: 1013.64
2018-12-28, (ma_period = 22) --- Terminal Value: 1021.24
2018-12-28, (ma_period = 23) --- Terminal Value: 1018.70
2018-12-28, (ma_period = 24) --- Terminal Value: 1018.70
2018-12-28, (ma_period = 25) --- Terminal Value: 1018.22
2018-12-28, (ma_period = 26) --- Terminal Value: 1009.37
2018-12-28, (ma_period = 27) --- Terminal Value: 1008.22
2018-12-28, (ma_period = 28) --- Terminal Value: 1011.92
2018-12-28, (ma_period = 29) --- Terminal Value: 1015.30
2018-12-28, (ma_period = 30) --- Terminal Value: 1013.13
```

We see that the strategy performed best for `ma_period = 22`.

# See also

Additional resources are available here:

- `https://www.zipline.io/`: An alternative framework for backtesting. Developed and actively maintained by Quantopian.

# Calculating Bollinger Bands and testing a buy/sell strategy

Bollinger Bands are a statistical method, used for deriving information about the prices and volatility of a certain asset over time. To obtain the Bollinger Bands, we need to calculate the moving average and standard deviation of the time series (prices), using a specified window (typically, 20 days). Then, we set the upper/lower bands at *K* times (typically, 2) the moving standard deviation above/below the moving average.

The interpretation of the bands is quite sample: the bands widen with an increase in volatility and contract with a decrease in volatility.

In this recipe, we build a simple trading strategy, with the following rules:

- Buy when the price crosses the lower Bollinger Band upwards.
- Sell (only if stocks are in possession) when the price crosses the upper Bollinger Band downward.
- All-in strategy—when creating a buy order, buy as many shares as possible.
- Short selling is not allowed.

We evaluate the strategy on Microsoft's stock in 2018. Additionally, we set the commission to be equal to 0.1%.

# How to do it...

Execute the following steps to backtest a strategy based on the Bollinger Bands.

1. Import the libraries:

```
import backtrader as bt
import datetime
import pandas as pd
```

2. The template of the strategy is presented:

```
class BBand_Strategy(bt.Strategy):
    params = (('period', 20),
              ('devfactor', 2.0),)

    def __init__(self):
        # some code
    def log(self, txt):
```

```
        # some code

    def notify_order(self, order):
        # some code

    def notify_trade(self, trade):
        # some code

    def next_open(self):
        # some code
```

The __init__ block is defined as:

```
def __init__(self):
    # keep track of close price in the series
    self.data_close = self.datas[0].close
    self.data_open = self.datas[0].open

    # keep track of pending orders/buy price/buy commission
    self.order = None
    self.price = None
    self.comm = None

    # add Bollinger Bands indicator and track the buy/sell signals
    self.b_band = bt.ind.BollingerBands(self.datas[0],
                                  period=self.p.period,
                                  devfactor=self.p.devfactor)
    self.buy_signal = bt.ind.CrossOver(self.datas[0],
                                  self.b_band.lines.bot)
    self.sell_signal = bt.ind.CrossOver(self.datas[0],
                                  self.b_band.lines.top)
```

The log block is defined as:

```
def log(self, txt):
        dt = self.datas[0].datetime.date(0).isoformat()
        print(f'{dt}, {txt}')
```

The notify_order block is defined as:

```
def notify_order(self, order):
        if order.status in [order.Submitted, order.Accepted]:
            return

        if order.status in [order.Completed]:
            if order.isbuy():
                self.log(
                    f'BUY EXECUTED --- Price:
```

```
{order.executed.price:.2f}, Cost: {order.executed.value:.2f},
Commission: {order.executed.comm:.2f}'
                )
                self.price = order.executed.price
                self.comm = order.executed.comm
            else:
                self.log(
                    f'SELL EXECUTED --- Price:
{order.executed.price:.2f}, Cost: {order.executed.value:.2f},
Commission: {order.executed.comm:.2f}'
                )

        elif order.status in [order.Canceled, order.Margin,
                                order.Rejected]:
            self.log('Order Failed')

        self.order = None
```

The `notify_trade` **block is defined as:**

```
def notify_trade(self, trade):
        if not trade.isclosed:
            return

        self.log(f'OPERATION RESULT --- Gross: {trade.pnl:.2f},
    Net: {trade.pnlcomm:.2f}')
```

The `next_open` **block is defined as:**

```
def next_open(self):
        if not self.position:
            if self.buy_signal > 0:
                size = int(self.broker.getcash() /
self.datas[0].open)
                self.log(f'BUY CREATED --- Size: {size}, Cash:
{self.broker.getcash():.2f}, Open: {self.data_open[0]}, Close:
{self.data_close[0]}')
                self.buy(size=size)
        else:
            if self.sell_signal < 0:
                self.log(f'SELL CREATED --- Size:
{self.position.size}')
                self.sell(size=self.position.size)
```

3. Download the data:

```
data = bt.feeds.YahooFinanceData(
    dataname='MSFT',
    fromdate=datetime.datetime(2018, 1, 1),
    todate=datetime.datetime(2018, 12, 31)
)
```

4. Set up the backtest:

```
cerebro = bt.Cerebro(stdstats = False, cheat_on_open=True)

cerebro.addstrategy(BBand_Strategy)
cerebro.adddata(data)
cerebro.broker.setcash(10000.0)
cerebro.broker.setcommission(commission=0.001)
cerebro.addobserver(bt.observers.BuySell)
cerebro.addobserver(bt.observers.Value)
cerebro.addanalyzer(bt.analyzers.Returns, _name='returns')
cerebro.addanalyzer(bt.analyzers.TimeReturn, _name='time_return')
```

5. Run the backtest:

```
print('Starting Portfolio Value: %.2f' % cerebro.broker.getvalue())
backtest_result = cerebro.run()
print('Final Portfolio Value: %.2f' % cerebro.broker.getvalue())
```

6. Plot the results:

```
cerebro.plot(iplot=True, volume=False)
```

The resulting graph is presented below:

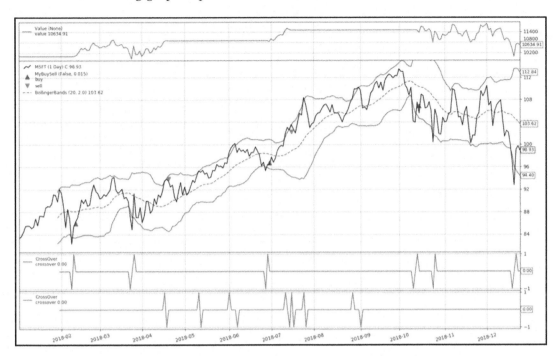

The log is presented below:

```
Starting Portfolio Value: 10000.00
2018-02-12, BUY CREATED --- Size: 115, Cash: 10000.00, Open: 86.54, Close: 86.92
2018-02-12, BUY EXECUTED --- Price: 86.54, Cost: 9952.10, Commission: 9.95
2018-04-19, SELL CREATED --- Size: 115
2018-04-19, SELL EXECUTED --- Price: 94.49, Cost: 9952.10, Commission: 10.87
2018-04-19, OPERATION RESULT --- Gross: 914.25, Net: 893.43
2018-06-29, BUY CREATED --- Size: 111, Cash: 10893.43, Open: 97.35, Close: 97.03
2018-06-29, BUY EXECUTED --- Price: 97.35, Cost: 10805.85, Commission: 10.81
2018-07-17, SELL CREATED --- Size: 111
2018-07-17, SELL EXECUTED --- Price: 102.94, Cost: 10805.85, Commission: 11.43
2018-07-17, OPERATION RESULT --- Gross: 620.49, Net: 598.26
2018-10-15, BUY CREATED --- Size: 106, Cash: 11491.69, Open: 107.58, Close: 106.29
2018-10-15, BUY EXECUTED --- Price: 107.58, Cost: 11403.48, Commission: 11.40
Final Portfolio Value: 10633.35
```

We can see that the strategy managed to make money, even after accounting for commission costs. We now turn to an inspection of the analyzers.

7. Run the following code to investigate different `returns` metrics:

```
print(backtest_result[0].analyzers.returns.get_analysis())
```

The output of the preceding line is as follows:

```
OrderedDict([('rtot', 0.06155731237239935),
             ('ravg', 0.00024622924948959743),
             ('rnorm', 0.06401530037885826),
             ('rnorm100', 6.401530037885826)])
```

8. Create a plot of daily portfolio returns:

```
returns_dict =
backtest_result[0].analyzers.time_return.get_analysis()
returns_df = pd.DataFrame(list(returns_dict.items()),
                          columns = ['report_date', 'return']) \
                   .set_index('report_date')
returns_df.plot(title='Portfolio returns')
```

Running the code results in the following plot:

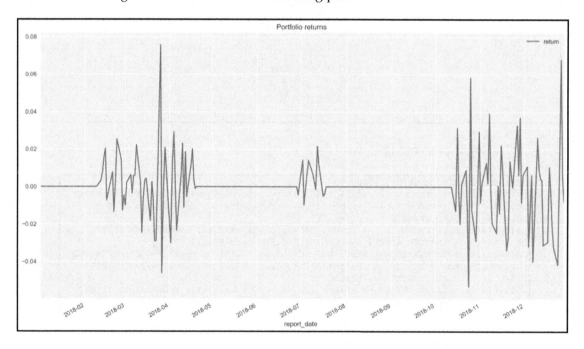

The flat lines represent periods when we have no open positions.

# How it works...

There are a lot of similarities between the code used for creating the Bollinger Bands-based strategy and that used in the previous recipe. That is why we only discuss the novelties, and refer you to the *Backtesting a strategy based on simple moving average* recipe for more details.

As we were going all-in in this strategy, we had to use a method called `cheat_on_open`. This means that we calculated the signals on day *t*'s close price, but calculated the number of shares we wanted to buy based on day *t+1*'s open price. To do so, we had to set `cheat_on_open=True` when creating the `bt.Cerebro` object. As a result, we also defined a `next_open` method instead of `next` within the `Strategy` class. This clearly indicated to `Cerebro` that we were cheating-on-open. Before creating a potential buy order, we calculated `size = int(self.broker.getcash() / self.datas[0].open)`, which is the maximum number of shares we could buy (the open price comes from day *t+1*). The last novelty was that we also added commission directly to `Cerebro` by using `cerebro.broker.setcommission(commission=0.001)`.

When calculating the buy/sell signals based on the Bollinger Bands, we used the `CrossOver` indicator. It returned the following:

- `1` if the first data (price) crossed the second data (indicator) upward
- `-1` if the first data (price) crossed the second data (indicator) downward

> We can also use `CrossUp` and `CrossDown` when we want to consider crossing from only one direction. The buy signal would look like this: `self.buy_signal = bt.ind.CrossUp(self.datas[0], self.b_band.lines.bot)`.

The last addition included utilizing analyzers—`backtrader` objects that help to evaluate what is happening with the portfolio. In the following example, we used two analyzers:

- `Returns`: A collection of different logarithmic returns, calculated on the entire timeframe: total compound return, the average return over the entire period, and the annualized return.
- `TimeReturn`: A collection of returns over time (using a provided time-frame, in this case, daily data).

**TIP**

We can obtain the same result as from the `TimeReturn` analyzer by adding an observer with the same name: `cerebro.addobserver(bt.observers.TimeReturn)`. The only difference is that the Observer will be plotted on the main results plot, which is not always desired.

# Calculating the relative strength index and testing a long/short strategy

The RSI is an indicator that uses the closing prices of an asset to identify oversold/overbought conditions. Most commonly, the RSI is calculated using a 14-day period, and it is measured on a scale from 0 to 100 (it is an oscillator). Traders usually buy an asset when it is oversold (if the RSI is below 30), and sell when it is overbought (if the RSI is above 70). More extreme high/low levels, such as 80-20, are used less frequently and, at the same time, imply stronger momentum.

In this recipe, we build a trading strategy with the following rules:

- We can go long and short.
- For calculating the RSI, we use 14 periods (trading days).
- Enter a long position if the RSI crosses the lower threshold (standard value of 30) upwards; exit the position when the RSI becomes larger than the middle level (value of 50).
- Enter a short position if the RSI crosses the upper threshold (standard value of 70) downwards; exit the position when the RSI becomes smaller than 50.
- Only one position can be open at a time.

We evaluate the strategy on Facebook's stock in 2018, and apply a commission of 0.1%.

# How to do it...

Execute the following steps to implement a strategy based on the RSI.

1. Import the libraries:

```
from datetime import datetime
import backtrader as bt
```

2. Define the signal strategy, **based on** `bt.SignalStrategy`:

```
class RsiSignalStrategy(bt.SignalStrategy):
    params = dict(rsi_periods=14, rsi_upper=70,
                  rsi_lower=30, rsi_mid=50)

    def __init__(self):
        rsi = bt.indicators.RSI(period=self.p.rsi_periods,
                                upperband=self.p.rsi_upper,
                                lowerband=self.p.rsi_lower)

        bt.talib.RSI(self.data, plotname='TA_RSI')
        rsi_signal_long = bt.ind.CrossUp(rsi, self.p.rsi_lower,
                                         plot=False)
        self.signal_add(bt.SIGNAL_LONG, rsi_signal_long)
        self.signal_add(bt.SIGNAL_LONGEXIT, -(rsi >
                                              self.p.rsi_mid))

        rsi_signal_short = -bt.ind.CrossDown(rsi, self.p.rsi_upper,
                                             plot=False)
        self.signal_add(bt.SIGNAL_SHORT, rsi_signal_short)
        self.signal_add(bt.SIGNAL_SHORTEXIT, rsi < self.p.rsi_mid)
```

3. Download the data:

```
data = bt.feeds.YahooFinanceData(dataname='FB',
                                 fromdate=datetime(2018, 1, 1),
                                 todate=datetime(2018, 12, 31))
```

4. Set up and run the backtest:

```
cerebro = bt.Cerebro(stdstats = False)

cerebro.addstrategy(RsiSignalStrategy)
cerebro.adddata(data)
cerebro.broker.setcash(1000.0)
cerebro.broker.setcommission(commission=0.001)
cerebro.addobserver(bt.observers.BuySell)
cerebro.addobserver(bt.observers.Value)

cerebro.run()
```

5. Plot the results:

```
cerebro.plot(iplot=True, volume=False)
```

Running the code results in the following graph:

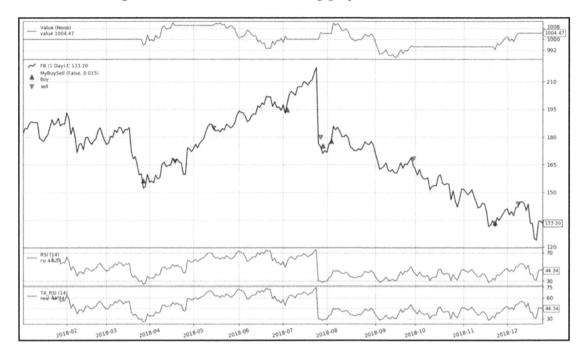

We look at the triangles in pairs. The first one indicates opening a position (going long if the triangle is blue and facing up; going short if the triangle is red and facing down). The next triangle (of the opposite color and direction) indicates closing a position. We can match the opening and closing of positions with the RSI below the chart. Sometimes, there are multiple triangles of the same color in sequence. That is because the RSI fluctuates around the line of opening a position, crossing it multiple times, as we can see on the preceding RSI chart. But the actual position is only opened on the first instance of a signal (no accumulation is the default setting).

# How it works...

In this recipe, we built a trading strategy on top of `bt.SignalStrategy`. First, we defined the indicator (RSI), with selected arguments. We also added `bt.talib.RSI(self.data,plotname='TA_RSI')`, just to show that `backtrader` provides an easy way to use indicators from the popular `TA-Lib` library (the `TA-Lib` library must be installed for the code to work). The trading strategy does not depend on this second indicator; it is only plotted for reference, and we could add an arbitrary number of indicators.

> Even when adding indicators for reference only, their existence influences the "warm-up period." For example, if we additionally included a 200-day SMA indicator, no trade would be carried out before there exists at least one value for the SMA indicator.

The next step was to define signals. To do so, we used the `bt.CrossUp`/`bt.CrossDown` indicators, which returned 1 if the first series (price) crossed the second (upper or lower RSI threshold) from below/above, respectively. For entering a short position, we made the signal negative, by adding a – in front of the `bt.CrossDown` indicator.

> We can disable printing any indicator, by adding `plot=False` to the function call.

As the last step of defining the strategy, we added tracking of all the signals, by using the `signal_add` method. For exiting the positions, the conditions we used (an RSI value higher/lower than 50) resulted in a Boolean, which we had to make negative in case of exiting a long position: `-True` is the same as `-1`.

Setting up and running the backtest is analogous to the previous recipe, so please refer to it if in doubt regarding any of the steps.

# Building an interactive dashboard for TA

In this recipe, we show how to build an interactive dashboard for technical analysis in Jupyter Notebook. Of course, the same result could be achieved without any interactivity, by writing the initial code, and then changing the parameter values inline multiple times. However, we believe it is much better to create an interactive tool that can ease the pain, as well as reduce the number of potential mistakes.

In order to do so, we leverage a tool called **IPython widgets** (**ipywidgets**), in combination with `plotly` and `cufflinks`. We select a few US tech stocks and three indicators (Bollinger Bands, MACD, and RSI) for the dashboard, but this selection can be extended to many more.

# Getting ready

After installing the `ipywidgets` library, we need to run the following line in Terminal to enable the extension:

```
jupyter nbextension enable --py widgetsnbextension
```

# How to do it...

Execute the following steps to create an interactive dashboard inside Jupyter Notebook.

1. Import the libraries:

```
import ipywidgets as wd
import cufflinks as cf
import pandas as pd
import yfinance as yf
from plotly.offline import iplot, init_notebook_mode
from ipywidgets import interact, interact_manual

init_notebook_mode()
```

2. Define the possible values for assets and technical indicators:

```
stocks = ['TWTR', 'MSFT', 'GOOGL', 'FB', 'TSLA', 'AAPL']
indicators = ['Bollinger Bands', 'MACD', 'RSI']
```

3. Define a function for creating the interactive plot:

```
def ta_dashboard(asset, indicator, start_date, end_date,
                 bb_k, bb_n, macd_fast, macd_slow, macd_signal,
                 rsi_periods, rsi_upper, rsi_lower):
    df = yf.download(asset,
                     start=start_date,
                     end=end_date,
                     progress=False,
                     auto_adjust=True)

    qf = cf.QuantFig(df, title=f'TA Dashboard - {asset}',
```

```
                              legend='right', name=f'{asset}')
            if 'Bollinger Bands' in indicator:
                qf.add_bollinger_bands(periods=bb_n,
                                        boll_std=bb_k)
            if 'MACD' in indicator:
                qf.add_macd(fast_period=macd_fast,
                            slow_period=macd_slow,
                            signal_period=macd_signal)
            if 'RSI' in indicator:
                qf.add_rsi(periods=rsi_periods,
                            rsi_upper=rsi_upper,
                            rsi_lower=rsi_lower,
                            showbands=True)

            return qf.iplot()
```

4. Define the selectors:

```
    stocks_selector = wd.Dropdown(
        options=stocks,
        value=stocks[0],
        description='Asset'
    )

    indicator_selector = wd.SelectMultiple(
        description='Indicator',
        options=indicators,
        value=[indicators[0]]
    )

    start_date_selector = wd.DatePicker(
        description='Start Date',
        value=pd.to_datetime('2018-01-01'),
        continuous_update=False
    )

    end_date_selector = wd.DatePicker(
        description='End Date',
        value=pd.to_datetime('2018-12-31'),
        continuous_update=False
    )
```

5. Define a label, and group the selectors inside a container:

```
main_selector_label = wd.Label('Main parameters',
                              layout=wd.Layout(height='45px'))

main_selector_box = wd.VBox(children=[main_selector_label,
                              stocks_selector,
                              indicator_selector,
                              start_date_selector,
                              end_date_selector])
```

6. Define the secondary selectors for the Bollinger Bands:

```
bb_label = wd.Label('Bollinger Bands')

n_param = wd.IntSlider(value=20, min=1, max=40, step=1,
                       description='N:', continuous_update=False)

k_param = wd.FloatSlider(value=2, min=0.5, max=4, step=0.5,
                         description='k:', continuous_update=False)

bollinger_box = wd.VBox(children=[bb_label, n_param, k_param])
```

7. Define the secondary selectors for the MACD:

```
macd_label = wd.Label('MACD')

macd_fast = wd.IntSlider(value=12, min=2, max=50, step=1,
                         description='Fast avg:',
                         continuous_update=False)

macd_slow = wd.IntSlider(value=26, min=2, max=50, step=1,
                         description='Slow avg:',
                         continuous_update=False)

macd_signal = wd.IntSlider(value=9, min=2, max=50, step=1,
                           description='MACD signal:',
                           continuous_update=False)

macd_box = wd.VBox(children=[macd_label, macd_fast,
                            macd_slow, macd_signal])
```

8. Define the secondary selectors for the RSI:

```
rsi_label = wd.Label('RSI')

rsi_periods = wd.IntSlider(value=14, min=2, max=50, step=1,
                           description='RSI periods:',
                           continuous_update=False)

rsi_upper = wd.IntSlider(value=70, min=1, max=100, step=1,
                         description='Upper Thr:',
                         continuous_update=False)

rsi_lower = wd.IntSlider(value=30, min=1, max=100, step=1,
                         description='Lower Thr:',
                         continuous_update=False)

rsi_box = wd.VBox(children=[rsi_label, rsi_periods,
                           rsi_upper, rsi_lower])
```

9. Create the labels and group the selectors into containers:

```
sec_selector_label = wd.Label('Secondary parameters',
                              layout=wd.Layout(height='45px'))
blank_label = wd.Label('', layout=wd.Layout(height='45px'))

sec_box_1 = wd.VBox([sec_selector_label, bollinger_box, macd_box])
sec_box_2 = wd.VBox([blank_label, rsi_box])

secondary_selector_box = wd.HBox([sec_box_1, sec_box_2])
```

10. Group the boxes and prepare the interactive output:

```
controls_dict = {'asset':stocks_selector,
                 'indicator':indicator_selector,
                 'start_date':start_date_selector,
                 'end_date':end_date_selector,
                 'bb_k':k_param,
                 'bb_n':n_param,
                 'macd_fast': macd_fast,
                 'macd_slow': macd_slow,
                 'macd_signal': macd_signal,
                 'rsi_periods': rsi_periods,
                 'rsi_upper': rsi_upper,
                 'rsi_lower': rsi_lower}

ui = wd.HBox([main_selector_box, secondary_selector_box])
out = wd.interactive_output(ta_dashboard, controls_dict)
```

11. Display the dashboard:

```
display(ui, out)
```

Running the last line displays the following **graphical user interface** (GUI):

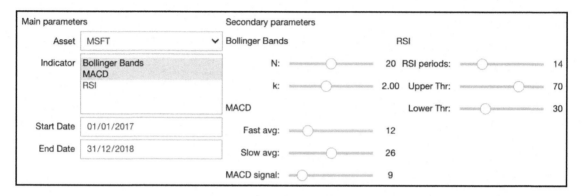

By selecting values of interest in the GUI, we can influence the interactive chart, for example, by changing the technical indicators we want to display.

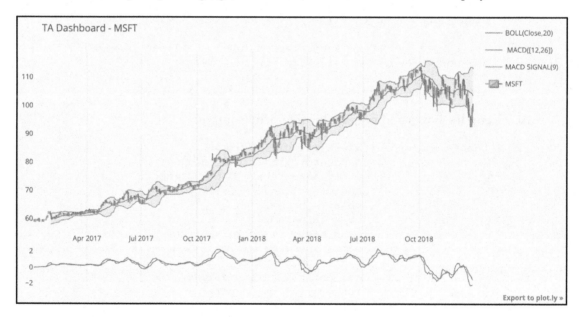

This time, we plotted both the Bollinger Bands and the MACD on top of the candlestick chart. Inside of the Notebook, we can zoom in on areas of interest, to further inspect the patterns.

# How it works...

After importing the libraries, we defined lists of possible assets (represented by their tickers), and the technical indicators from which to select.

In *Step 3*, we defined a function called `ta_dashboard`, which took as input all parameters we made configurable: asset, technical indicators, range of dates, and indicator-specific parameters. The function itself downloaded historical stock prices from Yahoo Finance and used `cufflinks` to draw a candlestick chart, as we presented in the *Creating a candlestick chart* recipe. Then, we added additional indicators to the figure, by using methods such as `add_bollinger_bands` and providing the required arguments. For a list of all supported technical indicators, please refer to the `cufflinks` documentation.

Having prepared the function, we started defining the elements of the GUI. In *Step 4* and *Step 5*, we defined the main selectors (such as the asset, technical indicators, and start/end dates for downloading the data) and grouped them inside a vertical box (`VBox`), which serves as storage for smaller elements and makes it easier to design the GUI. To indicate which selectors belonged to a given box, we provided a list of the objects as the `children` argument.

In *Steps 6* to *9*, we created the secondary container, this time with all the parameters responsible for tuning the technical indicators. Some general notes about using selectors and boxes are:

- We can turn off the continuous updating of sliders with `continuous_update=False`, so the plot only updates when a new value is set, not while moving it around.
- We can define the default value for a selector by providing the `value` argument.
- We can use blank labels (without any text) to align the elements of the boxes.

In *Step 10*, we used the `wd.interactive_output`, to indicate that the output of the `ta_dashboard` function would be modified by the interactive widgets (in a dictionary, we assigned widgets to certain arguments of the function). Lastly, we ran `display(ui, out)` to display the GUI, which in turn generated the plot.

## There's more...

The main advantage of the dashboard presented in this recipe is that it is embedded within Jupyter Notebook. However, we might want to move it outside of the local notebook and make it available for everyone as a web application. To do so, we could use **Dash**, which is Python's equivalent of R's vastly popular **Shiny** framework.

# 3
# Time Series Modeling

In this chapter, we will introduce the basics of time series modeling. We start by explaining the building blocks of time series and how to separate them using decomposition methods. Later, we will introduce the concept of stationarity—why it is important, how to test for it, and ultimately how to achieve it in case the original series is not stationary.

We will also look into two of the most widely used approaches to time series modeling—the exponential smoothing methods and ARIMA class models. In both cases, we will show you how to fit the models, evaluate the goodness of fit, and forecast future values of the time series. Additionally, we will present a novel approach to modeling a time series using the additive model from Facebook's Prophet library.

We cover the following recipes in this chapter:

- Decomposing time series
- Decomposing time series using Facebook's Prophet
- Testing for stationarity in time series
- Correcting for stationarity in time series
- Modeling time series with exponential smoothing methods
- Modeling time series with ARIMA class models
- Forecasting using ARIMA class models

# Decomposing time series

The goal of time series decomposition is to increase our understanding of the data by breaking down the series into multiple components. It provides insight in terms of modeling complexity and which approaches to follow in order to accurately capture each of the components.

These components can be divided into two types: systematic and non-systematic. The systematic ones are characterized by consistency and the fact that they can be described and modeled. By contrast, the non-systematic ones cannot be modeled directly.

The following are the **systematic components**:

- **level**: The mean value in the series.
- **trend**: An estimate of the trend, that is, the change in value between successive time points at any given moment. It can be associated with the slope (increasing/decreasing) of the series.
- **seasonality**: Deviations from the mean caused by repeating short-term cycles.

The following is the **non-systematic component**:

- **noise**: The random variation in the series

There are two types of models that are used for decomposing time series: additive and multiplicative.

The following are the characteristics of the **additive model**:

- Model's form: y(t) = level + trend + seasonality + noise
- Linear model: changes over time are consistent in size
- The trend is linear (straight line)
- Linear seasonality with the same frequency (width) and amplitude (height) of cycles over time

The following are the characteristics of the **multiplicative model**:

- Model's form: y(t) = level * trend * seasonality * noise
- **Non-linear model**: changes over time are not consistent in size, for example, exponential
- A curved, non-linear trend
- Non-linear seasonality with increasing/decreasing frequency and amplitude of cycles over time

It can be the case that we do not want to work with the multiplicative model. One possible solution is to apply certain transformations to make the trend/seasonality linear. One example of a transformation could be taking the log of a series in which we observe exponential growth.

In this recipe, we present how to carry out time-series decomposition of monthly gold prices downloaded from Quandl.

# How to do it...

Execute the following steps to carry out the time series decomposition.

1. Import the libraries:

```
import pandas as pd
import quandl
from statsmodels.tsa.seasonal import seasonal_decompose
```

2. Download the prices of gold for 2000-2011 and resample to monthly values:

```
QUANDL_KEY = '{key}' # replace {key} with your own API key
quandl.ApiConfig.api_key = QUANDL_KEY

df = quandl.get(dataset='WGC/GOLD_MONAVG_USD',
                start_date='2000-01-01',
                end_date='2011-12-31')

df.rename(columns={'Value': 'price'}, inplace=True)
df = df.resample('M').last()
```

There are some duplicate values in the series. For example, there is an entry for `2000-04-28` and `2000-04-30`, both with the same value. To deal with this issue, we resample to monthly data by only taking the last available value (this does not change any of the actual values; it only removes potential duplicates in each month).

3. Add the rolling mean and standard deviation:

```
WINDOW_SIZE = 12
df['rolling_mean'] = df.price.rolling(window=WINDOW_SIZE).mean()
df['rolling_std'] = df.price.rolling(window=WINDOW_SIZE).std()
df.plot(title='Gold Price')
```

Executing the code results in the following plot:

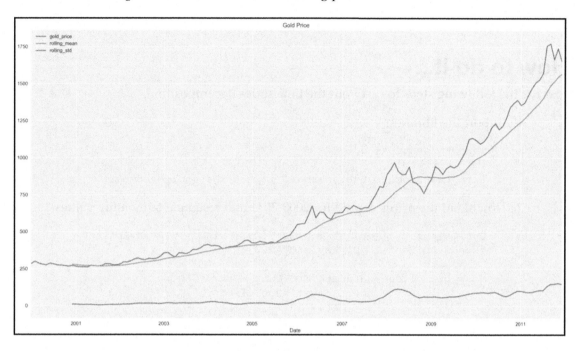

From the preceding plot, we can see that there is a non-linear growth pattern in the 12-month moving average and that the rolling standard deviation increases over time. That is why we decided to use the multiplicative model.

4. Carry out seasonal decomposition using the multiplicative model:

```
decomposition_results = seasonal_decompose(df.price,
                                        model='multiplicative')
decomposition_results.plot() \
                .suptitle('Multiplicative Decomposition',
                        fontsize=18);
```

The following decomposition plot is generated:

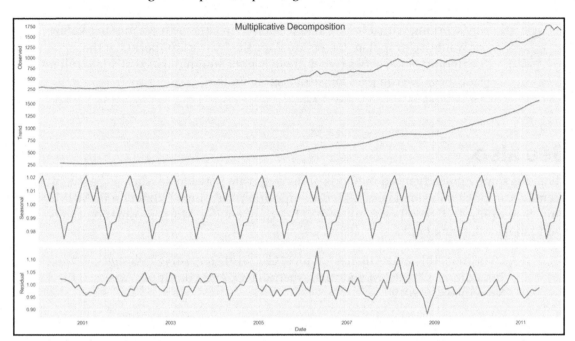

In the decomposition plot, we can see the extracted component series: trend, seasonal, and random (residual). To evaluate whether the decomposition makes sense, we can look at the random component. If there is no discernible pattern (in other words, the random component is indeed random), then the fit makes sense. For example, if we would have applied the additive model, there would be an increasing pattern in the residuals over time. In this case, it looks like the variance in the residuals is slightly higher in the second half of the dataset.

# How it works...

After downloading the data in *Step 2*, we made sure that the series only contained one data point per month (we enforced this by resampling the data to monthly frequency). To calculate the rolling statistics, we used the `rolling` method of a `pandas` DataFrame and specified the desired window size (12 months).

We used the `seasonal_decompose` function from the `statsmodels` library to carry out the classical decomposition. When doing so, we indicated what kind of model we would like to use—the possible values are `additive` and `multiplicative`.

When using `seasonal_decompose` with an array of numbers, we must specify the frequency of the observations (the `freq` argument) unless we are working with a `pandas` Series object. In case we have missing values or want to extrapolate the residual for the "warm-up" period at the beginning of the series (when there is not enough data to calculate rolling statistics), we can pass an extra argument, that is, `extrapolate_trend='freq'`.

# See also

There are some more advanced methods of decomposition available, such as Seasonal and Trend decomposition using Loess (STL decomposition), Seasonal Extraction in ARIMA Time Series (SEATS Decomposition), and X11 decomposition. More information can be found in the following book:

- Hyndman, R.J., and Athanasopoulos, G. (2018) *Forecasting: principles and practice*, 2nd edition, OTexts: Melbourne, Australia. OTexts.com/fpp2. Accessed on November 26, 2019.

# Decomposing time series using Facebook's Prophet

An alternative approach to time series decomposition is to use an additive model, in which a time series is represented as a combination of patterns on different time scales (daily, weekly, monthly, yearly, and so on) together with the overall trend. Facebook's Prophet does exactly that, along with more advanced functionalities such as accounting for changepoints (rapid changes in behavior), holidays, and much more. A practical benefit of using this library is that we are able to forecast future values of the time series, along with a confidence interval indicating the level of uncertainty.

In this recipe, we will try fitting Prophet's additive model to daily gold prices from 2000-2004 and predicting the prices over 2005.

# How to do it...

Execute the following steps to decompose the gold prices time series using Facebook's Prophet and create forecasts for one year ahead.

1. Import the libraries and authenticate with Quandl:

```
import pandas as pd
import seaborn as sns
import quandl
from fbprophet import Prophet

QUANDL_KEY = '{key}' # replace {key} with your own API key
quandl.ApiConfig.api_key = QUANDL_KEY
```

2. Download the daily gold prices and rename the columns:

```
df = quandl.get(dataset='WGC/GOLD_DAILY_USD',
                start_date='2000-01-01',
                end_date='2005-12-31')

df.reset_index(drop=False, inplace=True)
df.rename(columns={'Date': 'ds', 'Value': 'y'}, inplace=True)
```

3. Split the series into the training and test sets:

```
train_indices = df.ds.apply(lambda x: x.year) < 2005
df_train = df.loc[train_indices].dropna()
df_test = df.loc[~train_indices].reset_index(drop=True)
```

4. Create the instance of the model and fit it to the data:

```
model_prophet = Prophet(seasonality_mode='additive')
model_prophet.add_seasonality(name='monthly', period=30.5,
                              fourier_order=5)
model_prophet.fit(df_train)
```

5. Forecast the gold prices and plot the results:

```
df_future = model_prophet.make_future_dataframe(periods=365)
df_pred = model_prophet.predict(df_future)
model_prophet.plot(df_pred)
```

The resulting plot is as follows:

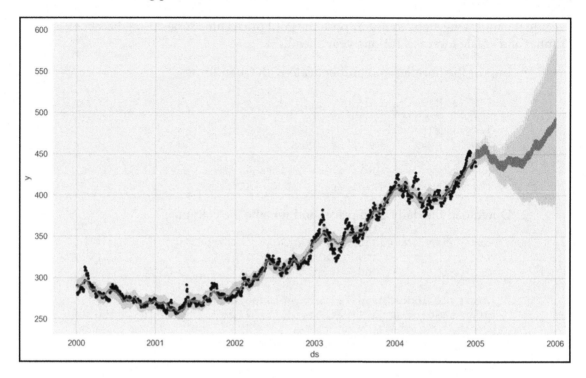

The black dots are the actual observations of the gold price. The blue line representing the fit does not match the observations exactly, as the model smooths out the noise in the data (also reducing the chance of overfitting). An important feature is that Prophet quantifies uncertainty, which is represented by the blue intervals around the fitted line.

6. Inspect the decomposition of the time series:

```
model_prophet.plot_components(df_pred)
```

The decomposition is presented in the following plot:

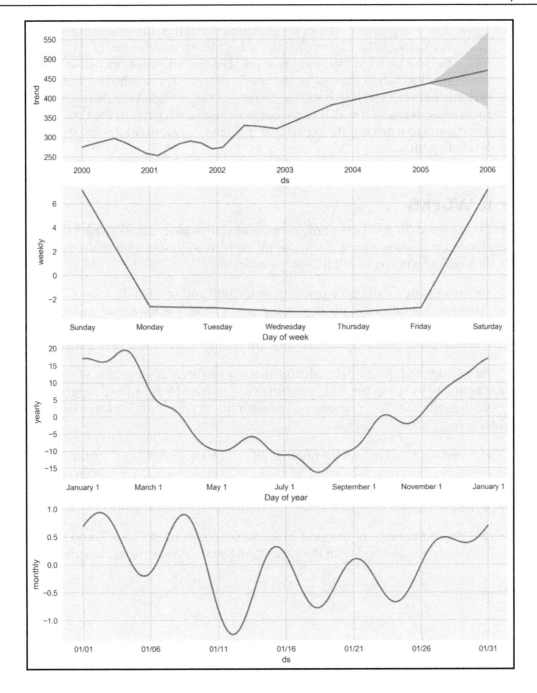

Upon closer inspection, we can see that the overall trend is increasing and that the gold price seems to be higher during the beginning and the end of the year, with a dip in the summer. On the monthly level, there is some movement, but the scale is much smaller than in the case of the yearly pattern. There is not a lot of movement in the weekly chart (we do not look at weekends as there are no prices for weekends), which makes sense because, with a decrease in the time scale, the noise starts to wash out the signal. For this reason, we might disable the weekly level altogether.

# How it works...

Prophet was designed for analyzing time series with daily observations (which does not mean that there are no ways to use weekly or monthly data) that exhibit patterns on different time scales (weekly, monthly, yearly, and so on).

In *Step 2*, we downloaded daily gold prices from Quandl and created a `pandas` DataFrame with two columns: `ds`, indicating the timestamp, and `y`, which is the target variable. This structure (column names) is required for working with Prophet. Then, we split the DataFrame into training (years 2000-2004) and test (the year 2005) sets by slicing over time.

In *Step 4*, we instantiated the model with additive seasonality. Additionally, we added the monthly seasonality by using the `add_seasonality` method with values suggested by Prophet's documentation. To fit the model, we used the `fit` method, which is known from the popular `scikit-learn` library.

In *Step 5*, we used the fitted model for predictions. To create forecasts with Prophet, we had to create a `future_dataframe` by using the `make_future_dataframe` method and indicating how many periods we wanted to obtain (by default, this is measured in days). We created the predictions using the `predict` method of the fitted model.

We inspected the components of the model (the decomposition) in *Step 6*. To do so, we used the `plot_components` method with the prediction DataFrame as the argument.

# There's more...

We are also interested in some basic performance evaluation of the fitted model. Execute the following steps to visually inspect the predicted versus actual gold prices in 2005.

1. Merge the test set with the forecasts:

```
selected_columns = ['ds', 'yhat_lower', 'yhat_upper', 'yhat']

df_pred = df_pred.loc[:, selected_columns].reset_index(drop=True)
df_test = df_test.merge(df_pred, on=['ds'], how='left')
df_test.ds = pd.to_datetime(df_test.ds)
df_test.set_index('ds', inplace=True)
```

We merged the test set with the prediction DataFrame. We used a left join, which returns all the rows from the left table (test set) and the matched rows from the right table (prediction DataFrame) while leaving the unmatched rows empty. This way, we also kept only the dates that were in the test set (Prophet created predictions for the next 365 days, including weekends and potential holidays).

2. Plot the test values versus predictions:

```
fig, ax = plt.subplots(1, 1)

ax = sns.lineplot(data=df_test[['y', 'yhat_lower', 'yhat_upper',
                                'yhat']])
ax.fill_between(df_test.index,
                df_test.yhat_lower,
                df_test.yhat_upper,
                alpha=0.3)
ax.set(title='Gold Price - actual vs. predicted',
       xlabel='Date',
       ylabel='Gold Price ($)')
```

Executing the code results in the following plot:

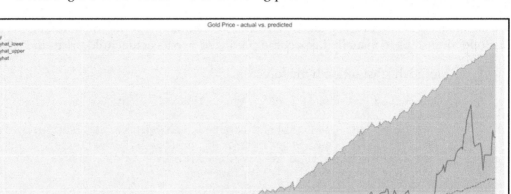

From the preceding plot, we can see that Prophet accurately (at least visually) predicted the price of gold over 2005. It was only over the first two months that the observed prices were outside of the confidence interval.

# Testing for stationarity in time series

A stationary time series is a series in which statistical properties such as mean, variance, and covariance are constant over time. Stationarity is a desired characteristic of time series as it makes modeling and extrapolating (forecasting) into the future more feasible. Some drawbacks of non-stationary data are:

- Variance can be misspecified by the model
- Worse model fit
- Cannot leverage valuable time-dependent patterns in the data

In this recipe, we show you how to test the time series for stationarity. To do so, we employ the following methods:

- The **Augmented Dickey-Fuller (ADF) test**
- The **Kwiatkowski-Phillips-Schmidt-Shin (KPSS) test**
- Plots of the **(partial) autocorrelation function (PACF/ACF)**

We investigate the stationarity of monthly gold prices from the years 2000-2011.

# Getting ready

We will use the same data that we used in the *Decomposing time series* recipe. In the plot presenting the rolling mean and standard deviation of the gold prices, we have already seen that the statistics seem to increase over time, suggesting non-stationarity.

# How to do it...

Execute the following steps to test the given time series for stationarity.

1. Import the libraries:

```
import pandas as pd
from statsmodels.graphics.tsaplots import plot_acf, plot_pacf
from statsmodels.tsa.stattools import adfuller, kpss
```

2. Define a function for running the ADF test:

```
def adf_test(x):
    indices = ['Test Statistic', 'p-value',
               '# of Lags Used', '# of Observations Used']
    adf_test = adfuller(x, autolag='AIC')
    results = pd.Series(adf_test[0:4], index=indices)
    for key, value in adf_test[4].items():
        results[f'Critical Value ({key})'] = value

    return results
```

Now, we can run the test:

```
adf_test(df.price)
```

The code generates the following summary:

```
Test Statistic                  3.510499
p-value                         1.000000
# of Lags Used                 14.000000
# of Observations Used        129.000000
Critical Value (1%)            -3.482088
Critical Value (5%)            -2.884219
Critical Value (10%)           -2.578864
```

The null hypothesis of the ADF test states that the time series is not stationary. With a p-value of 1 (or equivalently, the test statistic larger than the critical value for the selected confidence level), we have no reason to reject the null hypothesis, meaning that we can conclude that the series is not stationary.

3. Define a function for running the KPSS test:

```
def kpss_test(x, h0_type='c'):

    indices = ['Test Statistic', 'p-value', '# of Lags']
    kpss_test = kpss(x, regression=h0_type)
    results = pd.Series(kpss_test[0:3], index=indices)
    for key, value in kpss_test[3].items():
        results[f'Critical Value ({key})'] = value

    return results
```

Now, we can run the test:

```
kpss_test(df.price)
```

The code generates the following summary:

```
Test Statistic              0.985671
p-value                     0.010000
# of Lags                  14.000000
Critical Value (10%)        0.347000
Critical Value (5%)         0.463000
Critical Value (2.5%)       0.574000
Critical Value (1%)         0.739000
```

The null hypothesis of the KPSS test is that the time series is stationary. With a p-value of 0.01 (or test statistic greater than the selected critical value), we have reasons to reject the null hypothesis in favor of the alternative one, meaning that the series is not stationary.

4. Generate the ACF/PACF plots:

```
N_LAGS = 40
SIGNIFICANCE_LEVEL = 0.05

fig, ax = plt.subplots(2, 1)
plot_acf(df.price, ax=ax[0], lags=N_LAGS,
         alpha=SIGNIFICANCE_LEVEL)
plot_pacf(df.price, ax=ax[1], lags=N_LAGS,
          alpha=SIGNIFICANCE_LEVEL)
```

The output is as follows:

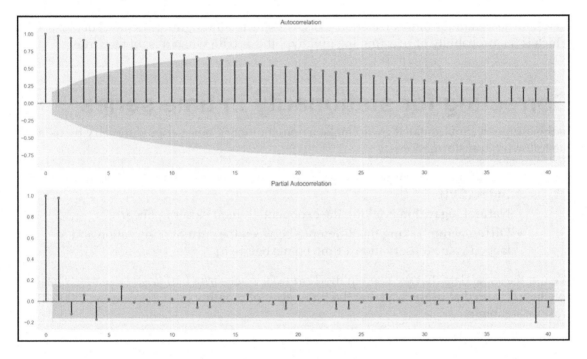

In the ACF plot, we can see that there are significant autocorrelations (above the 95% confidence interval, corresponding to the selected 5% significance level). There are also some significant autocorrelations at lags 1 and 4 in the PACF plot.

# How it works...

In *Step 2*, we defined a function used for running the ADF test and printing out the results. We specified `autolag='AIC'` in the `adfuller` function, so the number of considered lags is automatically selected based on the **Akaike Information Criterion (AIC)**. Alternatively, we could select this value manually.

For the `kpss` function (*Step 3*), we specified the `regression` argument. A value of `'c'` corresponds to the null hypothesis stating that the series is level-stationary, while `'ct'` corresponds to trend-stationary (removing the trend from the series would make it level-stationary).

For all the tests and the autocorrelation plots, we selected the significance level of 5%, which is the probability of rejecting the null hypothesis (*H0*) when it is, in fact, true.

# Correcting for stationarity in time series

In this recipe, we investigate how to make a non-stationary time series stationary by using the following transformations:

- **Deflation**: Accounting for inflation in monetary series using the **Consumer Price Index (CPI)**
- **Natural logarithm**: Making the exponential trend closer to linear
- **Differencing**: Taking the difference between the current observation and a lagged value (observation *x* time points before it)

We use the same data that we used in the *Testing for stationarity in time series* recipe. The conclusion from that recipe was that the time series of monthly gold prices from 2000-2011 was not stationary.

# How to do it...

Execute the following steps to transform the series from non-stationary to stationary.

1. Import the libraries and update the inflation data:

```
import cpi
import pandas as pd
from datetime import date
from statsmodels.graphics.tsaplots import plot_acf, plot_pacf
from statsmodels.tsa.stattools import adfuller, kpss
```

```
from chapter_3_utils import test_autocorrelation

# update the CPI data (if needed)
# cpi.update()
```

2. Deflate the gold prices (to 2011-12-31 USD values) and plot the results:

```
DEFL_DATE = date(2011, 12, 31)

df['dt_index'] = df.index.map(lambda x: x.to_pydatetime().date())
df['price_deflated'] = df.apply(lambda x:
                                        cpi.inflate(x.price,
                                                    x.dt_index,
                                                    DEFL_DATE),
                                axis=1)
df[['price', 'price_deflated']].plot(title='Gold Price
(deflated)');
```

We can observe the inflation-adjusted prices in the following plot:

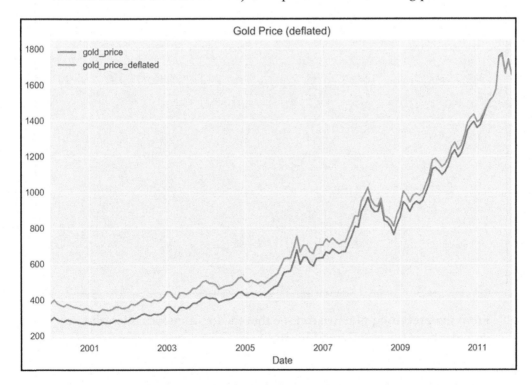

We could also adjust the gold prices to another point of time, as long as it is the same point for the entire series.

3. Deflate the series using a natural logarithm and plot it with the rolling metrics:

```
WINDOW = 12
selected_columns = ['price_log', 'rolling_mean_log',
                    'rolling_std_log']

df['price_log'] = np.log(df.price_deflated)
df['rolling_mean_log'] = df.price_log.rolling(window=WINDOW) \
                            .mean()
df['rolling_std_log'] = df.price_log.rolling(window=WINDOW) \
                            .std()

df[selected_columns].plot(title='Gold Price (logged)')
```

Executing the code results in the following output:

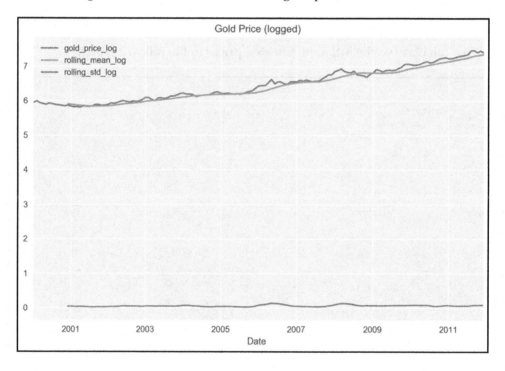

From the preceding plot, we can see that the log transformation did its job, that is, it made the exponential trend linear.

4. Use `test_autocorrelation` (the helper function for this chapter) to investigate whether the series became stationary:

```
test_autocorrelation(df.price_log)
```

Executing the code results in the following plot:

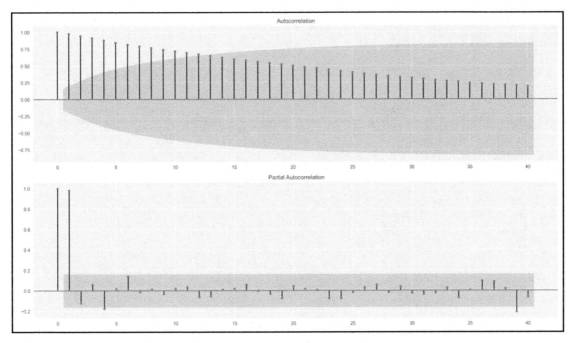

We also receive the results of the statistical tests:

```
ADF test statistic: 0.89 (p-val: 0.99)
KPSS test statistic: 1.04 (p-val: 0.01)
```

After inspecting the results of the statistical tests and the ACF/PACF plots, we can conclude that deflation and a natural algorithm were not enough to make the gold prices stationary.

5. Apply differencing to the series and plot the results:

```
selected_columns = ['price_log_diff','roll_mean_log_diff',
                    'roll_std_log_diff']
df['price_log_diff'] = df.price_log.diff(1)
df['roll_mean_log_diff'] = df.price_log_diff.rolling(WINDOW) \
                           .mean()
df['roll_std_log_diff'] = df.price_log_diff.rolling(WINDOW) \
                          .std()
df[selected_columns].plot(title='Gold Price (1st differences)')
```

Executing the code results in the following output:

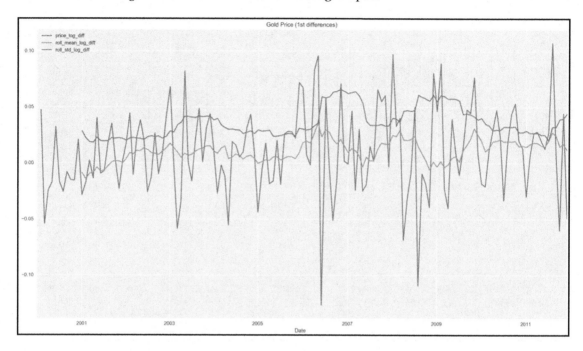

The transformed gold prices make the impression of being stationary – the series oscillates around 0 with more or less constant variance. At least there is no visible trend.

6. Test whether the series became stationary:

```
test_autocorrelation(df.price_log_diff.dropna())
```

Executing the preceding code results in the following plot:

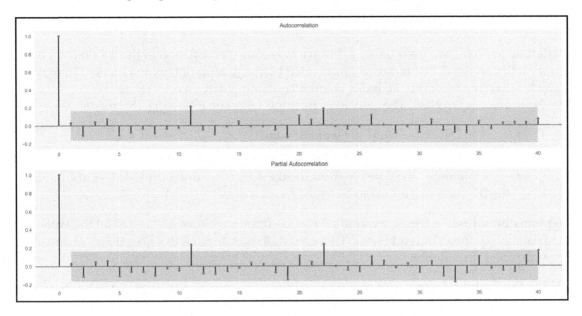

We also receive the results of the statistical tests:

```
ADF test statistic: -9.13 (p-val: 0.00)
KPSS test statistic: 0.37 (p-val: 0.09)
```

After applying the first differences, the series became stationary at the 5% significance level (according to both tests). In the ACF/PACF plots, we can see that there was a significant value of the function at lag 11 and 22. This might indicate some kind of seasonality or simply be a false signal. Using a 5% significance level means that 5% of the values might lie outside the 95% confidence interval – even when the underlying process does not show any autocorrelation or partial autocorrelation.

# How it works...

We address each transformation separately:

**Deflation:** In *Step 2*, we used the `cpi` library to account for inflation in the US dollar. The library relies on the CPI-U index recommended by the Bureau of Labor Statistics. To make it work, we created an artificial index column containing dates as objects of the `datetime.date` class. The `inflate` function takes the following arguments:

- `value`: The dollar value we want to adjust.
- `year_or_month`: The date that the dollar value comes from.
- `to`: Optionally, the date we want to adjust to. If we don't provide this argument, the function will adjust to the most recent year.

**Log transformation:** In *Step 3*, we applied the natural logarithm (`np.log`) to all the values to make the exponential trend linear. This operation was applied to prices that had already been corrected for inflation.

**Taking the first difference:** In *Step 5*, we used the `diff` method to calculate the difference between the value in time *t* and time *t-1* (the default setting corresponds to the first difference). We can specify a different number by changing the `period` argument.

# There's more...

The considered gold prices do not contain obvious seasonality. However, if the dataset shows seasonal patterns, there are a few potential solutions:

- **Adjustment by differencing**: Instead of using the first order differencing, use a higher-order one, for example, if there is yearly seasonality in monthly data, use `diff(12)`.
- **Adjustment by modeling**: We can directly model the seasonality and then remove it from the series. One possibility is to extract the seasonal component from `seasonal_decompose` or another more advanced automatic decomposition algorithm. In this case, we should subtract the seasonal component when using the additive model or divide by it if the model is multiplicative. Another solution is to use `np.polyfit()` to fit the best polynomial of a chosen order to the selected time series and then subtract it from the original series.

The **Box-Cox transformation** is another type of adjustment we can use on the time series data. It combines different exponential transformation functions to make the distribution more similar to the Normal (Gaussian) distribution. We can use `boxcox` from `scipy`, which allows us to automatically find the value of the `lambda` parameter for the best fit. One condition to be aware of is that all the values in the series must be positive, the transformation should not be used after 1st differences or any transformations that introduce negative values to the series.

A library called `pmdarima` (more on this library can be found in the *Modeling time series with ARIMA class models* recipe) contains two functions that employ statistical tests to determine how many times we should differentiate the series in order to achieve stationarity (and also remove seasonality, that is, seasonal stationarity).

We can employ the following tests to investigate stationarity: ADF, KPSS, and **Phillips–Perron (PP)**:

```
from pmdarima.arima import ndiffs, nsdiffs

print(f"Suggested # of differences (ADF): {ndiffs(df.price, test='adf')}")
print(f"Suggested # of differences (KPSS): {ndiffs(df.price,
test='kpss')}")
print(f"Suggested # of differences (PP): {ndiffs(df.price, test='pp')}")
```

The output of the preceding code is as follows:

```
Suggested # of differences (ADF): 1
Suggested # of differences (KPSS): 2
Suggested # of differences (PP): 1
```

For the KPSS test, we can also specify what type of null hypothesis we want to test against. The default is level stationarity (`null='level'`). The results of the tests suggest that the series (without any differencing) is not stationary.

The library also contains two tests for seasonal differences:

- **Osborn, Chui, Smith, and Birchenhall (OCSB)**
- **Canova-Hansen (CH)**

To run them, we also need to specify the frequency of our data (12, in our case) as we are working with monthly data:

```
print(f"Suggested # of differences (OSCB): {nsdiffs(df.price, m=12,
test='ocsb')}")
print(f"Suggested # of differences (CH): {nsdiffs(df.price, m=12,
test='ch')}")
```

The output is as follows:

```
Suggested # of differences (OSCB): 0
Suggested # of differences (CH): 0
```

The results suggest no seasonality in gold prices.

# Modeling time series with exponential smoothing methods

Exponential smoothing methods are suitable for non-stationary data (that is, data with a trend and/or seasonality) and work similarly to exponential moving averages. The forecasts are weighted averages of past observations. These models put more emphasis on recent observations as the weights become exponentially smaller with time. Smoothing methods are popular because they are fast (not a lot of computations are required) and relatively reliable when it comes to forecasts:

**Simple exponential smoothing:** The most basic model is called Simple Exponential Smoothing (SES). This class of models is most apt for cases when the considered time series does not exhibit any trend or seasonality. They also work well with series with only a few data points.

The model is parameterized by a smoothing parameter $\alpha$ with values between 0 and 1. The higher the value, the more weight is put to recent observations. When $\alpha = 0$, the forecasts for the future are equal to the average of historical data (the one that the model was fitted to). When $\alpha = 1$, all the forecasts have the same value as the last observation in the training data.

Simple Exponential Smoothing's forecast function is flat, that is, all the forecasts, regardless of the time horizon, are equal to the same value—the last level component. That is why this method is only suitable for series with neither trend nor seasonality.

**Holt's linear trend method:** Holt's model is an extension of SES that accounts for a trend in the series by adding the trend component into the model specification. This model should be used when there is a trend in the data, but no seasonality.

One issue with Holt's model is that the trend is constant in the future, which means that it increases/decreases indefinitely. That is why an extension of the model dampens the trend by adding the dampening parameter, $\varphi$. It makes the trend converge to a constant value in the future, effectively flattening it. Hyndman and Athanasopoulos (2018) state that $\varphi$ is rarely smaller than 0.8, as the dampening has a very strong effect for smaller values of $\varphi$.

The best practice is to restrict the values of φ so that they lie between 0.8 and 0.98, because for φ = 1 the damped model is equivalent to the model without dampening.

In this recipe, we show you how to apply smoothing methods to Google's monthly stock prices (non-stationary data with a trend and no visible seasonality). We fit the model to the prices from 2010-2017 and make forecasts for 2018.

# Getting ready

In the following recipes, we will be plotting multiple lines on the same plots, each of them representing a different model specification. That is why we want to make sure these lines are clearly distinguishable, especially in black and white. For that reason, from now until the last recipe of this chapter, we will be using a different color palette for the plots, that is, cubehelix:

```
plt.set_cmap('cubehelix')
sns.set_palette('cubehelix')

COLORS = [plt.cm.cubehelix(x) for x in [0.1, 0.3, 0.5, 0.7]]
```

In the preceding code, we defined a list of four colors. We will use these instead of using the standard color codes (red/green/blue/gray).

# How to do it...

Execute the following steps to use the exponential smoothing methods to create forecasts of Google's stock prices.

1. Import the libraries:

```
import pandas as pd
import numpy as np
import yfinance as yf
from datetime import date
from statsmodels.tsa.holtwinters import (ExponentialSmoothing,
                                         SimpleExpSmoothing,
                                         Holt)
```

2. Download the adjusted stock prices for Google:

```
df = yf.download('GOOG',
                 start='2010-01-01',
                 end='2018-12-31',
                 adjusted=True,
                 progress=False)
```

3. Aggregate to monthly frequency:

```
goog = df.resample('M') \
         .last() \
         .rename(columns={'Adj Close': 'adj_close'}) \
         .adj_close
```

4. Create the training/test split:

```
train_indices = goog.index.year < 2018
goog_train = goog[train_indices]
goog_test = goog[~train_indices]

test_length = len(goog_test)
```

5. Plot the prices:

```
goog.plot(title="Google's Stock Price")
```

The preceding code generates the following plot:

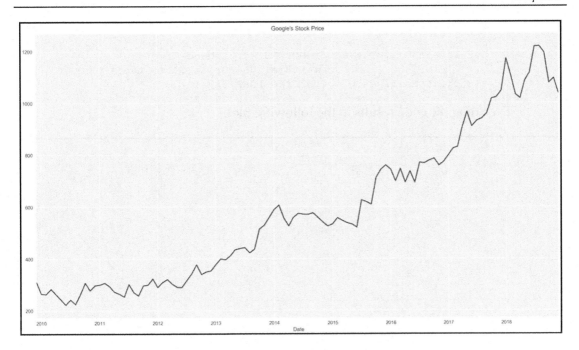

6. Fit three SES models and create forecasts for them:

```
ses_1 = SimpleExpSmoothing(goog_train).fit(smoothing_level=0.2)
ses_forecast_1 = ses_1.forecast(test_length)

ses_2 = SimpleExpSmoothing(goog_train).fit(smoothing_level=0.5)
ses_forecast_2 = ses_2.forecast(test_length)

ses_3 = SimpleExpSmoothing(goog_train).fit()
alpha = ses_3.model.params['smoothing_level']
ses_forecast_3 = ses_3.forecast(test_length)
```

7. Plot the original prices and the models' results:

```
goog.plot(color=COLORS[0],
          title='Simple Exponential Smoothing',
          label='Actual',
          legend=True)

ses_forecast_1.plot(color=COLORS[1], legend=True,
                    label=r'$\alpha=0.2$')
ses_1.fittedvalues.plot(color=COLORS[1])

ses_forecast_2.plot(color=COLORS[2], legend=True,
                    label=r'$\alpha=0.5$')
```

```
ses_2.fittedvalues.plot(color=COLORS[2])

ses_forecast_3.plot(color=COLORS[3], legend=True,
                     label=r'$\alpha={0:.4f}$'.format(alpha))
ses_3.fittedvalues.plot(color=COLORS[3])
```

Executing the code results in the following plot:

In the preceding plot, we can see the characteristic of the SES we described in the introduction to this recipe—the forecast is a flat line. We can also see that the optimal value that was selected by the `statsmodels` optimization routine is close to 1. Additionally, the fitted line of the third model is effectively the line of the observed prices shifted to the right.

8. Fit three variants of Holt's smoothing model and create forecasts:

```
# Holt's model with linear trend
hs_1 = Holt(goog_train).fit()
hs_forecast_1 = hs_1.forecast(test_length)

# Holt's model with exponential trend
hs_2 = Holt(goog_train, exponential=True).fit()
hs_forecast_2 = hs_2.forecast(test_length)

# Holt's model with exponential trend and damping
hs_3 = Holt(goog_train, exponential=False,
            damped=True).fit(damping_slope=0.99)
hs_forecast_3 = hs_3.forecast(test_length)
```

`Holt(goog_train, exponential=True)` is equivalent to
`ExponentialSmoothing(goog_train, trend='mul')`.

9. Plot the original prices and the models' results:

```
goog.plot(color=COLORS[0],
          title="Holt's Smoothing models",
          label='Actual',
          legend=True)

hs_1.fittedvalues.plot(color=COLORS[1])
hs_forecast_1.plot(color=COLORS[1], legend=True,
                   label='Linear trend')

hs_2.fittedvalues.plot(color=COLORS[2])
hs_forecast_2.plot(color=COLORS[2], legend=True,
                   label='Exponential trend')

hs_3.fittedvalues.plot(color=COLORS[3])
hs_forecast_3.plot(color=COLORS[3], legend=True,
                   label='Exponential trend (damped)')
```

Executing the code results in the following plot:

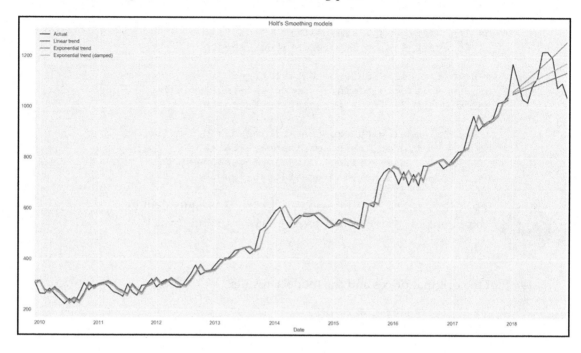

We can already observe an improvement since the lines are not flat anymore, as compared to SES.

# How it works...

In *Steps 2 to 5*, we downloaded Google's stock prices from 2010-2018, resampled the values to a monthly frequency, split the data into training (2010-2017) and test (2018) sets, and plotted the series.

In *Step 6*, we fitted three different SES models using the `SimpleExpSmoothing` class and its `fit` method. For fitting, we only used the training data. We could have manually selected the value of the smoothing parameter (`smoothing_level`), however, the best practice is to let `statsmodels` optimize it for the best fit. This optimization is done by minimizing the sum of squared residuals (errors). We created the forecasts using the `forecast` method, which requires the number of periods we want to forecast for (which is equal to the length of the test set). In *Step 7*, we visualized the results and compared them to the actual stock prices. We extracted the fitted values of the model by using the `fittedvalues` method of the fitted model.

In *Step 8*, we used the `Holt` class (which is a wrapper around the more general `ExponentialSmoothing` class) to fit Holt's linear trend model. By default, the trend in the model is linear, but we can make it exponential by specifying `exponential=True` and add dampening with `damped=True`. As in the case of SES, using the `fit` method with no arguments results in running the optimization routine to determine the optimal value of the parameter. We can access it by running `fitted_model.params`. In our example, we manually specified the value of the dampening parameter to be 0.99, as the optimizer selected 1 to be the optimal value, and this would be indistinguishable on the plot. In *Step 9*, we visualized the results.

# There's more...

There is an extension of Holt's method called **Holt-Winter's Seasonal Smoothing**. It accounts for seasonality in the time series. There is no separate class for this model, but we can tune the `ExponentialSmoothing` class by adding the `seasonal` and `seasonal_periods` arguments.

Without going into too much detail, this method is most suitable for data with trend and seasonality. There are two variants of this model and they have either additive or multiplicative seasonalities. In the former one, the seasonal variations are more or less constant throughout the time series. In the latter one, the variations change in proportion to the passing of time.

We begin by fitting the models:

```
SEASONAL_PERIODS = 12

# Holt-Winter's model with exponential trend
hw_1 = ExponentialSmoothing(goog_train,
                            trend='mul',
                            seasonal='add',
                            seasonal_periods=SEASONAL_PERIODS).fit()
hw_forecast_1 = hw_1.forecast(test_length)

# Holt-Winter's model with exponential trend and damping
hw_2 = ExponentialSmoothing(goog_train,
                            trend='mul',
                            seasonal='add',
                            seasonal_periods=SEASONAL_PERIODS,
                            damped=True).fit()
hw_forecast_2 = hw_2.forecast(test_length)
```

Then, we plot the results:

```
goog.plot(color=COLORS[0],
          title="Holt-Winter's Seasonal Smoothing",
          label='Actual',
          legend=True)

hw_1.fittedvalues.plot(color=COLORS[1])
hw_forecast_1.plot(color=COLORS[1], legend=True,
                   label='Seasonal Smoothing')

phi = hw_2.model.params['damping_slope']
plot_label = f'Seasonal Smoothing (damped with $\phi={phi:.4f}$)'

hw_2.fittedvalues.plot(color=COLORS[2])
hw_forecast_2.plot(color=COLORS[2], legend=True,
                   label=plot_label)
```

Executing the code results in the following plot:

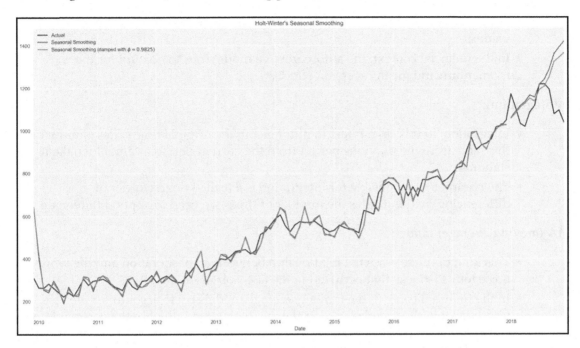

From the plotted forecasts, we can see that the model is more flexible in comparison to SES and Holt's linear trend models. The extreme fitted values at the beginning of the series are a result of not having enough observations to look back on (we selected `seasonal_periods=12` as we are dealing with monthly data).

# Modeling time series with ARIMA class models

ARIMA models are a class of statistical models that are used for analyzing and forecasting time series data. They aim to do so by describing the autocorrelations in the data. ARIMA stands for Autoregressive Integrated Moving Average and is an extension of a simpler ARMA model. The goal of the additional integration component is to ensure stationarity of the series, because, in contrast to the exponential smoothing models, the ARIMA class requires the time series to be stationary. In the next few paragraphs, we briefly go over the building blocks of ARIMA models.

## AR (autoregressive) model:

- This kind of model uses the relationship between an observation and its lagged values.
- In the financial context, the autoregressive model tries to account for the momentum and mean reversion effects.

## I (integration):

- Integration, in this case, refers to differencing the original time series (subtracting the value from the previous period from the current period's value) to make it stationary.
- The parameter responsible for integration is $d$ (called degree/order of differencing) and indicates the number of times we need to apply differencing.

## MA (moving average) model:

- This kind of model uses the relationship between an observation and the white noise terms (shocks that occurred in the last $q$ observations).
- In the financial context, the moving average models try to account for the unpredictable shocks (observed in the residuals) that influence the observed time series. Some examples of such shocks could be natural disasters, breaking news connected to a certain company, and so on.

All of these components fit together and are directly specified in the commonly used notation known as ARIMA (p,d,q).

By setting the parameters of the ARIMA model, we can obtain some special cases:
- ARIMA (0,0,0): White noise
- ARIMA (0,1,0) without constant: Random walk
- ARIMA (p,0,q): ARMA(p, q)
- ARIMA (p, 0, 0): AR(p) model
- ARIMA (0, 0, q): MA(q) model
- ARIMA (0,1,2): Damped Holt's model
- ARIMA (0,1,1) without constant: SES model
- ARIMA (0,2,2): Holt's linear method with additive errors

One of the known weaknesses of the ARIMA class models in the financial context is their inability to capture volatility clustering that is observed in most of the financial assets.

In this recipe, we go through all the necessary steps to correctly estimate an ARIMA model and learn how to verify that it is a proper fit to the data. For this example, we use Google's weekly stock prices from 2015-2018.

# How to do it...

Execute the following steps to fit and evaluate an ARIMA model using Google's stock price.

1. Import the libraries:

```python
import yfinance as yf
import pandas as pd
import numpy as np
from statsmodels.tsa.arima_model import ARIMA
import statsmodels.api as sm
from statsmodels.graphics.tsaplots import plot_acf
from statsmodels.stats.diagnostic import acorr_ljungbox
import scipy.stats as scs
from chapter_3_utils import test_autocorrelation
```

2. Download Google's stock prices and resample them to weekly frequency:

```python
df = yf.download('GOOG',
                 start='2015-01-01',
                 end='2018-12-31',
                 adjusted=True,
                 progress=False)

goog = df.resample('W') \
         .last() \
         .rename(columns={'Adj Close': 'adj_close'}) \
         .adj_close
```

3. Apply the first differences to the price series and plot them together:

```python
goog_diff = goog.diff().dropna()

fig, ax = plt.subplots(2, sharex=True)
goog.plot(title = "Google's stock price", ax=ax[0])
goog_diff.plot(ax=ax[1], title='First Differences')
```

In the following plot, we can see a more or less linear trend in Google's stock price, which indicates non-stationarity:

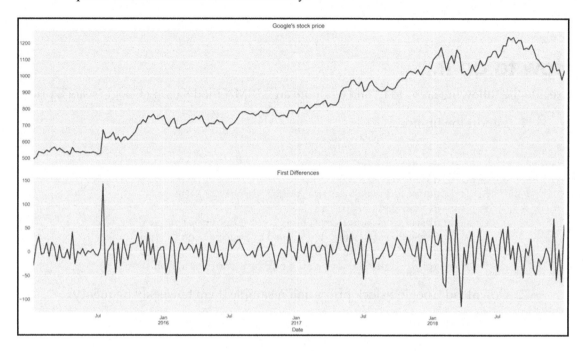

4. Test the differenced series for stationarity:

```
test_autocorrelation(goog_diff)
```

Executing the code results in the following plot:

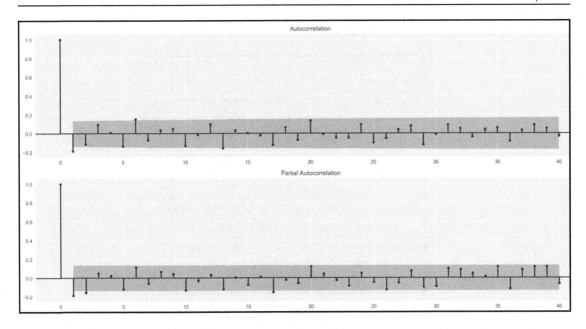

We also receive the results of the statistical tests:

```
ADF test statistic: -12.79 (p-val: 0.00)
KPSS test statistic: 0.11 (p-val: 0.10)
```

The results indicate that the differenced prices are stationary.

5.  Based on the results of the tests, specify the ARIMA model and fit it to the data:

```
arima = ARIMA(goog, order=(2, 1, 1)).fit(disp=0)
arima.summary()
```

We get the following output:

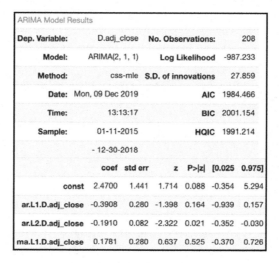

ARIMA Model Results

| Dep. Variable: | D.adj_close | No. Observations: | 208 |
|---|---|---|---|
| Model: | ARIMA(2, 1, 1) | Log Likelihood | -987.233 |
| Method: | css-mle | S.D. of innovations | 27.859 |
| Date: | Mon, 09 Dec 2019 | AIC | 1984.466 |
| Time: | 13:13:17 | BIC | 2001.154 |
| Sample: | 01-11-2015 | HQIC | 1991.214 |
| | - 12-30-2018 | | |

| | coef | std err | z | P>\|z\| | [0.025 | 0.975] |
|---|---|---|---|---|---|---|
| const | 2.4700 | 1.441 | 1.714 | 0.088 | -0.354 | 5.294 |
| ar.L1.D.adj_close | -0.3908 | 0.280 | -1.398 | 0.164 | -0.939 | 0.157 |
| ar.L2.D.adj_close | -0.1910 | 0.082 | -2.322 | 0.021 | -0.352 | -0.030 |
| ma.L1.D.adj_close | 0.1781 | 0.280 | 0.637 | 0.525 | -0.370 | 0.726 |

6. Prepare a function for diagnosing the fit of the model based on its residuals:

```
def arima_diagnostics(resids, n_lags=40):
    # create placeholder subplots
    fig, ((ax1, ax2), (ax3, ax4)) = plt.subplots(2, 2)

    r = resids
    resids = (r - np.nanmean(r)) / np.nanstd(r)
    resids_nonmissing = resids[~(np.isnan(resids))]

    # residuals over time
    sns.lineplot(x=np.arange(len(resids)), y=resids, ax=ax1)
    ax1.set_title('Standardized residuals')

    # distribution of residuals
    x_lim = (-1.96 * 2, 1.96 * 2)
    r_range = np.linspace(x_lim[0], x_lim[1])
    norm_pdf = scs.norm.pdf(r_range)
    sns.distplot(resids_nonmissing, hist=True, kde=True,
                 norm_hist=True, ax=ax2)
    ax2.plot(r_range, norm_pdf, 'g', lw=2, label='N(0,1)')
    ax2.set_title('Distribution of standardized residuals')
    ax2.set_xlim(x_lim)
    ax2.legend()

    # Q-Q plot
    qq = sm.qqplot(resids_nonmissing, line='s', ax=ax3)
    ax3.set_title('Q-Q plot')
```

```
# ACF plot
plot_acf(resids, ax=ax4, lags=n_lags, alpha=0.05)
ax4.set_title('ACF plot')

return fig
```

7.  Test the residuals of the fitted ARIMA model:

```
arima_diagnostics(arima.resid, 40)
```

The distribution of the standardized residuals does resemble the Normal distribution:

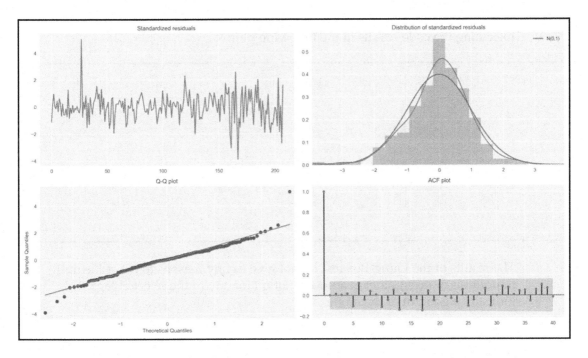

The average of the residuals is close to 0 (-0.05), and inspecting the ACF plot leads to the conclusion that the residuals are not correlated. These two characteristics speak in favor of a good fit. However, the tails of the distribution are slightly heavier than under normality, which we can observe in the Q-Q plot.

8. Apply the Ljung-Box test for no autocorrelation in the residuals and plot the results:

```
ljung_box_results = acorr_ljungbox(arima.resid)

fig, ax = plt.subplots(1, figsize=[16, 5])
sns.scatterplot(x=range(len(ljung_box_results[1])),
                y=ljung_box_results[1],
                ax=ax)
ax.axhline(0.05, ls='--', c='r')
ax.set(title="Ljung-Box test's results",
       xlabel='Lag',
       ylabel='p-value')
```

Executing the code results in the following plot:

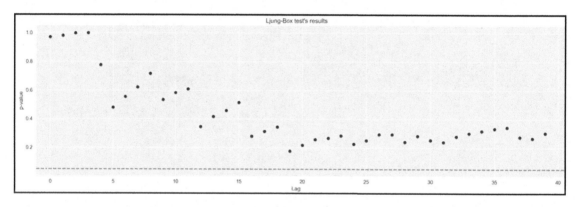

The results of the Ljung-Box test do not give us any reasons to reject the null hypothesis of no significant autocorrelation for any of the selected lags. This indicates a good fit of the model.

# How it works...

We started by downloading Google's stock prices from the given years and resampling them to weekly frequency by taking the last (adjusted) close price in every week. In *Step 3*, we applied the first difference in order to make the series stationary.

If we want to difference a given series more than once, we should use the `np.diff` function as it implements recursive differencing. Using the `diff` method of a DataFrame/Series with `periods` > 1 results in taking the difference between the current observations and the one from that many periods before.

*Step 4* is very important because, because we determined the order of the ARIMA model based on these results. We tested for stationarity using a custom function called `test_autocorrelation`. First, the series turned out to be stationary, so we knew that the order of integration was *d=1*. We determined the suggested lag order (*p*) by looking at the last lag after the PACF function crossed the confidence interval. In this case, it was *p=2*. Analogically, for the moving average order, we looked at the ACF plot to determine *q=1*. This way, we specified the model as ARIMA(2,1,1) in *Step 5*. We printed a summary using the `summary` method of the fitted model.

Hyndman and Athanasopoulos (2018) warned that if both *p* and *q* are positive, the ACF/PACF plots might not be helpful in determining the specification of the ARIMA model.

In *Step 6* and *Step 7*, we investigated the goodness of fit by looking at the model's residuals. If the fit is good, the residuals should be similar to the white noise. That is why we used four different types of plots to investigate how closely the residuals resemble the white noise.

Finally, we employed the Ljung-Box test (the `acorr_ljungbox` function from `statsmodels`) for no significant correlation and plotted the results.

Different sources suggest a different number of lags to consider in the Ljung-Box test. The default value in `statsmodels` is `min((nobs // 2 - 2), 40)`, while other commonly used variants include `min(20, nobs - 1)` and `ln(nobs)`.

# There's more...

**AUTO-ARIMA**: As manual selection of the ARIMA parameters might not lead to discovering the optimal model specification, there is a library called `pmdarima` (which ports the functionalities of the famous R package called `forecast` to Python). The key class of the library is called `auto_arima` and it automatically fits the best model for our time series.

In order to do so, we need to introduce a metric that the function will optimize. A popular choice is the **Akaike Information Criterion (AIC)**, which provides a trade-off between the goodness of fit of the model and its simplicity —AIC deals with the risks of overfitting and underfitting. When we compare multiple models, the lower the value of AIC, the better the model.

`auto_arima` iterates over the specified range of possible parameters and selects the model with the lowest AIC. It also facilitates estimation of SARIMA models.

We would like to verify whether the model we selected based on the ACF/PACF plots is the best one we could have selected.

1. Import the libraries:

   ```
   import pmdarima as pm
   ```

2. Run `auto_arima` with the majority of the settings set to the default values (only exclude potential seasonality):

   ```
   model = pm.auto_arima(goog,
                         error_action='ignore',
                         suppress_warnings=True,
                         seasonal=False)
   model.summary()
   ```

   Running the code generates the following summary:

| ARIMA Model Results | | | |
|---|---|---|---|
| **Dep. Variable:** | D.y | **No. Observations:** | 208 |
| **Model:** | ARIMA(0, 1, 1) | **Log Likelihood** | -988.749 |
| **Method:** | css-mle | **S.D. of innovations** | 28.065 |
| **Date:** | Mon, 09 Dec 2019 | **AIC** | 1983.497 |
| **Time:** | 13:17:54 | **BIC** | 1993.510 |
| **Sample:** | 1 | **HQIC** | 1987.546 |

| | coef | std err | z | P>|z| | [0.025 | 0.975] |
|---|---|---|---|---|---|---|
| **const** | 2.4561 | 1.486 | 1.653 | 0.100 | -0.456 | 5.368 |
| **ma.L1.D.y** | -0.2376 | 0.071 | -3.339 | 0.001 | -0.377 | -0.098 |

It looks like a simpler model provides a better fit. ARIMA(0,1,1) actually corresponds to one of the special cases—SES.

3. In the next step, we try to tune the search of the optimal parameters:

```
model = pm.auto_arima(goog,
                    error_action='ignore',
                    suppress_warnings=True,
                    seasonal=False,
                    stepwise=False,
                    approximation=False,
                    n_jobs=-1)
model.summary()
```

We receive the following summary:

| ARIMA Model Results | | | | | | |
|---|---|---|---|---|---|---|
| **Dep. Variable:** | | D.y | **No. Observations:** | | | 208 |
| **Model:** | ARIMA(3, 1, 2) | | **Log Likelihood** | | | -982.698 |
| **Method:** | | css-mle | **S.D. of innovations** | | | 27.235 |
| **Date:** | Mon, 09 Dec 2019 | | | | **AIC** | 1979.397 |
| **Time:** | | 13:18:06 | | | **BIC** | 2002.759 |
| **Sample:** | | 1 | | | **HQIC** | 1988.843 |

| | coef | std err | z | P>\|z\| | [0.025 | 0.975] |
|---|---|---|---|---|---|---|
| **const** | 2.4675 | 1.478 | 1.670 | 0.096 | -0.429 | 5.364 |
| **ar.L1.D.y** | -1.5445 | 0.124 | -12.445 | 0.000 | -1.788 | -1.301 |
| **ar.L2.D.y** | -1.1844 | 0.132 | -8.982 | 0.000 | -1.443 | -0.926 |
| **ar.L3.D.y** | -0.3043 | 0.072 | -4.230 | 0.000 | -0.445 | -0.163 |
| **ma.L1.D.y** | 1.3587 | 0.116 | 11.731 | 0.000 | 1.132 | 1.586 |
| **ma.L2.D.y** | 0.7929 | 0.119 | 6.655 | 0.000 | 0.559 | 1.026 |

This time, the suggested model is ARIMA(3,1,2), which has lower AIC. So, why did the initial run not discover this model? The reason is that, by default, `auto_arima` uses a stepwise algorithm to traverse the parameter space. Additionally, there are some approximations to speed up the search. Generally, a much larger set of models will be fitted if we disable both `stepwise` and `approximation`. We set `n_jobs = -1` to use all the cores for the search.

We can use the `plot_diagnostics` method of a fitted `pm.auto_arima` model to obtain a similar evaluation of the residuals to the one we obtained via the custom `arima_diagnostics` function for the models estimated using `statsmodels`.

There are also many different settings we can experiment with, such as the following:

- Selecting the starting value for the search.
- Capping the maximum values of parameters in the search.
- Selecting different statistical tests for determining the number of differences (also seasonal).
- Selecting an out-of-sample evaluation period (`out_of_sample_size`). This will make the algorithm fit the models on the data up until a certain point in time (the last observation—`out_of_sample_size`) and evaluate on the held-out set.

We list some of the notable extensions to the ARIMA framework:

- **ARIMAX**: Adds exogenous variable(s) to the model.
- **SARIMA (Seasonal ARIMA)**: Extends ARIMA to account for seasonality in the time series. The full specification is SARIMA(p,d,q)(P,D,Q)m, where the capitalized parameters are analogous to the original ones, but they refer to the seasonal component of the time series. *m* refers to the period of seasonality.

In `statsmodels`, ARIMA models can be fitted using two classes: `ARIMA` and `SARIMAX`. The latter one is more flexible and allows us to include exogenous variables, as well as account for the seasonal component. However, models in these two classes use a different formulation of ARIMA, where the latter one uses the state-space formulation. That is why fitting the same ARIMA(1,1,1) using these two classes will produce slightly different results.

# See also

For more information, you can refer to the following:

- `Chapter 3`, *Time Series Modeling*, (Residual diagnostics) from Hyndman, R.J., and Athanasopoulos, G. (2018) Forecasting: principles and practice, 2nd edition.

# Forecasting using ARIMA class models

In this recipe, we focus on using the ARIMA class models to forecast future observations of a given time series.

We compare the forecasting performance of the models we built in the *Modeling time series with ARIMA class models* recipe, where we investigated Google's stock prices in 2015-2018. We manually selected an ARIMA(2,1,1) model, while `auto_arima` suggested ARIMA(3,1,2). In this recipe, we use both models as they were initially estimated using different libraries, offering slightly different possibilities in terms of forecasting.

We forecast Google's weekly stock prices over the first 3 months of 2019.

# Getting ready

The ARIMA(2,1,1) model from the *Modeling time series with ARIMA class models* recipe is stored in the `arima` object, while the ARIMA(3,1,2) model is stored in the `auto_arima` object. The original data from 2015-2018 is stored in the `goog` object.

# How to do it...

Execute the following steps to forecast Google's stock prices using ARIMA models.

1. Download additional test data and resample it weekly frequency:

```
df = yf.download('GOOG',
                 start='2019-01-01',
                 end='2019-03-31',
                 adjusted=True,
                 progress=False)

test = df.resample('W') \
         .last() \
         .rename(columns={'Adj Close': 'adj_close'}) \
         .adj_close
```

2. Obtain the forecasts from the first model and store them in a DataFrame:

```
n_forecasts = len(test)

arima_pred = arima.forecast(n_forecasts)

arima_pred = [pd.DataFrame(arima_pred[0], columns=['prediction']),
```

```
                      pd.DataFrame(arima_pred[2], columns=['ci_lower',
                                                           'ci_upper'])]
      arima_pred = pd.concat(arima_pred,
                             axis=1).set_index(test.index)
```

3. **Obtain the forecasts from the second model and store them in a DataFrame:**

```
      auto_arima_pred = auto_arima.predict(n_periods=n_forecasts,
                                           return_conf_int=True,
                                           alpha=0.05)


      auto_arima_pred = [pd.DataFrame(auto_arima_pred[0],
                                      columns=['prediction']),
                         pd.DataFrame(auto_arima_pred[1],
                                      columns=['ci_lower', 'ci_upper'])]
      auto_arima_pred = pd.concat(auto_arima_pred,
                                  axis=1).set_index(test.index)
```

4. **Plot the results:**

```
      fig, ax = plt.subplots(1)

      ax = sns.lineplot(data=test, color=COLORS[0], label='Actual')

      ax.plot(arima_pred.prediction, c=COLORS[1], label='ARIMA(2,1,1)')
      ax.fill_between(arima_pred.index,
                      arima_pred.ci_lower,
                      arima_pred.ci_upper,
                      alpha=0.3,
                      facecolor=COLORS[1])

      ax.plot(auto_arima_pred.prediction, c=COLORS[2],
              label='ARIMA(3,1,2)')
      ax.fill_between(auto_arima_pred.index,
                      auto_arima_pred.ci_lower,
                      auto_arima_pred.ci_upper,
                      alpha=0.2,
                      facecolor=COLORS[2])

      ax.set(title="Google's stock price - actual vs. predicted",
             xlabel='Date',
             ylabel='Price ($)')
      ax.legend(loc='upper left')
```

We get the following output:

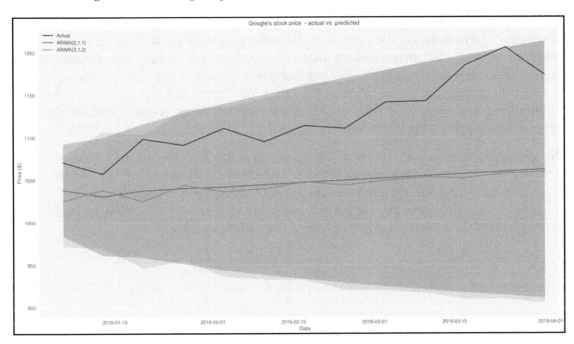

From the preceding plot, we can see that the forecasts from the ARIMA(2,1,1) model are smoother and that there is less volatility in them. Over time, the forecast error increases, however, the actual observations lie within the confidence interval of both models.

# How it works...

In *Step 2*, we obtained forecasts from the models that were fitted using `statsmodels`. To do so, we used the `forecast` method of the fitted object. We specified the length of the forecast (by default, it is 1 period ahead). The resulting object contained the forecasts, standard deviations, and confidence intervals (using the default significance level of 5%). For simplicity, we stored the necessary information in a `pandas` DataFrame.

In *Step 3*, we worked with the auto-ARIMA model from the `pmdarima` library. We used the `predict` method and also specified the number of periods that we wanted to forecast for.

Finally, we plotted all the results, along with the Google's stock prices.

# There's more...

When working with the `statsmodels` library, we can also use two different methods for forecasting. The first one is called `predict`. We need to specify the start and end of the prediction interval. We can use indices (in the case of the out of sample, `start` needs to be the first value after the last index of the training data), a string (`'2019-03-15'`), or a `datetime` type (`pd.datetime(1990, 12, 25)`). We should also specify `typ` -in case any differencing was done and we want to receive the forecasts in the original scale, we should use `'levels'` as the value (the default is `'linear'`).

The second method—`plot_predict`—an extension of the first one. Additional parameters include `plot_insample` (indicates whether we want to plot the in-sample fit) and `dynamic`. The second one affects the in-sample prediction (fitted values). If `dynamic=False`, the in-sample lagged values are used for prediction. Otherwise, the in-sample predictions are used in place of lagged dependent variables.

# 4
# Multi-Factor Models

This chapter is devoted to estimating various factor models in Python. The idea behind these models is to explain the excess returns (over the risk-free rate) of a certain portfolio or asset using one or more factors (features). These risk factors can be considered a tool for understanding the cross-section of (expected) returns.

In general, factor models can be used to identify interesting assets that can be added to the investment portfolio, which— in turn—should lead to better performing portfolios.

By the end of this chapter, we will have constructed some of the most popular factor models. We will start with the simplest, yet very popular, one-factor model (the **Capital Asset Pricing Model**, or **CAPM**) and then explain how to estimate more advanced three-, four-, and five-factor models. We will also cover the interpretation of what these factors represent and give a high-level overview of how they are constructed.

In this chapter, we cover the following recipes:

- Implementing the CAPM in Python
- Implementing the Fama-French three-factor model in Python
- Implementing the rolling three-factor model on a portfolio of assets
- Implementing the four- and five-factor models in Python

## Implementing the CAPM in Python

In this recipe, we learn how to estimate the famous **Capital Asset Pricing Model (CAPM)** and obtain the beta coefficient. This model represents the relationship between the expected return on a risky asset and the market risk (also known as systematic or undiversifiable risk). CAPM can be considered a one-factor model, on top of which more complex factor models were built.

CAPM is represented by the following equation:

$$E(r_i) = r_f + \beta_i (E(r_m) - r_f)$$

Here, $E(r_i)$ denotes the expected return on asset $i$, $r_f$ is the risk-free rate (such as a government bond), $E(r_m)$ is the expected return on the market, and $\beta$ is the beta coefficient.

Beta can be interpreted as the level of the asset return's sensitivity, as compared to the market in general. Some possible examples include:

- `beta <= -1`: The asset moves in the opposite direction as the benchmark and in a greater amount than the negative of the benchmark.
- `-1 < beta < 0`: The asset moves in the opposite direction to the benchmark.
- `beta = 0`: There is no correlation between the asset's price movement and the market benchmark.
- `0 < beta < 1`: The asset moves in the same direction as the market, but the amount is smaller. An example might be the stock of a company that is not very susceptible to day-to-day fluctuations.
- `beta = 1`: The asset and the market are moving in the same direction by the same amount.
- `beta > 1`: The asset moves in the same direction as the market, but the amount is greater. An example might be the stock of a company that is very susceptible to day-to-day market news.

CAPM can also be represented:

$$E(r_i) - r_f = \beta_i (E(r_m) - r_f)$$

Here, the left-hand side of the equation can be interpreted as the risk premium, while the right-hand side contains the market premium. The same equation can be reshaped into:

$$\beta = \frac{cov(R_i, R_m)}{var(R_m)}$$

Here, $R_i = E(r_i) - r_f$ and $R_m = E(r_m) - r_f$.

In this example, we consider the case of Amazon and assume that the S&P 500 index represents the market. We use 5 years (2014-2018) of monthly data to estimate the beta. In current times, the risk-free rate is so low that, for simplicity's sake, we assume it is equal to zero.

# How to do it...

Execute the following steps to implement the CAPM in Python.

1.  Import the libraries:

    ```
    import pandas as pd
    import yfinance as yf
    import statsmodels.api as sm
    ```

2.  Specify the risky asset and the time horizon:

    ```
    RISKY_ASSET = 'AMZN'
    MARKET_BENCHMARK = '^GSPC'
    START_DATE = '2014-01-01'
    END_DATE = '2018-12-31'
    ```

3.  Download the necessary data from Yahoo Finance:

    ```
    df = yf.download([RISKY_ASSET, MARKET_BENCHMARK],
                     start=START_DATE,
                     end=END_DATE,
                     adjusted=True,
                     progress=False)
    ```

4.  Resample to monthly data and calculate the simple returns:

    ```
    X = df['Adj Close'].rename(columns={RISKY_ASSET: 'asset',
                                        MARKET_BENCHMARK: 'market'}) \
                       .resample('M') \
                       .last() \
                       .pct_change() \
                       .dropna()
    ```

5.  Calculate `beta` using the covariance approach:

    ```
    covariance = X.cov().iloc[0,1]
    benchmark_variance = X.market.var()
    beta = covariance / benchmark_variance
    ```

    The result of the code is `beta = 1.6709`.

6. Prepare the input and estimate the CAPM as a linear regression:

```
y = X.pop('asset')
X = sm.add_constant(X)

capm_model = sm.OLS(y, X).fit()
print(capm_model.summary())
```

The following image shows the results of estimating the CAPM model:

```
                          OLS Regression Results
==============================================================================
Dep. Variable:                  asset   R-squared:                       0.381
Model:                            OLS   Adj. R-squared:                  0.370
Method:                 Least Squares   F-statistic:                     35.63
Date:                Mon, 02 Dec 2019   Prob (F-statistic):           1.53e-07
Time:                        20:37:50   Log-Likelihood:                 76.708
No. Observations:                  60   AIC:                            -149.4
Df Residuals:                      58   BIC:                            -145.2
Df Model:                           1
Covariance Type:            nonrobust
==============================================================================
                 coef    std err          t      P>|t|      [0.025      0.975]
------------------------------------------------------------------------------
const          0.0165      0.009      1.842      0.071      -0.001       0.035
market         1.6709      0.280      5.969      0.000       1.111       2.231
==============================================================================
Omnibus:                        3.375   Durbin-Watson:                   1.836
Prob(Omnibus):                  0.185   Jarque-Bera (JB):                2.673
Skew:                           0.508   Prob(JB):                        0.263
Kurtosis:                       3.194   Cond. No.                         31.6
==============================================================================
```

These results indicate that the beta (denoted as `market` here) is equal to 1.67, which means that Amazon's returns are 67% more volatile than the market (proxied by S&P 500). The value of the intercept is relatively small and statistically insignificant at the 5% significance level.

# How it works...

First, we specified the assets (Amazon and S&P 500) we wanted to use and the time frame. In *Step 3*, we downloaded the data from Yahoo Finance. Then, we only kept the last available price per month and calculated the monthly returns as the percentage change between the subsequent observations.

In *Step 5*, we calculated the beta as the ratio of the covariance between the risky asset and the benchmark to the benchmark's variance.

In *Step 6*, we separated the target (Amazon's stock returns) and the features (S&P 500 returns) using the `pop` method of a `pandas` DataFrame. Afterward, we added the constant to the features (effectively adding a column of ones) with the `add_constant` function. The idea behind adding the intercept to this regression is to investigate whether—after estimating the model—the intercept (in the case of the CAPM, also known as Jensen's alpha) is zero. If it is positive and significant, it means that– assuming the CAPM model is true—the asset or portfolio generates abnormally high risk-adjusted returns. There are two possible implications—either the market is inefficient or there are some other undiscovered risk factors that should be included in the model. This issue is known as the **joint hypothesis problem**.

We can also use the formula notation, which adds the constant automatically. To do so, we must import `statsmodels.formula.api` as `smf` and then run the slightly modified `capm_model = smf.ols(formula='asset ~ market', data=X).fit()`. The results of both approaches are the same.

Lastly, we ran the OLS regression and printed the summary. Here, we could see that the coefficient by the `market` variable (that is, the CAPM beta) is equal to the beta that was calculated using the covariance between the asset and the market in *Step 5*.

# There's more...

In the main example, we assumed there was no risk-free rate, which is a reasonable assumption to make nowadays. However, there might be cases when we would like to account for a non-zero risk-free rate. In this section, we present three possible approaches:

- Using data from prof. Kenneth French's website: The market premium ($r_m$- $r_f$) and the risk-free rate (approximated by the one-month Treasury bill) can be downloaded from Prof. Kenneth French's website (please refer to the *See also* section of this recipe for the link). Please bear in mind that the definition of the market benchmark used by prof. French is different than the S&P 500 index – a detailed description is available on his website. For a description of how to easily download the data, please refer to the *Implementing the Fama-French three-factor model in Python* recipe.

- The second option is to approximate the risk-free rate with, for example, the 13 Week (3-month) Treasury Bill (Yahoo finance ticker: ^IRX).

Follow these steps to learn how to download the data and convert it into the appropriate risk-free rate.

1. Define the length of the period in days:

```
N_DAYS = 90
```

2. Download the data from Yahoo Finance:

```
df_rf = yf.download('^IRX', start=START_DATE, end=END_DATE)
```

3. Resample the data to monthly frequency (by taking the last value for each month):

```
rf = df_rf.resample('M').last().Close / 100
```

4. Calculate the risk-free return (expressed as daily values) and convert the values to monthly:

```
rf = ( 1 / (1 - rf * N_DAYS / 360) )**(1 / N_DAYS)
rf = (rf ** 30) - 1
```

5. Plot the calculated risk-free rate:

```
rf.plot(title='Risk-free rate (13 Week Treasury Bill)')
```

The following plot shows the visualization of the risk-free rate over time:

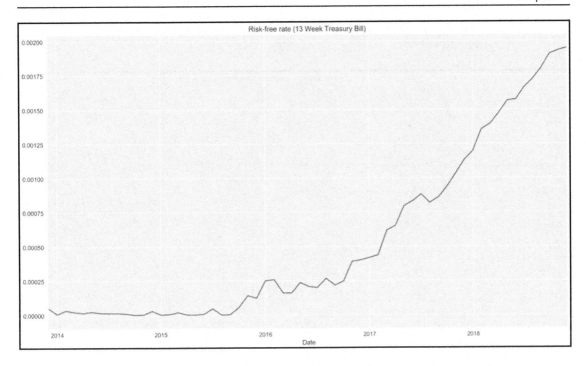

- The last approach is to approximate the risk-free rate using the 3-Month Treasury Bill (Secondary Market Rate), which can be downloaded from the **Federal Reserve Economic Data (FRED)** database. Follow these steps to learn how to download the data and convert it to a monthly risk-free rate:

1. Import the library:

```
import pandas_datareader.data as web
```

2. Download the data from the FRED database:

```
rf = web.DataReader('TB3MS', 'fred', start=START_DATE,
                    end=END_DATE)
```

3. Convert the obtained risk-free rate to monthly values:

```
rf = (1 + (rf / 100)) ** (1 / 12) - 1
```

4. Plot the calculated risk-free rate:

```
rf.plot(title='Risk-free rate (3-Month Treasury Bill)')
```

We can compare the results of the two methods by comparing the plots of the risk-free rates:

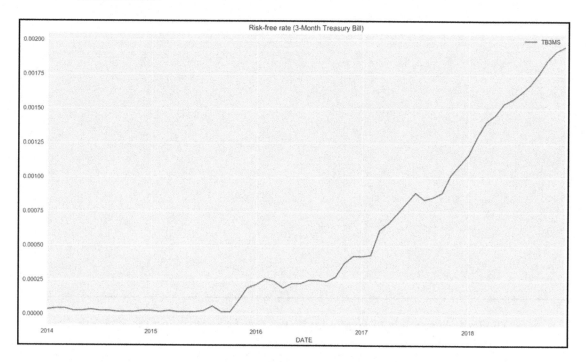

We can conclude that the plots look very similar.

# See also

Additional resources are available here:

- Sharpe, W. F. (1964). *Capital asset prices: A theory of market equilibrium under conditions of risk*. The journal of finance, 19(3), 425-442: `https://onlinelibrary.wiley.com/doi/full/10.1111/j.1540-6261.1964.tb02865.x`.
- Risk-free rate data on prof. Kenneth French's website: `http://mba.tuck.dartmouth.edu/pages/faculty/ken.french/ftp/F-F_Research_Data_Factors_CSV.zip`.

# Implementing the Fama-French three-factor model in Python

In their famous paper, Fama and French expanded the CAPM model by adding two additional factors explaining the excess returns of an asset or portfolio. The factors they considered are:

- **The market factor (MKT)**: It measures the excess return of the market, analogical to the one in the CAPM.
- **The size factor, SMB (Small Minus Big)**: It measures the excess return of stocks with a small market cap over those with a large market cap.
- **The value factor, HML (High Minus Low)**: It measures the excess return of value stocks over growth stocks. Value stocks have a high book-to-market ratio, while the growth stocks are characterized by a low ratio.

The model can be represented as follows:

$$E(r_i) = r_f + \alpha + \beta_{mkt}(E(r_m) - r_f) + \beta_{smb}SMB + \beta_{hml}HML$$

Or in its simpler form:

$$E(r_i) - r_f = \alpha + \beta_{mkt}MKT + \beta_{smb}SMB + \beta_{hml}HML$$

Here, $E(r_i)$ denotes the expected return on asset $i$, $r_f$ is the risk-free rate (such as a government bond), and $\alpha$ is the intercept. The reason for including the constant intercept is to make sure its value is equal to 0. This confirms that the three-factor model evaluates the relationship between the excess returns and the factors correctly.

In the case of a statistically significant, non-zero intercept, the model might not evaluate the asset/portfolio return correctly. However, the authors stated that the three-factor model is "fairly correct", even when it is unable to pass the statistical test.

Due to the popularity of this approach, these factors became collectively known as the **Fama-French Factors**, or the **Three-Factor Model**. They have been widely accepted in both academia and the industry as stock market benchmarks and they are often used to evaluate investment performance.

In this recipe, we estimate the three-factor model using 5 years (2014-2018) of monthly returns on Facebook.

# How to do it...

Follow these steps to implement the three-factor model in Python.

1. Import the libraries:

```
import pandas as pd
import yfinance as yf
import statsmodels.formula.api as smf
```

2. Download the necessary data from prof. French's website:

```
!wget
http://mba.tuck.dartmouth.edu/pages/faculty/ken.french/ftp/F-F_Rese
arch_Data_Factors_CSV.zip

!unzip -a F-F_Research_Data_Factors_CSV.zip

!rm F-F_Research_Data_Factors_CSV.zip
```

3. Define the parameters:

```
RISKY_ASSET = 'FB'
START_DATE = '2013-12-31'
END_DATE = '2018-12-31'
```

4. Load the data from the source CSV file and keep only the monthly data:

```
factor_df = pd.read_csv('F-F_Research_Data_Factors.csv',
                        skiprows=3)

STR_TO_MATCH = ' Annual Factors: January-December '
indices = factor_df.iloc[:, 0] == STR_TO_MATCH
start_of_annual = factor_df[indices].index[0]

factor_df = factor_df[factor_df.index < start_of_annual]
```

5. Rename the columns of the DataFrame, set a datetime index, and filter by dates:

```
factor_df.columns = ['date', 'mkt', 'smb', 'hml', 'rf']
factor_df['date'] = pd.to_datetime(factor_df['date'],
                                   format='%Y%m') \
                    .dt.strftime("%Y-%m")
factor_df = factor_df.set_index('date')
factor_df = factor_df.loc[START_DATE:END_DATE]
```

6. Convert the values into numeric values and divide by 100:

```
factor_df = factor_df.apply(pd.to_numeric,
                            errors='coerce') \
            .div(100)
```

The resulting data should be in the following form:

| | mkt | smb | hml | rf |
|---|---|---|---|---|
| **date** | | | | |
| **2014-01** | -0.0332 | 0.0085 | -0.0209 | 0.0 |
| **2014-02** | 0.0465 | 0.0034 | -0.0040 | 0.0 |
| **2014-03** | 0.0043 | -0.0189 | 0.0509 | 0.0 |
| **2014-04** | -0.0019 | -0.0424 | 0.0114 | 0.0 |
| **2014-05** | 0.0206 | -0.0186 | -0.0027 | 0.0 |

7. Download the prices of the risky asset:

```
asset_df = yf.download(RISKY_ASSET,
                       start=START_DATE,
                       end=END_DATE,
                       adjusted=True)
```

8. Calculate the monthly returns on the risky asset:

```
y = asset_df['Adj Close'].resample('M') \
                         .last() \
                         .pct_change() \
                         .dropna()

y.index = y.index.strftime('%Y-%m')
y.name = 'rtn'
```

9. Merge the datasets and calculate the excess returns:

```
ff_data = factor_df.join(y)
ff_data['excess_rtn'] = ff_data.rtn - ff_data.rf
```

10. Estimate the three-factor model:

```
ff_model = smf.ols(formula='excess_rtn ~ mkt + smb + hml',
                   data=ff_data).fit()
print(ff_model.summary())
```

The results of the three-factor model are presented below:

```
                            OLS Regression Results
==============================================================================
Dep. Variable:              excess_rtn   R-squared:                       0.217
Model:                             OLS   Adj. R-squared:                  0.175
Method:                  Least Squares   F-statistic:                     5.172
Date:                 Mon, 02 Dec 2019   Prob (F-statistic):            0.00317
Time:                         20:39:06   Log-Likelihood:                 88.388
No. Observations:                   60   AIC:                            -168.8
Df Residuals:                       56   BIC:                            -160.4
Df Model:                            3
Covariance Type:             nonrobust
==============================================================================
                 coef    std err          t      P>|t|      [0.025      0.975]
------------------------------------------------------------------------------
Intercept      0.0105      0.008      1.374      0.175      -0.005       0.026
mkt            0.5138      0.237      2.166      0.035       0.039       0.989
smb           -0.1611      0.301     -0.535      0.595      -0.764       0.442
hml           -0.9599      0.312     -3.073      0.003      -1.586      -0.334
==============================================================================
Omnibus:                         0.008   Durbin-Watson:                   1.780
Prob(Omnibus):                   0.996   Jarque-Bera (JB):                0.151
Skew:                           -0.006   Prob(JB):                        0.927
Kurtosis:                        2.755   Cond. No.                         44.5
==============================================================================
```

When interpreting the results of the three-factor model, we should pay attention to two issues:

- Whether the intercept is positive and statistically significant
- Which factors are statistically significant and if their direction matches past results (for example, from the literature) or our assumptions

In our case, the intercept is positive, but not statistically significant at the 5% significance level. Of the risk factors, only the SMB factor is not significant. However, a thorough literature study is required to formulate a hypothesis about the factors and their direction of influence.

We can also look at the F-statistic that was presented in the regression summary, which tests the joint significance of the regression. The null hypothesis states that coefficients of all features (factors, in this case), except for the intercept, have values equal to 0. We can see that the corresponding p-value is 0.00317, which gives us reason to reject the null hypothesis at the 5% significance level.

# How it works...

In *Step 2*, we downloaded the data directly from prof. French's website. To do so, we used the fact that we can execute bash commands in Jupyter Notebooks by preceding them with `!`. First, we downloaded the file using `wget` and then unzipped it using `unzip`. There are also ways to do this in Python only, but this seemed like a good place to introduce the possibility of mixing up bash script into the Notebooks. The link to the monthly data is always the same, and the file is updated every month.

In *Steps 4* to *6*, we wrangled the raw data from the CSV file into a form that can be used for modeling. The file also contained annual factors located below the monthly ones, so we only kept the relevant rows (we also skipped the first three rows containing unnecessary information). We only kept the required dates, converted all the values into numeric ones, and then divided them by 100 (for example, 3.45 in the dataset is actually 3.45%).

In *Steps 7* and *8*, we downloaded the prices of Facebook's stock. We obtained the monthly returns by calculating the percentage change of the end-of-month prices. In *Step 6*, we also changed the formatting of the index to `%Y-%m` (for example, `2000-12`) since the Fama-French factors contain dates in such a format. Then, we joined the two datasets in *Step 9*. Another noteworthy thing is that we must name the `pandas` Series by using `y.name = 'asset'`. This is a requirement for joining a DataFrame with a Series.

Finally, in *Step 10*, we ran the regression using the formula notation – we do not need to manually add an intercept when doing so. One thing worth mentioning is that the coefficient by the `mkt` variable will not be equal to the CAPM's beta, as there are also other factors in the model and the factors' influence on the excess returns is distributed differently.

# There's more...

We already showed how to download the factor-related data directly from prof. French's website. As an alternative, we can use the functionalities of `pandas_datareader` and avoid some manual preprocessing steps:

1. Import the libraries:

```
from pandas_datareader.famafrench import get_available_datasets
import pandas_datareader.data as web
```

2. Print the available datasets (only the first five):

```
get_available_datasets()[:5]
```

The preceding code results in the following output:

```
['F-F_Research_Data_Factors',
 'F-F_Research_Data_Factors_weekly',
 'F-F_Research_Data_Factors_daily',
 'F-F_Research_Data_5_Factors_2x3',
 'F-F_Research_Data_5_Factors_2x3_daily']
```

3. Download the selected dataset:

```
ff_dict = web.DataReader('F-F_Research_Data_Factors', 'famafrench',
                         start='2014-01-01')
```

The default behavior of `web.DataReader` downloads the last 5 years' worth of data. The resulting object is a dictionary and we can inspect its contents by running the following command:

```
ff_dict.keys()
```

This results in the following output:

```
dict_keys([0, 1, 'DESCR'])
```

4. Inspect the description of the dataset:

```
print(ff_dict['DESCR'])
```

The description is as follows:

```
F-F Research Data Factors
-------------------------
This file was created by CMPT_ME_BEME_RETS using the 201910 CRSP database. The 1-month TBill return is from Ibbotson
and Associates, Inc. Copyright 2019 Kenneth R. French
  0 : (70 rows x 4 cols)
  1 : Annual Factors: January-December (5 rows x 4 cols)
```

5. View the monthly dataset:

```
ff_dict[0].head()
```

The dataset looks like the one we manually downloaded from prof. French's website:

| Date ⇕ | Mkt-RF ⇕ | SMB ⇕ | HML ⇕ | RF ⇕ |
|---|---|---|---|---|
| 2014-01 | 3.32 | 0.85 | -2.09 | 0.0 |
| 2014-02 | 4.65 | 0.34 | -0.40 | 0.0 |
| 2014-03 | 0.43 | -1.89 | 5.09 | 0.0 |
| 2014-04 | 0.19 | -4.24 | 1.14 | 0.0 |
| 2014-05 | 2.06 | -1.86 | -0.27 | 0.0 |

The yearly values are stored under the key of 1 and can be accessed by using `ff_dict[1]`.

# See also

Additional resources are available here:

- For details on how all the factors were calculated, please refer to prof. French's website at `http://mba.tuck.dartmouth.edu/pages/faculty/ken.french/Data_Library/f-f_factors.html`.
- Fama, E. F., and French, K. R. (1993). *Common risk factors in the returns on stocks and bonds.* Journal of financial economics, 33(1), 3-56: `http://citeseerx.ist.psu.edu/viewdoc/download?doi=10.1.1.139.5892rep=rep1type=pdf`.

# Implementing the rolling three-factor model on a portfolio of assets

In this recipe, we learn how to estimate the three-factor model in a rolling fashion. What we mean by rolling is that we always consider an estimation window of a constant size (60 months, in this case) and roll it through the entire dataset, one period at a time. A potential reason for doing such an experiment is to test the stability of the results.

In contrast to the previous recipes, this time, we use portfolio returns instead of a single asset. To keep things simple, we assume that our allocation strategy is to have an equal share of the total portfolio's value in each of the following stocks: Amazon, Google, Apple, and Microsoft. For this experiment, we use stock prices from the years 2010-2018.

# How to do it...

Follow these steps to implement the rolling three-factor model in Python.

1. Import the libraries:

```python
import pandas as pd
import yfinance as yf
import statsmodels.formula.api as smf
import pandas_datareader.data as web
```

2. Define the parameters:

```python
ASSETS = ['AMZN', 'GOOG', 'AAPL', 'MSFT']
WEIGHTS = [0.25, 0.25, 0.25, 0.25]
START_DATE = '2009-12-31'
END_DATE = '2018-12-31'
```

3. Download the factor-related data:

```python
df_three_factor = web.DataReader('F-F_Research_Data_Factors',
                                 'famafrench', start=START_DATE)[0]
df_three_factor = df_three_factor.div(100)
df_three_factor.index = df_three_factor.index.format()
```

4. Download the prices of risky assets from Yahoo Finance:

```python
asset_df = yf.download(ASSETS,
                       start=START_DATE,
                       end=END_DATE,
                       adjusted=True,
                       progress=False)
```

5. Calculate the monthly returns on the risky assets:

```python
asset_df = asset_df['Adj Close'].resample('M') \
                                .last() \
                                .pct_change() \
                                .dropna()
asset_df.index = asset_df.index.strftime('%Y-%m')
```

6. Calculate the portfolio returns:

```python
asset_df['portfolio_returns'] = np.matmul(asset_df[ASSETS].values,
                                          WEIGHTS)
```

7. Merge the datasets:

```
ff_data = asset_df.join(df_three_factor).drop(ASSETS, axis=1)
ff_data.columns = ['portf_rtn', 'mkt', 'smb', 'hml', 'rf']
ff_data['portf_ex_rtn'] = ff_data.portf_rtn - ff_data.rf
```

8. Define a function for the rolling *n*-factor model:

```
def rolling_factor_model(input_data, formula, window_size):
    coeffs = []

    for start_index in range(len(input_data) - window_size + 1):
        end_index = start_index + window_size

        ff_model = smf.ols(
            formula=formula,
            data=input_data[start_index:end_index]
        ).fit()
        coeffs.append(ff_model.params)

    coeffs_df = pd.DataFrame(
        coeffs,
        index=input_data.index[window_size - 1:]
    )

    return coeffs_df
```

 For a version with a docstring explaining the input/output, please refer to this book's GitHub repository.

9. Estimate the rolling three-factor model and plot the results:

```
MODEL_FORMULA = 'portf_ex_rtn ~ mkt + smb + hml'
results_df = rolling_factor_model(ff_data,
                                  MODEL_FORMULA,
                                  window_size=60)
results_df.plot(title = 'Rolling Fama-French Three-Factor model')
```

Executing the code results in the following plot:

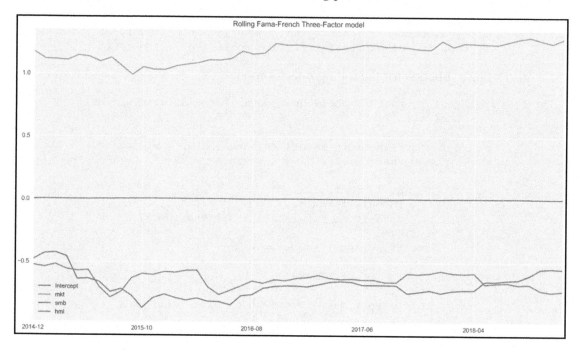

By inspecting the preceding plot, we can see the following:

- The intercept is almost constant and very close to 0.
- There is some variability in the factors, but no sudden reversals or unexpected jumps.

# How it works...

In *Steps 2* and *3*, we downloaded data using `pandas_datareader` and `yfinance`. This is very similar to what we did in the *Implementing the Fama-French three-factor model in Python* recipe, so at this point, we will not go into too much detail about this.

In *Step 4*, we calculated the portfolio returns as a weighted average of the portfolio constituents. This is possible as we are working with simple returns – for more details, please refer to the *Converting prices to returns* recipe in `Chapter 1`, *Financial Data and Preprocessing*. Bear in mind that this simple approach assumes that, at the end of each month, we have exactly the same asset allocation (as indicated by the weights). This can be achieved with portfolio rebalancing, that is, adjusting the allocation after a specified period of time to always match the intended weights' distribution.

Afterward, we merged the two datasets in *Step 5*. In *Step 6*, we defined a function for estimating the *n*-factor model using a rolling window. The main idea is to loop over the DataFrame we prepared in previous steps and for each month, estimate the Fama-French model using the last 5 years' worth of data (60 months). By appropriately slicing the input DataFrame, we made sure that we only estimate the model from the 60th month onwards, to make sure we always have a full window of observations.

 Proper software engineering best practices would suggest writing some assertions to make sure the types of the inputs are as we intended them to be, or whether the input DataFrame contains the necessary columns. However, we have not done this here for brevity.

Finally, we applied the defined function to the prepared DataFrame and plotted the results.

# Implementing the four- and five-factor models in Python

In this recipe, we implement two extensions of the Fama-French three-factor model.

**Carhart's Four-Factor model:** The underlying assumption of this extension is that, within a short period of time, a winner stock will remain a winner, while a loser will remain a loser. An example of a criterion for classifying winners and losers could be the last 12-month cumulative total returns. After identifying the two groups, we long the winners and short the losers within a certain holding period.

The **momentum factor** (WML; Winners Minus Losers) measures the excess returns of the winner stocks over the loser stocks in the past 12 months (please refer to the *See also* section of this recipe for references on the calculations of the momentum factor).

The four-factor model can be expressed:

$$E(r_i) - r_f = \alpha + \beta_{mkt}MKT + \beta_{smb}SMB + \beta_{hml}HML + \beta_{wml}WML$$

**Fama-French's Five-Factor model:** Fama and French expanded their three-factor model by adding two factors:

- **Robust Minus Weak (RMW)** measures the excess returns of companies with high profit margins (robust profitability) over those with lower profits (weak profitability).
- **Conservative Minus Aggressive (CMA)** measures the excess returns of firms with low investment policies (conservative) over those investing more (aggressive).

The five-factor model can be expressed as follows:

$$E(r_i) - r_f = \alpha + \beta_{mkt}MKT + \beta_{smb}SMB + \beta_{hml}HML + \beta_{rmw}RMW + \beta_{cma}CMA$$

Like in all factor models, if the exposure to the risk factors captures all possible variations in expected returns, the intercept ($\alpha$) for all the assets/portfolios should be equal to zero.

In this recipe, we explain monthly returns on Amazon from 2014-2018 with the four- and five-factor models.

# How to do it...

Follow these steps to implement the four- and five-factor models in Python.

1. Import the libraries:

```
import pandas as pd
import yfinance as yf
import statsmodels.formula.api as smf
import pandas_datareader.data as web
```

2. Specify the risky asset and the time horizon:

```
RISKY_ASSET = 'AMZN'
START_DATE = '2013-12-31'
END_DATE = '2018-12-31'
```

3. Download the risk factors from prof. French's website:

```
# three factors
df_three_factor = web.DataReader('F-F_Research_Data_Factors',
                                 'famafrench', start=START_DATE)[0]
df_three_factor.index = df_three_factor.index.format()

# momentum factor
df_mom = web.DataReader('F-F_Momentum_Factor', 'famafrench',
                        start=START_DATE)[0]
df_mom.index = df_mom.index.format()

# five factors
df_five_factor = web.DataReader('F-F_Research_Data_5_Factors_2x3',
                                'famafrench',
                                start=START_DATE)[0]
df_five_factor.index = df_five_factor.index.format()
```

4. Download the data of the risky asset from Yahoo Finance:

```
asset_df = yf.download(RISKY_ASSET,
                       start=START_DATE,
                       end=END_DATE,
                       adjusted=True,
                       progress=False)
```

5. Calculate the monthly returns:

```
y = asset_df['Adj Close'].resample('M') \
                         .last() \
                         .pct_change() \
                         .dropna()

y.index = y.index.strftime('%Y-%m')
y.name = 'return'
```

6. Merge the datasets for the four-factor model:

```
# join all datasets on the index
four_factor_data = df_three_factor.join(df_mom).join(y)

# rename columns
four_factor_data.columns = ['mkt', 'smb', 'hml', 'rf', 'mom',
                            'rtn']

# divide everything (except returns) by 100
four_factor_data.loc[:, four_factor_data.columns != 'rtn'] /= 100
```

```
# convert index to datetime
four_factor_data.index = pd.to_datetime(four_factor_data.index,
                                        format='%Y-%m')

# select period of interest
four_factor_data = four_factor_data.loc[START_DATE:END_DATE]

# calculate excess returns
four_factor_data['excess_rtn'] = four_factor_data.rtn -
four_factor_data.rf
```

7. Merge the datasets for the five-factor model:

```
# join all datasets on the index
five_factor_data = df_five_factor.join(y)

# rename columns
five_factor_data.columns = ['mkt', 'smb', 'hml', 'rmw', 'cma',
                            'rf', 'rtn']

# divide everything (except returns) by 100
five_factor_data.loc[:, five_factor_data.columns != 'rtn'] /= 100

# convert index to datetime
five_factor_data.index = pd.to_datetime(five_factor_data.index,
                                        format='%Y-%m')

# select period of interest
five_factor_data = five_factor_data.loc[START_DATE:END_DATE]

# calculate excess returns
five_factor_data['excess_rtn'] = five_factor_data.rtn -
five_factor_data.rf
```

8. Estimate the four-factor model:

```
four_factor_model = smf.ols(formula='excess_rtn ~ mkt + smb + hml +
                            mom', data=four_factor_data).fit()

print(four_factor_model.summary())
```

The following summary shows the results:

```
                          OLS Regression Results
==============================================================================
Dep. Variable:             excess_rtn   R-squared:                      0.550
Model:                            OLS   Adj. R-squared:                 0.517
Method:                 Least Squares   F-statistic:                    16.78
Date:                Mon, 02 Dec 2019   Prob (F-statistic):          4.80e-09
Time:                        20:40:43   Log-Likelihood:                86.248
No. Observations:                  60   AIC:                           -162.5
Df Residuals:                      55   BIC:                           -152.0
Df Model:                           4
Covariance Type:            nonrobust
==============================================================================
                 coef    std err          t      P>|t|      [0.025      0.975]
------------------------------------------------------------------------------
Intercept      0.0094      0.008      1.165      0.249      -0.007       0.025
mkt            1.7202      0.256      6.712      0.000       1.207       2.234
smb           -0.5547      0.315     -1.762      0.084      -1.186       0.076
hml           -1.0756      0.391     -2.748      0.008      -1.860      -0.291
mom            0.3251      0.294      1.104      0.274      -0.265       0.915
==============================================================================
Omnibus:                        5.028   Durbin-Watson:                  1.700
Prob(Omnibus):                  0.081   Jarque-Bera (JB):               4.598
Skew:                           0.678   Prob(JB):                       0.100
Kurtosis:                       3.034   Cond. No.                        57.6
==============================================================================
```

9. Estimate the five-factor model:

```
five_factor_model = smf.ols(
    formula='excess_rtn ~ mkt + smb + hml + rmw + cma',
    data=five_factor_data
).fit()

print(five_factor_model.summary())
```

The following summary shows the results:

```
                         OLS Regression Results
===============================================================================
Dep. Variable:           excess_rtn   R-squared:                      0.595
Model:                          OLS   Adj. R-squared:                 0.557
Method:               Least Squares   F-statistic:                    15.85
Date:              Mon, 02 Dec 2019   Prob (F-statistic):          1.38e-09
Time:                      20:40:44   Log-Likelihood:                89.415
No. Observations:                60   AIC:                           -166.8
Df Residuals:                    54   BIC:                           -154.3
Df Model:                         5
Covariance Type:          nonrobust
===============================================================================
                 coef    std err          t      P>|t|      [0.025      0.975]
-------------------------------------------------------------------------------
Intercept      0.0101      0.008      1.308      0.197      -0.005       0.025
mkt            1.5508      0.246      6.303      0.000       1.058       2.044
smb           -0.7826      0.342     -2.288      0.026      -1.468      -0.097
hml           -0.5938      0.423     -1.404      0.166      -1.442       0.254
rmw           -0.7025      0.571     -1.231      0.224      -1.847       0.442
cma           -1.4384      0.695     -2.071      0.043      -2.831      -0.046
===============================================================================
Omnibus:                      1.893   Durbin-Watson:                  1.734
Prob(Omnibus):                0.388   Jarque-Bera (JB):               1.496
Skew:                         0.387   Prob(JB):                       0.473
Kurtosis:                     3.015   Cond. No.                       105.
===============================================================================
```

According to the five-factor model, Amazon's excess returns are negatively exposed to most of the factors (all but the market factor). Here, we present an example of the interpretation of the coefficients: an increase by 1 percentage point in the market factor results in an increase of 0.015 p.p. In other words, for a 1% return by the market factor, we can expect our portfolio (Amazon's stock) to return 1.5508 * 1% in excess of the risk-free rate.

Similarly to the three-factor model, if the five-factor model fully explains the excess stock returns, the estimated intercept should be statistically indistinguishable from zero (which is the case for the considered problem).

# How it works...

In *Step 2*, we defined the parameters (the ticker of the considered stock and timeframes) for later use.

In *Step 3*, we downloaded the necessary datasets using `pandas_datareader`, which provides us with a convenient way of downloading the risk-factors-related data without manually downloading the CSV files. For more information on this process, please refer to the *There's more* section in the *Implementing the Fama-French three-factor model in Python* recipe. One thing to note here is that we applied the `format` method to the index, as we had to remove `PeriodIndex` in order to join multiple datasets later.

In *Steps 4* and *5*, we downloaded Amazon's stock prices and calculated the monthly returns using the previously explained methodology.

In *Steps 6* and *7*, we joined all the datasets, renamed the columns, selected the period of interest, and calculated the excess returns. When using the `join` method without specifying what we want to join on (the `on` argument), the default is the index of the DataFrames.

This way, we prepared all the necessary inputs for the four- and five-factor models. We also had to divide all the data we downloaded from prof. French's website by 100 to arrive at the correct scale.

 The SMB factor in the five-factor dataset is calculated differently compared to how it is in the three-factor dataset. For more details, please refer to the link in the *See also* section of this recipe.

In *Step 8* and *Step 9*, we estimated the models using the functional form of OLS regression from the `statsmodels` library. The functional form automatically adds the intercept to the regression equation.

# See also

For details on the calculation of the factors, please refer to the following links:

- Momentum factor: `https://mba.tuck.dartmouth.edu/pages/faculty/ken.french/Data_Library/det_mom_factor.htmlF`
- Five-factor model: `https://mba.tuck.dartmouth.edu/pages/faculty/ken.french/Data_Library/f-f_5_factors_2x3.html`

For papers introducing the four- and five-factor models, please refer to the following links:

- Carhart, M. M. (1997). *On persistence in mutual fund performance.* The Journal of Finance, 52(1), 57-82: `https://onlinelibrary.wiley.com/doi/pdf/10.1111/j.1540-6261.1997.tb03808.x`.
- Fama, E. F., & French, K. R. (2015). *A five-factor asset pricing model.* Journal of financial economics, 116(1), 1-22: `https://tevgeniou.github.io/EquityRiskFactors/bibliography/FiveFactor.pdf`.

# Modeling Volatility with GARCH Class Models

In Chapter 3, *Time Series Modeling*, we looked at various approaches to modeling time series. However, models such as **ARIMA (Autoregressive Integrated Moving Average)** cannot account for volatility that is not constant over time (heteroskedastic). We have already explained that some transformations (such as log or Box-Cox transformations) can be used to adjust for modest changes in volatility, but we would like to go a step further, and model it.

In this chapter, we focus on conditional heteroskedasticity, which is a phenomenon caused when an increase in volatility is correlated with a further increase in volatility. An example might help to understand this concept. Imagine the price of an asset going down significantly—due to some breaking news related to the company. Such a sudden price drop could trigger certain risk management tools of investment funds, which start selling the stocks as the result of the previous decrease in price. This could result in the price plummeting even further. Conditional heteroskedasticity was also clearly visible in the *Investigating stylized facts of asset returns* recipe, in which we showed that returns exhibit volatility clustering.

We would like to briefly explain the motivation for this chapter. Volatility is an incredibly important concept in finance. It is synonymous with risk and has many applications in quantitative finance. Firstly, it is used in options pricing, as the Black-Scholes model relies on the volatility of the underlying asset. Secondly, volatility has a significant impact on risk management, where it is used to calculate metrics such as the **Value-at-Risk (VaR)** of a portfolio, the Sharpe ratio, and many more. Thirdly, volatility is also present in trading, as it can be directly traded in the form of the CBOE Volatility Index (ticker symbol: VIX). The name comes from the Chicago Board Options Exchange, by which the index is calculated in real time.

By the end of the chapter, we will have covered a selection of **GARCH (Generalized Autoregressive Conditional Heteroskedasticity)** models—both univariate and multivariate—which are one of the most popular ways of modeling volatility. Knowing the basics, it is quite simple to implement even more advanced models. We have already mentioned the importance of volatility in finance. By knowing how to model it, we can use such forecasts to replace the previously used naïve ones in many practical use cases in the fields of risk management or derivatives valuation.

In this chapter, we cover the following recipes:

- Explaining stock returns' volatility with ARCH models
- Explaining stock returns' volatility with GARCH models
- Implementing a CCC-GARCH model for multivariate volatility forecasting
- Forecasting a conditional covariance matrix using DCC-GARCH

# Explaining stock returns' volatility with ARCH models

In this recipe, we approach the problem of explaining the conditional volatility of stock returns, with the **Autoregressive Conditional Heteroskedasticity (ARCH)** model.

The logic of the ARCH method can be represented by the following equations:

$$r_t = \mu + \epsilon_t$$

$$\epsilon_t = \sigma_t z_t$$

$$\sigma_t^2 = \omega + \sum_{i=1}^{q} \alpha_i \epsilon_{t-i}^2$$

The first equation represents the return series as a combination of the expected return μ and the unexpected return $\epsilon_t$. The latter one is also known as the mean-corrected return, error term, or innovations. $\epsilon_t$ has white noise properties—the conditional mean equal to zero and the time-varying conditional variance $\sigma^2_t$. Error terms are serially uncorrelated but do not need to be serially independent, as they can exhibit conditional heteroskedasticity.

A zero mean process implies that the returns are only described by the residuals, $r_t = \epsilon_t$. Other popular options include constant mean $r_t = \mu + \epsilon_t$, autoregressive mean, **Autoregressive-Moving-Average (ARMA)**, and so on.

In the second equation, we represent the error series in terms of a stochastic component $z_t \sim N(0,1)$ and a conditional standard deviation $\sigma_t$, which governs the typical size of the residuals. The stochastic component can also be interpreted as standardized residuals.

The third equation presents the ARCH formula, where $\omega > 0$ and $\alpha_i \geq 0$.

Some important points about the ARCH model:

- The ARCH model explicitly recognizes the difference between the unconditional and the conditional variance of the time series.
- It models the conditional variance as a function of past residuals (errors) from a mean process.
- It assumes the unconditional variance to be constant over time.
- We must specify the number of prior residuals ($q$) in the model—similarly to the autoregressive model.
- ARCH models should only be applied to residuals obtained after fitting another model (such as ARIMA) to the given time series.
- The residuals should look like observations of a discrete white noise—zero mean, stationary (no trends or seasonal effects, that is, no evident serial correlation).

In the original ARCH notation, as well as in the `arch` library in Python, the lag hyperparameter is denoted with $p$. However, we use $q$ as the symbol, in line with the GARCH notation introduced in the next recipe, *Explaining stock returns' volatility with GARCH models*.

In this recipe, we apply the ARCH(1) model to Google's daily stock returns from the years 2015-2018.

# How to do it...

Execute the following steps to estimate the ARCH(1) model.

1. Import the libraries:

```
import pandas as pd
import yfinance as yf
from arch import arch_model
```

2. Specify the risky asset and the time horizon:

```
RISKY_ASSET = 'GOOG'
START_DATE = '2015-01-01'
END_DATE = '2018-12-31'
```

3. Download data from Yahoo Finance:

```
df = yf.download(RISKY_ASSET,
                 start=START_DATE,
                 end=END_DATE,
                 adjusted=True)
```

4. Calculate daily returns:

```
returns = 100 * df['Adj Close'].pct_change().dropna()
returns.name = 'asset_returns'
returns.plot(title=f'{RISKY_ASSET} returns: {START_DATE} -
{END_DATE}')
```

Running the code generates the following plot:

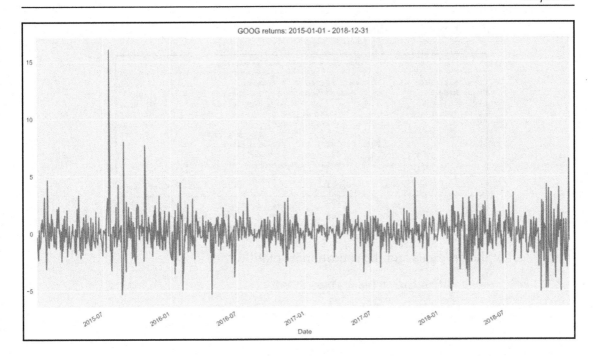

In the plot, we can observe a few sudden spikes and examples of volatility clustering.

5.  Specify the ARCH model:

```
model = arch_model(returns, mean='Zero', vol='ARCH', p=1, o=0, q=0)
```

6.  Estimate the model and print the summary:

```
model_fitted = model.fit(disp='off')
print(model_fitted.summary())
```

Running the code results in the following summary:

```
                    Zero Mean - ARCH Model Results
==============================================================================
Dep. Variable:            asset_returns   R-squared:                   0.000
Mean Model:                   Zero Mean   Adj. R-squared:              0.001
Vol Model:                         ARCH   Log-Likelihood:           -1800.60
Distribution:                    Normal   AIC:                       3605.20
Method:          Maximum Likelihood       BIC:                       3615.02
                                          No. Observations:             1005
Date:                Mon, Dec 02 2019     Df Residuals:                 1003
Time:                        23:05:48     Df Model:                        2
                             Volatility Model
==============================================================================
                 coef    std err        t      P>|t|     95.0% Conf. Int.
------------------------------------------------------------------------------
omega          1.6323      0.167      9.794  1.196e-22  [  1.306,    1.959]
alpha[1]       0.3342      0.168      1.993  4.631e-02  [5.461e-03,  0.663]
==============================================================================
```

7. Plot the residuals and the conditional volatility:

```
model_fitted.plot(annualize='D')
```

Running the code results in the plots shown below:

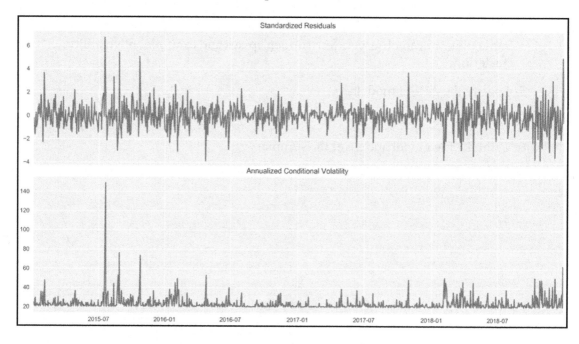

We can observe some standardized residuals that are large (in magnitude) and correspond to highly volatile periods.

# How it works...

In *Step 2* to *4*, we downloaded Google's daily stock prices and calculated simple returns. When working with (G)ARCH models, convergence warnings are likely to occur in the case of very small numbers. This is caused by instabilities in the underlying `scipy`'s optimization algorithms. To overcome this issue, we multiplied the returns by 100 to express them as percentages.

In *Step 5*, we defined the ARCH(1) model. For the mean model, we selected the zero-mean approach, which is suitable for many liquid financial assets. Another viable choice here could be a constant mean.

In *Step 6*, we fitted the model, using the `fit` method. Additionally, we passed `disp='off'` to the `fit` method to suppress output from the optimization steps. To fit the model using the `arch` library, we had to take similar steps to the familiar `scikit-learn` approach: we first defined the model and then fitted it to the data. We printed the model's summary by using the `summary` method.

In *Step 7*, we also inspected the standardized residuals and the conditional volatility series by plotting them. The standardized residuals were computed by dividing the residuals by the conditional volatility. By passing `annualize='D'` to the `plot` method, we indicated that we wanted to annualize the conditional volatility series from daily data.

# There's more...

A few more noteworthy points about ARCH models:

- Selecting the zero-mean process is useful when working on residuals from a separately estimated model.
- To detect ARCH effects, we can look at the correlogram of the squared residuals from a certain model (such as the ARIMA model). We need to make sure that the mean of these residuals is equal to zero. We can use the **Partial Autocorrelation Function (PACF)** plot to infer the value of $q$, similarly to the approach used in the case of the **Autoregressive (AR)** model (please refer to the *Modeling time series with ARIMA class models* recipe in `Chapter 3`, *Time Series Modeling*, for more details).
- To test the validity of the model, we can inspect whether the standardized residuals and squared standardized residuals exhibit no serial autocorrelation (for example, using the Box-Pierce test—`acorr_ljungbox` from `statsmodels`). Also, we can employ the **Lagrange Multiplier (LM)** test to make sure that the model captures all ARCH effects (`het_arch` from `statsmodels`).

# See also

Additional resources are available here:

- Engle, R. F. (1982). Autoregressive conditional heteroscedasticity with estimates of the variance of United Kingdom inflation. *Econometrica: Journal of the Econometric Society*, 987-1007: `http://www.econ.uiuc.edu/~econ508/Papers/engle82.pdf`

# Explaining stock returns' volatility with GARCH models

In this recipe, we present how to work with an extension of the ARCH model, namely the **Generalized Autoregressive Conditional Heteroskedasticity (GARCH)** model. GARCH can be considered an ARMA model applied to the variance of a time series—the AR component was already expressed in the ARCH model, while GARCH additionally adds the moving average part. In other words, the ARCH model specifies the conditional variance as a linear function of past sample variances, while the GARCH model adds lagged conditional variances to the specification.

The equation of the GARCH model can be presented as:

$$r_t = \mu + \epsilon_t$$

$$\epsilon_t = \sigma_t z_t$$

$$\sigma_t^2 = \omega + \sum_{i=1}^{q} \alpha_i \epsilon_{t-i}^2 + \sum_{i=1}^{p} \beta_i \sigma_{t-i}^2$$

While the interpretation is very similar to the ARCH model presented in the previous recipe, the difference lies in the last equation, where there is an additional component. Parameters are constrained to meet the following: $\omega > 0$, $\alpha_i \geq 0$, and $\beta_i \geq 0$.

 In the GARCH model, there are additional constraints on coefficients. For example, in the case of a GARCH(1,1) model, $\alpha_1 + \beta_1$ must be less than 1, otherwise, the model is unstable.

The two hyperparameters of the GARCH model can be described as:

- *p:* The number of lag variances
- *q:* The number of lag residual errors from a mean process

 A GARCH(0, *q*) model is equivalent to an ARCH(*q*) model.

In this recipe, we apply the GARCH(1,1) model to the same data as in the previous recipe, *Explaining stock returns' volatility with ARCH models*, to clearly see the difference between the two modeling approaches.

# How to do it...

Execute the following steps to estimate the GARCH(1,1) model in Python.

1. Specify the GARCH model:

```
model = arch_model(returns, mean='Zero', vol='GARCH', p=1, o=0,
                   q=1)
```

2. Estimate the model and print the summary:

```
model_fitted = model.fit(disp='off')
print(model_fitted.summary())
```

This results in the following screenshot:

```
                    Zero Mean - GARCH Model Results
================================================================================
Dep. Variable:         asset_returns   R-squared:                       0.000
Mean Model:                Zero Mean   Adj. R-squared:                  0.001
Vol Model:                     GARCH   Log-Likelihood:                -1764.88
Distribution:                 Normal   AIC:                            3535.76
Method:           Maximum Likelihood   BIC:                            3550.50
                                       No. Observations:                 1005
Date:              Mon, Dec 02 2019   Df Residuals:                      1002
Time:                      23:07:25   Df Model:                             3
                            Volatility Model
================================================================================
                 coef    std err          t      P>|t|      95.0% Conf. Int.
--------------------------------------------------------------------------------
omega          0.1781      0.157      1.134      0.257   [ -0.130,    0.486]
alpha[1]       0.1799      0.124      1.446      0.148   [-6.394e-02,  0.424]
beta[1]        0.7616      0.153      4.991  6.008e-07   [  0.463,    1.061]
================================================================================
```

3. Plot the residuals and the conditional volatility:

```
model_fitted.plot(annualize='D')
```

In the plots shown below, we can observe the effect of including the extra component (lagged conditional volatility) into the model specification:

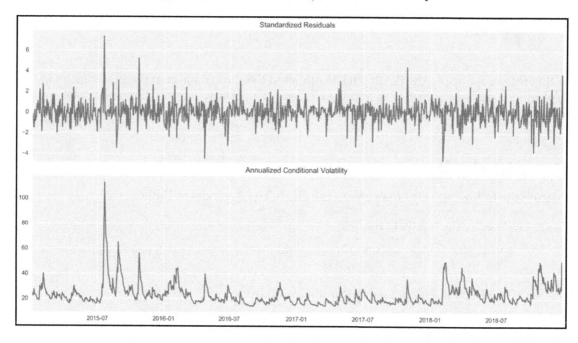

When using ARCH, the conditional volatility series exhibits many spikes, and then immediately returns to the low level. In the case of GARCH, as the model also includes lagged conditional volatility, it takes more time to return to the level observed before the spike.

# How it works...

In this recipe, we used the same data as in the previous one, in order to compare the results of the ARCH and GARCH models. For more information on downloading data, please refer to *Step 1* to *4* in the *Explaining stock returns' volatility with ARCH models* recipe.

Due to the convenience of the `arch` library, it was very easy to adjust the code used previously to fit the ARCH model. To estimate the GARCH model, we had to specify the type of volatility model we wanted to use, and set q=1.

For comparison's sake, we left the mean process as a zero-mean process.

# There's more...

In this chapter, we have already used two models to explain and potentially forecast the conditional volatility of a time series. However, there are numerous extensions of the GARCH model, as well as different configurations with which we can experiment in order to find the best-fitting model.

In the GARCH framework, aside from the hyperparameters (such as $p$ and $q$, in the case of the vanilla GARCH model), we can modify the models described next.

## Conditional mean model

As explained before, we apply the GARCH class models to residuals obtained after fitting another model to the series. Some popular choices for the mean model are:

- Zero-mean
- Constant mean
- Any variant of the ARIMA model (including potential seasonality adjustment, as well as external regressors)—some popular choices in the literature are ARMA, or even AR models
- Regression models

## Conditional volatility model

There are numerous extensions to the GARCH framework. Some popular models include:

- **GJR-GARCH**: A variant of the GARCH model that takes into account the asymmetry of the returns (negative returns tend to have a stronger impact on volatility than positive ones)
- **EGARCH**: Exponential GARCH
- **TGARCH**: Threshold GARCH

- **FIGARCH**: Fractionally integrated GARCH, used with non-stationary data
- **GARCH-MIDAS**: In this class of models, volatility is decomposed into a short-term GARCH component and a long-term component driven by an additional explanatory variable
- Multivariate GARCH models, such as CCC-/DCC-GARCH

The first three models use slightly different approaches to introduce asymmetry into the conditional volatility specification. This is in line with the belief that negative shocks have a stronger impact on volatility than positive shocks.

## Distribution of errors

In the *Investigating stylized facts of asset returns* recipe in `Chapter 1`, *Financial Data and Preprocessing*, we saw that the distribution of returns is not Normal (skewed, with heavy tails). That is why distributions other than Gaussian might be more fitting for errors in the GARCH model.

Some possible choices are:

- Student's t-distribution
- Skew-t distribution (Hansen, 1994)
- **Generalized Error Distribution** (GED)
- **Skewed Generalized Error Distribution** (SGED)

The `arch` library provides most of the models and distributions mentioned, and also allows for the use of your own volatility models/distributions of errors, as long as they fit into a predefined format. For more information on this, please refer to the excellent documentation at `https://arch.readthedocs.io/en/latest/index.html`.

## See also

Additional resources are available here:

- Bollerslev, T. (1986). Generalized autoregressive conditional heteroskedasticity. *Journal of Econometrics*, 31(3), 307-327. — `http://www.u.arizona.edu/~rlo/readings/278762.pdf`

- Glosten, L. R., Jagannathan, R., and Runkle, D. E. (1993). On the relation between the expected value and the volatility of the nominal excess return on stocks. *The Journal of Finance*, 48(5), 1779-1801. — `https://onlinelibrary.wiley.com/doi/full/10.1111/j.1540-6261.1993.tb05128.x`
- Hansen, B. E. (1994). Autoregressive conditional density estimation. *International Economic Review*, 35(3), 705–730. — `http://www.ssc.wisc.edu/~bhansen/papers/ier_94.pdf`

# Implementing a CCC-GARCH model for multivariate volatility forecasting

In this chapter, we have already considered multiple univariate conditional volatility models. That is why in this recipe, we move to the multivariate setting. As a starting point, we consider Bollerslev's **Constant Conditional Correlation GARCH (CCC-GARCH)** model. The idea behind it is quite simple. The model consists of $N$ univariate GARCH models, related to each other via a constant conditional correlation matrix **R**.

Like before, we start with the model's specification:

- $r_t = \mu + \epsilon_t$
- $\epsilon_t \sim N(0, \Sigma_t)$
- $\Sigma_t = D_t R D_t$

In the first equation, we represent the return series. The key difference between this representation and the one presented in previous recipes is the fact that, this time, we are considering multivariate returns, so $r_t$ is actually a vector of returns $r_t = (r_{1t}, \ldots, r_{nt})$. The mean and error terms are represented analogically. To highlight this, we use the bold font when considering vectors or matrices.

The second equation shows that the error terms come from a Multivariate Normal distribution with zero means and a conditional covariance matrix: $\Sigma_t$ (of size N x N).

The elements of the conditional covariance matrix can be defined as:

- diagonal: $\sigma_{ii,t}^2 = \omega_{ii} + \sum_{i=1}^{q} \alpha_{ii} \epsilon_{i,t-i}^2 + \sum_{i=1}^{p} \beta_{ii} \sigma_{i,t-i}^2$ for $i = 1, \ldots, N$
- off-diagonal: $\sigma_{ij,t}^2 = \rho_{i,j} \sigma_{ii,t} \sigma_{jj,t}$ for $i \neq j$

The third equation presents the decomposition of the conditional covariance matrix. $D_t$ is a matrix containing the conditional standard deviations on the diagonal, and $R$ is a correlation matrix.

Key ideas of the model:

- It avoids the problem of guaranteeing positive definiteness of $\Sigma_t$ by splitting it into variances and correlations.
- The conditional correlations between error terms are constant over time.
- Individual conditional variances follow a univariate GARCH(1,1) model.

In this recipe, we estimate the CCC-GARCH model on a series of stock returns for three US tech companies. For more details about the estimation of the CCC-GARCH model, please refer to the *How it works...* section.

# How to do it...

Execute the following steps to estimate the CCC-GARCH model in Python.

1. Import the libraries:

```
import pandas as pd
import yfinance as yf
from arch import arch_model
```

2. Specify the risky assets and the time horizon:

```
RISKY_ASSETS = ['GOOG', 'MSFT', 'AAPL']
N = len(RISKY_ASSETS)
START_DATE = '2015-01-01'
END_DATE = '2018-12-31'
```

3. Download data from Yahoo Finance:

```
df = yf.download(RISKY_ASSETS,
                 start=START_DATE,
                 end=END_DATE,
                 adjusted=True)
```

4. Calculate daily returns:

```
returns = 100 * df['Adj Close'].pct_change().dropna()
returns.plot(subplots=True,
             title=f'Stock returns: {START_DATE} - {END_DATE}');
```

This results in the plot shown below:

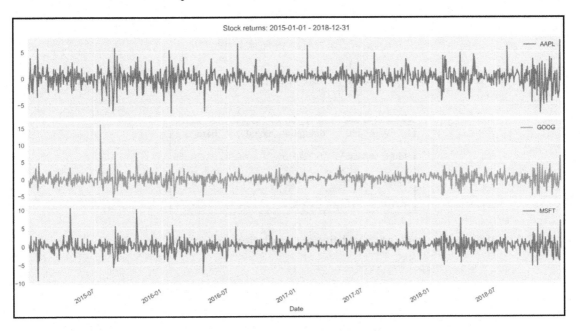

5. Define lists for storing objects:

```
coeffs = []
cond_vol = []
std_resids = []
models = []
```

6. Estimate the univariate GARCH models:

```
for asset in returns.columns:
    model = arch_model(returns[asset], mean='Constant',
                       vol='GARCH', p=1, o=0,
                       q=1).fit(update_freq=0, disp='off')
    coeffs.append(model.params)
    cond_vol.append(model.conditional_volatility)
    std_resids.append(model.resid / model.conditional_volatility)
    models.append(model)
```

7.  Store the results in DataFrames:

```
coeffs_df = pd.DataFrame(coeffs, index=returns.columns)
cond_vol_df = pd.DataFrame(cond_vol).transpose() \
                                    .set_axis(returns.columns,
                                              axis='columns',
                                              inplace=False)
std_resids_df = pd.DataFrame(std_resids).transpose() \
                                    .set_axis(returns.columns,
                                              axis='columns',
                                              inplace=False)
```

The following image shows a table containing the estimated coefficients for each series:

| ⬍ | mu ⬍ | omega ⬍ | alpha[1] ⬍ | beta[1] ⬍ |
|---|---|---|---|---|
| **AAPL** | 0.123511 | 0.221315 | 0.126038 | 0.784369 |
| **GOOG** | 0.080484 | 0.193113 | 0.187870 | 0.747876 |
| **MSFT** | 0.119715 | 0.384615 | 0.253280 | 0.624706 |

8.  Calculate the constant conditional correlation matrix (R):

```
R = std_resids_df.transpose() \
            .dot(std_resids_df) \
            .div(len(std_resids_df))
```

9.  Calculate the one-step-ahead forecast of the conditional covariance matrix:

```
diag = []
D = np.zeros((N, N))

for model in models:
    diag.append(model.forecast(horizon=1).variance.values[-1][0])
diag = np.sqrt(np.array(diag))
np.fill_diagonal(D, diag)

H = np.matmul(np.matmul(D, R.values), D)
```

The end result is:

```
array([[6.98457361, 3.26885359, 3.73865239],
       [3.26885359, 6.15816116, 4.47315426],
       [3.73865239, 4.47315426, 7.51632679]])
```

We can compare this matrix to the one obtained using a more complex DCC-GARCH model, which we cover in the next recipe.

# How it works...

In *Steps 2* and *Step 3*, we downloaded the daily stock prices of Google, Microsoft, and Apple. Then, we calculated simple returns and multiplied them by 100 to avoid encountering convergence errors.

In *Step 5*, we defined empty lists for storing elements required at later stages: GARCH coefficients, conditional volatilities, standardized residuals, and the models themselves (used for forecasting). In *Step 6*, we iterated over the columns of the DataFrame containing the stock returns and fitted a univariate GARCH model to each of the series. We stored the results in the predefined lists. Then, we wrangled the data in order to have objects such as residuals in DataFrames, to make work with them and visual inspection easier.

In *Step 8*, we calculated the constant conditional correlation matrix (**R**) as the unconditional correlation matrix of $z_i$:

$$R = \frac{1}{T}\Sigma_{t=1}^T z_t z_t'$$

where $z_t$ stands for time $t$ standardized residuals from the univariate GARCH models.

In the last step, we obtained one-step-ahead forecasts of the conditional covariance matrix $H_{t+1}$. To do so, we did the following:

- We created a matrix $D_{t+1}$ of zeros, using `np.zeros`.
- We stored the one-step-ahead forecasts of conditional variances from univariate GARCH models in a list called `diag`.
- Using `np.fill_diagonal`, we placed the elements of the list called `diag` on the diagonal of the matrix $D_{t+1}$.
- Following equation 3 from the introduction, we obtained the one-step-ahead forecast using matrix multiplication (`np.matmul`).

# See also

Additional resources are available here:

- Bollerslev, T. (1990), Modeling the Coherence in Short-Run Nominal Exchange Rates: A Multivariate Generalized ARCH Approach, *Review of Economics and Statistics*, 72, 498–505.—http://public.econ.duke.edu/~boller/Published_Papers/restat_90.pdf

# Forecasting the conditional covariance matrix using DCC-GARCH

In this recipe, we cover an extension of the CCC-GARCH model: Engle's **Dynamic Conditional Correlation GARCH (DCC-GARCH)** model. The main difference between the two is that in the latter, the conditional correlation matrix is not constant over time—we have $R_t$ instead of $R$.

There are some nuances in terms of estimation, but the outline is similar to the CCC-GARCH model:

- Estimate the univariate GARCH models for conditional volatility
- Estimate the DCC model for conditional correlations

In the second step of estimating the DCC model, we use a new matrix $Q_t$, representing a proxy correlation process.

- $R_t = diag(Q_t)^{-1/2} Q_t diag(Q_t)^{-1/2}$
- $Q_t = (1 - \gamma - \delta)\bar{Q} + \gamma z_{t-1} z'_{t-1} + \delta Q_{t-1}$
- $\bar{Q} = \frac{1}{T}\Sigma_{t=1}^{T} z_t z'_t$

The first equation describes the relationship between the conditional correlation matrix $R_t$ and the proxy process $Q_t$. The second equation represents the dynamics of the proxy process. The last equation shows the definition of $\bar{Q}$, which is defined as the unconditional correlation matrix of standardized residuals from the univariate GARCH models.

This representation of the DCC model—the one with $\bar{Q}$—uses an approach called correlation targeting. It means that we are effectively reducing the number of parameters we need to estimate to two: $\gamma$ and $\delta$. This is similar to volatility targeting in the case of univariate GARCH models, further described in the *There's more...* section.

At the time of writing, there is no Python library to estimate DCC-GARCH models. One solution would be to write such a library from scratch. Another, more time-efficient solution would be to use a well-established R package for that task. That is why in this recipe, we also introduce how to efficiently make Python and R work together in one Jupyter Notebook (this can also be done in a normal `.py` script). The `rpy2` library is an interface between both languages. It enables us to not only run both R and Python in the same Notebook, but also to transfer objects between the two.

In this recipe, we use the same data as in the previous one, in order to highlight the differences in the approach and results.

# Getting ready

For details on how to easily install R, please refer to `https://cran.r-project.org/` or `https://docs.anaconda.com/anaconda/user-guide/tasks/using-r-language/`.

# How to do it...

Execute the following steps to estimate a DCC-GARCH model in Python (using R).

1. Import the library:

```
%load_ext rpy2.ipython
```

2. Install the `rmgarch` R package (run only once) and load it:

```
%%R

#install.packages('rmgarch', repos =
"http://cran.us.r-project.org")
library(rmgarch)
```

3. Import the dataset into R:

```
%%R -i returns
print(head(returns))
```

Using the preceding command, we print the first five rows of the R `data.frame`:

```
         AAPL       GOOG       MSFT
1 -0.9564189 -0.3028802  0.6714628
2 -2.8173221 -2.0845673 -0.9290138
3  0.0102438 -2.3162783 -1.4666987
4  1.4032572 -0.1717973  1.2689117
5  3.8484848  0.3141697  2.9397590
```

4. Define the model specification:

```
%%R

# define GARCH(1,1) model
univariate_spec <- ugarchspec(
    mean.model = list(armaOrder = c(0,0)),
    variance.model = list(garchOrder = c(1,1),
                          model = "sGARCH"),
    distribution.model = "norm"
)

# define DCC(1,1) model
n <- dim(returns)[2]
dcc_spec <- dccspec(
    uspec = multispec(n, univariate_spec)),
    dccOrder = c(1,1),
    distribution = "mvnorm"
)
```

5. Estimate the model:

```
%%R
dcc_fit <- dccfit(dcc_spec, data=returns)
dcc_fit
```

The following image shows a table containing the model's specification summary, estimated coefficients, as well as some test statistics:

```
*---------------------------------*
*          DCC GARCH Fit          *
*---------------------------------*
Distribution        :  mvnorm
Model               :  DCC(1,1)
No. Parameters      :  17
[VAR GARCH DCC UncQ] : [0+12+2+3]
No. Series          :  3
No. Obs.            :  1005
Log-Likelihood      :  -4889.521
Av.Log-Likelihood   :  -4.87

Optimal Parameters
---------------------------------------
                Estimate  Std. Error  t value  Pr(>|t|)
[AAPL].mu       0.123569    0.046497   2.65760  0.007870
[AAPL].omega    0.225659    0.088530   2.54895  0.010805
[AAPL].alpha1   0.128393    0.035263   3.64103  0.000272
[AAPL].beta1    0.780760    0.052609  14.84074  0.000000
[GOOG].mu       0.080476    0.042767   1.88174  0.059872
[GOOG].omega    0.193072    0.161134   1.19820  0.230838
[GOOG].alpha1   0.187833    0.126945   1.47964  0.138969
[GOOG].beta1    0.747919    0.154264   4.84831  0.000001
[MSFT].mu       0.121999    0.044221   2.75883  0.005801
[MSFT].omega    0.014938    0.092794   0.16098  0.872109
[MSFT].alpha1   0.024745    0.074276   0.33314  0.739025
[MSFT].beta1    0.969867    0.109462   8.86033  0.000000
[Joint]dcca1    0.034478    0.013725   2.51197  0.012006
[Joint]dccb1    0.843667    0.038480  21.92490  0.000000

Information Criteria
---------------------
Akaike        9.7642
Bayes         9.8473
Shibata       9.7637
Hannan-Quinn  9.7958
```

6. Calculate five-step-ahead forecasts:

```
forecasts <- dccforecast(dcc_fit, n.ahead = 5)
```

7. Access the forecasts:

```
%%R

# conditional covariance matrix
forecasts@mforecast$H
# conditional correlation matrix
forecasts@mforecast$R
# proxy correlation process
```

```
forecasts@mforecast$Q
# conditional mean forecasts
forecasts@mforecast$mu
```

The following image shows the five-step-ahead forecasts of the conditional covariance matrix:

```
[[1]]
, , 1

          [,1]      [,2]      [,3]
[1,] 6.996757 4.237756 4.018266
[2,] 4.237756 6.157358 4.240759
[3,] 4.018266 4.240759 5.257858

, , 2
          [,1]      [,2]      [,3]
[1,] 6.586779 3.931634 3.792690
[2,] 3.931634 5.954830 4.102074
[3,] 3.792690 4.102074 5.244462

, , 3

          [,1]      [,2]      [,3]
[1,] 6.214045 3.663597 3.593009
[2,] 3.663597 5.765315 3.976738
[3,] 3.593009 3.976738 5.231138

, , 4

          [,1]      [,2]      [,3]
[1,] 5.875174 3.428138 3.415793
[2,] 3.428138 5.587975 3.863163
[3,] 3.415793 3.863163 5.217885

, , 5
          [,1]      [,2]      [,3]
[1,] 5.567088 3.220645 3.258122
[2,] 3.220645 5.422030 3.759978
[3,] 3.258122 3.759978 5.204704
```

We can now compare this forecast (the first step) to the one obtained using a simpler CCC-GARCH model.

# How it works...

In this recipe, we used the same data as in the previous recipe, in order to compare the results of the CCC- and DCC-GARCH models. For more information on downloading the data, please refer to *Step 1 to 4* in the *Implementing CCC-GARCH model for multivariate volatility forecasting* recipe.

To work with Python and R at the same time, we used the `rpy2` library. Here, we presented how to use the library in combination with Jupyter Notebook. For more details on how to use the library in a `.py` script, please refer to the official documentation (`https://rpy2.readthedocs.io`). Also, we do not delve into the details of R code in general, as this is outside the scope of this book.

In *Step 1*, aside from loading any libraries, we also had to use the following magic command: `%load_ext rpy2.ipython`. It enabled us to run R code by adding `%%R` to the beginning of a cell in the Notebook. For that reason, please assume that any code block in this chapter is a separate Notebook cell (see the Jupyter Notebook in the accompanying GitHub repository for more information).

In *Step 2*, we had to install the required R dependencies. To do so, we used the `install.packages` function and specified the repository we wanted to use.

In *Step 3*, we moved the `pandas` DataFrame into the R environment. To do so, we passed the extra code `-i returns`, together with the `%%R` magic command. We could have imported the data in any of the ensuing steps.

When you want to move a Python object to R, do some manipulation/modeling, and move the final results back to Python, you can use the following syntax: `%%R -i input_object -o output_object`.

In *Step 4*, we defined the DCC-GARCH model's specification. First, we defined the univariate GARCH specification (for conditional volatility estimation), using `ugarchspec`. This function comes from a package called `rugarch`, which is the framework for univariate GARCH modeling. By not specifying the ARMA parameters, we chose a constant mean model. For the volatility, we used a GARCH(1,1) model with normally distributed innovations. Secondly, we also specified the DCC model. To do so, we:

- Replicated the univariate specification for each returns series—three, in this case
- Specified the order of the DCC model—DCC(1,1) in this case
- Specified the multivariate distribution—Multivariate Normal

We could see the summary of the specification by calling the dcc_spec object.

In *Step 5*, we estimated the model by calling the dccfit function with the specification and data as arguments. Afterward, we obtained five-step-ahead forecasts by using the dccforecast function, which returned nested objects such as:

- H: Conditional covariance matrix
- R: Conditional correlation matrix
- Q: The proxy process for the correlation matrix
- mu: Conditional mean

Each one of them contained five-step forecasts, stored in lists.

# There's more...

In this section, we would also like to go over a few more details on estimating GARCH.

- **Estimation details:** In the first step of estimating the DCC-GARCH model, we can additionally use an approach called **variance targeting**. The idea is to reduce the number of parameters we need to estimate in the GARCH model.

  To do so, we can slightly modify the GARCH equation. The original equation runs as follows:

$$\sigma_t^2 = \omega + \sum_{i=1}^{q} \alpha_i \epsilon_{t-i}^2 + \sum_{i=1}^{p} \beta_i \sigma_{t-i}^2$$

  The unconditional volatility is defined as $\bar{\sigma} = \omega/(1 - \alpha - \beta)$. We can now plug it into the GARCH equation and produce the following:

$$\sigma_t^2 = \bar{\sigma}(1 - \alpha - \beta) + \sum_{i=1}^{q} \alpha_i \epsilon_{t-i}^2 + \sum_{i=1}^{p} \beta_i \sigma_{t-i}^2$$

  In the last step, we replace the unconditional volatility with the sample variance of the returns:

$$\hat{\sigma} = \frac{1}{T} \Sigma_{t=1}^{T} \epsilon_t^2$$

By doing so, we have one less parameter to estimate for each GARCH equation. Also, the unconditional variance implied by the model is guaranteed to be equal to the unconditional sample variance. To use variance targeting in practice, we add an extra argument to the `ugarchspec` function call: `ugarchspec(...,  variance.targeting = TRUE)`.

- **Univariate and multivariate GARCH models:** It is also worth mentioning that `rugarch` and `rmgarch` work nicely together, as they were both developed by the same author and created as a one go-to environment for GARCH class estimation in R. We have already experienced this when we used the `ugarchspec` function in the first step in estimating the DCC-GARCH model. There is much more to discover in terms of that package.
- **Parallelizing the estimation of multivariate GARCH models:** Lastly, the estimation process of the DCC-GARCH model can be easily parallelized, with the help of the `parallel` R package.

To potentially speed up computations with parallelization, we reused the majority of the code from this recipe and added a few extra lines. First, we had to set up a cluster by using `makePSOCKcluster` from the `parallel` package, and indicated that we would like to use three cores. Then, we defined the parallelizable specification using `multifit`. Lastly, we fitted the DCC-GARCH model. The difference here, compared to the previously used code, is that, this time, we additionally passed the `fit` and `cluster` arguments to the function call.

When we are done with the estimation, we stop the cluster:

```
%%R

# parallelized DCC-GARCH(1,1)

library('parallel')

# set up the cluster
cl <- makePSOCKcluster(3)

# define parallelizable specification
parallel_fit <- multifit(multispec(replicate(n, univariate_spec)),
                         returns,
                         cluster = cl)

# fit the DCC-GARCH model
dcc_fit <- dccfit(dcc_spec,
                  data = returns,
```

```
                              fit.control = list(eval.se = TRUE),
                              fit = parallel_fit,
                              cluster = cl)
        # stop the cluster
        stopCluster(cl)
```

Using the preceding code, we can significantly speed up the estimation of the DCC-GARCH model. The improvement in performance is mostly visible when dealing with large volumes of data. Also, the approach of using the `parallel` package together with `multifit` can be used to speed up the calculations of various GARCH and ARIMA models from the `rugarch` and `rmgarch` packages.

# See also

Additional resources are available here:

- Engle, R.F. (2002). *Dynamic Conditional Correlation: A Simple Class of Multivariate Generalized Autoregressive Conditional Heteroskedasticity Models. Journal of Business and Economic Statistics* 20, 339–350: `https://amstat.tandfonline.com/doi/pdf/10.1198/073500102288618487`
- Ghalanos, A. (2019). *The rmgarch models: Background and properties.* (Version 1.3-0): `https://cran.r-project.org/web/packages/rmgarch/vignettes/The_rmgarch_models.pdf`

# 6
# Monte Carlo Simulations in Finance

Monte Carlo simulations are a class of computational algorithms that use repeated random sampling to solve any problems that have a probabilistic interpretation. In finance, one of the reasons they gained popularity is that they can be used to accurately estimate integrals. The main idea of Monte Carlo simulations is to produce a multitude of sample paths—possible scenarios/outcomes, often over a given period of time. The horizon is then split into a specified number of time steps and the process of doing so is called **discretization**. Its goal is to approximate continuous time, since the pricing of financial instruments happens in continuous time.

The results from all these simulated sample paths can be used to calculate metrics such as the percentage of times an event occurred, the average value of an instrument at the last step, and so on. Historically, the main problem with the Monte Carlo approach was that it required heavy computational power to calculate all possible scenarios. Nowadays, it is becoming less of a problem as we can run fairly advanced simulations on a desktop computer or a laptop.

By the end of this chapter, we will have seen how we can use Monte Carlo methods in various scenarios and tasks. In some of them, we will create the simulations from scratch, while in others, we will use modern Python libraries to make the process even easier. Due to the method's flexibility, Monte Carlo is one of the most important techniques in computational finance. It can be adapted to various problems, such as pricing derivatives with no closed-form solution (American/Exotic options), valuating bonds (for example, a zero-coupon bond), estimating the uncertainty of a portfolio (for example, by calculating Value-at-Risk and Expected Shortfall), or carrying out stress-tests in risk management. We show how to solve some of these problems in this chapter.

In this chapter, we cover the following recipes:

- Simulating stock price dynamics using Geometric Brownian Motion
- Pricing European options using simulations
- Pricing American options with Least Squares Monte Carlo
- Pricing American options using Quantlib
- Estimating value-at-risk using Monte Carlo

# Simulating stock price dynamics using Geometric Brownian Motion

Thanks to the unpredictability of financial markets, simulating stock prices plays an important role in the valuation of many derivatives, such as options. Due to the aforementioned randomness in price movement, these simulations rely on **stochastic differential equations (SDE)**.

A stochastic process is said to follow the **Geometric Brownian Motion (GBM)** when it satisfies the following SDE:

$$dS = \mu S dt + \sigma S dW_t$$

Here, we have the following:

- S: Stock price
- $\mu$: The drift coefficient, that is, the average return over a given period or the instantaneous expected return
- $\sigma$: The diffusion coefficient, that is, how much volatility is in the drift
- $W_t$: The Brownian Motion

We will not investigate the properties of the Brownian Motion in too much depth, as it is outside the scope of this book. Suffice to say, Brownian increments are calculated as a product of a Standard Normal random variable ($rv \sim N(0,1)$) and the square root of the time increment. Another way to say this is that the Brownian increment comes from $rv \sim N(0,t)$, where $t$ is the time increment. We obtain the Brownian path by taking the cumulative sum of the Brownian increments.

The SDE has a closed-form solution (only a few SDEs have it):

$$S(t) = S_0 e^{(\mu - \frac{1}{2}\sigma^2)t + \sigma W_t}$$

Here, $S_0 = S(0)$ is the initial value of the process, which in this case is the initial price of a stock. The preceding equation presents the relationship compared to the initial stock price.

For simulations, we can use the following recursive formula:

$$S(t_{i+1}) = S(t_i)exp(\mu - \frac{1}{2}\sigma^2)(t_{i+1} - t_i) + \sigma\sqrt{t_{i+1} - t_i}Z_{i+1}$$

Here, $Z_i$ is a Standard Normal random variable and $i = 0, \ldots, T - 1$ is the time index. This specification is possible because the increments of $W$ are independent and normally distributed.

 GBM is a process that does not account for mean-reversion and time-dependent volatility. That is why it is often used for stocks and not for bond prices, which tend to display long-term reversion to the face value.

In this recipe, we use Monte Carlo methods and the Geometric Brownian Motion to simulate Microsoft's stock prices one month ahead.

# How to do it...

Execute the following steps to simulate Microsoft's stock prices one month ahead.

1. Import the libraries:

```
import numpy as np
import pandas as pd
import yfinance as yf
```

2. Define the parameters for downloading the data:

```
RISKY_ASSET = 'MSFT'
START_DATE = '2019-01-01'
END_DATE = '2019-07-31'
```

3. Download data from Yahoo Finance:

```
df = yf.download(RISKY_ASSET, start=START_DATE,
                 end=END_DATE, adjusted=True)
```

4. Calculate the daily returns:

```
adj_close = df['Adj Close']
returns = adj_close.pct_change().dropna()
print(f'Average return: {100 * returns.mean():.2f}%')
returns.plot(title=f'{RISKY_ASSET} returns: {START_DATE} -
{END_DATE}')
```

The code produces the following plot:

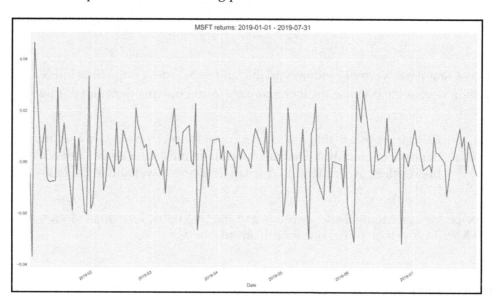

And the following line:

```
Average return: 0.24%
```

5. Split the data into training and test sets:

```
train = returns['2019-01-01':'2019-06-30']
test = returns['2019-07-01':'2019-07-31']
```

6. Specify the parameters of the simulation:

```
T = len(test)
N = len(test)
S_0 = adj_close[train.index[-1].date()]
N_SIM = 100
mu = train.mean()
sigma = train.std()
```

7. Define the function for simulations:

```
def simulate_gbm(s_0, mu, sigma, n_sims, T, N):
    dt = T/N
    dW = np.random.normal(scale = np.sqrt(dt),
                          size=(n_sims, N))
    W = np.cumsum(dW, axis=1)

    time_step = np.linspace(dt, T, N)
    time_steps = np.broadcast_to(time_step, (n_sims, N))

    S_t = s_0 * np.exp((mu - 0.5 * sigma ** 2) * time_steps
                       + sigma * W)
    S_t = np.insert(S_t, 0, s_0, axis=1)
    return S_t
```

8. Run the simulations:

```
gbm_simulations = simulate_gbm(S_0, mu, sigma, N_SIM, T, N)
```

9. Plot the simulation results:

```
# prepare objects for plotting
LAST_TRAIN_DATE = train.index[-1].date()
FIRST_TEST_DATE = test.index[0].date()
LAST_TEST_DATE = test.index[-1].date()
PLOT_TITLE = (f'{RISKY_ASSET} Simulation '
              f'({FIRST_TEST_DATE}:{LAST_TEST_DATE})')

selected_indices = adj_close[LAST_TRAIN_DATE:LAST_TEST_DATE].index
index = [date.date() for date in selected_indices]

gbm_simulations_df = pd.DataFrame(np.transpose(gbm_simulations),
                                  index=index)

# plotting
ax = gbm_simulations_df.plot(alpha=0.2, legend=False)
line_1, = ax.plot(index, gbm_simulations_df.mean(axis=1),
                  color='red')
line_2, = ax.plot(index, adj_close[LAST_TRAIN_DATE:LAST_TEST_DATE],
                  color='blue')
ax.set_title(PLOT_TITLE, fontsize=16)
ax.legend((line_1, line_2), ('mean', 'actual'))
```

In the following plot, we observe that the average value from the simulations exhibits a positive trend due to the positive drift term:

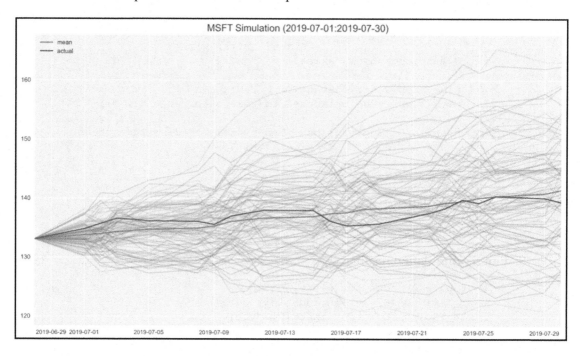

Bear in mind that this visualization is only feasible for a reasonable number of sample paths. In real-life cases, we want to use significantly more sample paths than 100, as usually the more sample paths, the more accurate/reliable the results are.

# How it works...

In *Steps 2* to *4*, we downloaded Microsoft's stock prices and calculated simple returns. In the next step, we divided the data into the training and test sets. We calculated the average and standard deviation of the returns from the training set to obtain the drift (`mu`) and diffusion (`sigma`) coefficients, which we used later for simulations. Additionally, in Step 6, we defined the following parameters:

- `T`: Forecasting horizon; in this case, the number of days in the test set.
- `N`: Number of time increments in the forecasting horizon.

- `S_0`: Initial price. For this simulation, we take the last observation from the training set.
- `N_SIM`: Number of simulated paths.

Monte Carlo simulations use a process called **discretization**. The idea is to approximate the continuous pricing of financial assets by splitting the considered time horizon into a large number of discrete intervals. That is why, except for considering the forecasting horizon, we also need to indicate the number of time increments to fit into the horizon.

*Step 7* is where we defined the function for running the simulations. It is good practice to define a function/class for such a problem, as it will also come in handy in the following recipes. We started by defining the time increment (`dt`) and the Brownian increments (`dW`). In the matrix of increments (size: `n_sims x N`), each row describes one sample path. From there, we calculated the Brownian paths (`W`) by running a cumulative sum (`np.cumsum`) over the rows. Then, we created a matrix containing the time steps (`time_steps`). To do so, we created an array of evenly spaced values within an interval (the horizon of the simulation). For that, we used `np.linspace`. Afterward, we broadcasted the array to the intended shape using `np.broadcast_to`. We used the closed-form formula to calculate the stock price at each point in time. Finally, we inserted the initial value into the first position of each row.

There was no explicit need to broadcast the vector containing time steps. It would have been done automatically to match the required dimensions (the dimension of `W`). However, in languages such as R, there is no automatic broadcasting. This also gives us more control over what we are doing and makes the code easier to debug.

In the preceding steps, we can recognize the drift as `(mu - 0.5 * sigma ** 2) * time_steps` and the diffusion as `sigma * W`.

While defining this function, we followed the vectorized approach. By doing so, we avoided writing any `for` loops, which would be inefficient in the case of large simulations.

For reproducible results, use `np.random.seed` before simulating the paths.

In *Step 8*, we visualized the simulated sample paths. To do so, we transposed the data and converted it into a `pandas` DataFrame. We did the transposition so that we had one path per column, which simplifies using the `plot` method of `pandas` DataFrame. This can also be done using pure `matplotlib`.

Aside from the main plot, we added two extra lines. The first one represents the average value of all sample paths at a given point in time. The second one is the actual stock price of Microsoft in the test set. To visualize the simulated stock prices, we chose `alpha=0.2` to make the lines transparent. By doing this, it is easier to see the two extra lines.

## There's more...

There are some statistical methods that make working with Monte Carlo simulations easier (higher accuracy, faster computations). One of them is a variance reduction method called **antithetic variates**. In this approach, we try to reduce the variance of the estimator by introducing negative dependence between pairs of random draws. This translates into the following: when creating sample paths, for each $[\epsilon_1, \ldots, \epsilon_t]$, we also take the antithetic values $[-\epsilon_1, \ldots, -\epsilon_t]$.

The advantages of this approach are:

- Reduction (by half) of the number of Standard Normal samples to be drawn in order to generate N paths
- Reduction of the sample path variance, while at the same time, improving the accuracy

We implemented this approach in the `simulate_gbm` function. Additionally, we made the function shorter by putting the majority of the calculations into one line.

Before we implemented these changes, we timed the old version of the function:

```
%timeit gbm_simulations = simulate_gbm(S_0, mu, sigma, N_SIM, T, N)
# 188 µs ± 3.75 µs per loop (mean ± std. dev. of 7 runs, 10000 loops each)
```

The new function is defined as follows:

```
def simulate_gbm(s_0, mu, sigma, n_sims, T, N, antithetic_var=False):
    dt = T/N
    if antithetic_var:
        dW_ant = np.random.normal(scale = np.sqrt(dt),
                                  size=(int(n_sims/2), N + 1))
        dW = np.concatenate((dW_ant, -dW_ant), axis=0)
    else:
```

```
dW = np.random.normal(scale = np.sqrt(dt),
                      size=(n_sims, N + 1))
S_t = s_0 * np.exp(np.cumsum((mu - 0.5 * sigma ** 2) * dt + sigma * dW,
                   axis=1))
S_t[:, 0] = s_0
return S_t
```

First, we run the simulations without antithetic variables:

```
%timeit gbm_simulations = simulate_gbm(S_0, mu, sigma, N_SIM, T, N)
# 106 µs ± 9.68 µs per loop (mean ± std. dev. of 7 runs, 10000 loops each)
```

Then, we run the simulations with them:

```
%timeit gbm_simulations = simulate_gbm(S_0, mu, sigma, N_SIM, T, N,
antithetic_var=True)
# 71.5 µs ± 1.89 µs per loop (mean ± std. dev. of 7 runs, 10000 loops each)
```

We succeeded in making the function faster. If you are interested in pure performance, these simulations can be further expedited using `Numba`, `Cython`, or `multiprocessing`.

Other possible variance reduction techniques include:

- Control variates
- Common random numbers

# See also

In this recipe, we have shown how to simulate stock prices using Geometric Brownian Motion. However, there are other stochastic processes that could be used as well, some of which are:

- **Jump-diffusion model**: Merton, Robert (1976): Option Pricing When the Underlying Stock Returns Are Discontinuous. *Journal of Financial Economics*, Vol. 3, No. 3, pp. 125–144.
- **Square-root diffusion model**: Cox, John, Jonathan Ingersoll, and Stephen Ross (1985): *A Theory of the Term Structure of Interest Rates. Econometrica*, Vol. 53, No. 2, pp. 385–407.
- **Stochastic volatility model**: Heston, S. L. (1993). A closed-form solution for options with stochastic volatility with applications to bond and currency options. *The review of financial studies*, 6(2), 327-343.

# Pricing European options using simulations

Options are a type of derivative instrument because their price is linked to the price of the underlying security, such as stock. Buying an options contract grants the right, but not the obligation, to buy or sell an underlying asset at a set price (known as a strike) on/before a certain date. The main reason for the popularity of options is because they hedge away exposure to an asset's price moving in an undesirable way.

A European call/put option gives us the right (but again, no obligation) to buy/sell a certain asset on a certain expiry date (commonly denoted as $T$).

Some popular methods of options' valuation:

- Using analytic formulas
- Binomial tree approach
- Finite differences
- Monte Carlo simulations

European options are an exception in the sense that there exist an analytical formula for their valuation, which is not the case for more advanced derivatives, such as American or Exotic options.

To price options using Monte Carlo simulations, we use risk-neutral valuation, under which the fair value of a derivative is the expected value of its future payoff(s). In other words, we assume that the option premium grows at the same rate as the risk-free rate, which we use for discounting to the present value. For each of the simulated paths, we calculate the option's payoff at maturity, take the average of all the paths, and discount it to the present value.

In this recipe, we show how to code the closed-form solution to the Black-Scholes model and then use the simulation approach. For simplicity, we use fictitious input data, but real-life data could be used analogically.

# How to do it...

Execute the following steps to price European options using Monte Carlo simulations.

1. Import the libraries:

```
import numpy as np
from scipy.stats import norm
from chapter_6_utils import simulate_gbm
```

2. Define the parameters for the valuation:

```
S_0 = 100
K = 100
r = 0.05
sigma = 0.50
T = 1 # 1 year
N = 252 # 252 days in a year
dt = T / N # time step
n_sims = 10 ** 6
discount_factor = np.exp(-r * T)
```

3. Define the function using the analytical solution:

```
def black_scholes_analytical(S_0, K, T, r, sigma, type='call'):
    d1 = (np.log(S_0/K) + (r + 0.5 * sigma**2) * T)
                        /(sigma * np.sqrt(T))
    d2 = (np.log(S_0/K) + (r - 0.5 * sigma**2) * T)
                        /(sigma * np.sqrt(T))
    if type == 'call':
        val = (S_0*norm.cdf(d1, 0, 1)-K*np.exp(-r*T)
                *norm.cdf(d2, 0, 1))
    elif type == 'put':
        val = (K*np.exp(-r*T)*norm.cdf(-d2, 0, 1)-S_0
                *norm.cdf(-d1, 0, 1))
    return val
```

4. Valuate a call option using the specified parameters:

```
black_scholes_analytical(S_0=S_0, K=K, T=T, r=r,
                        sigma=sigma, type='call')
```

The price of a European call option with the specified parameters is 21.7926.

5. Simulate the stock path using the `simulate_gbm` function:

```
gbm_sims = simulate_gbm(s_0=S_0, mu=r, sigma=sigma,
                        n_sims=N_SIMS, T=T, N=N)
```

6. Calculate the option premium:

```
premium = discount_factor * np.average(np.maximum(0,
                            gbm_sims[:, -1] - K))
```

The calculated option premium is 21.7562.

Here, we can see that the option premium that we calculated using Monte Carlo simulations is close to the one from a closed-form solution of the Black-Scholes model. To increase the accuracy of the simulation, we could increase the number of simulated paths (using the n_sims parameter).

# How it works...

In *Step 2*, we defined the parameters that we used for this recipe:

- S_0: Initial stock price
- K: Strike price, that is, the one we can buy/sell for at maturity
- r: Annual risk-free rate
- sigma: Underlying stock volatility (annualized)
- T: Time until maturity in years
- N: Number of time increments for simulations
- n_sims: Number of simulated sample paths
- discount_factor: Discount factor, which is used to calculate the present value of the future payoff

In *Step 3*, we defined a function for calculating the option premium using the closed-form solution to the Black-Scholes model (for non-dividend-paying stocks). We used it in *Step 4* to calculate the benchmark for the Monte Carlo simulations.

The analytical solution to the call and put options is:

$$C(S_t, t) = N(d_1)S_t - N(d_2)Ke^{-r(T-t)}$$

$$P(S_t, t) = N(-d_2)Ke^{-r(T-t)} - N(-d_1)S_t.$$

$$d_1 = \frac{1}{\sigma\sqrt{T-t}}[ln(\frac{S_t}{K}) + (r + \frac{\sigma^2}{2})(T-t)]$$

$$d_2 = d1 - \sigma\sqrt{T-t}$$

Here, *N()* stands for the **cumulative distribution function (CDF)** of the Standard Normal distribution and *T - t* is the time to maturity expressed in years. Equation 1 represents the formula for the price of a European call option, while equation 2 represents the price of the European put option. Informally, the two terms in equation 1 can be thought of as:

- The current price of the stock, weighted by the probability of exercising the option to buy the stock ($N(d_1)$) – in other words, what we could receive.
- The discounted price of exercising the option (strike), weighted by the probability of exercising the option ($N(d_2)$) – in other words, what we are going to pay.

In *Step 5*, we used the GBM simulation function from the previous recipe to obtain 1,000,000 possible paths of the underlying asset. To calculate the option premium, we only looked at the terminal values, and for each path, calculated the payoff as follows:

- $max(S_T - K, 0)$ for the call option
- $max(K - S_T, 0)$ for the put option

In *Step 6*, we took the average of the payoffs and discounted it to present the value by using the discount factor.

# There's more...

In the previous steps, we showed you how to reuse the GBM simulation to calculate the European call option premium. However, we can make the calculations faster, as in the case of European options we are only interested in the terminal stock price. The intermediate steps do not matter. That is why we only need to simulate the price at time *T* and use these values to calculate the expected payoff. We show how to do this by using an example of a European put option with the same parameters as we used before.

We start by calculating the option premium using the analytical formula:

```
black_scholes_analytical(S_0=S_0, K=K, T=T, r=r, sigma=sigma, type='put')
```

The calculated option premium is 16.9155.

Then, we define the modified simulation function, which only looks at the terminal values of the simulation paths:

```
def european_option_simulation(S_0, K, T, r, sigma, n_sims, type):
    rv = np.random.normal(0, 1, size=n_sims)
    S_T = S_0 * np.exp((r - 0.5 * sigma**2) * T + sigma * np.sqrt(T) * rv)
```

```
if type == 'call':
    payoff = np.maximum(0, S_T - K)
elif type == 'put':
    payoff = np.maximum(0, K - S_T)
else:
    raise ValueError('Wrong input for type!')
premium = np.mean(payoff) * np.exp(-r * T)
return premium
```

Then, we run the simulations:

```
european_option_simulation(S_0, K, T, r, sigma, n_sims, type='put')
```

The resulting value is 16.9482. The two values are close to each other. Further increasing the number of simulated paths should increase the accuracy of the valuation.

# Pricing American options with Least Squares Monte Carlo

In this recipe, we learn how to valuate American options. The key difference between European and American options is that the latter can be exercised at any time before and including the maturity date – basically, whenever the underlying asset's price moves favorably for the option holder.

This behavior introduces additional complexity to the valuation and there is no closed-form solution to this problem. When using Monte-Carlo simulations, we cannot only look at the terminal value on each sample path, as the option's exercise can happen anywhere along the path. That is why we need to employ a more sophisticated approach called **Least Squares Monte Carlo (LSMC)**, which was introduced by Longstaff and Schwartz (2001).

First of all, the time axis spanning [0, T] is discretized into a finite number of equally spaced intervals and the early exercise can happen only at those particular time-steps. Effectively, the American option is approximated by a Bermudan one. For any time step *t*, the early exercise is performed in case the payoff from immediate exercise is larger than the continuation value.

This is expressed by the following formula:

$$V_t(s) = max(h_t(s), C_t(s))$$

Here, $h_t(s)$ stands for the option's payoff (also called the option's inner value, calculated as in the case of European options) and $C_t(s)$ is the continuation value of the option, which is defined as :

$$C_t(s) = E_t^Q[e^{-rdt}V_{t+dt}(S_{t+dt})|S_t = s]$$

Here, $r$ is the risk-free rate, $dt$ is the time increment, and $E_t^Q(\dots|St = s)$ is the risk-neutral expectation given the underlying price. The continuation value is basically the expected payoff from not exercising the option at a given time.

When using Monte Carlo simulations, we can define the continuation value for each path and time as $e^{-rdt}V_t+d_{t,i}$, where $i$ indicates the sample path. Using this value directly is not possible as this would imply perfect foresight. That is why the LSMC algorithm uses linear regression to estimate the expected continuation value. In the algorithm, we regress the discounted future values (obtained from keeping the option) onto a set of basis functions of the spot price (time $t$ price). The simplest way to approach this is to use an $x$-degree polynomial regression. Other options for the basis functions include Legendre, Hermite, Chebyshev, Gegenbauer, or Jacobi polynomials.

We iterate this algorithm backward (from time *T-1* to *0*) and at the last step take the average discounted value as the option premium. The premium of a European option represents the lower bound to the American option's premium. The difference is usually called the early exercise premium.

# How to do it...

Execute the following steps to price American options using the Least Squares Monte Carlo method.

1. Import the libraries:

```
import numpy as np
from chapter_6_utils import (simulate_gbm,
                             black_scholes_analytical,
                             lsmc_american_option)
```

2. Define the parameters:

```
S_0 = 36
K = 40
r = 0.06
sigma = 0.2
T = 1 # 1 year
```

```
N = 50
dt = T / N
N_SIMS = 10 ** 5
discount_factor = np.exp(-r * dt)
OPTION_TYPE = 'put'
POLY_DEGREE = 5
```

3. Simulate the stock prices using GBM:

```
gbm_sims = simulate_gbm(s_0=S_0, mu=r, sigma=sigma, n_sims=N_SIMS,
                        T=T, N=N)
```

4. Calculate the payoff matrix:

```
payoff_matrix = np.maximum(K - gbm_sims, np.zeros_like(gbm_sims))
```

5. Define the value matrix and fill in the last column (time T):

```
value_matrix = np.zeros_like(payoff_matrix)
value_matrix[:, -1] = payoff_matrix[:, -1]
```

6. Iteratively calculate the continuation value and the value vector in the given time:

```
for t in range(N - 1, 0 , -1):
    regression = np.polyfit(gbm_sims[:, t],
                            value_matrix[:, t + 1] *
                            discount_factor,
                            POLY_DEGREE)
    continuation_value = np.polyval(regression, gbm_sims[:, t])
    value_matrix[:, t] = np.where(
        payoff_matrix[:, t] > continuation_value,
        payoff_matrix[:, t],
        value_matrix[:, t + 1] * discount_factor
    )
```

7. Calculate the option premium:

```
option_premium = np.mean(value_matrix[:, 1] * discount_factor)
```

The premium on the specified American put option is 4.465.

8. Calculate the premium of a European put with the same parameters:

```
black_scholes_analytical(S_0=S_0, K=K, T=T, r=r, sigma=sigma,
                         type='put')
```

The price of the European put option with the same parameters is 3.84.

9. As an extra check, calculate the prices of the American and European call options:

```
european_call_price = black_scholes_analytical(S_0=S_0, K=K, T=T,
                                                r=r, sigma=sigma)
american_call_price = lsmc_american_option(S_0=S_0, K=K, T=T, r=r,
                                            sigma=sigma,
                                            n_sims=N_SIMS,
                                            option_type='call',
                                            poly_degree=POLY_DEGREE)
```

The price of the European call is 2.17, while the American call's price (using 100,000 simulations) is 2.10.

# How it works...

In *Step 2*, we once again defined the parameters of the considered American option. For comparison's sake, we took the same values that Longstaff and Schwartz (2001) did. In *Step 3*, we simulated the stock's evolution using the `simulate_gbm` function from the previous recipe. Afterward, we calculated the payoff matrix of the put option using the same formula that we used for the European options.

In *Step 5*, we prepared the matrix of option values over time, which we defined as a matrix of zeros of the same size as the payoff matrix. We filled the last column of the value matrix with the last column of the payoff matrix, as at the last step there are no further computations to carry out – the payoff is equal to the European option.

*Step 6* is where we ran the backward part of the algorithm from time *T-1* to 0. At each of these steps, we estimated the expected continuation value as a cross-sectional linear regression. We fitted the $5^{th}$-degree polynomial to the data using `np.polyfit`. Then, we evaluated the polynomial at specific values (using `np.polyval`), which is the same as getting the fitted values from a linear regression. We compared the expected continuation value to the payoff to see if the option should be exercised. If the payoff was higher than the expected value from continuation, we set the value to the payoff. Otherwise, we set it to the discounted one-step-ahead value. We used `np.where` for this selection.

It is also possible to use `scikit-learn` for the polynomial fit. To do so, you need to combine `LinearRegression` with `PolynomialFeatures`.

In *Step 7* of the algorithm, we obtained the option premium by taking the average value of the discounted `t = 1` value vector.

In the last two steps, we carried out some sanity checks regarding the implementation by calculating the option premiums of the European put and call options with the same parameters. To make this easier, we put the entire algorithm for LSMC into one function, which is available in this book's GitHub repository. For the call option, the premium on the American and European options should be equal, as it is never optimal to exercise the option when there are no dividends. Our results are very close, but we can obtain a more accurate price using more sample paths.

In principle, the Longstaff-Schwartz algorithm should underprice American options because the approximation of the continuation value by the basis functions is just that, an approximation. As a consequence, the algorithm will not always make the correct decision about exercising the option. This, in turn, means that the option's value will be lower than in the case of the optimal exercise.

# See also

Additional resources are available here:

- Longstaff, F. A., & Schwartz, E. S. (2001). Valuing American options by simulation: a simple least-squares approach. *The review of financial studies*, 14(1), 113-147. - https://escholarship.org/content/qt43n1k4jb/qt43n1k4jb.pdf.
- Broadie, M., Glasserman, P., & Jain, G. (1997). An alternative approach to the valuation of American options using the stochastic tree method. Enhanced Monte Carlo estimates for American option prices. *Journal of Derivatives*, 5, 25-44.

# Pricing American options using Quantlib

In the previous recipe, we showed how to manually code the Longstaff-Schwartz algorithm. However, we can also use already existing frameworks for valuation of derivatives. One of the most popular ones is QuantLib. It is an open source C++ library that provides tools for the valuation of financial instruments. By using **Simplified Wrapper and Interface Generator** (**SWIG**), it is possible to use QuantLib from Python (and some other programming languages, such as R or Julia). In this recipe, we show how to price the same American put option that we priced in the *Pricing American options with Least squares Monte Carlo* recipe, but the library itself has many more interesting features to explore.

# How to do it...

Execute the following steps to price American options using Quantlib.

1. Import the library:

```
import QuantLib as ql
```

2. Specify the calendar and the day counting convention:

```
calendar = ql.UnitedStates()
day_counter = ql.ActualActual()
```

3. Specify the valuation date and the expiry date of the option:

```
valuation_date = ql.Date(1, 1, 2018)
expiry_date = ql.Date(1, 1, 2019)
ql.Settings.instance().evaluationDate = valuation_date
```

4. Define the option type (call/put), type of exercise, and the payoff:

```
if OPTION_TYPE == 'call':
    option_type_ql = ql.Option.Call
elif OPTION_TYPE == 'put':
    option_type_ql = ql.Option.Put
exercise = ql.AmericanExercise(valuation_date, expiry_date)
payoff = ql.PlainVanillaPayoff(option_type_ql, K)
```

5. Prepare the market-related data:

```
u = ql.SimpleQuote(S_0)
r = ql.SimpleQuote(r)
sigma = ql.SimpleQuote(sigma)
```

6. Specify market-related curves:

```
underlying = ql.QuoteHandle(u)
volatility = ql.BlackConstantVol(0, ql.TARGET(),
                                 ql.QuoteHandle(sigma),
                                 day_counter)
risk_free_rate = ql.FlatForward(0, ql.TARGET(),
                                ql.QuoteHandle(r),
                                day_counter)
```

7. Plug the market-related data into the BS process:

```
bsm_process = ql.BlackScholesProcess(
    underlying,
    ql.YieldTermStructureHandle(risk_free_rate),
    ql.BlackVolTermStructureHandle(volatility),
)
```

8. Instantiate the Monte Carlo engine for the American options:

```
engine = ql.MCAmericanEngine(bs_process, 'PseudoRandom',
                             timeSteps=N,
                             polynomOrder=POLY_DEGREE,
                             seedCalibration=42,
                             requiredSamples=N_SIMS)
```

9. Instantiate the `option` object and set its pricing engine:

```
option = ql.VanillaOption(payoff, exercise)
option.setPricingEngine(engine)
```

10. Calculate the option premium:

```
option_premium_ql = option.NPV()
```

The value of the American put option is 4.463.

# How it works...

Since we wanted to compare the results we obtained here with those in the previous recipes, we used the same problem setup as we did there. For brevity, we will not look at all the code here, but we should run *Step 2* from the previous recipe.

In *Step 2*, we specified the calendar and the day-counting convention. The day counting convention determines the way interest accrues over time for various financial instruments, such as bonds. The `actual/actual` convention means that we use the actual number of elapsed days and the actual number of days in a year – 365 or 366. There are many other conventions such as `actual/365 fixed`, `actual/360`, and so on.

In *Step 3*, we selected two dates – valuation and expiry – as we are interested in pricing an option that expires in a year. It is important to set `ql.Settings.instance().evaluationDate` to the considered evaluation date to make sure the calculations are performed correctly. In this case, the dates only determine the passage of time, meaning that the option expires within a year. We would get the same results (with some margin of error due to the random component of the simulations) using different dates with the same interval between them.

We can check the time to expiry (in years) by running the following code:

```
T = day_counter.yearFraction(valuation_date, expiry_date)
print(f'Time to expiry in years: {T}')
# Time to expiry in years: 1.0
```

Next, we defined the option type (call/put), the type of exercise (European, American, or Bermudan), and the payoff (Vanilla). In *Step 5*, we prepared the market data. We wrapped the values in quotes (`ql.SimpleQuote`) so that the values can be changed and the changes are registered in the instrument. This is important for calculating Greeks in the *There's more* section.

In *Step 6*, we defined the relevant curves. Simply put, `TARGET` is a calendar that contains information on which days are holidays.

In this step, we specified the three important components of the **Black-Scholes** (**BS**) process, which are:

- The price of the underlying instrument
- Volatility, which is constant as per our assumptions
- The risk-free rate, which is also constant over time

We passed all these objects to the Black-Scholes process (`ql.BlackScholesProcess`), which we defined in *Step 7*. Then, we passed the process object into the special engine used for pricing American options using Monte Carlo simulations (there are many predefined engines for different types of options and pricing methods). At this point, we provided the desired number of simulations, the number of time steps for discretization, and the degree/order of the polynomial in the LSMC algorithm.

In *Step 9*, we created an instance of `ql.VanillaOption` by providing previously defined types of payoff and exercise. We also set the pricing engine using the `setPricingEngine` method.

Finally, we obtained the price of the option using the `NPV` method.

By doing this, we can see that the option premium we obtained using QuantLib is very similar to the one we calculated previously, which further validates our results. The important thing to note here is that the workflow is similar for the valuation of a wide array of different derivatives, so it is good to be familiar with it. We could just as well price a European option using Monte Carlo simulations by substituting a few commands with their European option equivalents.

# There's more...

QuantLib also allows us to use variance reduction techniques such as antithetic values or **control variates**.

Now that we have completed the preceding steps, we can calculate Greeks. Greeks (from the letters of the Greek alphabet) represent the sensitivity of the price of derivatives (for example, the option premium) to a change in one of the underlying parameters (such as the price of the underlying asset, time to expiry, volatility, the interest rate, and so on). When there is an analytical formula available for the Greeks (when the QuantlLib engine is using analytical formulas), we could just access it by running, for example, `option.delta()`. However, in cases such as valuations using binomial trees or simulations, there is no analytical formula and we would receive an error (`RuntimeError: delta not provided`). This does not mean that it is impossible to calculate it, but we need to employ numerical differentiation and calculate it ourselves.

In this example, we will only extract the delta. Therefore, the relevant two-sided formula is:

$$\Delta = \frac{P(S_0 + h) - P(S_0 - h)}{2h}$$

Here, $P(S)$ is the price of the instrument given the underlying's price $S$; $h$ is a very small increment.

Run the following block of code to calculate the delta:

```
u_0 = u.value() # original value
h = 0.01

u.setValue(u_0 + h)
```

```
P_plus_h = option.NPV()

u.setValue(u_0 - h)
P_minus_h = option.NPV()

u.setValue(u_0) # set back to the original value

delta = (P_plus_h - P_minus_h) / (2 * h)
```

The simplest interpretation of the delta is that the option's delta being equal to -1.25 indicates that, if the underlying stock increases in price by $1 per share, the option on it will decrease by $1.25 per share; otherwise, everything will be equal.

# Estimating value-at-risk using Monte Carlo

**Value-at-risk** is a very important financial metric that measures the risk associated with a position, portfolio, and so on. It is commonly abbreviated to VaR, not to be confused with Vector Autoregression. VaR reports the worst expected loss – at a given level of confidence – over a certain horizon under normal market conditions. The easiest way to understand it is by looking at an example. Let's say that the 1-day 95% VaR of our portfolio is $100. This means that 95% of the time (under normal market conditions), we will not lose more than $100 by holding our portfolio over one day.

It is common to present the loss given by VaR as a positive (absolute) value. That is why in this example, a VaR of $100 means losing no more than $100.

There are several ways to calculate VaR, some of which are:

- Parametric Approach (Variance-Covariance)
- Historical Simulation Approach
- Monte Carlo simulations

In this recipe, we only consider the last method. We assume that we are holding a portfolio consisting of two assets (Facebook and Google) and that we want to calculate a 1-day value-at-risk.

# How to do it...

Execute the following steps to estimate the value-at-risk using Monte Carlo.

1. Import the libraries:

```
import numpy as np
import pandas as pd
import yfinance as yf
import seaborn as sns
```

2. Define the parameters that will be used for this exercise:

```
RISKY_ASSETS = ['GOOG', 'FB']
SHARES = [5, 5]
START_DATE = '2018-01-01'
END_DATE = '2018-12-31'
T = 1
N_SIMS = 10 ** 5
```

3. Download the data from Yahoo Finance:

```
df = yf.download(RISKY_ASSETS, start=START_DATE,
                 end=END_DATE, adjusted=True)
```

4. Calculate the daily returns:

```
adj_close = df['Adj Close']
returns = adj_close.pct_change().dropna()
plot_title = f'{" vs. ".join(RISKY_ASSETS)} returns: {START_DATE} -
                                                    {END_DATE}'

returns.plot(title=plot_title)
```

We also plot the calculated returns and calculate the Pearson's correlation of the two series:

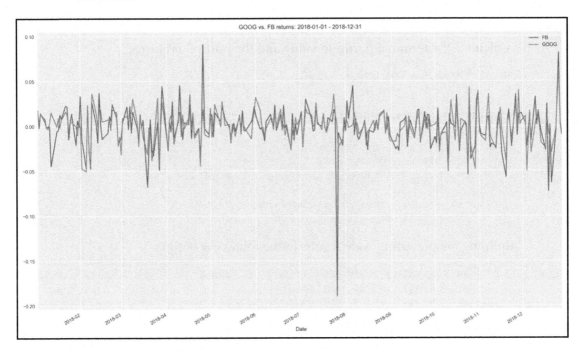

The correlation between the two series is 0.62.

5. Calculate the covariance matrix:

```
cov_mat = returns.cov()
```

6. Perform the Cholesky decomposition of the covariance matrix:

```
chol_mat = np.linalg.cholesky(cov_mat)
```

7. Draw the correlated random numbers from the Standard Normal distribution:

```
rv = np.random.normal(size=(N_SIMS, len(RISKY_ASSETS)))
correlated_rv = np.transpose(np.matmul(chol_mat, np.transpose(rv)))
```

8. Define the metrics that will be used for simulations:

```
r = np.mean(returns, axis=0).values
sigma = np.std(returns, axis=0).values
S_0 = adj_close.values[-1, :]
P_0 = np.sum(SHARES * S_0)
```

9. Calculate the terminal price of the considered stocks:

```
S_T = S_0 * np.exp((r - 0.5 * sigma ** 2) * T +
                    sigma * np.sqrt(T) * correlated_rv)
```

10. Calculate the terminal portfolio value and the portfolio returns:

```
P_T = np.sum(SHARES * S_T, axis=1)
P_diff = P_T - P_0
```

11. Calculate the VaR for the selected confidence levels:

```
P_diff_sorted = np.sort(P_diff)
percentiles = [0.01, 0.1, 1.]
var = np.percentile(P_diff_sorted, percentiles)

for x, y in zip(percentiles, var):
    print(f'1-day VaR with {100-x}% confidence: {-y:.2f}$')
```

Running the preceding code results in the following output:

```
1-day VaR with 99.99% confidence: 8.49$
1-day VaR with 99.9% confidence: 7.23$
1-day VaR with 99.0% confidence: 5.78$
```

12. Present the results on a graph:

```
ax = sns.distplot(P_diff, kde=False)
ax.set_title('''Distribution of possible 1-day changes
            in portfolio value
            1-day 99% VaR''', fontsize=16)
ax.axvline(var[2], 0, 10000);
```

Running the code results in the following plot:

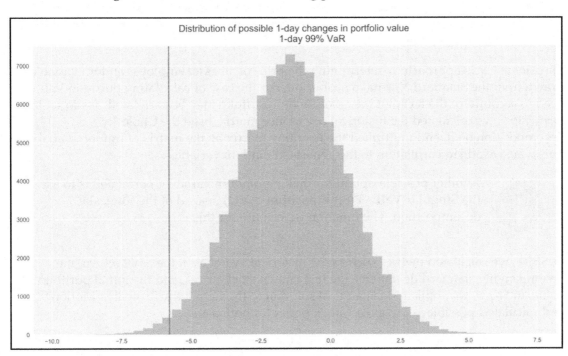

The preceding plot shows the distribution of possible 1-day ahead portfolio values. We present the value-at-risk with the vertical line.

# How it works...

In *Steps 2* to *4*, we downloaded the daily stock prices of Google and Facebook, extracted the adjusted close prices, and converted them into simple returns. We also defined a few parameters, such as the number of simulations and the number of shares we have in our portfolio.

There are two ways to approach VaR calculations:

- **Calculate VaR from prices**: Using the number of shares and the asset prices, we can calculate the worth of the portfolio now and its possible value X days ahead.

- **Calculate VaR from returns**: Using the percentage weights of each asset in the portfolio and the assets' expected returns, we can calculate the expected portfolio return X days ahead. Then, we can express VaR as the dollar amount based on that return and the current portfolio value.

The Monte Carlo approach to determining the price of an asset employs random variables drawn from the Standard Normal distribution. For the case of calculating portfolio VaR, we need to account for the fact that the assets in our portfolio may be correlated. To do so, in *Steps 5* to *7*, we calculated the historical covariance matrix, used the Cholesky decomposition on it, and multiplied the resulting matrix by the matrix of random variables. This way, we added correlation to the generated random variables.

Another possible option for making random variables correlated is to use the **Singular Value Decomposition (SVD)** instead of the Cholesky decomposition. The function we can use for this is np.linalg.svd.

In *Step 8*, we calculated metrics such as the historical averages of the asset return, the accompanying standard deviations, the last known stock prices, and the initial portfolio value. In *Step 9*, we applied the analytical solution to the Geometric Brownian Motion SDE and calculated possible 1-day-ahead stock prices for both assets.

To calculate the portfolio VaR, we calculated the possible 1-day-ahead portfolio values and the accompanying differences ($P_T - P_0$) and sorted them in ascending order. The X% VaR is simply the (1-X)-th percentile of the sorted portfolio differences.

Banks frequently calculate the 1-day and 10-day VaR. To arrive at the latter, they can simulate the value of their assets over a 10-day interval using 1-day steps (discretization). However, they can also calculate the 1-day VaR and multiply it by the square root of 10. This might be beneficial for the bank if it leads to lower capital requirements.

# There's more...

Calculating VaR using different approaches has its drawbacks, some of which are:

- Assuming a parametric distribution (variance-covariance approach).
- Not capturing enough tail risk.
- Not considering the so-called Black Swan events (unless they are already in the historical sample).

- Historical VaR can be slow to adapt to new market conditions.
- The Historical Simulation Approach assumes that past returns are sufficient to evaluate future risk (connects to the previous points).

Another general drawback of VaR is that it does not contain information about the size of the potential loss when it exceeds the threshold given by VaR. This is when **Expected Shortfall** (also known as conditional VaR or expected tail loss) comes into play. It simply states what the expected loss is in the worst X% of scenarios.

There are many ways to calculate the Expected Shortfall, but here, we present the one that is easily connected to the VaR and can be estimated using Monte Carlo.

Following on from the example of a two-asset portfolio, we would like to know the following: if the loss exceeds the VaR, how big will it be? To obtain that number, we need to filter out all losses that are higher than the value given by VaR and calculate their expected value by taking the average.

We can do this by using the following code:

```
var = np.percentile(P_diff_sorted, 5)
expected_shortfall = P_diff_sorted[P_diff_sorted<=var].mean()
```

Please bear in mind that, for Expected Shortfall, we only use a small fraction of all the simulations that were used to obtain the VaR. That is why, in order to have reasonable results for the Expected Shortfall, the overall sample must be large enough.

The 1-day 95% VaR is $4.48, while the accompanying Expected Shortfall is $5.27. We can interpret these results as follows: if the loss exceeds the 95% VaR, we can expect to lose $5.27 by holding our portfolio for 1 day.

# 7
# Asset Allocation in Python

Asset allocation is the most important decision that any investor needs to face, and there is no one-size-fits-all solution that can work for each and every investor. By asset allocation, we mean spreading the investor's total investment amount over certain assets (be it stocks, options, bonds, or any other financial instruments). When considering the allocation, the investor wants to balance the risk and the potential reward. At the same time, the allocation is dependent on factors such as the individual goals (expected return), risk tolerance (how much risk is the investor willing to accept), or the investment horizon (short or long-term investment).

The key framework in asset allocation is the **modern portfolio theory** (**MPT**, also known as **mean-variance analysis**). It was introduced by the Nobel recipient Harry Markowitz and describes how risk-averse investors can construct portfolios to maximize their expected returns (profits) for a given level of risk. The main insight from MPT is that investors should not evaluate an asset's performance alone (by metrics such as expected return or volatility), but instead investigate how it would impact the performance of their portfolio of assets.

MPT is closely related to the concept of diversification, which simply means that owning different kinds of assets reduces risk, as the loss or gain of a particular security has less impact on the portfolio's performance. Another key concept to be aware of is that while the portfolio return is the weighted average of the individual asset returns, this is not true for the risk (volatility). It is also dependent on the correlations between the assets. What is interesting is that thanks to optimized asset allocation, it is possible to have a portfolio with lower volatility than the lowest individual volatility of the assets in the portfolio. In principle, the lower the correlation between the assets we hold, the better it is for diversification. With a perfect negative correlation, we could diversify all the risk.

The main assumptions of modern portfolio theory are:

- Investors are rational and aim to maximize their returns, while avoiding risks whenever possible.
- Investors share the goal to maximize their expected returns.
- All investors have the same level of information about potential investments.
- Commissions, taxes, and transaction costs are not taken into account.
- Investors can borrow and lend money (without limits) at a risk-free rate.

In this chapter, we start with the most basic asset allocation strategy, and on its basis learn how to evaluate the performance of portfolios (also applicable to individual assets). Later on, we show three different approaches to obtaining the Efficient Frontier, while also relaxing some of the assumptions of MPT. One of the main benefits of learning how to approach optimization problems is that they can be easily refactored, for example, optimizing a different objective function. This requires only slight modifications to the code, while the majority of the framework stays the same.

We cover the following recipes in this chapter:

- Evaluating the performance of a basic *1/n* portfolio
- Finding the Efficient Frontier using Monte Carlo simulations
- Finding the Efficient Frontier using optimization with `scipy`
- Finding the Efficient Frontier using convex optimization with `cvxpy`

# Evaluating the performance of a basic *1/n* portfolio

We begin with inspecting the most basic asset allocation strategy: the **1/n portfolio**. The idea is to assign equal weights to all the considered assets, thus diversifying the portfolio. As simple as that might sound, DeMiguel, Garlappi, and Uppal (2007) show that it can be difficult to beat the performance of the 1/n portfolio by using more advanced asset allocation strategies.

The goal of the recipe is to show how to create a 1/n portfolio, calculate its returns, and then use a Python library called `pyfolio` to quickly obtain all relevant portfolio evaluation metrics in the form of a tear sheet. Historically, a tear sheet is a concise, usually one-page, document, summarizing important information about public companies.

# How to do it...

Execute the following steps to create and evaluate the 1/n portfolio.

1. Import the libraries:

```
import yfinance as yf
import numpy as np
import pandas as pd
import pyfolio as pf
```

2. Set up the parameters:

```
RISKY_ASSETS = ['AAPL', 'IBM', 'MSFT', 'TWTR']
START_DATE = '2017-01-01'
END_DATE = '2018-12-31'

n_assets = len(RISKY_ASSETS)
```

3. Download the stock prices from Yahoo Finance:

```
prices_df = yf.download(RISKY_ASSETS, start=START_DATE,
                        end=END_DATE, adjusted=True)
```

4. Calculate individual asset returns:

```
returns = prices_df['Adj Close'].pct_change().dropna()
```

5. Define the weights:

```
portfolio_weights = n_assets * [1 / n_assets]
```

6. Calculate the portfolio returns:

```
portfolio_returns = pd.Series(np.dot(portfolio_weights, returns.T),
                              index=returns.index)
```

7. Create the tear sheet (simple variant):

```
pf.create_simple_tear_sheet(portfolio_returns)
```

The preceding line of code generates the simple tear sheet, and the first table looks like this:

| | |
|---:|:---|
| **Start date** ⬍ | 2017-01-04 ⬍ |
| **End date** ⬍ | 2018-12-28 ⬍ |
| **Total months** ⬍ | 23 ⬍ |
| ⬍ | **Backtest** ⬍ |
| **Annual return** | 17.7% |
| **Cumulative returns** | 38.1% |
| **Annual volatility** | 21.8% |
| **Sharpe ratio** | 0.86 |
| **Calmar ratio** | 0.70 |
| **Stability** | 0.87 |
| **Max drawdown** | -25.3% |
| **Omega ratio** | 1.17 |
| **Sortino ratio** | 1.21 |
| **Skew** | -0.29 |
| **Kurtosis** | 3.93 |
| **Tail ratio** | 0.88 |
| **Daily value at risk** | -2.7% |

We describe the metrics presented in the first table of the tear sheet in the following section.

# How it works...

In *Steps 1* to *4*, we followed the already established approach—imported the libraries, set up the parameters, downloaded stock prices of four US tech companies (Apple, IBM, Microsoft, and Twitter) over the years 2017-2018, and calculated simple returns, using the adjusted close prices.

In *Step 5*, we created a list of weights, each one equal to 1 / n_assets, where n_assets is the number of assets we want to have in our portfolio. Next, we calculated the portfolio returns as a matrix multiplication (also known as the dot product—np.dot) of the portfolio weights and a transposed matrix of asset returns. To transpose the matrix, we used the T method of a pandas DataFrame. Then, we stored the portfolio returns as a pandas Series object, because that is the input for the ensuing step.

Lastly, we created a tear sheet using `pf.create_simple_tear_sheet`. We decided to use a simple variant, containing the most relevant portfolio metrics and plots.

The most important metrics that we saw in the preceding table are:

- **Sharpe ratio**: One of the most popular performance evaluation metrics, it measures the excess return (over the risk-free rate) per unit of standard deviation. When no risk-free rate is provided, the default assumption is that it is equal to 0%. The greater the Sharpe ratio, the better the portfolio's risk-adjusted performance.
- **Max drawdown**: A metric of the downside risk of a portfolio, it measures the largest peak-to-valley loss (expressed as a percentage) during the course of the investment. The lower the maximum drawdown, the better.
- **Calmar ratio**: The ratio is defined as the average annual compounded rate of return divided by the maximum drawdown for that same time period. The higher the ratio, the better.
- **Stability**: Measured as the R-squared of a linear fit to the cumulative log returns. In practice, this means regressing a range of integers (serving as the time index) on cumulative log returns.
- **Omega ratio**: The probability-weighted ratio of gains over losses for a determined return target threshold (default set to 0). Its main advantage over the Sharpe ratio is that the Omega ratio—by construction—considers all moments of the returns distribution, while the former only considers the first two (mean and variance).
- **Sortino ratio**: A modified version of the Sharpe ratio, where the standard deviation in the denominator is replaced with downside deviation.
- **Skew**: Skewness measures the degree of asymmetry, that is, how much is the given distribution (here, of portfolio returns) more skewed than the Normal distribution. Negative skewness (left-skewed distributions) means that large negative returns occur more frequently than large positive ones.
- **Kurtosis**: Measures extreme values in either of the tails. Distributions with large kurtosis exhibit tail data exceeding the tails of the Gaussian distribution, meaning that large and small returns occur more frequently.
- **Tail ratio**: The ratio (absolute) between the 95th and 5th percentile of the daily returns. A tail ratio of ~0.8 means that losses are ~1.25 times as bad as profits.
- **Daily value at risk**: Calculated as $\mu - 2\sigma$, where $\mu$ is the average portfolio return over the period, and $\sigma$ the corresponding standard deviation.

Downside deviation is similar to standard deviation; however, it only considers negative returns—it discards all positive changes from the series. It also allows us to define different levels of minimum acceptable returns (dependent on the investor), and returns below that threshold are used to calculate the downside deviation.

The tear sheet also contains the following plots:

- **Cumulative returns plot**: It presents the evolution of the portfolio's worth over time:

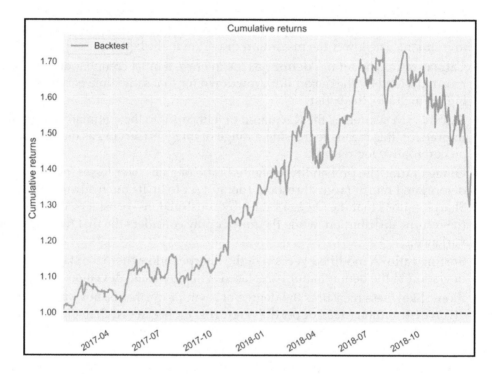

- **Rolling Sharpe ratio**: Instead of reporting one number over time, it is also interesting to see how stable the Sharpe ratio was. That is why the following plot presents this metric calculated on a rolling basis, using 6 months' worth of data:

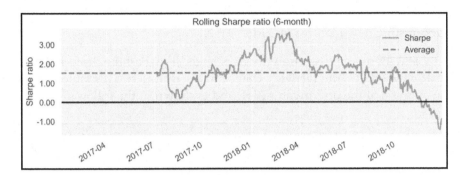

- **Underwater plot (also known as the underwater equity curve)**: This plot presents the investment from a pessimistic point of view, as it focuses on losses. It plots all the drawdown periods and how long they lasted—until the value rebounded to a new high. One of the insights we can draw from this is how long the periods of losses lasted:

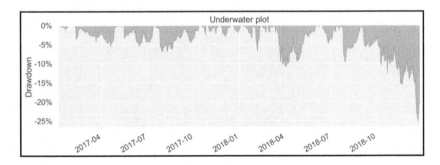

To obtain all the plots, we used the `pf.create_simple_tear_sheet` function. However, we can also obtain only the selected plots from the tear sheets. For example, to create the rolling Sharpe ratio plot seen previously, we can use the `pf.plot_rolling_sharpe` function. By calling the specific functions directly, we can make the plots more tailored to our needs. In this case, one of the parameters of the function corresponds to the rolling window's length.

# There's more...

Previously, we used the `pf.create_simple_tear_sheet` function, as it already contains a lot of useful metrics. To obtain even more details, we can use the `pf.create_returns_tear_sheet` function.

Some of the interesting new features include:

- A table with the top five drawdown periods: how bad the drawdown was, the peak/valley dates, the recovery date, and the duration. This table complements the analysis of the underwater plot, and is shown in the following image:

| Worst drawdown periods ⬍ | Net drawdown in % ⬍ | Peak date ⬍ | Valley date ⬍ | Recovery date ⬍ | Duration ⬍ |
|---|---|---|---|---|---|
| 0 | 25.32 | 2018-07-25 | 2018-12-24 | NaT | NaN |
| 1 | 10.93 | 2018-03-12 | 2018-04-02 | 2018-06-01 | 60 |
| 2 | 6.93 | 2017-07-20 | 2017-07-31 | 2017-10-12 | 61 |
| 3 | 6.71 | 2018-02-01 | 2018-02-05 | 2018-02-12 | 8 |
| 4 | 5.47 | 2017-02-08 | 2017-04-19 | 2017-05-01 | 59 |

- The top five drawdown periods are also visualized on a separate plot:

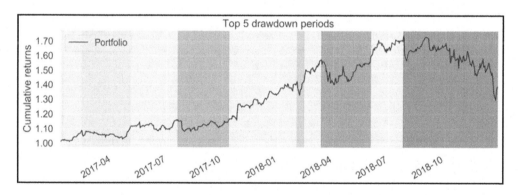

- Plots describing the distribution of the portfolio returns: a summary of what the returns were over certain months/years, how the monthly returns were distributed, and the returns' quantiles, using different frequencies. All that information is presented below:

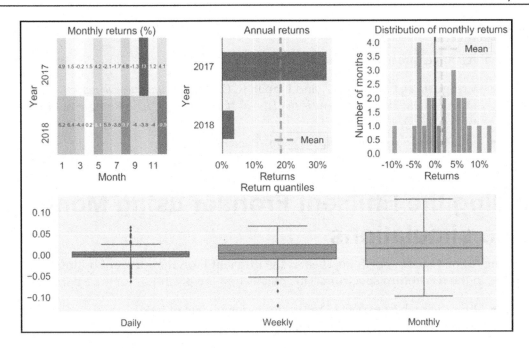

pyfolio was developed by the Quantopian team and works really well as a standalone library. However, it can also be combined with zipline—a Quantopian-developed backtesting and live-trading framework. Similarly to backtrader, it is a framework facilitating backtesting of trading strategies. When we add extra information (such as transaction/position details obtained from zipline) to the pyfolio function calls, we receive even more information in the tear sheet.

We can create Bayesian tear sheets by running the pf.create_bayesian_tear_sheet function. These are based on PyMC3 and require additional dependencies.

Most of the performance/risk metrics presented in the pyfolio tear sheets are actually calculated using a library called empyrical, also developed by Quantopian. We can use it directly if we are only interested in calculating a specific metric, such as the Omega ratio.

# See also

Additional resources are available here:

- DeMiguel, V., Garlappi, L., and Uppal, R. (2007). *Optimal versus naive diversification: How inefficient is the 1/N portfolio strategy?* The Review of Financial Studies, 22(5), 1915-1953.
- Quantopian's website: `https://www.quantopian.com/`

# Finding the Efficient Frontier using Monte Carlo simulations

According to the Modern Portfolio Theory, the Efficient Frontier is a set of optimal portfolios in the risk-return spectrum. This means that the portfolios on the frontier:

- Offer the highest expected return for a given level of risk
- Offer the lowest level of risk for a given level of expected returns

All portfolios located under the Efficient Frontier curve are considered sub-optimal, so it is always better to choose the ones on the frontier instead.

In this recipe, we show how to find the Efficient Frontier using Monte Carlo simulations. We build thousands of portfolios, using randomly assigned weights, and visualize the results. To do so, we use the returns of four US tech companies from 2018.

# How to do it...

Execute the following steps to find the Efficient Frontier using Monte Carlo simulations.

1. Import the libraries:

```
import yfinance as yf
import numpy as np
import pandas as pd
```

2. Set up the parameters:

```
N_PORTFOLIOS = 10 ** 5
N_DAYS = 252
RISKY_ASSETS = ['FB', 'TSLA', 'TWTR', 'MSFT']
RISKY_ASSETS.sort()
START_DATE = '2018-01-01'
END_DATE = '2018-12-31'

n_assets = len(RISKY_ASSETS)
```

3. Download the stock prices from Yahoo Finance:

```
prices_df = yf.download(RISKY_ASSETS, start=START_DATE,
                        end=END_DATE, adjusted=True)
```

4. Calculate annualized average returns and the corresponding standard deviation:

```
returns_df = prices_df['Adj Close'].pct_change().dropna()
avg_returns = returns_df.mean() * N_DAYS
cov_mat = returns_df.cov() * N_DAYS
```

5. Simulate random portfolio weights:

```
np.random.seed(42)
weights = np.random.random(size=(N_PORTFOLIOS, n_assets))
weights /= np.sum(weights, axis=1)[:, np.newaxis]
```

6. Calculate the portfolio metrics:

```
portf_rtns = np.dot(weights, avg_returns)

portf_vol = []
for i in range(0, len(weights)):
    portf_vol.append(np.sqrt(np.dot(weights[i].T,
                                    np.dot(cov_mat, weights[i]))))
portf_vol = np.array(portf_vol)
portf_sharpe_ratio = portf_rtns / portf_vol
```

7. Create a DataFrame containing all the data:

```
portf_results_df = pd.DataFrame({'returns': portf_rtns,
                                 'volatility': portf_vol,
                                 'sharpe_ratio':
                                 portf_sharpe_ratio})
```

8.  Locate the points creating the Efficient Frontier:

```
N_POINTS = 100
portf_vol_ef = []
indices_to_skip = []

portf_rtns_ef = np.linspace(portf_results_df.returns.min(),
                            portf_results_df.returns.max(),
                            N_POINTS)
portf_rtns_ef = np.round(portf_rtns_ef, 2)
portf_rtns = np.round(portf_rtns, 2)

for point_index in range(N_POINTS):
    if portf_rtns_ef[point_index] not in portf_rtns:
        indices_to_skip.append(point_index)
        continue
    matched_ind = np.where(portf_rtns ==
                           portf_rtns_ef[point_index])
    portf_vol_ef.append(np.min(portf_vol[matched_ind]))

portf_rtns_ef = np.delete(portf_rtns_ef, indices_to_skip)
```

9.  Plot the Efficient Frontier:

```
MARKS = ['o', 'X', 'd', '*']

fig, ax = plt.subplots()
portf_results_df.plot(kind='scatter', x='volatility',
                      y='returns', c='sharpe_ratio',
                      cmap='RdYlGn', edgecolors='black',
                      ax=ax)
ax.set(xlabel='Volatility',
       ylabel='Expected Returns',
       title='Efficient Frontier')
ax.plot(portf_vol_ef, portf_rtns_ef, 'b--')
for asset_index in range(n_assets):
    ax.scatter(x=np.sqrt(cov_mat.iloc[asset_index, asset_index]),
               y=avg_returns[asset_index],
               marker=MARKS[asset_index],
               s=150,
               color='black',
               label=RISKY_ASSETS[asset_index])
ax.legend()
```

Executing the preceding code generates the plot with all the randomly created portfolios, four points indicating the individual assets, and the Efficient Frontier:

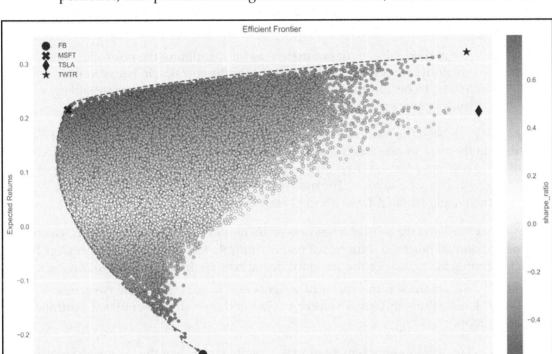

In the preceding plot, we see the typical, bullet-like shape of the Efficient Frontier.

# How it works...

In *Step 2*, we defined parameters used for this recipe, such as the considered timeframe, the risky assets we wanted to use for building the portfolio, and the number of simulations. An important thing to note here is that we also ran RISKY_ASSETS.sort(), to sort the list alphabetically. This matters when interpreting the results as when downloading data from Yahoo Finance using the yfinance library, the obtained prices are ordered alphabetically, not as specified in the provided list. Having downloaded the stock prices, we calculated simple returns using the pct_change method of a pandas DataFrame, and dropped the first row containing NaNs.

For evaluating the potential portfolios, we needed the average (expected) annual return and the corresponding covariance matrix. We obtained them by using the `mean()` and `cov()` methods of the DataFrame. We also annualized both metrics by multiplying them by 252 (the average number of trading days in a year).

 We needed the covariance matrix, as for calculating the portfolio volatility, we also needed to account for the correlation between the assets. To benefit from significant diversification, the assets should have low positive or negative correlations.

In *Step 5*, we calculated the random portfolio weights. Following the assumptions of the MPT (refer to the chapter introduction for reference), the weights needed to be positive and sum up to 1. To achieve this, we first generated a matrix of random numbers (between 0 and 1), using `np.random.random`. The matrix was of size `N_SIMULATIONS` x `N_ASSETS`. To make sure the weights totaled 1, we divided each row of the matrix by its sum.

In *Step 6*, we calculated the portfolio metrics—returns and standard deviation. To calculate the expected annual portfolio returns, we had to multiply the weights by the previously calculated annual averages. For the standard deviations, we had to use the following formula: $\omega^T \Sigma \omega$, where $\omega$ is the vector of weights and $\Sigma$ is the historical covariance matrix. To calculate the standard deviation, we iterated over all the simulated portfolios, using a `for` loop.

 The `for` loop implementation is actually faster than the vectorized matrix equivalent: `np.diag(np.sqrt(np.dot(weights, np.dot(cov_mat, weights.T))))`. The reason for that is the quickly increasing number of off-diagonal elements to be calculated, which, in the end, does not matter for the metrics of interest. This approach is faster than the `for` loop for only a relatively small number of simulations (~100).

For this example, we assumed that the risk-free rate was 0%, so the Sharpe ratio of the portfolio could be calculated as portfolio returns/portfolio volatility. Another possible approach would be to calculate the average annual risk-free rate over 2018, and to use the portfolio excess returns for calculating the ratio.

The last three steps led to visualizing the results. First, we put all the relevant metrics into a `pandas` DataFrame. Second, we created an array of expected returns from the sample. To do so, we used `np.linspace`, with the min and max values from the calculated portfolio returns. We rounded the numbers to two decimals, to make the calculations smoother. For each expected return, we found the minimum observable volatility. In cases where there was no match, as can happen with equally spread points on the linear space, we skipped that point.

In the very last step, we plotted the simulated portfolios, the individual assets, and the approximated Efficient Frontier in one plot. The shape of the frontier was a bit jagged, which can be expected when using only simulated values that are not that frequent in some extreme areas. Additionally, we colored the dots representing the simulated portfolios by the value of the Sharpe ratio.

You can find the available colormaps here: `https://matplotlib.org/` `examples/color/colormaps_reference.html`. Depending on the problem at hand, a different colormap might be more suitable (sequential, diverging, qualitative, and so on).

# There's more...

Having simulated 100,000 random portfolios, we can also investigate which one has the highest Sharpe ratio (maximum expected return per unit of risk, also known as the **Tangency Portfolio**) or minimum volatility. To locate these portfolios among the simulated ones, we use `np.argmin` and `np.argmax`, which return the index of a minimum/maximum value in the array.

The code is as follows:

```
max_sharpe_ind = np.argmax(portf_results_df.sharpe_ratio)
max_sharpe_portf = portf_results_df.loc[max_sharpe_ind]

min_vol_ind = np.argmin(portf_results_df.volatility)
min_vol_portf = portf_results_df.loc[min_vol_ind]
```

We can also investigate the constituents of these portfolios:

```
print('Maximum Sharpe ratio portfolio ----')
print('Performance')
for index, value in max_sharpe_portf.items():
    print(f'{index}: {100 * value:.2f}% ', end="", flush=True)
print('\nWeights')
for x, y in zip(RISKY_ASSETS,
weights[np.argmax(portf_results_df.sharpe_ratio)]):
    print(f'{x}: {100*y:.2f}% ', end="", flush=True)
```

The maximum Sharpe ratio portfolio allocates the majority of the resources (~75%) to Microsoft and virtually nothing to Facebook. That is because Facebook's annualized average returns for 2018 were negative:

```
Maximum Sharpe Ratio portfolio ----
Performance
returns: 23.42% volatility: 29.77% sharpe_ratio: 78.67%
Weights
FB: 0.01% MSFT: 75.18% TSLA: 5.80% TWTR: 19.00%
```

The minimum volatility portfolio assigns ~79% of the weight to Microsoft, as it is the stock with the lowest volatility (this can be inspected by viewing the covariance matrix):

```
Minimum Volatility portfolio ----
Performance
returns: 13.45% volatility: 27.56% sharpe_ratio: 48.79%
Weights
FB: 17.80% MSFT: 78.75% TSLA: 2.94% TWTR: 0.50%
```

Lastly, we mark these two portfolios on the Efficient Frontier plot. To do so, we add two extra scatterplots, each with one point corresponding to the selected portfolio. We then define the marker shape with the `marker` argument, and the marker size with the `s` argument. We increase the size of the markers to make the portfolios more visible among all others.

The code is as follows:

```
fig, ax = plt.subplots()
portf_results_df.plot(kind='scatter', x='volatility',
                      y='returns', c='sharpe_ratio',
                      cmap='RdYlGn', edgecolors='black',
                      ax=ax)
ax.scatter(x=max_sharpe_portf.volatility,
           y=max_sharpe_portf.returns,
           c='black', marker='*',
           s=200, label='Max Sharpe Ratio')
ax.scatter(x=min_vol_portf.volatility,
           y=min_vol_portf.returns,
           c='black', marker='P',
           s=200, label='Minimum Volatility')
ax.set(xlabel='Volatility', ylabel='Expected Returns',
       title='Efficient Frontier')
ax.legend()
```

Executing the code generates the following plot:

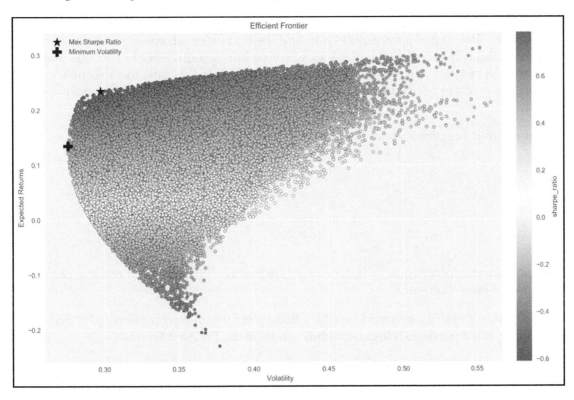

We did not plot the individual assets and the Efficient Frontier's line, to avoid the plot becoming too cluttered.

# Finding the Efficient Frontier using optimization with scipy

In the previous recipe, *Finding the Efficient Frontier using Monte Carlo simulations*, we used a brute-force approach based on Monte Carlo simulations to visualize the Efficient Frontier. In this recipe, we use a more refined method to determine the frontier.

From its definition, the Efficient Frontier is formed by a set of portfolios offering the highest expected portfolio return for a certain volatility, or offering the lowest risk (volatility) for a certain level of expected returns. We can leverage this fact, and use it in numerical optimization. The goal of optimization is to find the best (optimal) value of the objective function by adjusting the target variables and taking into account some boundaries and constraints (which have an impact on the target variables). In this case, the objective function is a function returning portfolio volatility, and the target variables are portfolio weights.

Mathematically, the problem can be expressed as:

$$\min w^T \Sigma w$$

$$s.t. \quad w^T \mathbf{1} = 1$$
$$w \geq 0$$
$$w^T \mu = \mu_p$$

Here, $w$ is a vector of weights, $\Sigma$ is the covariance matrix, $\mu$ is a vector of returns, and $\mu_p$ is the expected portfolio return.

We iterate the optimization routine used for finding the optimal portfolio weights over a range of expected portfolio returns, and this results in the Efficient Frontier.

In this recipe, we work with the same dataset as in the previous one, in order to show that the results obtained by both approaches are similar.

# Getting ready

This recipe requires all the code from the *Finding the Efficient Frontier using Monte Carlo simulations* recipe to be run.

# How to do it...

Execute the following steps to find the Efficient Frontier using optimization with `scipy`.

1. Import the libraries:

```
import numpy as np
import scipy.optimize as sco
```

2. Define functions for calculating portfolio returns and volatility:

```
def get_portf_rtn(w, avg_rtns):
    return np.sum(avg_rtns * w)

def get_portf_vol(w, avg_rtns, cov_mat):
    return np.sqrt(np.dot(w.T, np.dot(cov_mat, w)))
```

3. Define the function calculating the Efficient Frontier:

```
def get_efficient_frontier(avg_rtns, cov_mat, rtns_range):
    efficient_portfolios = []
    n_assets = len(avg_returns)
    args = (avg_returns, cov_mat)
    bounds = tuple((0,1) for asset in range(n_assets))
    initial_guess = n_assets * [1. / n_assets, ]
    for ret in rtns_range:
        constraints = ({'type': 'eq',
                        'fun': lambda x: get_portf_rtn(x, avg_rtns)
                        - ret},
                       {'type': 'eq',
                        'fun': lambda x: np.sum(x) - 1})
        efficient_portfolio = sco.minimize(get_portf_vol,
                                           initial_guess,
                                           args=args,
                                           method='SLSQP',
                                           constraints=constraints,
                                           bounds=bounds)
        efficient_portfolios.append(efficient_portfolio)
    return efficient_portfolios
```

4. Define the considered range of returns:

```
rtns_range = np.linspace(-0.22, 0.32, 200)
```

5. Calculate the Efficient Frontier:

```
efficient_portfolios = get_efficient_frontier(avg_returns,
                                              cov_mat,
                                              rtns_range)
```

6. Extract the volatilities of the efficient portfolios:

```
vols_range = [x['fun'] for x in efficient_portfolios]
```

7. Plot the calculated Efficient Frontier, together with the simulated portfolios:

```
fig, ax = plt.subplots()
portf_results_df.plot(kind='scatter', x='volatility',
                      y='returns', c='sharpe_ratio',
                      cmap='RdYlGn', edgecolors='black',
                      ax=ax)
ax.plot(vols_range, rtns_range, 'b--', linewidth=3)
ax.set(xlabel='Volatility',
       ylabel='Expected Returns',
       title='Efficient Frontier')
```

The following image presents a graph of the Efficient Frontier, calculated using numerical optimization:

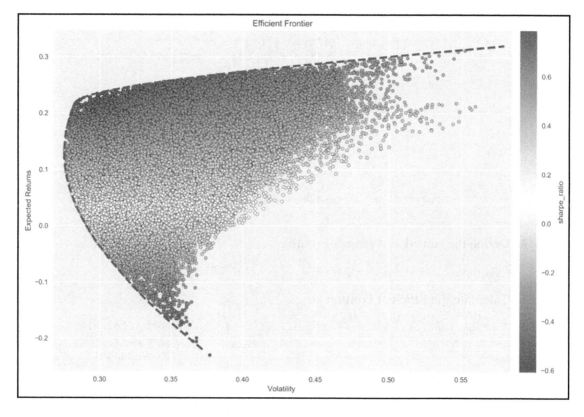

We see that the Efficient Frontier has a very similar shape to the one obtained using Monte Carlo simulations. The only difference is that the line is smoother.

8. Identify the minimum volatility portfolio:

```
min_vol_ind = np.argmin(vols_range)
min_vol_portf_rtn = rtns_range[min_vol_ind]
min_vol_portf_vol = efficient_portfolios[min_vol_ind]['fun']

min_vol_portf = {'Return': min_vol_portf_rtn,
                 'Volatility': min_vol_portf_vol,
                 'Sharpe Ratio': (min_vol_portf_rtn /
                                  min_vol_portf_vol)}
```

9. Print the performance summary:

```
print('Minimum volatility portfolio ----')
print('Performance')

for index, value in min_vol_portf.items():
    print(f'{index}: {100 * value:.2f}% ', end="", flush=True)

print('\nWeights')
for x, y in zip(RISKY_ASSETS,
efficient_portfolios[min_vol_ind]['x']):
    print(f'{x}: {100*y:.2f}% ', end="", flush=True)
```

Running the code results in the following summary:

```
Minimum Volatility portfolio ----
Performance
Return: 13.01% Volatility: 27.54% Sharpe Ratio: 47.22%
Weights
FB: 18.65% MSFT: 77.34% TSLA: 4.01% TWTR: 0.00%
```

The minimum volatility portfolio is achieved by investing mostly in Microsoft and Facebook, while not investing in Twitter at all.

# How it works...

As mentioned in the introduction, we continued the example from the previous recipe. That is why we had to run *Step 1* to *Step 4* from the previous recipe, *Finding the Efficient Frontier using Monte Carlo simulations* (not shown here for brevity), to have all the required data. As an extra prerequisite, we had to import the optimization module from scipy.

In *Step 2*, we defined two functions, which returned the expected portfolio return and volatility, given historical data and the portfolio weights. We had to define these functions instead of calculating these metrics directly, as we used them in the optimization procedure. The algorithm iteratively tries different weights and needs to be able to use the current values of the target variables (weights) to arrive at the metric it tries to optimize.

In *Step 3*, we defined a function called `get_efficient_frontier`. Its goal is to return a list containing the efficient portfolios, given historical metrics and the considered range of returns. This was the most important step of the recipe and contained a lot of nuances.

We describe the logic of the function sequentially:

- The outline of the function is that it runs the optimization procedure for each expected return in the considered range, and stores the resulting optimal portfolio in a list.
- Outside of the `for` loop, we define a couple of objects that we pass into the optimizer:
    - The arguments that are passed to the objective function. In this case, these are the historical average returns and the covariance matrix. The function that we optimize must accept the arguments as inputs. That is why we pass the returns to the `get_portfolio_volatility` function, even though they are not necessary for calculations.
    - Bounds (a nested tuple)—for each target variable (weight), a tuple containing the boundaries—minimum and maximum allowable values. In this case, the values span the range from 0 to 1 (no negative weights, as per the MPT).
    - `initial_guess`, which is the initial guess of the target variables. The goal of using the initial guess is to make the optimization run faster and more efficiently. In this case, the guess is the *1/n* allocation.
- Inside the `for` loop, we define the last element used for the optimization—the constraints. We define two constraints:
    - The expected portfolio return must be equal to the provided value.
    - The sum of the weights must be equal to 1.

- The first constraint is the reason why the constraint's tuple is defined within the loop—as the loop passes over the considered range of expected portfolio returns, and for each value, we find the optimal risk level.
- We run the optimizer with the **Sequential Least-Squares Programming (SLSQP)** algorithm, which is frequently used for generic minimization problems. For the function to be minimized, we pass the specially prepared `get_portfolio_volatility` function.

> The optimizer sets the equality (eq) constraint to 0. That is why the intended constraint, `np.sum(weights) == 1`, is expressed as `np.sum(weights) - 1 == 0`.

In *Steps 4* and *5*, we defined the range of expected portfolio returns (based on the range we empirically observed in the previous recipe) and ran the optimization function.

In *Step 6*, we iterated over the list of efficient portfolios and extracted the optimal volatilities. We extracted the volatility from the `scipy.optimize.OptimizeResult` object by accessing the `fun` element. This stands for the optimized objective function—in this case, the portfolio volatility.

In *Step 7*, we added the calculated Efficient Frontier on top of the plot from the previous recipe, *Finding the Efficient Frontier using Monte Carlo simulations*. All the simulated portfolios lie on or below the Efficient Frontier, which is what we expected to happen.

In *Steps 8* and *9*, we identified the minimum volatility portfolio, printed the performance metrics, and showed the portfolio's weights (extracted from the Efficient Frontier).

We can now compare the two minimum volatility portfolios: the one obtained using Monte Carlo simulations, and the one we received from optimization. The prevailing pattern in the allocation is the same—allocate the majority of the available resources to Facebook and Microsoft. We can also see that the volatility of the optimized strategy is slightly lower. This means that among the 100,000 portfolios, we have not simulated the actual minimum volatility portfolio.

# There's more...

We can also use the optimization approach to find the weights that generate a portfolio with the highest expected Sharpe ratio—the Tangency Portfolio. To do so, we first need to define the objective function, which is the negative of the Sharpe ratio. The reason why we use the negative is that the optimization algorithms run minimization problems. We can easily approach the maximization problems by changing the sign of the objective metric:

1. Define the objective function (negative Sharpe ratio):

```
def neg_sharpe_ratio(w, avg_rtns, cov_mat, rf_rate):
    portf_returns = np.sum(avg_rtns * w)
    portf_volatility = np.sqrt(np.dot(w.T, np.dot(cov_mat, w)))
    portf_sharpe_ratio = (portf_returns - rf_rate) /
                         portf_volatility
    return -portf_sharpe_ratio
```

The second step is very similar to what we have already done with the Efficient Frontier, this time without the `for` loop, as we are only searching for one set of weights. We include the risk-free rate in the arguments (though we assume it is 0%, for simplicity) and only use one constraint—the sum of the target variables must be equal to 1.

2. Find the optimized portfolio:

```
n_assets = len(avg_returns)
RF_RATE = 0

args = (avg_returns, cov_mat, RF_RATE)
constraints = ({'type': 'eq',
                'fun': lambda x: np.sum(x) - 1})
bounds = tuple((0,1) for asset in range(n_assets))
initial_guess = n_assets * [1. / n_assets]

max_sharpe_portf = sco.minimize(neg_sharpe_ratio,
                                x0=initial_guess,
                                args=args,
                                method='SLSQP',
                                bounds=bounds,
                                constraints=constraints)
```

3. Extract information about the maximum Sharpe ratio portfolio:

```
max_sharpe_portf_w = max_sharpe_portf['x']
max_sharpe_portf = {'Return': get_portf_rtn(max_sharpe_portf_w,
                                             avg_returns),
                    'Volatility': get_portf_vol(max_sharpe_portf_w,
                                                 avg_returns,
                                                 cov_mat),
                    'Sharpe Ratio': -max_sharpe_portf['fun']}
```

4. Print the performance summary:

```
print('Maximum Sharpe Ratio portfolio ----')
print('Performance')

for index, value in max_sharpe_portf.items():
    print(f'{index}: {100 * value:.2f}% ', end="", flush=True)

print('\nWeights')
for x, y in zip(RISKY_ASSETS, max_sharpe_portf_w):
    print(f'{x}: {100*y:.2f}% ', end="", flush=True)
```

The following image contains a summary of the portfolio maximizing the Sharpe ratio:

```
Maximum Sharpe Ratio portfolio ----
Performance
Return: 23.10% Volatility: 29.25% Sharpe Ratio: 78.96%
Weights
FB: 0.00% MSFT: 81.48% TSLA: 2.79% TWTR: 15.72%
```

To achieve maximum Sharpe ratio, the investor should invest mostly in Microsoft and Twitter, with a 0% allocation to Facebook, as Facebook's average return over 2018 was negative.

# Finding the Efficient Frontier using convex optimization with cvxpy

In the previous recipe, *Finding the Efficient Frontier using optimization with scipy*, we found the Efficient Frontier, using numerical optimization with `scipy`. We used the portfolio volatility as the metric we wanted to minimize. However, it is also possible to state the same problem a bit differently and use convex optimization to find the Efficient Frontier.

We can reframe the mean-variance optimization problem into a risk-aversion framework, in which the investor wants to maximize the risk-adjusted return:

$$\max \quad w^T \mu - \gamma w^T \Sigma w$$

$$s.t. \quad w^T \mathbf{1} = 1$$
$$w \geq 0$$

Here, $\gamma \in [0, \infty)$ is the risk-aversion parameter, and the constraints specify that the weights must sum up to 1, and short-selling is not allowed. The higher the value of $\gamma$, the more risk-averse the investor is.

In this recipe, we use the same data as in the previous two recipes, to make sure the results are comparable.

# Getting ready

This recipe requires all the code to be run from the previous recipes listed here:

- *Finding the Efficient Frontier using Monte Carlo simulations*
- *Finding the Efficient Frontier using optimization with scipy*

# How to do it...

Execute the following steps to find the Efficient Frontier using convex optimization.

1. Import the library:

```
import cvxpy as cp
```

2. Convert the annualized average returns and the covariance matrix to `numpy` arrays:

```
avg_returns = avg_returns.values
cov_mat = cov_mat.values
```

3. Set up the optimization problem:

```
weights = cp.Variable(n_assets)
gamma = cp.Parameter(nonneg=True)
portf_rtn_cvx = avg_returns * weights
portf_vol_cvx = cp.quad_form(weights, cov_mat)
objective_function = cp.Maximize(portf_rtn_cvx - gamma *
portf_vol_cvx)
problem = cp.Problem(objective_function,
                     [cp.sum(weights) == 1, weights >= 0])
```

4. Calculate the Efficient Frontier:

```
N_POINTS = 25
portf_rtn_cvx_ef = np.zeros(N_POINTS)
portf_vol_cvx_ef = np.zeros(N_POINTS)
weights_ef = []
gamma_range = np.logspace(-3, 3, num=N_POINTS)

for i in range(N_POINTS):
    gamma.value = gamma_range[i]
    problem.solve()
    portf_vol_cvx_ef[i] = cp.sqrt(portf_vol_cvx).value
    portf_rtn_cvx_ef[i] = portf_rtn_cvx.value
    weights_ef.append(weights.value)
```

5. Plot the allocation for different values of the risk-aversion parameter:

```
weights_df = pd.DataFrame(weights_ef,
                          columns=RISKY_ASSETS,
                          index=np.round(gamma_range, 3))
ax = weights_df.plot(kind='bar', stacked=True)
ax.set(title='Weights allocation per risk-aversion level',
       xlabel=r'$\gamma$',
       ylabel='weight')
ax.legend(bbox_to_anchor=(1,1))
```

In the following plot, we see the asset allocation for the considered range of risk-aversion parameters:

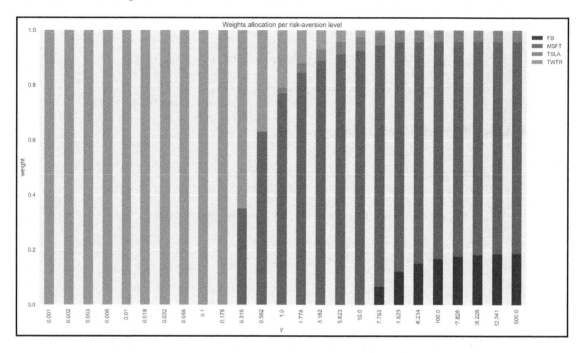

6. Plot the Efficient Frontier, together with the individual assets:

```
fig, ax = plt.subplots()
ax.plot(portf_vol_cvx_ef, portf_rtn_cvx_ef, 'g-')
for asset_index in range(n_assets):
    plt.scatter(x=np.sqrt(cov_mat[asset_index, asset_index]),
                y=avg_returns[asset_index],
                marker=MARKS[asset_index],
                label=RISKY_ASSETS[asset_index],
                s=150)
ax.set(title='Efficient Frontier',
       xlabel='Volatility',
       ylabel='Expected Returns', )
ax.legend()
```

The following image shows a plot of the Efficient Frontier, generated by solving the convex optimization problem:

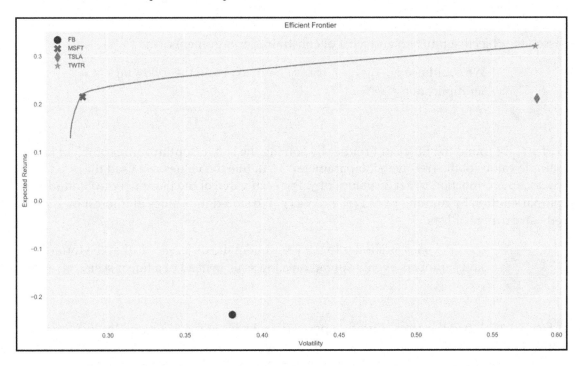

In the *There's more...* section, we also compare the frontier to the one obtained in the previous recipe, *Finding the Efficient Frontier using optimization with scipy*.

# How it works...

As mentioned in the introduction, we continued the example from the previous two recipes. That is why we had to run *Step 1* to *4* from the *Finding the Efficient Frontier using Monte Carlo simulations* recipe (not shown here for brevity) to have all the required data. As an extra step, we had to import the cvxpy convex optimization library. We additionally converted the historical average returns and the covariance matrix into numpy arrays.

In *Step 5*, we set up the optimization problem. We started by defining the target variables (`weights`), the risk-aversion parameter `gamma`, the portfolio returns and volatility (both using the previously defined `weights` variable), and lastly, the objective function—the risk-adjusted returns we want to maximize. Then, we created the `cp.Problem` object, and passed the objective function and a list of constraints as arguments.

 We could use `cp.quad_form (x, y)` to obtain the following multiplication $w^T y w$.

In *Step 6*, we found the Efficient Frontier by solving the convex optimization problem for multiple values of the risk-aversion parameter. To define the values, we used the `np.logspace` function to get 25 values of $\gamma$. For each value of the parameter, we found the optimal solution by running `problem.solve()`. We stored the values of interest in dedicated arrays or lists.

 `np.logspace` is similar to `np.linspace`; the difference is that the former finds numbers evenly spread on a log scale instead of a linear scale.

In *Step 7*, we plotted the asset allocation per various levels of risk aversion. In the plot, we could see that for very small values of $\gamma$, the investor would allocate 100% of their resources to Twitter. As we increased the risk aversion, the allocation to Twitter grew smaller, and more weight was allocated to Microsoft and the other assets. At the other end of the considered values for the parameter, the investor would allocate 0% to Twitter.

In *Step 8*, we plotted the Efficient Frontier, together with the individual assets.

# There's more...

We can also plot the two Efficient Frontiers for comparison—the one calculated by minimizing the volatility per expected level of return, and the other one using the convex optimization and maximizing the risk-adjusted return.

The code is as follows:

```
x_lim = [0.25, 0.6]
y_lim = [0.125, 0.325]

fig, ax = plt.subplots(1, 2)
```

```
ax[0].plot(vols_range, rtns_range, 'g-', linewidth=3)
ax[0].set(title='Efficient Frontier - Minimized Volatility',
          xlabel='Volatility',
          ylabel='Expected Returns',
          xlim=x_lim,
          ylim=y_lim)

ax[1].plot(portf_vol_cvx_ef, portf_rtn_cvx_ef, 'g-', linewidth=3)
ax[1].set(title='Efficient Frontier - Maximized Risk-Adjusted Return',
          xlabel='Volatility',
          ylabel='Expected Returns',
          xlim=x_lim,
          ylim=y_lim)
```

The only thing to note is that the one obtained using minimization is smoother, as we used more points to calculate the frontier:

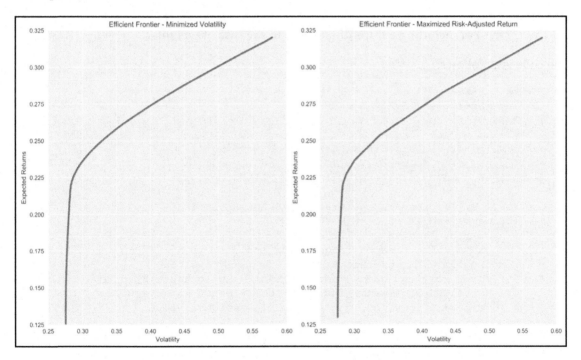

Another interesting concept we can incorporate into the analysis is the maximum allowable leverage. We replace the non-negativity constraints on the weights with a max leverage constraint, using the norm of a vector.

In the following code, we only show what was added to the previous code block:

```
max_leverage = cp.Parameter()
problem_with_leverage = cp.Problem(objective_function,
                        [cp.sum(weights) == 1,
                         cp.norm(weights, 1) <= max_leverage])
```

In the following code block, we modify the code, this time to include two loops—one over potential values of the risk-aversion parameter, and the other one indicating the maximum allowable leverage. Max leverage equal to 1 (meaning no leverage) results in a case similar to the previous optimization problem (only this time, there is no non-negativity constraint).

We also redefine the objects, storing the results to be either larger 2D matrices (np.ndarrays) or including a third dimension, in the case of weights.

The code is as follows:

```
LEVERAGE_RANGE = [1, 2, 5]
len_leverage = len(LEVERAGE_RANGE)
N_POINTS = 25

portf_vol_l_ef = np.zeros((N_POINTS, len_leverage))
portf_rtn_l_ef = np.zeros(( N_POINTS, len_leverage))
weights_ef = np.zeros((len_leverage, N_POINTS, n_assets))

for lev_ind, leverage in enumerate(LEVERAGE_RANGE):
    for gamma_ind in range(N_POINTS):
        max_leverage.value = leverage
        gamma.value = gamma_range[gamma_ind]
        problem_with_leverage.solve()
        portf_vol_l_ef[gamma_ind, lev_ind] = cp.sqrt(portf_vol_cvx).value
        portf_rtn_l_ef[gamma_ind, lev_ind] = portf_rtn_cvx.value
        weights_ef[lev_ind, gamma_ind, :] = weights.value
```

In the following code block, we plot the Efficient Frontiers for different maximum leverages. We can clearly see that higher leverage increases returns and, at the same time, allows for greater volatility:

```
fig, ax = plt.subplots()

for leverage_index, leverage in enumerate(LEVERAGE_RANGE):
    plt.plot(portf_vol_l_ef[:, leverage_index],
            portf_rtn_l_ef[:, leverage_index],
```

```
                label=f'{leverage}')

ax.set(title='Efficient Frontier for different max leverage',
        xlabel='Volatility',
        ylabel='Expected Returns')
ax.legend(title='Max leverage');
```

Executing the preceding code generates the following plot:

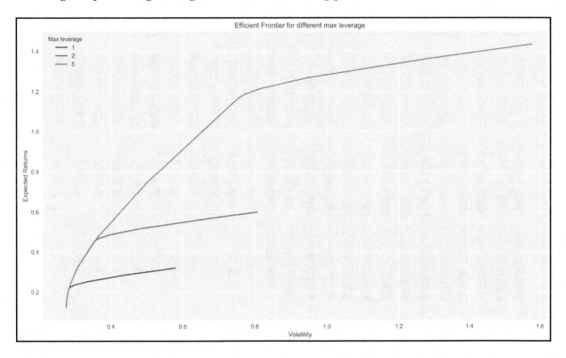

Lastly, we also recreate the plot showing weight allocation per varying risk-aversion levels. With a maximum leverage of 1, there is no short-selling.

The code is as follows:

```
fig, ax = plt.subplots(len_leverage, 1, sharex=True)

for ax_index in range(len_leverage):
    weights_df = pd.DataFrame(weights_ef[ax_index],
                              columns=RISKY_ASSETS,
                              index=np.round(gamma_range, 3))
    weights_df.plot(kind='bar',
                    stacked=True,
```

```
                        ax=ax[ax_index],
                        legend=None)
        ax[ax_index].set(ylabel=(f'max_leverage = {LEVERAGE_RANGE[ax_index]}'
                            '\n weight'))

    ax[len_leverage - 1].set(xlabel=r'$\gamma$')
    ax[0].legend(bbox_to_anchor=(1,1))
    ax[0].set_title('Weights allocation per risk-aversion level',
                fontsize=16)
```

Executing the preceding code generates the following plot:

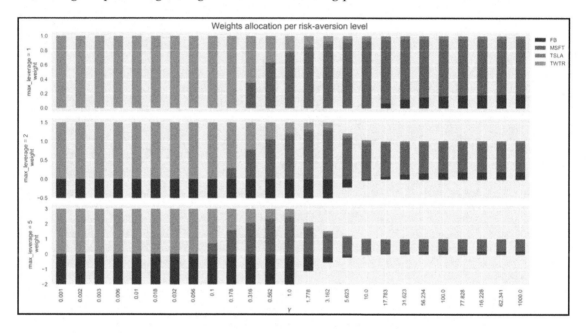

We can spot a pattern where, with an increase in risk aversion, investors stop using leverage altogether, and converge to a similar allocation for all levels of maximum permitted leverage.

# 8

# Identifying Credit Default with Machine Learning

In recent years, we have witnessed machine learning gaining more and more popularity in solving traditional business problems. Every so often, a new algorithm is published, beating the current state of the art. It is only natural for businesses (in all industries) to try to leverage the incredible powers of machine learning in their core functionalities.

Before specifying a problem, we provide a brief introduction to the field of machine learning. Machine learning can be broken down into two main areas: supervised learning and unsupervised learning. In the former, we have a target variable (label), which we try to predict as accurately as possible. In the latter, there is no target, and we try to use different techniques to draw some insights from the data. An example of unsupervised learning might be clustering, which is often used for customer segmentation.

We can further break down supervised problems into regression problems (where a target variable is a continuous number, such as income or the price of a house) and classification problems (where the target is a class, either binary or multi-class).

In this chapter, we tackle a binary classification problem set in the financial industry. We work with a dataset contributed to the UCI Machine Learning Repository (a very popular data repository).

The dataset used in this chapter was collected in a Taiwanese bank in October 2005. The study was motivated by the fact that—at that time—more and more banks were giving cash (and credit card) credit to willing customers. On top of that, more and more people, regardless of their repayment capabilities, accumulated significant amounts of debt, which in turn resulted in defaults.

The goal of the study was to use some basic information about customers (such as gender, age, and education level), together with their past repayment history, to predict who was likely to default. The setting can be described as follows—using the previous 6 months of repayment history (April-September 2005), we try to predict whether the customer will default in October 2005.

By the end of this chapter, you will be familiar with a real-life approach to a machine learning task, from gathering and cleaning data to building and tuning a classifier. Another takeaway is understanding the general approach to machine learning projects, which can then be applied to many different tasks, be it churn prediction or estimating the price of new real estate in a neighborhood.

In this chapter, we focus on the following recipes:

- Loading data and managing data types
- Exploratory data analysis
- Splitting data into training and test sets
- Dealing with missing values
- Encoding categorical variables
- Fitting a decision tree classifier
- Implementing scikit-learn's pipelines
- Tuning hyperparameters using grid search and cross-validation

# Loading data and managing data types

In this recipe, we show how to load a dataset into Python. In order to show the entire pipeline—including working with messy data—we apply some transformation to the original dataset. For more information on applied changes, please refer to the accompanying GitHub repository.

## How to do it...

Execute the following steps to load a dataset into Python.

1. Import the libraries:

```
import pandas as pd
```

2. Preview a CSV file:

```
!head -n 5 credit_card_default.csv
```

The output looks like this:

```
,limit_bal,sex,education,marriage,age,payment_status_sep,payment_status_aug,payment_status_jul,payment_status_jun,pay
ment_status_may,payment_status_apr,bill_statement_sep,bill_statement_aug,bill_statement_jul,bill_statement_jun,bill_s
tatement_may,bill_statement_apr,previous_payment_sep,previous_payment_aug,previous_payment_jul,previous_payment_jun,p
revious_payment_may,previous_payment_apr,default_payment_next_month
0,20000,Female,University,Married,24,Payment delayed 2 months,Payment delayed 2 months,Payed duly,Payed duly,Unknown,
Unknown,3913,3102,689,0,0,0,689,0,0,0,0,1
1,120000,Female,University,Single,26,Payed duly,Payment delayed 2 months,Unknown,Unknown,Unknown,Payment delayed 2 mo
nths,2682,1725,2682,3272,3455,3261,0,1000,1000,1000,0,2000,1
2,90000,Female,University,Single,34,Unknown,Unknown,Unknown,Unknown,Unknown,Unknown,29239,14027,13559,14331,14948,155
49,1518,1500,1000,1000,1000,5000,0
3,50000,Female,University,Married,37,Unknown,Unknown,Unknown,Unknown,Unknown,Unknown,46990,48233,49291,28314,28959,29
547,2000,2019,1200,1100,1069,1000,0
```

3. Load the data from the CSV file:

```
df = pd.read_csv('credit_card_default.csv', index_col=0,
                   na_values='')
```

The DataFrame has 30,000 rows and 24 columns.

4. Separate the features from the target:

```
X = df.copy()
y = X.pop('default_payment_next_month')
```

After running this block of code, X no longer contains the target column.

# How it works...

In *Step 1*, we imported the `pandas` library. Then, we used the bash command `head` (with an additional argument `-n 5`) to preview the first five rows of the CSV file. This can come in handy when we want to determine what kind of data we are dealing with, without opening a potentially large text file.

Inspecting a few rows of the dataset raised the following questions:

- What is the separator?
- Are there any special characters that need to be escaped?

- Are there any missing values and, if so, what scheme (NA, empty string, nan and so on) is used for them?
- What variables types (floats, integers, strings) are in the file? Based on that information, we can try to optimize memory usage while loading the file.

In *Step 3*, we loaded the CSV file by using the pd.read_csv function. When doing so, we indicated that the first column (zero-indexed) contained the index, and empty strings should be interpreted as missing values. In the last step, we separated the features from the target by using the pop method. It assigned the given column to the new variable, while removing it from the source DataFrame.

In the following, we provide a simplified description of the variables:

- limit_bal: The amount of the given credit (NT dollar)
- sex: Gender
- education: Level of education
- marriage: Marital status
- age: Age of the customer
- payment_status_{month}: Status of payments in one of the previous 6 months
- bill_statement_{month}: The amount of bill statements (NT dollars) in one of the previous 6 months
- previous_payment_{month}: The amount of previous payments (NT dollars) in one of the previous 6 months

The target variable indicates whether the customer defaulted on the payment in the following month.

# There's more...

In general, pandas tries to load and store data efficiently. It automatically assigns data types (which we can inspect by calling the dtypes method of a pandas DataFrame). However, there are some tricks that can lead to much better memory allocation, which definitely make working with larger tables (in hundreds of MBs, or even GBs) easier.

1. We start by inspecting the data types in our DataFrame:

```
df.dtypes
```

We only show a snippet of all the columns, for brevity:

```
limit_bal                int64
sex                     object
education               object
marriage                object
age                    float64
payment_status_sep      object
payment_status_aug      object
payment_status_jul      object
payment_status_jun      object
payment_status_may      object
payment_status_apr      object
bill_statement_sep       int64
bill_statement_aug       int64
```

In the preceding image, we see a few distinct data types: floats (floating-point numbers, such as 3.42), integers, and objects. The last ones are the `pandas` representation of string variables. The number next to `float` and `int` indicates how many bits this type uses to represent a particular value. The default types use 64 bits of memory.

The basic `int8` type covers integers in the following range: -128 to 127. `uint8` stands for unsigned integer and covers the same total span, but only the non-negative values: 0 to 255. By knowing the range of values covered by specific data types (please refer to the link in the *See also* section), we can try to optimize allocated memory. For example, for features such as the month of purchase (represented by numbers in the range 1-12), there is no point in using the default `int64`, as a much smaller type would suffice.

We also leverage a special type called `category`. The underlying idea is that string variables are encoded as integers, and `pandas` uses a special mapping dictionary to decode them back into their original form. This is especially useful when dealing with a limited number of distinct string values (for example, certain levels of education, country of origin, and so on).

We should know when it is actually profitable (from the memory perspective) to use the `categorical` data type. A rule of thumb is to use it for variables with a ratio of unique observations to the overall number of observations lower than 50%.

2. We define a function, which we use to inspect how much memory (in MBs) a DataFrame actually uses:

```
def get_df_memory_usage(df, top_columns=5):
    print('Memory usage ----')
    memory_per_column = df.memory_usage(deep=True) / 1024 ** 2
    print(f'Top {top_columns} columns by memory (MB):')
    print(memory_per_column.sort_values(ascending=False) \
                           .head(top_columns))
    print(f'Total size: {memory_per_column.sum():.4f} MB')
```

3. Inspect the size of the initial DataFrame (just as we loaded it from the source CSV file):

```
get_df_memory_usage(df)
```

This results in the following code block:

```
Memory usage ----
Top 5 columns by memory (MB):
education 1.965001
payment_status_sep 1.954342
payment_status_aug 1.920288
payment_status_jul 1.916343
payment_status_jun    1.904229
dtype: float64
Total size: 20.7012 MB
```

In total, the DataFrame uses ~20.7 MB of memory, with ~82% of that used by columns with the `object` data type. This is still very small in terms of the current machines' capabilities, however, the memory-saving principles we show here apply just as well to DataFrames measured in gigabytes.

We create a copy of the original DataFrame and change the types of the `object` columns to `category`. We first select the names of the columns with variables of the `object` type (using the `select_dtypes` method), and then convert them to a categorical type using the `astype` method.

Remember to check the number of unique values in a column before converting it to `category`!

4. Convert `object` columns to categorical:

```
df_cat = df.copy()
object_columns = df_cat.select_dtypes(include='object').columns
df_cat[object_columns] = df_cat[object_columns].astype('category')
```

5. Inspect the size of the DataFrame:

```
get_df_memory_usage(df_cat)
```

This results in the following code block:

```
Memory usage ----
Top 5 columns by memory (MB):
default_payment_next_month    0.228882
bill_statement_may            0.228882
limit_bal                     0.228882
age                           0.228882
previous_payment_apr          0.228882
dtype: float64
Total size: 3.9266 MB
```

With this simple transformation, we managed to reduce the size (memory-wise) of the DataFrame by ~80%. We could also downcast the integer columns (currently using the `int64` type) to something much smaller memory-wise, but for that, we would need to inspect the min and max values for each column and determine which type would be the best fit. We do not do this here; however, the process of using `astype` is the same.

6. It is also possible to specify the types of variables while loading the CSV file into Python. We need to pass a dictionary (with pairs of column names and desired data types) to the `dtype` argument in the call to `pd.read_csv`.

```
column_dtypes = {'education': 'category',
                 'marriage': 'category',
                 'sex': 'category',
                 'payment_status_sep': 'category',
                 'payment_status_aug': 'category',
                 'payment_status_jul': 'category',
                 'payment_status_jun': 'category',
                 'payment_status_may': 'category',
                 'payment_status_apr': 'category'}
df_cat2 = pd.read_csv('credit_card_default.csv', index_col=0,
                      na_values='', dtype=column_dtypes)
```

We obtain a DataFrame identical to the one created using the `astype` method.

7. Check whether the two DataFrames contain the same objects:

```
df_cat.equals(df_cat2)
# True
```

For simplicity, in the rest of the chapter, we will use the default loading data version, with the `object` data type for categorical variables.

# See also

Additional resources:

- Dua, D. and Graff, C. (2019). UCI Machine Learning Repository [`http://archive.ics.uci.edu/ml`]. Irvine, CA: University of California, School of Information and Computer Science.
- Yeh, I. C., & Lien, C. H. (2009). The comparisons of data mining techniques for the predictive accuracy of probability of default of credit card clients. *Expert Systems with Applications*, 36(2), 2473-2480. - `https://bradzzz.gitbooks.io/ga-dsi-seattle/content/dsi/dsi_05_classification_databases/2.1-lesson/assets/datasets/DefaultCreditCardClients_yeh_2009.pdf`
- List of different data types used in Python: `https://docs.scipy.org/doc/numpy-1.13.0/user/basics.types.html`.

# Exploratory data analysis

The second step, after loading the data, is to carry out **Exploratory Data Analysis** (**EDA**). By doing this, we get to know the data we are supposed to work with. Some insights we try to gather are:

- What kind of data do we actually have, and how should we treat different types?
- What is the distribution of the variables?
    - Are there outliers in the data, and how can we treat them?
    - Are any transformations required? For example, some models work better with (or require) normally distributed variables, so we might want to use techniques such as log transformation.
    - Does the distribution vary per group (for example, gender or education level)?
- Do we have cases of missing data? How frequent are these, and in which variables?
- Is there a linear relationship between some variables (correlation)?
- Can we create new features using the existing set of variables? An example might be deriving hour/minute from a timestamp, day of the week from a date, and so on.
- Are there any variables that we can remove as they are not relevant for the analysis? An example might be a randomly generated customer identifier.

EDA is extremely important in all data science projects, as it enables analysts to develop an understanding of the data, facilitates asking better questions, and makes it easier to pick modeling approaches suitable for the type of data being dealt with.

In real-life cases, it makes sense to carry out univariate analysis (one feature at a time) for all relevant features to get a good understanding of them, and then proceed to multivariate analysis (comparing distributions per group, correlations, and so on). For brevity, we only show some popular approaches on selected features, but a deeper analysis is highly encouraged.

# How to do it...

Execute the following steps to carry out EDA.

1.  Import the libraries:

```
import pandas as pd
import seaborn as sns
import numpy as np
```

2.  Get summary statistics for numeric variables:

```
df.describe().transpose().round(2)
```

This results in the following table:

| | count | mean | std | min | 25% | 50% | 75% | max |
|---|---|---|---|---|---|---|---|---|
| limit_bal | 30000.0 | 167484.32 | 129747.66 | 10000.0 | 50000.00 | 140000.0 | 240000.00 | 1000000.0 |
| age | 29850.0 | 35.49 | 9.22 | 21.0 | 28.00 | 34.0 | 41.00 | 79.0 |
| bill_statement_sep | 30000.0 | 51223.33 | 73635.86 | -165580.0 | 3558.75 | 22381.5 | 67091.00 | 964511.0 |
| bill_statement_aug | 30000.0 | 49179.08 | 71173.77 | -69777.0 | 2984.75 | 21200.0 | 64006.25 | 983931.0 |
| bill_statement_jul | 30000.0 | 47013.15 | 69349.39 | -157264.0 | 2666.25 | 20088.5 | 60164.75 | 1664089.0 |
| bill_statement_jun | 30000.0 | 43262.95 | 64332.86 | -170000.0 | 2326.75 | 19052.0 | 54506.00 | 891586.0 |
| bill_statement_may | 30000.0 | 40311.40 | 60797.16 | -81334.0 | 1763.00 | 18104.5 | 50190.50 | 927171.0 |
| bill_statement_apr | 30000.0 | 38871.76 | 59554.11 | -339603.0 | 1256.00 | 17071.0 | 49198.25 | 961664.0 |
| previous_payment_sep | 30000.0 | 5663.58 | 16563.28 | 0.0 | 1000.00 | 2100.0 | 5006.00 | 873552.0 |
| previous_payment_aug | 30000.0 | 5921.16 | 23040.87 | 0.0 | 833.00 | 2009.0 | 5000.00 | 1684259.0 |
| previous_payment_jul | 30000.0 | 5225.68 | 17606.96 | 0.0 | 390.00 | 1800.0 | 4505.00 | 896040.0 |
| previous_payment_jun | 30000.0 | 4826.08 | 15666.16 | 0.0 | 296.00 | 1500.0 | 4013.25 | 621000.0 |
| previous_payment_may | 30000.0 | 4799.39 | 15278.31 | 0.0 | 252.50 | 1500.0 | 4031.50 | 426529.0 |
| previous_payment_apr | 30000.0 | 5215.50 | 17777.47 | 0.0 | 117.75 | 1500.0 | 4000.00 | 528666.0 |
| default_payment_next_month | 30000.0 | 0.22 | 0.42 | 0.0 | 0.00 | 0.0 | 0.00 | 1.0 |

3.  Get summary statistics for categorical variables:

```
df.describe(include='object').transpose()
```

This results in the following table:

| | count ⬍ | unique ⬍ | top ⬍ | freq ⬍ |
|---|---|---|---|---|
| **sex** | 29850 | 2 | Female | 18027 |
| **education** | 29850 | 4 | University | 13960 |
| **marriage** | 29850 | 3 | Single | 15891 |
| **payment_status_sep** | 30000 | 10 | Unknown | 17496 |
| **payment_status_aug** | 30000 | 10 | Unknown | 19512 |
| **payment_status_jul** | 30000 | 10 | Unknown | 19849 |
| **payment_status_jun** | 30000 | 10 | Unknown | 20803 |
| **payment_status_may** | 30000 | 9 | Unknown | 21493 |
| **payment_status_apr** | 30000 | 9 | Unknown | 21181 |

4. Plot the distribution of age and, additionally, split it by gender:

```
fig, ax = plt.subplots()
sns.distplot(df.loc[df.sex=='Male', 'age'].dropna(),
             hist=False, color='green',
             kde_kws={"shade": True},
             ax=ax, label='Male')
sns.distplot(df.loc[df.sex=='Female', 'age'].dropna(),
             hist=False, color='blue',
             kde_kws={"shade": True},
             ax=ax, label='Female')
ax.set_title('Distribution of age')
ax.legend(title='Gender:')
```

Running the code results in the following plot:

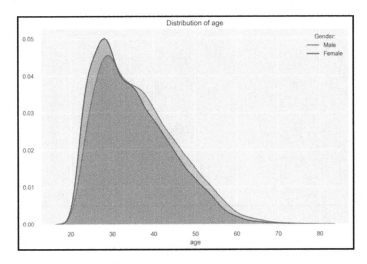

By analyzing the plot, we can say there is not much difference in the shape of the distribution per gender. The female sample is slightly younger, on average.

5. Plot a `pairplot` of selected variables:

```
pair_plot = sns.pairplot(df[['age', 'limit_bal',
                             'previous_payment_sep']])
pair_plot.fig.suptitle('Pairplot of selected variables', y=1.05)
```

Running the code results in the following plot:

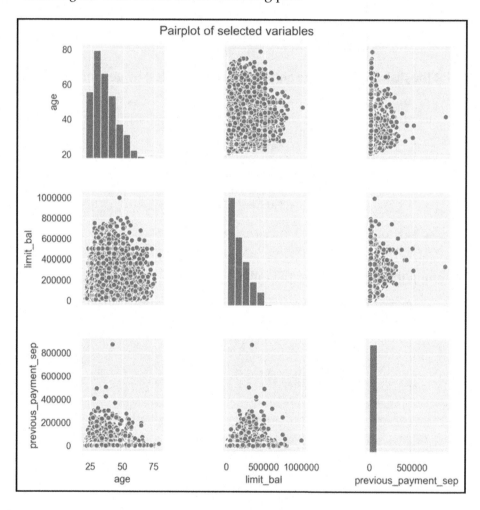

6. Define and run a function for plotting the correlation heatmap:

```
def plot_correlation_matrix(corr_mat):
    sns.set(style="white")
    mask = np.zeros_like(corr_mat, dtype=np.bool)
    mask[np.triu_indices_from(mask)] = True
    fig, ax = plt.subplots()
    cmap = sns.diverging_palette(240, 10, n=9, as_cmap=True)
    sns.heatmap(corr_mat, mask=mask, cmap=cmap, vmax=.3, center=0,
                square=True, linewidths=.5,
                cbar_kws={"shrink": .5}, ax=ax)
    ax.set_title('Correlation Matrix', fontsize=16)
    sns.set(style="darkgrid")

corr_mat = df.select_dtypes(include='number').corr()
plot_correlation_matrix(corr_mat)
```

Running the code results in the following plot:

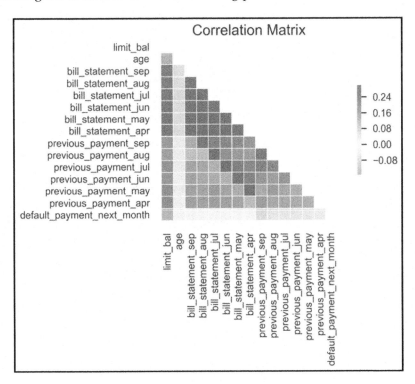

In the plot, we can see that age seems to be uncorrelated to any of the other features.

7. Plot the distribution of limit balance for each gender and education level:

```
ax = sns.violinplot(x='education', y='limit_bal',
                    hue='sex', split=True, data=df)
ax.set_title('Distribution of limit balance per education level',
             fontsize=16)
```

Running the code results in the following plot:

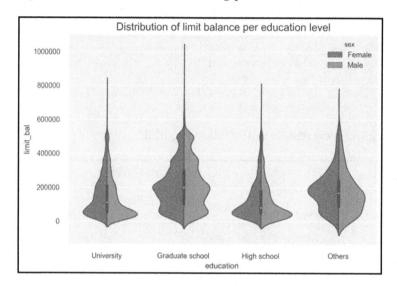

Inspecting the plot reveals a few interesting patterns:

- The largest balance appears in the group with the *Graduate school* level of education.
- The shape of the distribution is different per education level: the *Graduate school* level resembles the *Others* category, while the *High school* level is similar to the *University* level.
- In general, there are few differences between the genders.

8. Investigate the distribution of the target variable per gender and education level:

```
ax = sns.countplot('default_payment_next_month', hue='sex',
                   data=df, orient='h')
ax.set_title('Distribution of the target variable', fontsize=16)
```

Running the code results in the following plot:

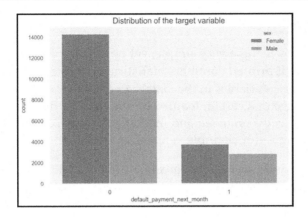

By analyzing the plot, we can say that the percentage of defaults is higher among male customers.

9.  Investigate the percentage of defaults per education level:

```
ax = df.groupby("education")['default_payment_next_month'] \
        .value_counts(normalize=True) \
        .unstack() \
        .plot(kind='barh', stacked='True')
ax.set_title('Percentage of default per education level',
                fontsize=16)
ax.legend(title='Default', bbox_to_anchor=(1,1))
```

Running the code results in the following plot:

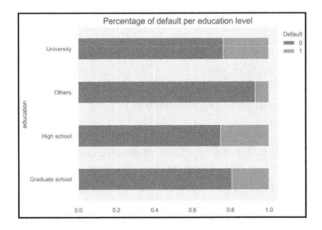

Relatively speaking, most defaults happen among customers with high-school education, while the fewest defaults happen in the *Others* category.

# How it works...

We started the analysis by using a very simple, yet powerful method of a `pandas` DataFrame—`describe`. It printed summary statistics, such as count, mean, min/max, and quartiles of all the numeric variables in the DataFrame. By inspecting these metrics, we could infer the value range of a certain feature, or whether the distribution was skewed (by looking at the difference between mean and median). Also, we could easily spot values outside the plausible range—for example, a negative or very small age.

We can include additional percentiles in the `describe` method by passing an extra argument `percentiles=[.99]` —in this case, we added the 99th percentile.

The count metric represents the number of non-null observations, so it is also a way to determine which numeric features contain missing values. Another way of investigating the presence of missing values is by running `df.isnull().sum()`. For more information on missing values, please see the *Dealing with missing values* recipe.

In the third step, we added the `include='object'` argument to the `describe` method, to inspect the categorical features separately. The output was different from the numeric features: we could see the count, the number of unique categories, which one was the most frequent, and how many times it appeared in the dataset.

We can use `include='all'` to display summary metrics for all features—only the metrics available for a given data type will be present; the rest will be filled with `NA` values.

In *Step 4*, we showed a way of investigating the distribution of a variable, in this case, the age of the customers. To do so, we called `sns.distplot` twice, each time with a different subset of the data (corresponding to age values per gender). Additionally, we had to remove existing `NA` values using the `dropna` method.

Together with a histogram, this is one of the most popular methods of inspecting the distribution of a single feature. To create a histogram, we can call `sns.distplot` with the following default value: `hist=True`. Alternatively, we can use the `plot` method of a `pandas` DataFrame, while specifying `kind='hist'`.

An extension of this analysis can be done by using a pair-plot. It creates a matrix of plots, where the diagonal shows the univariate histogram, while the off-diagonal plots are scatterplots of two features. This way, we can also try to see if there is a relationship between two features. In this case, we only plotted three features. That is because, with 30,000 observations, it can take quite some time to render this for all numeric columns, not to mention losing readability with so many small plots in one matrix. When using pair-plots, we can also specify the `hue` argument to add a split for a category (such as gender, or education level).

In *Step 6*, we defined a function for plotting a heatmap representing the correlation matrix. In the function, we used a couple of operations to mask the upper triangular matrix, together with the diagonal (all correlations equal to 1 on the diagonal). This way, the output was easier to interpret.

To calculate the correlations, we used the `corr` method of a DataFrame, which by default calculated Pearson's correlation coefficient. We did this only for numeric features. There are also methods for calculating the correlation of categorical features, but this is beyond the scope of this chapter. Inspecting correlations is crucial, especially when using machine learning algorithms that assume linear independence of the features (such as linear regression).

In *Step 7*, we used violin plots to investigate the distribution of the limit balance feature per level of education and gender. We created them by using `sns.violinplot`. We indicated the education level as the x argument. Additionally, we set `hue='sex'` and `split=True`. By doing so, each half of the violin represented a different gender.

In the violin plots, we can find the following information:

- Median, represented by a white dot.
- **Interquartile range (IQR)**, represented as the black bar in the center of a violin.
- The lower and upper adjacent values, represented by the black lines stretched from the bar. The lower adjacent value is defined as the first quartile – 1.5 IQR, while the upper is defined as the third quartile + 1.5 IQR.

 Adjacent values can be used in a simple outlier detection technique (called **Tukey's fences**). The idea is to treat observations lying outside the fences (created by the adjacent values) as outliers.

Violin plots are a combination of a box plot (which can be created using `sns.boxplot`) and a kernel density estimate plot. A definite advantage of a violin plot over a box plot is that the former enables us to clearly see the shape of the distribution. This is especially useful when dealing with multimodal distributions (distributions with multiple peaks), such as the limit balance violin in the *Graduate school* education category.

In the last step, we investigated the distribution of the target variable (default) per gender and education. In the first case, we used `sns.countplot` to display the count of occurrences of both possible outcomes for each gender. In the second case, we opted for a different approach. We wanted to plot the percentage of defaults per education level, as comparing percentages between groups is easier than comparing nominal values. To do so, we first grouped by education level, selected the variable of interest, calculated the percentages per group (using `value_counts(normalize=True)`), unstacked (to remove multi-index), and—finally—generated a plot using the `plot` method.

# There's more...

In this recipe, we introduced a range of possible approaches to investigate the data at hand. However, this requires many lines of code each time we want to carry out the EDA. Thankfully, there is a Python library that simplifies the process. The library is called `pandas_profiling` and, with a single line of code, it generates a comprehensive summary of the dataset in the form of an HTML report.

To create a report, we need to run the following:

```
import pandas_profiling
df.profile_report()
```

For brevity, we only mention some selected elements of the report:

- An overview giving information about the size of the DataFrame (number of features/rows, missing values, duplicated rows, memory size, breakdown per data type)
- A list of warnings, including: duplicated rows, variables with a high percentage of zeros, variables with high correlation (they are automatically rejected in further reporting), skewness in the features, and so on
- Detailed univariate analysis of each feature (more details are available by clicking *Toggle details* in the report)
- Different measures of correlation (Pearson's, Spearman's, Kendall's, and more)
- Detailed analysis of missing values

# Splitting data into training and test sets

Having completed the EDA, the next step is to split the dataset into training and test sets. The idea is to have two separate datasets:

- Training set—On this part of the data, we train a machine learning model
- Test set—This part of the data was not seen by the model during training, and is used to evaluate the performance

What we want to achieve by splitting the data is preventing overfitting. Overfitting is a phenomenon whereby a model finds too many patterns in data used for training and performs well only on that particular data. In other words, it fails to generalize to unseen data.

This is a very important step in the analysis, as doing it incorrectly can introduce bias, for example, in the form of **data leakage**. Data leakage can occur when, during the training phase, a model observes information to which it should not have access. We follow up with an example. A common scenario is that of imputing missing values with the feature's average. If we had done this before splitting the data, we would have also used data from the test set to calculate the average, introducing data leakage. That is why the proper order would be to split the data into training and test sets first and then carry out the imputation, using the data observed in the training set.

Additionally, this approach ensures consistency, as unseen data in the future (new customers that will be scored by the model) will be treated in the same way as the ones data in the test set.

# How to do it...

Execute the following steps to split the dataset into training and test sets.

1. Import the function from `sklearn`:

```
from sklearn.model_selection import train_test_split
```

2. Split the data into training and test sets:

```
X_train, X_test, y_train, y_test = train_test_split(X, y,
test_size=0.2, random_state=42)
```

3. Split the data into training and test sets without shuffling:

```
X_train, X_test, y_train, y_test = train_test_split(X, y,
test_size=0.2, shuffle=False)
```

4. Split the data into training and test sets with stratification:

```
X_train, X_test, y_train, y_test = train_test_split(X, y,
test_size=0.2, stratify=y, random_state=42)
```

5. Verify that the ratio of the target is preserved:

```
y_train.value_counts(normalize=True)
y_test.value_counts(normalize=True)
```

In both sets, the percentage of defaults is ~22.12%.

# How it works...

We first imported the `train_test_split` function from the `model_selection` module of `scikit-learn`. In the second step, we showed how to do the most basic split. We passed `X` and `y` objects to the `train_test_split` function. Additionally, we specified the size of the test set, as a fraction of all observations. For reproducibility, we also specified the random state. We also had to assign the output of the function to four new objects.

In *Step 3*, we took a different approach. By specifying `shuffle=False`, we assigned the first 80% of the data to the training set and the remaining 20% to the test set. This might come in handy when dealing with time series, where the order of observations matters.

In the last step, we also specified the stratification argument by passing the target variable (`stratify=y`). Splitting the data with stratification means that both the training and test sets will have a possibly identical distribution of the specified variable. This parameter is very important when dealing with imbalanced data, such as in cases of fraud detection. If 99% of data is normal and only 1% covers fraudulent cases, a random split can result in the training set not having any fraudulent cases. That is why, when dealing with imbalanced data, it is important to split it correctly.

In the rest of the chapter, we will use the data obtained from the stratified split.

# There's more...

It is also common to split data into three sets: training, validation, and test. The validation set is used for frequent evaluation and tuning of the model's hyperparameters. Suppose we want to train a decision tree classifier and find the optimal value of the `max_depth` hyperparameter, which decides the maximum depth of the tree. To do so, we can train the model multiple times using the training set, and each time with a different value of the hyperparameter. Then, we can evaluate the performance of all these models, using the validation set. We pick the best model of those, and then, finally, evaluate its performance on the test set.

In the following code block, we illustrate a possible way of creating a train-validation-test split, using the same `train_test_split` function:

```
# define the size of the validation and test sets
VALID_SIZE = 0.1
TEST_SIZE = 0.2

# create the initial split - training and temp
X_train, X_temp, y_train, y_temp = train_test_split(X, y,
test_size=(VALID_SIZE + TEST_SIZE), stratify=y, random_state=42)

# calculate the new test size
NEW_TEST_SIZE = np.around(TEST_SIZE / (VALID_SIZE + TEST_SIZE), 2)

# create the valid and test sets
X_valid, X_test, y_valid, y_test = train_test_split(X_temp, y_temp,
test_size=NEW_TEST_SIZE, stratify=y_temp, random_state=42)
```

We basically ran `train_test_split`; however, we had to adjust the sizes of the `test_size` input in such a way that the initially defined proportions (70-10-20) were preserved.

Sometimes, we do not have enough data to split it into three sets, either because we do not have that many observations in general or because the data can be highly imbalanced, and we would remove valuable training samples from the training set. That is why practitioners often use a method called cross-validation, which we describe in the *Tuning hyperparameters using grid search and cross-validation* recipe.

# Dealing with missing values

In most real-life cases, we do not work with clean, complete data. One of the potential problems we are bound to encounter is that of missing values. We can categorize missing values by the reason they occur:

- **Missing completely at random (MCAR)**—The reason for the missing data is unrelated to the rest of the data. An example could be a respondent accidentally missing a question in a survey.
- **Missing at random (MAR)**—The missingness of the data can be inferred from data in another column(-s). For example, the missingness to a response to a certain survey question can be to some extent determined conditionally by other factors such as gender, age, lifestyle, and so on.
- **Missing not at random (MNAR)**—When there is some underlying reason for the missing values. For example, people with very high incomes tend to be hesitant about revealing it.
- **Structurally missing data**—Often a subset of MNAR, the data is missing because of a logical reason. For example, when a variable representing the age of a spouse is missing, we can infer that a given person has no spouse.

While some machine learning algorithms can account for missing data (for example, decision trees can treat missing values as a separate and unique value), many algorithms cannot, or their popular implementations (such as the ones in `scikit-learn`) do not incorporate this functionality.

 We should only impute features, not the target variable!

Some popular solutions include:

- Drop observations with one, or more, missing values—While this is the easiest approach, it is not always a good one, especially in the case of small datasets. Even if there is only a small fraction of missing values per feature, they do not necessarily occur for the same observations (rows), so the actual number of rows to remove can be much higher. Additionally, in the case of data missing not at random, removing such observations from the analysis can introduce bias into the results.

- Replace the missing values with a value far outside the possible range, so that algorithms such as decision trees can treat it as a special value, indicating missing data.
- In the case of dealing with time series, we can use forward-filling (take the last-known observation before the missing one), backward-filling (take the first-known observation after the missing one), or interpolation (linear or more advanced).
- Replace the missing values with an aggregate metric—for continuous data, we can use the mean (when there are no clear outliers in the data) or median (when there are outliers). In the case of categorical variables, we can use mode (the most common value in the set). A potential disadvantage of mean/median imputation is the reduction of variance in the dataset.
- Replace the missing values with aggregate metrics calculated per group—for example, when dealing with body-related metrics, we can calculate the mean or median per gender, to more accurately replace the missing data.
- ML-based approaches—We can treat the considered feature as a target, and use complete cases to train a model and predict values for the missing observations.

# How to do it...

Execute the following steps to investigate and deal with missing values in the dataset.

1. Import the libraries:

```
import pandas as pd
import missingno
from sklearn.impute import SimpleImputer
```

2. Inspect the information about the DataFrame:

```
X.info()
```

Running the code results in the following table:

```
Int64Index: 30000 entries, 0 to 29999
Data columns (total 23 columns):
limit_bal              30000 non-null int64
sex                    29850 non-null object
education              29850 non-null object
marriage               29850 non-null object
age                    29850 non-null float64
payment_status_sep     30000 non-null object
payment_status_aug     30000 non-null object
payment_status_jul     30000 non-null object
payment_status_jun     30000 non-null object
payment_status_may     30000 non-null object
payment_status_apr     30000 non-null object
bill_statement_sep     30000 non-null int64
bill_statement_aug     30000 non-null int64
bill_statement_jul     30000 non-null int64
bill_statement_jun     30000 non-null int64
bill_statement_may     30000 non-null int64
bill_statement_apr     30000 non-null int64
previous_payment_sep   30000 non-null int64
previous_payment_aug   30000 non-null int64
previous_payment_jul   30000 non-null int64
previous_payment_jun   30000 non-null int64
previous_payment_may   30000 non-null int64
previous_payment_apr   30000 non-null int64
dtypes: float64(1), int64(13), object(9)
memory usage: 5.5+ MB
```

3. Visualize the nullity of the DataFrame:

```
missingno.matrix(X)
```

Running the line of code results in the following plot:

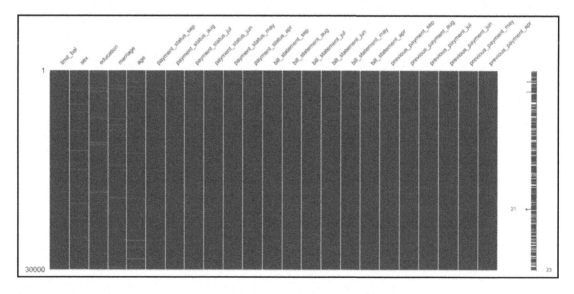

The white bars visible in the columns represent missing values. The line on the right side of the plot describes the shape of data completeness. The two numbers indicate the maximum and minimum nullity in the dataset (there are 23 columns in total, and the row with the most missing values contains 2—hence the 21).

4. Define columns with missing values per data type:

```
NUM_FEATURES = ['age']
CAT_FEATURES = ['sex', 'education', 'marriage']
```

5. Impute numerical features:

```
for col in NUM_FEATURES:
    num_imputer = SimpleImputer(strategy='median')
    num_imputer.fit(X_train[[col]])
    X_train.loc[:, col] = num_imputer.transform(X_train[[col]])
    X_test.loc[:, col] = num_imputer.transform(X_test[[col]])
```

6. Impute categorical features:

```
for col in CAT_FEATURES:
    cat_imputer = SimpleImputer(strategy='most_frequent')
    cat_imputer.fit(X_train[[col]])
    X_train.loc[:, col] = cat_imputer.transform(X_train[[col]])
    X_test.loc[:, col] = cat_imputer.transform(X_test[[col]])
```

7. Verify that there are no missing values:

```
X_train.info()
```

We can inspect the output, to confirm that there are no missing values in X.

# How it works...

In *Step 1*, we imported the required libraries. Then, we used the `info` method of a pandas DataFrame to view information about the columns, such as their type and the number of non-null observations. Another possible way of inspecting the number of missing values per column is to run `X.isnull().sum()`.

Instead of imputing, we could also drop the observations (or even columns) containing missing values. To drop all rows containing any missing value, we could use `X_train.dropna(how='any', inplace=True)`. In our sample case, the number of missing values is not large, however, in a real-life dataset it can be considerable or, alternatively, the dataset can be too small for the analysts to be able to remove observations.

In *Step 3*, we visualized the nullity of the DataFrame, with the help of the `missingno` library.

In *Step 4*, we defined lists containing features we wanted to impute, one list per data type. The reason for this is the fact that numeric features are imputed using different strategies than the categorical features. For basic imputation, we used the `SimpleImputer` class from `scikit-learn`.

In *Step 5*, we iterated over the numerical features (in this case, only the `age` feature), and used the `median` to replace the missing values. Inside the loop, we defined the `imputer` object with the correct strategy (`median`), fitted it to the given column of the training data, and transformed both the training and test data. This way, the median was estimated by only using the training data, preventing potential data leakage.

In this recipe, we used `scikit-learn` to deal with the imputation of missing values. However, we can also do this manually. To do so, for each column with any missing values (either in the training or test set), we need to calculate the given statistic (mean/median/mode) using the training set, for example, `age_median = X_train.age.median()`. Afterward, we need to use this median to fill inthe missing values for the `age` column (in both the training and test sets) using the `fillna` method.

*Step 6* is analogical to *Step 5*, where we used the same approach to iterate over categorical columns. The difference lies in the selected strategy—we used the most frequent value (`most_frequent`) in the given column. This strategy can be used for both categorical and numerical features; in the latter case, this is the mode.

# There's more...

In this recipe, we mentioned how to impute missing values. Approaches such as replacing the missing value with one large value or the mean/median/mode are called **single imputation approaches**, as they replace missing values with one specific value. However, there are also **multiple imputation approaches**, and one of those is **Multiple Imputation by Chained Equations** (**MICE**). In short, the algorithm runs multiple regression models, and each missing value is determined conditionally on the basis of the non-missing data points. A potential benefit of using an ML-based approach to imputation is the reduction of bias introduced by single imputation.

The MICE algorithm is available in `scikit-learn`, under the name of `IterativeImputer`, in the `impute` module.

# See also

Additional resources are available here:

- Azur, M. J., Stuart, E. A., Frangakis, C., and Leaf, P. J. (2011). Multiple imputation by chained equations: what is it and how does it work? *International Journal of Methods in Psychiatric Research*, 20(1), 40-49.—`https://www.ncbi.nlm.nih.gov/pmc/articles/PMC3074241/`.
- Buck, S. F. (1960). A method of estimation of missing values in multivariate data suitable for use with an electronic computer. *Journal of the Royal Statistical Society: Series B* (Methodological), 22(2), 302-306.—`https://www.jstor.org/stable/2984099`.
- van Buuren, S. and Groothuis-Oudshoorn, K. (2011). MICE: Multivariate Imputation by Chained Equations in R. *Journal of Statistical Software* 45 (3): 1–67.—`https://ris.utwente.nl/ws/portalfiles/portal/6433591/Buuren11mice.pdf`.

# Encoding categorical variables

In the previous recipes, we have seen that some features are categorical variables (originally represented as either `object` or `category` data types). However, most machine learning algorithms work exclusively with numeric data. That is why we need to encode categorical features into a representation compatible with the models.

In this recipe, we cover some popular encoding approaches:

- Label encoding
- One-hot encoding

In **label encoding**, we replace the categorical value with a numeric value between 0 and # of classes - 1—for example, with three distinct classes, we use {0, 1, 2}.

 This is already very similar to the outcome of converting to the `category` class in `pandas`. We can access the codes of the categories by running `df_cat.education.cat.codes`. Additionally, we can recover the mapping by running `dict(zip(df_cat.education.cat.codes, df_cat.education))`.

One potential issue with label encoding is that, most of the time, there is no relationship of any kind between categories, while label encoding introduces a relationship. In a three-classes example, the relationship looks as follows: 0 < 1 < 2. This does not make much sense if the categories are, for example, countries. However, this can work for features that represent some kind of order (ordinal variables), for example, a rating of service received, on a scale of Bad-Neutral-Good.

To overcome the preceding problem, we can use **one-hot encoding**. In this approach, for each category of a feature, we create a new column (sometimes called a dummy variable) with binary encoding to denote whether a particular row belongs to this category. A potential drawback of this method is a significant increase in the dimensionality of the dataset (see **Curse of Dimensionality**).

 Creating dummy variables introduces a form of redundancy to the dataset. In fact, if a feature has three categories, we only need to have two dummy variables because, if an observation is neither of the two, it must be the third one. This is often referred to as the **dummy-variable trap**, and it is best practice to always remove one column (known as the reference) from such an encoding.

Summing up, we should avoid label encoding when it introduces false order to the data, which can, in turn, lead to incorrect conclusions. Tree-based methods (decision trees, Random Forest, and so on) can work with categorical data and label encoding. However, for algorithms such as linear regression, models calculating distance metrics between features (k-means clustering, k-Nearest Neighbors, and so on) or **Artificial Neural Networks (ANN)**, the natural representation is one-hot encoding.

# How to do it...

Execute the following steps to encode categorical variables.

1. Import the libraries:

```
import pandas as pd
from sklearn.preprocessing import LabelEncoder, OneHotEncoder
from sklearn.compose import ColumnTransformer
```

2. Use Label Encoder to encode a selected column:

```
COL = 'education'

X_train_copy = X_train.copy()
X_test_copy = X_test.copy()

label_enc = LabelEncoder()
label_enc.fit(X_train_copy[COL])
X_train_copy.loc[:, COL] = label_enc.transform(X_train_copy[COL])
X_test_copy.loc[:, COL] = label_enc.transform(X_test_copy[COL])
```

We created a copy of X_train and X_test, just to show how to work with LabelEncoder, but we do not want to modify the DataFrames.

3. Select categorical features for one-hot encoding:

```
CAT_FEATURES = X_train.select_dtypes(include='object') \
                      .columns \
                      .to_list()
```

4. Instantiate the OneHotEncoder object:

```
one_hot_encoder = OneHotEncoder(sparse=False,
                                handle_unknown='error',
                                drop='first')
```

5. Create the column transformer using the one-hot encoder:

```
one_hot_transformer = ColumnTransformer(
    [("one_hot", one_hot_encoder, CAT_FEATURES)]
)
```

6. Fit the transformer:

```
one_hot_transformer.fit(X_train)
```

7. Apply the transformations to both the training and the test set:

```
col_names = one_hot_transformer.get_feature_names()

X_train_cat = pd.DataFrame(one_hot_transformer.transform(X_train),
                           columns=col_names,
                           index=X_train.index)
X_train_ohe = pd.concat([X_train, X_train_cat], axis=1) \
                .drop(CAT_FEATURES, axis=1)

X_test_cat = pd.DataFrame(one_hot_transformer.transform(X_test),
                          columns=col_names,
                          index=X_test.index)
X_test_ohe = pd.concat([X_test, X_test_cat], axis=1) \
               .drop(CAT_FEATURES, axis=1)
```

In the preceding snippet, `X_train_cat` and `X_test_cat` were only used as helper objects used to create the final DataFrames.

## How it works...

First, we imported the necessary libraries. In the second step, we selected the column we wanted to encode using label encoding, instantiated the `LabelEncoder`, fitted it to the training data, and transformed both the training and the test data. We did not want to keep the label encoding, and for that reason, we operated on copies of the DataFrames.

In *Step 3*, we started the preparations for one-hot encoding by creating a list of all the categorical features (using `select_dtypes`). Then, we created an instance of `OneHotEncoder`. We specified that we did not want to work with a sparse matrix (a special kind of data type, suitable for storing matrices with a very high percentage of zeros), we dropped the first column per feature (to avoid the dummy variable trap), and we specified what to do in case the encoder finds an unknown value while applying the transformation (`handle_unknown='error'`).

In *Step 5*, we defined the `ColumnTransformer`, which is a convenient approach to applying the same transformation (in this case, the one-hot encoder) to multiple columns. We passed a list of steps, where each step was defined by a tuple. In this case, it was a single tuple with the name of the step, the transformation to be applied, and the features to which we wanted to apply the transformation. When creating the `ColumnTransformer`, we could have also specified another argument, `remainder='passthrough'`, which would have effectively fitted and transformed only the specified columns, while leaving the rest intact. The default value for `remainder` was `drop`, which dropped the unused columns.

`ColumnTransformer` returned a `numpy` array, and we were also interested in recovering the names of the features (for the sake of interpreting and understanding machine learning models). At the time of writing, it is impossible to specify `remainder='passthrough'` and then use the `get_feature_names` method of the `ColumnTransformer`.

In *Step 6*, we fitted the transformer using the `fit` method. Lastly, we had to apply a small trick to overcome the issue mentioned above. We started by extracting the names of the features, by using the `get_feature_names` method. Then, we created a `pandas` DataFrame using the transformed features, the new column names, and the old indices (to keep everything in order). Afterward, we concatenated the original DataFrame (`X_train`), with the newly encoded categorical features (`X_train_cat`) and dropped the original categorical columns (encoded as `object`).

# There's more...

We would like to mention a few more things regarding encoding categorical variables.

## Using pandas.get_dummies for one-hot encoding

`pandas` contains a very useful function we can use for one-hot encoding, namely `pd.get_dummies`. The example syntax looks like the following:

```
X_train = pd.get_dummies(X_train, prefix_sep='_', drop_first=True)
```

## Specifying possible categories for OneHotEncoder

When creating `ColumnTransformer`, we could have additionally provided a list of possible categories for all the considered features. A simplified example follows:

```
one_hot_encoder = OneHotEncoder(
    categories=[['Male', 'Female', 'Unknown']],
    sparse=False,
    handle_unknown='error',
    drop='first'
)

one_hot_transformer = ColumnTransformer(
    [("one_hot", one_hot_encoder, ['sex'])]
)
```

```
one_hot_transformer.fit(X_train)

one_hot_transformer.get_feature_names()
#['one_hot__x0_Female', 'one_hot__x0_Unknown']
```

By passing a list (of lists) containing possible categories for each feature, we are taking into account the possibility that the specific value does not appear in the training set, but might appear in the test set. If this were the case, we would run into errors.

In the preceding code block, we added an extra category called 'Unknown' to the column representing gender. As a result, we will end up with an extra "dummy" column for that category.

# Category Encoders library

Aside from using pandas and scikit-learn, we can also use another library called Category Encoders. It belongs to a set of libraries compatible with scikit-learn and provides a selection of encoders using a similar fit-transform approach. That is why it is also possible to use them together with ColumnTransformer and Pipeline.

We show two of the available encoders. The first one will be an alternative implementation of the one-hot encoder.

Import the library:

```
import category_encoders as ce
```

Create the encoder object:

```
one_hot_encoder_ce = ce.OneHotEncoder(use_cat_names=True)
```

Additionally, we could specify an argument called drop_invariant, to indicate that we want to drop columns with a 0 variance. This could help reduce the number of features.

Fit the encoder, and transform the data:

```
one_hot_encoder_ce.fit(X_train)
X_train_ce = one_hot_encoder_ce.transform(X_train)
```

This implementation of the one-hot encoder automatically encodes only the columns containing strings (unless we specify only a subset of categorical columns by passing a list to the `cols` argument). By default, it also returns a `pandas` DataFrame (in comparison to the `numpy` array, in the case of `scikit-learn`'s implementation) with the adjusted column names. The only drawback of this implementation is that it does not allow for dropping the one redundant dummy column of each feature.

The second interesting approach to encoding categorical features available in the `Category Encoders` library is target encoding. This approach is useful for classification tasks and relies on using the mean of the dependent variable (target) to replace categories. We can also interpret mean encoding as a probability of the target variable, conditional on each value of the feature. In the case of a simple variable with gender and a Boolean target, target encoding would replace the categories with the percentage of positive cases per gender.

```
target_encoder = ce.TargetEncoder(smoothing=0)
target_encoder.fit(X_train.sex, y_train)
target_encoder.transform(X_train.sex).head()
```

Running the code generates a preview of the table, as shown in the following screenshot:

| | sex |
|---|---|
| 22788 | 0.206563 |
| 29006 | 0.206563 |
| 16950 | 0.243825 |
| 22280 | 0.206563 |
| 11346 | 0.206563 |

It looks as though ~20.7% of females and ~24.4% of males defaulted in the training set. We set the `smoothing` argument to zero, to remove regularization and keep the pure mean value.

The benefits of using target encoding include:

- Improved model performance.
- Target encoding tends to group the classes of the target together, while the distribution of the target is quite random in the case of label encoding.

- The number of features is reduced, instead of using one-hot encoding with a large number of columns. This is especially helpful with gradient-boosted trees, as they have trouble handling high-cardinality categorical features, due to the limited depth of the trees.

The biggest drawback of target encoding is its potential to cause overfitting. As a remedy, we could apply k-fold target encoding.

**A warning about one-hot encoding and decision tree-based algorithms**

While regression-based models can naturally handle the OR condition of one-hot encoded features, this is not that simple using decision tree-based algorithms. In theory, decision trees are capable of handling categorical features without the need for encoding.

However, its popular implementation in `scikit-learn` still requires all features to be numerical. Without going into too much detail, such an approach favors continuous numerical features over one-hot-encoded dummies, as a single dummy can only bring a fraction of the total feature information into the model. A possible solution is to use either a different kind of encoding (label/target encoding) or an implementation that handles categorical features, such as Random Forest in the `h2o` library.

# See also

Library documentation:

- `http://contrib.scikit-learn.org/categorical-encoding`
- `http://docs.h2o.ai/h2o/latest-stable/h2o-docs/data-science/drf.html`

# Fitting a decision tree classifier

A decision tree classifier is a relatively simple, yet very important machine learning algorithm, for both regression and classification problems. The name comes from the fact that the model creates a set of rules (for example: `if x_1 > 50 and x_2 < 10 then y = 'default'`), which taken together can be visualized in the form of a tree. The decision trees segment the feature space into a number of smaller regions, by repeatedly splitting the features at a certain value. To do so, they use a greedy algorithm (together with some heuristics) to find a split that minimizes the combined impurity of the children nodes (measured using the Gini impurity or entropy).

In the case of a binary classification problem, the algorithm tries to obtain nodes that contain as many observations from one class as possible, thus minimizing the impurity. The prediction in a terminal node (leaf) is made on the basis of mode, in the case of classification, and mean for regression problems.

> Decision trees are a base for many complex algorithms, such as Random Forest, Gradient Boosted Trees, XGBoost, LightGBM, CatBoost, and so on.

**Advantages of decision trees:**

- Easily visualized in the form of a tree—high interpretability
- Fast training and prediction stages
- A small number of hyperparameters to tune

- Support numerical and categorical features
- Handle non-linearity in data
- Can be further improved with feature engineering, though no explicit need
- Do not require scaling and normalization of features
- Implement their version of feature selection by choosing the features on which to split the sample
- Non-parametric model—no assumptions about the distribution of the features/target

**Disadvantages of decision trees:**

- Instability—The trees are very sensitive to the noise in input data; a small change in the data can change the model significantly.
- Overfitting—If we do not provide maximum values or stopping criteria, the trees tend to grow very deep and do not generalize well.
- The trees can only interpolate, but not extrapolate—they make constant predictions for observations that lie beyond the boundary region established on the feature space of the training data.
- The underlying greedy algorithm does not guarantee the selection of a globally optimal decision tree.
- Class imbalance can lead to biased trees.
- Information gain (a decrease in entropy) in a decision tree with categorical variables results in a biased outcome for features with a higher number of categories.

# How to do it...

Execute the following steps to fit a decision tree classifier.

1. Import the libraries:

```
from sklearn.tree import DecisionTreeClassifier, export_graphviz
from sklearn import metrics

from chapter_8_utils import performance_evaluation_report

from io import StringIO
import seaborn as sns
from ipywidgets import Image
import pydotplus
```

2. Create an instance of the model, fit it to the training data, and create the prediction:

```
tree_classifier = DecisionTreeClassifier()
tree_classifier.fit(X_train_ohe, y_train)
y_pred = tree_classifier.predict(X_test_ohe)
```

3. Evaluate the results:

```
LABELS = ['No Default', 'Default']
tree_perf = performance_evaluation_report(tree_classifier,
                                          X_test_ohe,
                                          y_test, labels=LABELS,
                                          show_plot=True)
```

Running the code results in the following plot:

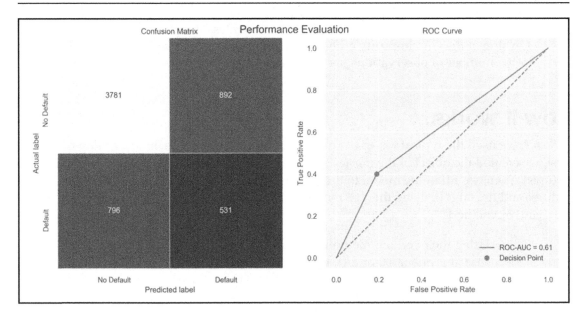

4. Plot the simplified decision tree:

```
small_tree = DecisionTreeClassifier(max_depth=3)
small_tree.fit(X_train_ohe, y_train)

tree_dot = StringIO()
export_graphviz(small_tree, feature_names=X_train_ohe.columns,
                class_names=LABELS, rounded=True,
                out_file=tree_dot,
                proportion=False, precision=2, filled=True)
tree_graph = pydotplus.graph_from_dot_data(tree_dot.getvalue())
Image(value=tree_graph.create_png())
```

Running the code results in the following plot:

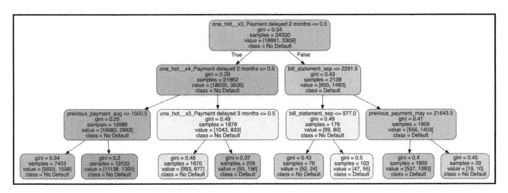

For each node, we can see the split criterion (unless it is the terminal node), the value of the Gini impurity criterion, the number of observations, a list containing the number of observations per class, and the majority class.

# How it works...

In *Step 2*, we used the typical `scikit-learn` approach to train a machine learning model. First, we created the object of the `DecisionTreeClassifier` class (using all the default settings). Then, we fitted the model to the training data (we needed to pass both the features and the target), using the `fit` method. Lastly, we obtained the predictions by using the `predict` method.

Using the `predict` method results in an array of predicted classes (in this case, it is either a 0 or a 1). However, there are cases when we are interested in the assigned probabilities. To obtain them, we can use the `predict_proba` method and obtain an `n_test_observations x n_classes` array, where each row contains all the possible class probabilities (they sum up to 1). In the case of binary classification, the `predict` method automatically assigns a positive class when the corresponding probability is > 50%.

In *Step 3*, we evaluated the performance of the model. We used a custom function to display all the results. We will not go deeper into its specifics, as it is quite standard and is built using functions from the `metrics` module of `scikit-learn`. For a detailed description of the function, please refer to the accompanying GitHub repository.

The **confusion matrix** summarizes all possible combinations of the predicted values as opposed to the actual target. It has a structure that looks like the following:

```
TN | FP
-------
FN | TP
```

The values are as follows:

- **True positive (TP)**: The model predicts a default, and the client defaulted.
- **False positive (FP)**: The model predicts a default, but the client did not default.
- **True negative (TN)**: The model predicts a good customer, and the client did not default.
- **False negative (FN)**: The model predicts a good customer, but the client defaulted.

Using these values, we can further build multiple evaluation criteria:

- Accuracy (`(TP + TN) / (TP + FP + TN + FN)`)—Measures the model's overall ability to correctly predict the class of the observation.
- Precision (`TP / (TP + FP)`)—Out of all predictions of the positive class (in our case, the default), how many observations indeed defaulted.
- Recall (`TP / (TP + FN)`)—Out of all positive cases, how many were predicted correctly. Also called **sensitivity** or the **true positive rate**.
- F-1 Score—A harmonic average of precision and recall. The reason for a harmonic mean instead of a standard mean is that it punishes extreme outcomes, such as precision = 1 and recall = 0, or vice versa.
- Specificity (`TN / (TN + FP)`)—Measures what fraction of negative cases (clients without a default) actually did not default.

Understanding the subtleties behind these metrics is very important for the correct evaluation of the model's performance. Accuracy can be highly misleading in the case of class imbalance. Imagine a case when 99% of data is not fraudulent and only 1% is fraudulent. Then, a naïve model classifying each observation as non-fraudulent achieves 99% accuracy, while it is actually worthless. That is why, in such cases, we should refer to precision or recall. When we try to achieve as high precision as possible, we will get fewer false positives, at the cost of more false negatives. When optimizing for recall, we will achieve fewer false negatives, at the cost of more false positives. The metric on which we try to optimize should be selected based on the use case.

The second plot contains the **Receiver Operating Characteristic (ROC)** curve. The ROC curve presents a trade-off between the true-positive rate and the false-positive rate for different probability thresholds. A probability threshold determines the predicted probability above which we decide that the observation belongs to the positive class (by default, it is 50%). The ideal point is (0, 1), and a skillful model's curve would be as close to it as possible. On the other hand, a model with no skill will have a line close to the diagonal (45°) line.

 A model with a curve below the diagonal line is actually possible and better than the "no-skill" one, as its predictions can be simply inverted to obtain better performance.

To summarize the performance of a model with one number, we can look at the **area under the ROC curve (AUC)**. It is a metric with values between 0.5 (no skill) and 1 (ideal model). We can interpret the AUC in probabilistic terms. An AUC of 75% means that, if we randomly take two observations from the predictions, with a 75% probability they will be ordered in the correct way. This also explains the minimal AUC of 0.5, as a random model will result in a 50% probability of being correctly ordered.

Lastly, we may use the ROC curve to select a threshold that results in an appropriate balance between false positives and false negatives.

In *Step 4*, we visualized the decision tree. We started by retraining a tree, this time with a maximum depth of 3. This way, we ensured that the image was readable. We used the `export_graphviz` function to create a `dot` file containing the visualized tree and captured it using `StringIO`. This way, we avoided storing a copy of the file on the HDD. Then, we recovered the file, using the `getvalue` method, and created the graph inside Jupyter Notebook.

# There's more...

The ROC curve loses its credibility when it comes to evaluating the performance of the model when we are dealing with class imbalance. That is why, in such cases, we should use another curve—the Precision-Recall curve. That is because, for calculating both precision and recall, we do not use the true negatives, and only consider the correct prediction of the minority class (the positive one).

Calculate precision and recall for different thresholds:

```
y_pred_prob = tree_classifier.predict_proba(X_test_ohe)[:, 1]
precision, recall, thresholds = metrics.precision_recall_curve(y_test,
                                                        y_pred_prob)
```

Having calculated the required elements, we can plot the curve:

```
ax = plt.subplot()
ax.plot(recall, precision,
        label=f'PR-AUC = {metrics.auc(recall, precision):.2f}')
ax.set(title='Precision-Recall Curve',
       xlabel='Recall',
       ylabel='Precision')
ax.legend()
```

Running the code results in the following plot:

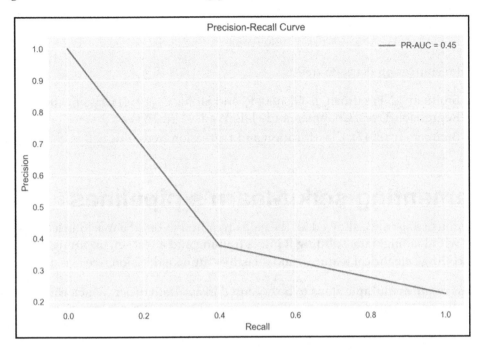

As a summary metric, we can approximate the area under the Precision-Recall curve by calling `metrics.auc(recall, precision)`. In contrast to the ROC-AUC, the PR-AUC ranges from 0 to 1, where 1 indicates the perfect model. A model with a PR-AUC of 1 can identify all the positive observations (perfect recall), while not wrongly labeling a single negative observation as a positive one (perfect precision). We can consider models that bow towards the (1, 1) point as skillful.

# See also

Information on the dangers of using ROC-AUC as a performance evaluation metric:

- Lobo, J. M., Jiménez-Valverde, A., & Real, R. (2008). AUC: a misleading measure of the performance of predictive distribution models. *Global Ecology and Biogeography*, 17(2), 145-151. — `http://www2.unil.ch/biomapper/Download/ Lobo-GloEcoBioGeo-2007.pdf`

- Sokolova, M., & Lapalme, G. (2009). A systematic analysis of performance measures for classification tasks. *Information Processing and Management*, 45(4), 427-437. — `http://rali.iro.umontreal.ca/rali/sites/default/files/publis/SokolovaLapalme-JIPM09.pdf`

Additional resources on decision trees:

- Breiman, L., Friedman, J., Olshen, R. and Stone, C. (1984) Classification and Regression Trees. Chapman and Hall, Wadsworth, New York.
- Breiman, L. (2017). Classification and regression trees. Routledge.

# Implementing scikit-learn's pipelines

In the previous recipes, we showed all the steps required to build a machine learning model—starting with loading data, splitting it into a training and a test set, imputing missing values, encoding categorical features, and—lastly—fitting a decision tree classifier.

The process requires multiple steps to be executed in a certain order, which can sometimes be tricky with a lot of modifications to the pipeline mid-work. That is why `scikit-learn` introduced Pipelines. By using Pipelines, we can sequentially apply a list of transformations to the data, and then train a given estimator (model).

One important point to be aware of is that the intermediate steps of the Pipeline must have the `fit` and `transform` methods (the final estimator only needs the `fit` method, though). Using Pipelines has several benefits:

- The flow is much easier to read and understand—the chain of operations to be executed on given columns is clear
- The order of steps is enforced by the Pipeline
- Increased reproducibility

In this recipe, we show how to create the entire project's pipeline, from loading the data to training the classifier.

# How to do it...

Execute the following steps to build the project's pipeline.

1. Import the libraries:

```
import pandas as pd
from sklearn.model_selection import train_test_split
from sklearn.impute import SimpleImputer
from sklearn.preprocessing import OneHotEncoder
from sklearn.compose import ColumnTransformer
from sklearn.tree import DecisionTreeClassifier
from sklearn.pipeline import Pipeline
from chapter_8_utils import performance_evaluation_report
```

2. Load the data, separate the target, and create the stratified train-test split:

```
df = pd.read_csv('credit_card_default.csv', index_col=0,
                  na_values='')

X = df.copy()
y = X.pop('default_payment_next_month')

X_train, X_test, y_train, y_test = train_test_split(X, y,
                                                    test_size=0.2,
                                                    stratify=y)
```

3. Store lists of numerical/categorical features:

```
num_features = X_train.select_dtypes(include='number') \
                      .columns \
                      .to_list()
cat_features = X_train.select_dtypes(include='object') \
                      .columns \
                      .to_list()
```

4. Define the numerical Pipeline:

```
num_pipeline = Pipeline(steps=[
    ('imputer', SimpleImputer(strategy='median'))
])
```

5. Define the categorical Pipeline:

```
cat_list = [list(X_train[col].dropna().unique()) for col in
cat_features]

cat_pipeline = Pipeline(steps=[
    ('imputer', SimpleImputer(strategy='most_frequent')),
    ('onehot', OneHotEncoder(categories=cat_list, sparse=False,
                             handle_unknown='error', drop='first'))
])
```

6. Define the column transformer object:

```
preprocessor = ColumnTransformer(transformers=[
    ('numerical', num_pipeline, num_features),
    ('categorical', cat_pipeline, cat_features)],
    remainder='drop')
```

7. Create a joint Pipeline:

```
dec_tree = DecisionTreeClassifier(random_state=42)

tree_pipeline = Pipeline(steps=[('preprocessor', preprocessor),
                                ('classifier', dec_tree)])
```

8. Fit the Pipeline to the data:

```
tree_pipeline.fit(X_train, y_train)
```

9. Evaluate the performance of the entire Pipeline:

```
LABELS = ['No Default', 'Default']
tree_perf = performance_evaluation_report(tree_pipeline, X_test,
                                          y_test, labels=LABELS,
                                          show_plot=True)
```

Running the code results in the following plot:

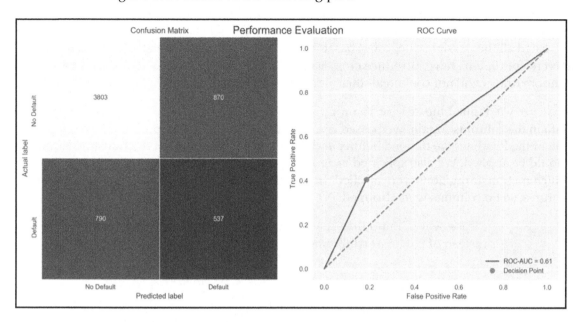

We see that the performance of the model is very similar to what we achieved by carrying out all the steps separately. This is what we expected to achieve.

# How it works...

In *Step 1*, we imported the required libraries. The list can look a bit daunting, but that is due to the fact that we need to combine multiple functions/classes used in the previous recipes.

In *Step 2*, we loaded the data from a CSV file, separated the target variable and created the stratified train-test split. Next, we also created two lists containing the names of the numerical/categorical features—we will apply different transformations depending on the type of the feature. To select the appropriate columns, we used the `select_dtypes` method.

In *Step 4*, we started preparing the separate Pipelines. For the numerical one, we only wanted to impute the missing values of the features using the column median. For the `Pipeline`, we provided a list of tuples containing the steps, each of the tuples containing the name of the step (for easier identification) and the class we wanted to use, in this case, it was the `SimpleImputer`.

In *Step 5*, we prepared a similar Pipeline for categorical features. This time, however, we chained two different operations—the imputer (using the most frequent value), and the one-hot encoder. For the encoder, we also specified a list of lists called `cat_list`, in which we listed all the possible categories, based on `X_train`. We did so mostly for the sake of the next recipe, in which we introduce cross-validation, and it can happen that some of the random draws will not contain all the categories.

In *Step 6*, we defined the `ColumnTransformer` object, which we used to manipulate the data in the columns. Again, we passed a list of tuples, where each tuple contained a name, one of the Pipelines we defined before, and a list of columns to which the transformations should be applied. We also specified `remainder='drop'`, to drop any extra columns to which no transformations were applied. In this case, the transformations were applied to all features, so no columns were dropped.

 Please bear in mind that `ColumnTransformer` returns `numpy` arrays instead of `pandas` DataFrames!

In *Step 7*, we once again used `Pipeline` to chain the `preprocessor` (the previously defined `ColumnTransformer` object) with the decision tree classifier (for comparability, we set the random state to 42). The last two steps involved fitting the entire Pipeline to the data and using the custom function to measure the performance of the model. The `performance_evaluation_report` function was built in such a way that it works with any estimator or `Pipeline` that has the `predict` and `predict_proba` methods, used to create predictions.

# There's more...

In this recipe, we showed how to create the entire pipeline for a data science project. However, there are many other transformations we can apply to data as preprocessing steps. Some of them include:

- **Scaling numerical features**: In other words, changing the range of the features due to the fact that different features are measured on different scales; and this can introduce bias to the model. We should mostly be concerned with feature scaling when dealing with models that calculate some kind of distance between features (such as K-Nearest Neighbors). In general, methods based on decision trees do not require any scaling. Some popular options from `scikit-learn` include `StandardScaler` and `MinMaxScaler`.

- **Discretizing continuous variables**: We can transform a continuous variable (such as age) into a finite number of bins (such as below 25, between 25 and 50, and older than 50). When we want to create specific bins, we can use the `pd.cut` function, while `pd.qcut` is used for splitting based on quantiles.
- **Transforming/removing outliers**: During the EDA, we often see some feature values that are extreme and can be caused by some kind of error (for example, adding an extra digit to the age) or are simply incompatible with the rest (for example, a multimillionaire among a sample of middle-class citizens). Such outliers can skew the results of the model, and it is good practice to somehow deal with them. One solution would be to remove them at all, but this can have an impact on the model's ability to generalize. We can also bring them closer to regular values.

> We can also create new (or transformed) features within Pipelines. To explicitly add a new column, we should first create an appropriate transformer/Pipeline, and then use `FeatureUnion` to add it within the Pipeline.

In this example, we show how to create a custom transformer to detect and modify outliers. We apply the 3σ rule—we cap the values above/below the average +/- 3 standard deviations. We create a dedicated transformer for this task, so we can incorporate the outlier treatment into the previously established Pipeline.

1. Import the base estimator and transformer from `sklearn`:

   ```
   from sklearn.base import BaseEstimator, TransformerMixin
   ```

   We want to make a custom transformer that is compatible with `scikit-learn`'s Pipelines. For that, it must come with methods such as `fit`, `transform`, `fit_transform`, `get_params`, and `set_params`. We could write them all manually, but a definitely more appealing approach is to use Python's class inheritance, to make the process easier. That is why we imported `BaseEstimator` and `TransformerMixin` from `scikit-learn`. By inheriting from `TransformerMixin`, we do not need to specify the `fit_transform` method, while inheriting from `BaseEstimator` automatically provides the `get_params` and `set_params` methods.

2. Define the `OutlierRemover` class:

   ```
   class OutlierRemover(BaseEstimator, TransformerMixin):
       def __init__(self, n_std=3):
           self.n_std = n_std
       def fit(self, X, y = None):
   ```

```
            if np.isnan(X).any(axis=None):
                raise ValueError('''There are missing values in the
                                    array! Please remove them.''')

        mean_vec = np.mean(X, axis=0)
        std_vec = np.std(X, axis=0)
        self.upper_band_ = mean_vec + self.n_std * std_vec
        self.lower_band_ = mean_vec - self.n_std * std_vec
        self.n_features_ = len(self.upper_band_)
        return self
    def transform(self, X, y = None):
        X_copy = pd.DataFrame(X.copy())
        upper_band = np.repeat(
            self.upper_band_.reshape(self.n_features_, -1),
            len(X_copy),
            axis=1).transpose()
        lower_band = np.repeat(
            self.lower_band_.reshape(self.n_features_, -1),
            len(X_copy),
            axis=1).transpose()

        X_copy[X_copy >= upper_band] = upper_band
        X_copy[X_copy <= lower_band] = lower_band
        return X_copy.values
```

We designed the class similarly to the ones in `scikit-learn`, meaning we can train it on the training set, and only use the transformation on the test set.

In the __init__ method, we stored the number of standard deviations that determines whether observations will be treated as outliers (the default is 3). In the `fit` method, we stored the upper and lower thresholds for being considered an outlier, as well as the number of features in general. In the `transform` method, we capped all the values, according to the $3\sigma$ symbol rule.

One known limitation of this class is that it does not handle missing values. That is why we raise a `ValueError` when there are any missing values. In the Pipeline, we use the `OutlierRemover` after the imputation in order to avoid the issue. We could, of course, account for the missing values in the transformer, however, this would make the code longer and less readable. Please refer to the definition of `SimpleImputer` in `scikit-learn` for an example of how to mask missing values while building transformers.

3. Add the `OutlierRemover` to the numerical Pipeline:

```
num_pipeline = Pipeline(steps=[
    ('imputer', SimpleImputer(strategy='median')),
    ('outliers', OutlierRemover())
])
```

4. Run the rest of the Pipeline, to compare the results:

```
preprocessor = ColumnTransformer(transformers=[
    ('numerical', num_pipeline, num_features),
    ('categorical', cat_pipeline, cat_features)],
    remainder='drop')

dec_tree = DecisionTreeClassifier(random_state=42)

tree_pipeline = Pipeline(steps=[('preprocessor', preprocessor),
                                ('classifier', dec_tree)])

tree_pipeline.fit(X_train, y_train)

tree_perf = performance_evaluation_report(tree_pipeline, X_test,
                                          y_test, labels=LABELS,
                                          show_plot=True)
```

Running the code results in the following plot:

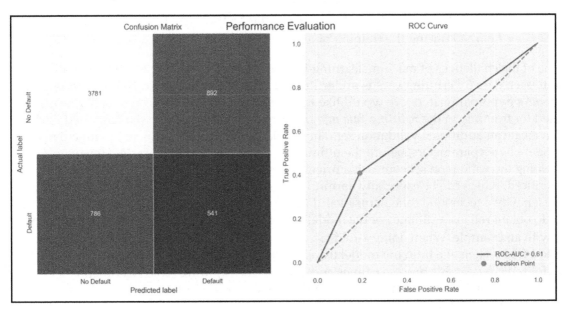

Including the outlier-capping transformation did not result in any significant changes in the performance of the entire Pipeline.

# Tuning hyperparameters using grid searches and cross-validation

Cross-validation, together with grid search, is commonly used to tune the hyperparameters of the model in order to achieve better performance. Below, we outline the differences between hyperparameters and parameters.

**Hyperparameters**:

- External characteristic of the model
- Not estimated based on data
- Can be considered the model's settings
- Set before the training phase
- Tuning them can result in better performance

**Parameters**:

- Internal characteristic of the model
- Estimated based on data, for example, the coefficients of linear regression
- Learned during the training phase

One of the challenges of machine learning is training models that are able to generalize well to unseen data (overfitting versus underfitting; a bias-variance trade-off). While tuning the model's hyperparameters, we would like to evaluate its performance on data that was not used for training. In the *Splitting data into training and test sets* recipe, we mentioned that we can create an additional validation set. The validation set is used explicitly to tune the model's hyperparameters, before the ultimate evaluation using the test set. However, creating the validation set comes at a price: data used for training (and possibly testing) is sacrificed, which can be especially harmful when dealing with small datasets. That is the reason why a technique called **cross-validation** became so popular. Cross-validation allows us to obtain reliable estimates of the model's generalization error. It is easiest to understand it with an example. When doing $k$-fold cross-validation, we randomly split the training data into $k$ folds. Then, we train the model using $k$-1 folds and evaluate the performance on the $k^{th}$ fold. We repeat this process $k$ times and average the resulting scores. A potential drawback of cross-validation is the computational cost, especially when paired together with a grid search for hyperparameter tuning.

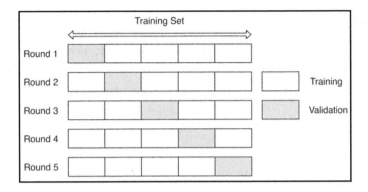

We already mentioned **grid search** as a technique used for tuning hyperparameters. The idea is to create a grid of all possible hyperparameter combinations and train the model using each one of them. Due to its exhaustive search, grid search guarantees to find the optimal parameter within the grid. The drawback is that the size of the grid grows exponentially with adding more parameters or more considered values. The number of required model fits and predictions increases significantly if we also use cross-validation!

As a solution to the problems encountered with grid search, we can also use the **random search** (also called **randomized grid search**). In this approach, we choose a random set of hyperparameters, train the model (also using cross-validation), return the scores, and repeat the entire process until we reach a predefined number of iterations or the computational time limit. Random search is preferred over grid search when dealing with a very large grid. That is because the former can explore a wider hyperparameter space and often find a hyperparameter set that performs very similarly to the optimal one (obtained from a full grid search) in a much shorter time. The only problematic question is: how many iterations are sufficient to find a good solution? However, there is no simple answer to that; most of the time, it is indicated by the available resources.

# Getting ready

For this recipe, we use the decision tree pipeline created in the *Implementing scikit-learn's pipelines* recipe, including the outlier removal from the *There's more...* section.

# How to do it...

Execute the following steps to run both grid search and randomized search on the decision tree pipeline we have created in the *Implementing scikit-learn's pipelines* recipe.

1. Import the libraries:

```
from sklearn.model_selection import (GridSearchCV, cross_val_score,
                                      RandomizedSearchCV,
                                      cross_validate,
                                      StratifiedKFold)
```

2. Define a cross-validation scheme:

```
k_fold = StratifiedKFold(5, shuffle=True, random_state=42)
```

3. Evaluate the Pipeline using cross-validation:

```
cross_val_score(tree_pipeline, X_train, y_train, cv=k_fold)
```

This results in an array containing the estimator's default score (accuracy) values:

```
array([0.73193085, 0.735625, 0.71458333, 0.72395833, 0.72619296])
```

4. Add extra metrics to the cross-validation:

```
cross_validate(tree_pipeline, X_train, y_train, cv=k_fold,
               scoring=['accuracy', 'precision', 'recall',
                        'roc_auc'])
```

This results in the array shown in the following array:

```
{'fit_time': array([1.51690102, 1.7562921 , 1.51606917, 1.33704495,
1.19413209]),
 'score_time': array([0.18366694, 0.16472888, 0.20106912,
0.13241482, 0.14992499]),
 'test_accuracy': array([0.73193085, 0.735625  , 0.71458333,
0.72395833, 0.72619296]),
 'test_precision': array([0.39515377, 0.40832595, 0.36200717,
0.37902484, 0.3825441 ]),
 'test_recall': array([0.3992467 , 0.43408663, 0.38041431,
0.38794727, 0.38831291]),
 'test_roc_auc': array([0.61259443, 0.6278503 , 0.59531745,
0.6034391 , 0.60667299])}
```

5. Define the parameter grid:

```
param_grid = {'classifier__criterion': ['entropy', 'gini'],
              'classifier__max_depth': range(3, 11),
              'classifier__min_samples_leaf': range(2, 11),
              'preprocessor__numerical__outliers__n_std': [3, 4]}
```

6. Run the grid search:

```
classifier_gs = GridSearchCV(tree_pipeline, param_grid,
                             scoring='recall',
                             cv=k_fold, n_jobs=-1, verbose=1)
classifier_gs.fit(X_train, y_train)

print(f'Best parameters: {classifier_gs.best_params_}')
print(f'Recall (Training set): {classifier_gs.best_score_:.4f}')
print(f'Recall (Test set): {metrics.recall_score(y_test,
classifier_gs.predict(X_test)):.4f}')
```

The best model is:

```
Best parameters: {'classifier__criterion': 'gini',
'classifier__max_depth': 10,
'classifier__min_samples_leaf': 3,
'preprocessor__numerical__outliers__n_std': 3}

Recall (Training set): 0.3905

Recall (Test set): 0.3828
```

7. Evaluate the performance of the grid search:

```
LABELS = ['No Default', 'Default']
tree_gs_perf = performance_evaluation_report(classifier_gs, X_test,
                                             y_test, labels=LABELS,
                                             show_plot=True)
```

Running the code results in the following plot:

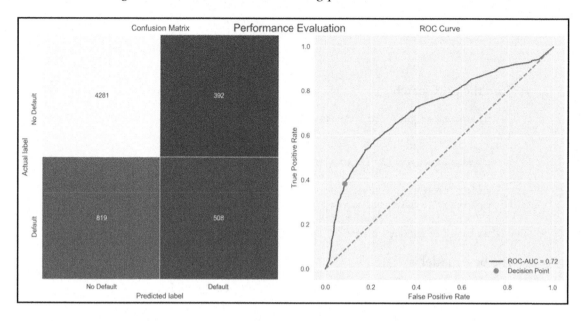

8. Run the randomized grid search:

```
classifier_rs = RandomizedSearchCV(tree_pipeline, param_grid,
                                    scoring='recall',
                                    cv=k_fold, n_jobs=-1, verbose=1,
                                    n_iter=100, random_state=42)

print(f'Best parameters: {classifier_rs.best_params_}')
print(f'Recall (Training set): {classifier_rs.best_score_:.4f}')
print(f'Recall (Test set): {metrics.recall_score(y_test,
classifier_rs.predict(X_test)):.4f}')
```

The best model is:

```
Best parameters: {'preprocessor__numerical__outliers__n_std': 4,
'classifier__min_samples_leaf': 5,
'classifier__max_depth': 10, 'classifier__criterion': 'gini'}

Recall (Training set): 0.3905

Recall (Test set): 0.3723
```

In the randomized search, we looked at 100 random sets of hyperparameters, which correspond to ~1/3 of all possibilities. The search did not find the best possible model indicated by the exhaustive grid search. Even though the recall on the training set is the same (up to 4 decimals), the same metric on the test set is worse.

# How it works...

In *Step 2*, we defined the cross-validation scheme. As there is no inherent order in the data, we used shuffling and specified the random state for reproducibility. Stratification ensured that each fold received a similar ratio of classes in the target variable.

In *Step 3*, we evaluated the Pipeline created in the *Implementing scikit-learn's pipelines* recipe using `cross_val_score`. We passed the estimator (the entire Pipeline), the training data, and the cross-validation scheme as arguments to the function. We could have also provided a number to the `cv` argument (the default is 5)—if it had been a classification problem, it would have automatically applied the stratified k-fold cross-validation. However, by providing a custom scheme, we also ensured that the random state was defined and that the results were reproducible.

In *Step 4*, we generally ran the same cross-validation, however, we used `cross_validate`. This function is more flexible in the way it allows us to use multiple evaluation criteria (we used accuracy, precision, and recall). Additionally, it records the time spent in both the training and inference steps.

In *Step 5*, we defined the parameter grid to be used for the grid search. An important point to remember here is the naming convention when working with Pipelines. Keys in the grid dictionary are built from the name of the step/model concatenated with the hyperparameter name using a double underscore. In this example, we searched a space created on top of three hyperparameters of the decision tree classifier:

- `criterion`: The metric used for determining a split, either entropy or Gini importance
- `max_depth`: The maximum depth of the tree
- `min_samples_leaf`: The minimum number of observations in a leaf; this prevents the creation of trees with very few observations in leaves

Additionally, we experimented with the outlier transformer, by using either three or four standard deviations from the mean to indicate whether an observation was an outlier. Please pay attention to the construction of the name, where we first indicated the step (`preprocessor`), before which Pipeline (`numerical`) and which step of it (`outliers`), and—lastly—the hyperparameter name.

 When only tuning the estimator (model), we should use hyperparameter names directly.

We decided to select the best performing decision tree model based on recall: the percentage of all defaults correctly identified by the model. This evaluation metric makes sense not only for a default detection problem but also possibly for fraud detection, as the target class in such a problem is often imbalanced. This can make optimization difficult unless there is a way to account for the class imbalance (more on this in the *Investigating different approaches to handling imbalanced data* recipe). In real life, there is often a different cost for a false negative (predicting no default when the user actually defaulted) and a false positive (predicting that a good customer defaults). To predict defaults, we decided that we could accept the cost of more false positives, in return for reducing the number of false negatives (missed defaults).

In *Step 6*, we created an instance of the Grid Search class. We provided the Pipeline and parameter grid, and specified recall as the scoring metric to be used for selecting the best model (different metrics could have been used here). We also used our custom CV scheme and indicated that we wanted to use all available cores to speed up the computations (`n_jobs=-1`). We then fitted the Grid Search object, just like any other estimator in `scikit-learn`. From the output, we saw that the grid contained 288 different combinations of the hyperparameters and, for each, we fitted five models (5-fold cross-validation).

 `GridSearchCV`'s default setting (`refit=True`) means that after the entire grid search, the best model has automatically been fitted once again, this time to the entire training set. We can then directly use that estimator (specified by the indicated criterion) for inference by running `classifier_gs.predict(X_test)`.

In *Step 8*, we created an instance of a randomized grid search. It is similar to a regular grid search, except that the maximum number of iterations was specified. In this case, we tested 100 different combinations from the parameter grid, which was roughly 1/3 of all combinations.

# There's more...

We can also create a grid containing multiple classifiers. To do so, we first import another classifier from `scikit-learn`, the logistic regression classifier:

```
from sklearn.linear_model import LogisticRegression
```

Again, we need to define the parameter grid. This time, it is a list containing multiple dictionaries—one dictionary per classifier. The hyperparameters for the decision tree are the same as before, and we do not explore the meaning of the logistic regression's hyperparameters. One extra thing worth mentioning is that, if we want to tune some other hyperparameters in the Pipeline, we need to specify them in each of the dictionaries in the list. That is why `'preprocessor__numerical__outliers__n_std'` is included twice:

```
param_grid = [{'classifier': [LogisticRegression()],
               'classifier__penalty': ['l1', 'l2'],
               'classifier__C': np.logspace(0, 3, 10, 2),
               'preprocessor__numerical__outliers__n_std': [3, 4]},
              {'classifier': [DecisionTreeClassifier(random_state=42)],
               'classifier__criterion': ['entropy', 'gini'],
               'classifier__max_depth': range(3,11),
               'classifier__min_samples_leaf': range(2, 11),
               'preprocessor__numerical__outliers__n_std': [3, 4]}]
```

The rest of the process is exactly the same:

```
classifier_gs_2 = GridSearchCV(tree_pipeline, param_grid, scoring='recall',
                               cv=k_fold, n_jobs=-1, verbose=1)

classifier_gs_2.fit(X_train, y_train)

print(f'Best parameters: {classifier_gs_2.best_params_}')
print(f'Recall (Training set): {classifier_gs_2.best_score_:.4f}')
print(f'Recall (Test set): {metrics.recall_score(y_test,
classifier_gs_2.predict(X_test)):.4f}')
```

Running the code results in the following output:

```
Best parameters: {'classifier': DecisionTreeClassifier(...),
'classifier__criterion': 'gini', 'classifier__max_depth': 10,
'classifier__min_samples_leaf': 3,
'preprocessor__numerical__outliers__n_std': 3}
Recall (Training set): 0.3905
Recall (Test set): 0.3828
```

The best model is the same as the one found by the initial grid search.

# See also

Additional resources are available here:

- Bergstra, J., & Bengio, Y. (2012). Random search for hyper-parameter optimization. *Journal of Machine Learning Research*, 13(Feb), 281-305.—http://www.jmlr.org/papers/volume13/bergstra12a/bergstra12a.pdf

# 9
# Advanced Machine Learning Models in Finance

In Chapter 8, *Identifying Credit Default with Machine Learning*, we introduced the workflow of solving a real-life problem using machine learning. We went over the entire pipeline, from cleaning the data to training a model (a classifier, in that case) and evaluating its performance. However, this is rarely the end of the project. We used a simple decision tree classifier, which most of the time can be used as a benchmark or **minimum viable product (MVP)**. We will now approach a few more advanced topics.

We start the chapter by presenting how to use more advanced classifiers (also based on decision trees). Some of them (such as XGBoost or LightGBM) are frequently used for winning machine learning competitions (such as those found on Kaggle). Additionally, we introduce the concept of stacking multiple machine learning models, to further improve prediction performance.

In the finance industry (but not exclusively), it is crucial to understand the logic behind the model's prediction. For example, a bank needs to have actual reasons for declining a credit request or can try to limit its losses by predicting which customers are likely to default on a loan. That is why we introduce a few methods to investigate feature importance, some of which are model-agnostic.

Another common real-life problem concerns dealing with imbalanced data, that is, when one class (such as default or fraud) is rarely observed in practice, which makes it difficult to train a model to accurately capture the minority class observations. We introduce a few common approaches to handling class imbalance and compare their performance on a credit card fraud dataset.

Lastly, we expand on hyperparameter tuning, explained in the previous chapter. There, we used either an exhaustive grid search or a randomized search, both of which are uninformed. This means that there is no underlying logic in selecting the next set of hyperparameters to investigate. This time, we introduce Bayesian optimization, whereby the past attempts are used to select the next set. This approach can significantly speed up the tuning phase of our projects.

In this chapter, we present the following recipes:

- Investigating advanced classifiers
- Using stacking for improved performance
- Investigating the feature importance
- Investigating different approaches to handling imbalanced data
- Bayesian hyperparameter optimization

# Investigating advanced classifiers

In Chapter 8, *Identifying Credit Default with Machine Learning*, we learned how to build an entire pipeline, with the goal of predicting customer default, that is, their inability to repay their debts. For the machine learning part, we used a decision tree classifier, which is one of the basic algorithms.

There are a few ways to possibly improve the performance of the model, some of them include:

- Gathering more observations
- Adding extra features—either by gathering additional data or through feature engineering
- Using more advanced models
- Tuning the hyperparameters

There is a common rule that data scientists spend 80% of their time on a project gathering and cleaning data while spending only 20% on the actual modeling. In line with this, adding more data might greatly improve a model's performance, especially when dealing with imbalanced classes in a classification problem. But finding new data is not always possible, or might simply be too complicated. Then, the other solution may be to use more advanced models or to tune the hyperparameters to squeeze out some extra performance.

In the default prediction model we worked on in Chapter 8, *Identifying Credit Default with Machine Learning*, it was not feasible to gather additional data. We can also assume we did our best to manually create new features. In this recipe, we focus on using more advanced classifiers (based on decision trees).

# Getting ready

In this recipe, we build on top of what we already established in the *Implementing scikit-learn's pipelines* recipe from the previous chapter, where we created the default prediction pipeline, from loading the data to training the classifier. We use the variant without the outlier removal procedure (introduced in the *There's more...* section of that recipe). In this recipe, we will be replacing the last step (the estimator) with different, more advanced ones. Additionally, we fit the decision tree pipeline to the data to obtain the baseline model for performance comparison. For your convenience, we reiterate all the required steps in the Notebook accompanying this chapter.

# How to do it...

Execute the following steps to train the advanced classifiers.

1. Import the libraries:

```
from sklearn.ensemble import (RandomForestClassifier,
                              GradientBoostingClassifier)
from xgboost.sklearn import XGBClassifier
from lightgbm import LGBMClassifier
```

2. Define and fit the Random Forest pipeline:

```
rf = RandomForestClassifier(random_state=42)
rf_pipeline = Pipeline(steps=[('preprocessor', preprocessor),
                              ('classifier', rf)
                              ])

rf_pipeline.fit(X_train, y_train)
rf_perf = performance_evaluation_report(rf_pipeline, X_test,
                                        y_test, labels=LABELS,
                                        show_plot=True,
                                        show_pr_curve=True)
```

The performance of the Random Forest can be summarized by the following plot:

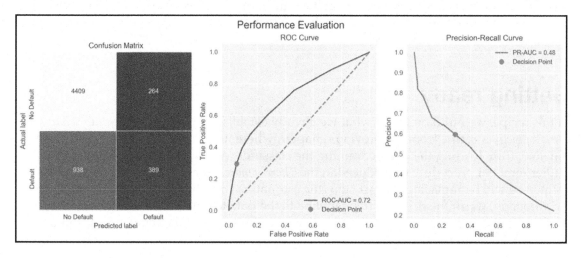

3. Define and fit the Gradient Boosted Trees pipeline:

```
gbt =  GradientBoostingClassifier(random_state=42)
gbt_pipeline = Pipeline(steps=[('preprocessor', preprocessor),
                               ('classifier', gbt)
                               ])

gbt_pipeline.fit(X_train, y_train)
gbt_perf = performance_evaluation_report(gbt_pipeline, X_test,
                                         y_test, labels=LABELS,
                                         show_plot=True,
                                         show_pr_curve=True)
```

The performance of the Gradient Boosted Trees can be summarized by the following plot:

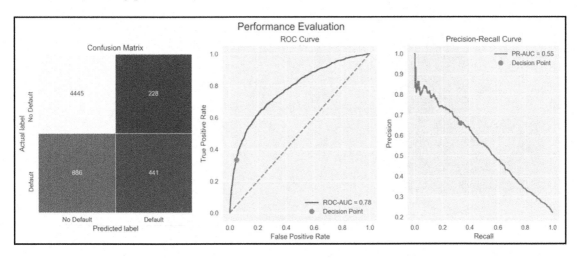

4. Define and fit an XGBoost pipeline:

```
xgb = XGBClassifier(random_state=42)
xgb_pipeline = Pipeline(steps=[('preprocessor', preprocessor),
                               ('classifier', xgb)
                               ])

xgb_pipeline.fit(X_train, y_train) xgb_perf =
performance_evaluation_report(xgb_pipeline, X_test,
                              y_test, labels=LABELS,
                              show_plot=True,
                              show_pr_curve=True)
```

The performance of the XGBoost can be summarized by the following plot:

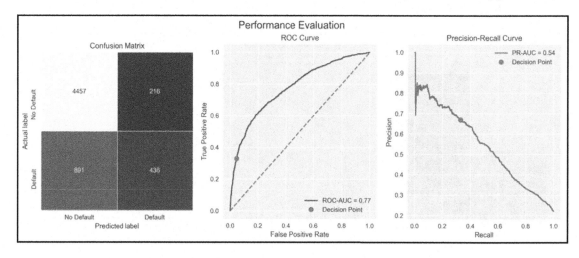

5. Define and fit the LightGBM pipeline:

```
lgbm = LGBMClassifier(random_state=42)
lgbm_pipeline = Pipeline(steps=[('preprocessor', preprocessor),
                                ('classifier', lgbm)
                                ])

lgbm_pipeline.fit(X_train, y_train)
lgbm_perf = performance_evaluation_report(lgbm_pipeline, X_test,
                                y_test, labels=LABELS,
                                show_plot=True,
                                show_pr_curve=True)
```

The performance of the LightGBM can be summarized by the following plot:

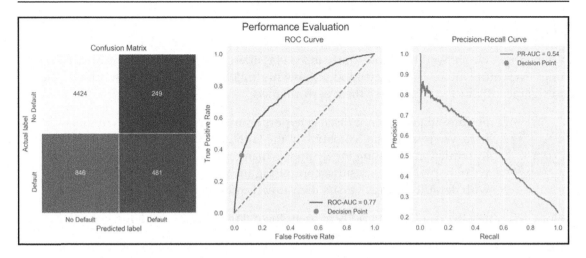

From the reports, it looks like the shape of the ROC Curve and the Precision-Recall Curve was very similar for all the models.

# How it works...

This recipe shows how easy it is to use different classifiers, as long as we want to use the default settings. In the first step, we imported the classifiers from their respective libraries.

In *Steps 2* to *5*, we created a special pipeline for each classifier. We combined the already established `ColumnTransformer` preprocessor with the corresponding classifier. Then, we fitted each pipeline to the training data and showed the performance evaluation report.

Classifiers such as XGBoost and LightGBM offer their own approaches to training models. First, you need to convert the `pandas` DataFrame to an acceptable data format (`xgb.DMatrix`, in the case of XGBoost, and `lightgbm.Dataset` for LightGBM), then use the `train` and `cv` functions to actually train the models. However, as `scikit-learn` is the leading library for training machine learning models in Python, both libraries provide `scikit-learn`-compatible APIs, which we used in this recipe. Using the native approaches can yield extra benefits, in terms of using features such as automatic handling of categorical variables by LightGBM, or using early stopping (stopping the training of the model when the validation score ceases to improve meaningfully), for both XGBoost and LightGBM.

# There's more...

In this recipe, we showed how to use advanced classifiers to achieve better results. To make things even more interesting, these models have multiple hyperparameters to tune, which can significantly increase/decrease their performance.

 For brevity, we do not discuss hyperparameter tuning of these models here. We refer to the Notebook in the GitHub repository for a short introduction to tuning these models using randomized grid search. Here, we only present the results, comparing the performance of the models with default settings versus their tuned counterparts.

Before describing the results, we briefly go over the details of the considered classifiers:

**Random Forest**: Random Forest is the first of the models we consider in this recipe, and it is an example of an ensemble of models. It trains a series of smaller models (decision trees) and uses them to create predictions. In the case of a regression problem, it takes the average value of all the underlying trees. For classification, it uses a majority vote. There are several aspects that make Random Forest stand out:

- It uses **bagging** (bootstrap aggregation)—each tree is trained on a subset of all available observations (drawn randomly with replacement, so—unless specified otherwise—the total number of observations used for each tree is the same as the total in the training set). Even though a single tree might have high variance with respect to a particular dataset (due to bagging), the forest will have lower variance overall, without increasing the bias. Additionally, this can also reduce the effect of any outliers in the data, as they will not be used in all of the trees.
- Additionally, each tree only considers a subset of all features to create the splits.
- Thanks to the two mechanisms above, the trees in the forest are not correlated with each other and are built independently.

Random Forest is a good algorithm to be familiar with, as it provides a good trade-off between complexity and performance. Often—without any tuning—we can get much better performance than when using simpler algorithms, such as decision trees or linear/logistic regression. That is because Random Forest has lower bias (due to its flexibility) and reduced variance (due to aggregating predictions of multiple models).

**Gradient Boosted Trees**: Gradient Boosted Trees is another type of ensemble model. The idea is to train many weak learners (decision trees/stumps) and combine them, to obtain a strong learner. In contrast to Random Forest, Gradient Boosted Trees is a sequential/iterative algorithm. We start with the first weak learner, and each of the subsequent learners tries to learn from the mistakes of the previous one. They do this by being fitted to the residuals (error terms) of the previous models.

The term *gradient* comes from the fact that the trees are built using **gradient descent**, which is an optimization algorithm. Without going into too much detail, it uses the gradient (slope) of the loss function to minimize the overall loss and achieve the best performance. The loss function represents the difference between actual values and the predicted ones. In practice, to perform the gradient descent procedure in the Gradient Boosted Trees, we add such a tree to the model that reduces the value of the loss function (that is, it follows the gradient).

> The reason why we create an ensemble of weak learners instead of strong learners is that in the case of the strong learners, the errors/mislabeled data points would most likely be the noise in the data, so the overall model would end up overfitting to the training data.

**Extreme Gradient Boosting (XGBoost)**: XGBoost is an implementation of Gradient Boosted Trees that incorporates a series of improvements resulting in superior performance (both in terms of evaluation metrics and time). Since being published, the algorithm was successfully used to win many data science competitions. In this recipe, we only present a high-level overview of the distinguishable features. For a more detailed overview, please refer to the original paper or documentation. The key concepts of XGBoost are:

- XGBoost combines a pre-sorted algorithm with a histogram-based algorithm to calculate the best splits. This tackles a significant inefficiency of Gradient Boosted Trees, that is, for creating a new branch, they consider the potential loss for all possible splits (especially important when considering hundreds, or thousands, of features).
- The algorithm uses the Newton-Raphson method for boosting (instead of gradient descent)—it provides a direct route to the minimum/minima of the loss function.
- XGBoost has an extra randomization parameter to reduce the correlation between the trees.

- XGBoost combines Lasso (L1) and Ridge (L2) regularization to prevent overfitting.
- It offers a different (more efficient) approach to tree pruning.
- XGBoost has a feature called monotonic constraints (that other models, such as LightGBM, lack)—the algorithm sacrifices some accuracy, and increases the training time to improve model interpretability.
- XGBoost does not take categorical features as input—we must use some kind of encoding.
- The algorithm can handle missing values in the data.

**LightGBM**: LightGBM, released by Microsoft, is another competition-winning implementation of Gradient Boosted Trees. Due to some improvements, LightGBM results in a similar performance to XGBoost, but with faster training time. Some key features include the following:

- The difference in speed is caused by the approach to growing trees. In general, algorithms (such as XGBoost) use a level-wise (horizontal) approach. LightBGM, on the other hand, grows trees leaf-wise (vertically). The leaf-wise algorithm chooses the leaf with the maximum reduction in the loss function. This function was later added to XGBoost as well (`grow_policy = 'lossguide'`).
- LightGBM uses a technique called **Gradient-based One-Side Sampling (GOSS)**, to filter out the data instances for finding the best split value. Intuitively, observations with small gradients are already well trained, while those with large gradients have more room for improvement. GOSS retains instances with large gradients and, additionally, samples randomly from observations with small gradients.
- LightGBM uses **Exclusive Feature Bundling (EFB)** to take advantage of sparse datasets and bundles together features that are mutually exclusive (they never have values of zero at the same time). This leads to a reduction in the complexity (dimensionality) of the feature space.
- The model can easily overfit for small datasets.

Having described the models, we present the results of the default and tuned variants of the classifiers:

| | accuracy | precision | recall | specificity | f1_score | cohens_kappa | roc_auc | pr_auc |
|---|---|---|---|---|---|---|---|---|
| decision_tree_baseline | 0.723333 | 0.381663 | 0.404672 | 0.813824 | 0.392831 | 0.213880 | 0.609528 | 0.458925 |
| random_forest | 0.799667 | 0.595712 | 0.293142 | 0.943505 | 0.392929 | 0.289244 | 0.717612 | 0.478045 |
| random_forest_rs | 0.810833 | 0.621212 | 0.370761 | 0.935801 | 0.464370 | 0.358276 | 0.750332 | 0.510628 |
| gradient_boosted_trees | 0.814333 | 0.659193 | 0.332329 | 0.951209 | 0.441884 | 0.344736 | 0.775486 | 0.547474 |
| gradient_boosted_trees_rs | 0.816500 | 0.651070 | 0.366993 | 0.944147 | 0.469398 | 0.368741 | 0.771308 | 0.538203 |
| xgboost | 0.815500 | 0.668712 | 0.328561 | 0.953777 | 0.440627 | 0.345202 | 0.774324 | 0.544790 |
| xgboost_rs | 0.800167 | 0.575472 | 0.367747 | 0.922962 | 0.448736 | 0.333852 | 0.745122 | 0.503757 |
| light_gbm | 0.817500 | 0.658904 | 0.362472 | 0.946715 | 0.467671 | 0.368547 | 0.773868 | 0.543574 |
| light_gbm_rs | 0.815667 | 0.651994 | 0.357197 | 0.945859 | 0.461538 | 0.361588 | 0.775173 | 0.551186 |

For the models calibrated using the randomized search (including `rs` in the name), we used 100 random sets of hyperparameters. As the considered problem deals with imbalanced data (the minority class is ~20%), we look at recall for performance evaluation. It seems that the basic decision tree achieved the best recall score on the test set, at the cost of much lower precision than the more advanced models. That is why the F1 Score (a harmonic mean of precision and recall) is the lowest for the decision tree. The results by no means indicate that the more advanced models are inferior; they might simply require more tuning or a different set of hyperparameters. For example, the advanced models had enforced the maximum depth of the tree, while the decision tree had no such limit (it reached the depth of 37!). The more advanced the model, the more effort it requires to "get it right".

It is also worth mentioning that the training of the LightGBM model was by far the fastest. However, this could also be dependent on the random draw of the hyperparameters, so, this alone should not be used as a deciding argument about the speed of the algorithms.

There are many different classifiers available to experiment with. Some of the possibilities include:

- Logistic regression—Often a good starting point to get the baseline
- **Support vector machines (SVMs)**
- Naive Bayes classifier
- ExtraTrees classifier (also known as **Extremely Randomized Trees (ERT)**)
- AdaBoost—The first boosting algorithm
- CatBoost—A recently released algorithm, developed with special attention to dealing with categorical features
- Artificial neural networks

# See also

Additional resources are available here:

- Breiman, L. (2001). Random Forests. *Machine Learning*, 45(1), 5-32.
- Chen, T., & Guestrin, C. (2016, August). Xgboost: A scalable tree boosting system. In *Proceedings of the 22nd international conference on knowledge discovery and data mining* (pp. 785-794). ACM.
- Freund, Y., & Schapire, R. E. (1996, July). Experiments with a new boosting algorithm. In *Icml* (Vol. 96, pp. 148-156).
- Freund, Y., & Schapire, R. E. (1997). A decision-theoretic generalization of on-line learning and an application to boosting. *Journal of computer and system sciences*, 55(1), 119-139.
- Ke, G., Meng, Q., Finley, T., Wang, T., Chen, W., Ma, W., ... & Liu, T. Y. (2017). Lightgbm: A highly efficient gradient boosting decision tree. In *Advances in Neural Information Processing Systems* (pp. 3146-3154).

# Using stacking for improved performance

In the previous recipe, *Investigating advanced classifiers*, we introduced a few examples of ensemble models. They used multiple decision trees (each model in a slightly different way) to build a better model. The goal was to reduce the overall bias and/or variance. Similarly, stacking is a technique that combines multiple estimators. It is a very powerful and popular technique, used in many competitions.

We provide a high-level overview of the characteristics:

- The models used as base learners do not need to be homogeneous—we can use a combination of different estimators. For example, we can use a decision tree, a k-nearest neighbors classifier, and logistic regression.
- Stacking uses a meta learner (model) to combine the predictions of the base learners and create the final prediction.
- Stacking can be extended to multiple levels.

The following screenshot represents a one-level stacked ensemble:

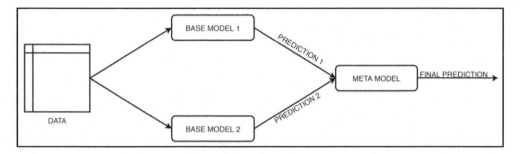

There are many variants of stacking. They differ in how they split data, and how they handle potential overfitting and data leakage. In this recipe, we use the credit card fraud dataset and follow the approach used in the `scikit-learn` library.

# How to do it...

Execute the following steps to create a stacked ensemble.

1.  Import the libraries:

    ```
    import pandas as pd
    from sklearn.model_selection import (train_test_split,
                                         StratifiedKFold)
    from sklearn import metrics
    from sklearn.preprocessing import StandardScaler

    from sklearn.naive_bayes import GaussianNB
    from sklearn.neighbors import KNeighborsClassifier
    from sklearn.tree import DecisionTreeClassifier
    from sklearn.ensemble import StackingClassifier
    from sklearn.linear_model import LogisticRegression
    ```

2.  Load and preprocess the data:

    ```
    RANDOM_STATE = 42
    k_fold = StratifiedKFold(5, shuffle=True, random_state=42)

    df = pd.read_csv('credit_card_fraud.csv')

    X = df.copy()
    y = X.pop('Class')

    X_train, X_test, y_train, y_test = train_test_split(X, y,
    ```

```
                                                    test_size=0.2,
                                                    stratify=y)

        scaler = StandardScaler()
        X_train = scaler.fit_transform(X_train)
        X_test = scaler.transform(X_test)
```

3. Define a list of classifiers to consider:

```
    clf_list = [('dec_tree', DecisionTreeClassifier()),
                ('log_reg', LogisticRegression()),
                ('knn', KNeighborsClassifier()),
                ('naive_bayes', GaussianNB())]
```

4. Iterate over the selected models, fit them to the data, and calculate recall using the test set:

```
    for model_tuple in clf_list:
        model = model_tuple[1]
        if 'random_state' in model.get_params().keys():
            model.set_params(random_state=RANDOM_STATE)
        model.fit(X_train, y_train)
        y_pred = model.predict(X_test)
        recall = metrics.recall_score(y_pred, y_test)
        print(f"{model_tuple[0]}'s recall score: {recall:.4f}")
```

Running the code results in the following output:

```
    dec_tree's recall score: 0.7526
    log_reg's recall score: 0.8312
    knn's recall score: 0.9186
    naive_bayes's recall score: 0.0588
```

5. Define and fit the stacking classifier:

```
    lr = LogisticRegression()
    stack_clf = StackingClassifier(clf_list,
                                   final_estimator=lr,
                                   cv=k_fold,
                                   n_jobs=-1)
    stack_clf.fit(X_train, y_train)
```

6. Create predictions, and evaluate the stacked ensemble:

```
y_pred = stacking_clf.predict(X_test)
recall = metrics.recall_score(y_pred, y_test)
print(f"The stacked ensemble's recall score: {recall:.4f}")
```

The stacked ensemble's recall score is 0.9398.

# How it works...

In *Step 1*, we imported the required libraries. The `StackingClassifier` is available in `scikit-learn` from version 0.22. In *Step 2*, we loaded the credit card fraud dataset into Python (for more details on the dataset, please refer to the *Investigating different approaches to handling imbalanced data* recipe), separated the target from the features, split the data into training and test sets, and—lastly—used scaling (`StandardScaler`) to obtain features with zero mean and unit variance. The transformation is not necessary for tree-based models, however, we later use different classifiers. For simplicity, we did not investigate different properties of the features, such as normality. Additionally, in this step, we also defined the 5-fold cross-validation scheme, for later use.

In *Step 3*, we defined a list of base learners for the stacked ensemble. We decided to use a few simple classifiers, such as decision tree, Naive Bayes, k-NN, and logistic regression (for brevity, we do not describe the properties of the selected classifiers here).

In *Step 4*, we iterated over the list of classifiers, fitted each model (with its default settings) to the training data, and calculated the recall score using the test set. Additionally, if the estimator had a `random_state` parameter, we set it to 42 for reproducibility. The goal of this step was to investigate the performance of the individual models, so that we could compare it to the stacked ensemble.

In *Step 5*, we defined the `StackingClassifier` by providing the list of classifiers as one of the arguments. Additionally, we specified that we wanted to use logistic regression as the meta learner, and then selected the cross-validation scheme. In the `scikit-learn` implementation of stacking, the base learners are fitted using the entire training set, and only the meta-estimator is trained using the cross-validated predictions of the base learners (it uses `cross_val_predict` for this).

 A possible shortcoming of this approach is that applying cross-validation only to the meta learner can result in overfitting, as a result of overfitting of the base learners. Different libraries (mentioned in the *There's more...* section) employ different approaches to cross-validation with stacked ensembles.

In the last step, we used the stacked ensemble for predictions and evaluated the recall score. With a value of 0.9398, the stacked model performed better than each of the individual base learners.

# There's more...

We presented a very basic example of stacking. Some possible extensions include:

- Adding more layers to the stacking ensemble
- Experimenting with different meta learners
- Using more diversified models (for example, SVMs)
- Tuning the hyperparameters of the base classifiers

The `ensemble` module of `scikit-learn` also contains a `VotingClassifier`, which can aggregate the predictions of multiple classifiers. `VotingClassifier` uses one of the two available voting schemes. The first one is `hard`, and it is simply the majority vote. The `soft` voting scheme uses the `argmax` of the sums of the predicted probabilities to predict the class label.

There are also other libraries providing stacking functionalities. Some of them are listed here:

- `vecstack`
- `mlxtend`
- `h2o`

These libraries also differ in the way they approach stacking. Please refer to the respective documentation for more details.

# See also

Additional resources are available here:

- Igor Ivanov, `Vecstack` (2016), GitHub
- Raschka, Sebastian (2018) `MLxtend: Providing machine learning and data science utilities and extensions to Python's scientific computing stack`. *J Open Source Softw* 3(24).
- Wolpert, D. H. (1992). Stacked generalization. *Neural networks*, 5(2), 241-259.

# Investigating the feature importance

We have already spent quite some time on creating the entire pipeline and tuning the models to achieve better performance. However, what is equally—or even more—important is the model's interpretability: so, not only giving an accurate prediction but also being able to explain the *why*. In the case of customer churn, an accurate model is important. However, knowing what are the actual predictors of the customers leaving might be helpful in improving the overall service and, potentially, making them stay longer. In a financial setting, banks often use machine learning in order to predict a customer's ability to repay credit. And, in many cases, they are obliged to justify their reasoning, in case they decline a credit application—why exactly this customer's application was not approved. In the case of very complicated models, this might be hard, or even impossible.

By knowing the features' importance, we can benefit in multiple ways, for example:

- By understanding the model's logic, we can theoretically verify its correctness (if a sensible feature is a good predictor), but also, try to improve the model by focusing only on the important variables.
- We can use the feature importances to only keep the $x$ most important features (contributing to a specified percentage of total importance), which can not only lead to better performance but also to shorter training time.
- In some real-life cases, it makes sense to sacrifice some accuracy (or any other performance metric) for the sake of interpretability.

It is also important to be aware that the more accurate (in terms of a specified performance metric) the model is, the more reliable the feature importances are. That is why we investigate the importance of the features after tuning the models.

In this recipe, we show how to calculate the feature importance on an example of a Random Forest classifier. However, most of the methods are model-agnostic. In other cases, there are often equivalent approaches (such as in the case of XGBoost and LightGBM). We briefly present three methods of calculating feature importance.

**Scikit-learn's feature importance**: The default feature importance used by Random Forest is the mean decrease in impurity. As we know, decision trees use a metric of impurity to create the best splits while growing. When training a decision tree, we can compute how much each feature contributes to decreasing the weighted impurity. To calculate the importance for the entire trees, the algorithm averages the decrease in impurity over all the trees.

Here are the advantages of this approach:

- Fast calculation
- Easy to retrieve

Here are the disadvantages of this approach:

- Biased—It tends to inflate the importance of continuous (numerical) features or high-cardinality categorical variables. This can sometimes lead to absurd cases, whereby an additional random variable (unrelated to the problem at hand) scores high in the feature importance ranking.
- Impurity-based importances are calculated on the basis of the training set and do not reflect the model's ability to generalize to unseen data.

**Permutation feature importance**: This approach directly measures feature importance. It observes how random re-shuffling of each predictor influences the model's performance. Additionally, the re-shuffling preserves the distribution of the variables.

The steps of the algorithm are:

1. Train the baseline model and record the score of interest (this can be done on either the training set or on the validation set, to gain some insight about the model's ability to generalize).
2. Randomly permute (re-shuffle) the values of one of the features, use the entire dataset (with one re-shuffled feature) to obtain predictions, and record the score. The feature importance is the difference between the baseline score and the one from the permuted dataset.
3. Repeat the second step for all features.

Here are the advantages of this approach:

- Model-agnostic
- Reasonably efficient—no need to retrain the model at every step

Here are the disadvantages of this approach:

- Computationally more expensive than the default feature importances
- Overestimates the importance of correlated predictors

**Drop column feature importance**: The idea behind this approach is very simple. We compare a model with all the features to a model with one of the features dropped for training and inference. We repeat this process for all the features.

Here are the advantages of this approach:

- Most accurate/reliable feature importance

Here are the disadvantages of this approach:

- Potentially high computation cost, caused by retraining the model for each variant of the dataset

# Getting ready

For this recipe, we use a fitted Random Forest pipeline (called `rf_pipeline`) from the *Investigating advanced classifiers* recipe.

# How to do it...

Execute the following steps to evaluate the feature importance of a Random Forest model.

1. Import the libraries:

```
from sklearn.base import clone
from eli5.sklearn import PermutationImportance
```

2. Extract the classifier and preprocessor from the pipeline:

```
rf_classifier = rf_pipeline.named_steps['classifier']
preprocessor = rf_pipeline.named_steps['preprocessor']
```

3. Recover feature names from the preprocessing transformer, and transform the training data:

```
feat_names = preprocessor.named_transformers_['categorical'] \
                        .named_steps['onehot'] \
                        .get_feature_names(
        input_features=cat_features
)
feat_names = np.r_[num_features, feat_names]

X_train_preprocessed = pd.DataFrame(
        preprocessor.transform(X_train),
        columns=feat_names
)
```

4. Extract the default feature importance and calculate the cumulative importance:

```
rf_feat_imp = pd.DataFrame(rf_classifier.feature_importances_,
                        index=feat_names,
                        columns=['mdi'])
rf_feat_imp = rf_feat_imp.sort_values('mdi', ascending=False)
rf_feat_imp['cumul_importance_mdi'] = np.cumsum(rf_feat_imp.mdi)
```

5. Define a function for plotting the top $x$ features in terms of their importance:

```
def plot_most_important_features(feat_imp, method='MDI',
                                n_features=10, bottom=False):
    if bottom:
        indicator = 'Bottom'
        feat_imp = feat_imp.sort_values(ascending=True)
    else:
        indicator = 'Top'
        feat_imp = feat_imp.sort_values(ascending=False)
    ax = feat_imp.head(n_features).plot.barh()
    ax.invert_yaxis()
    ax.set(title=('Feature importance - '
                f'{method} ({indicator} {n_features})'),
        xlabel='Importance',
        ylabel='Feature')
    return ax
```

We use the function as follows:

```
plot_most_important_features(rf_feat_imp.mdi,
                                method='MDI')
```

Running the code results in the following plot:

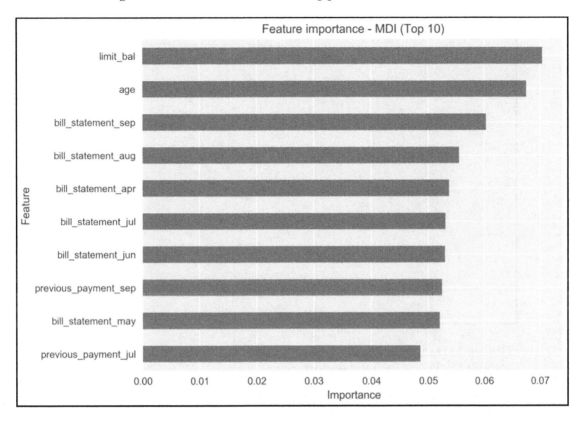

The list of most important features is dominated by numerical ones: `limit_balance`, `age`, and various bill statements from the previous months.

6. Plot the cumulative importance of the features:

```
x_values = range(len(feat_names))

fig, ax = plt.subplots()

ax.plot(x_values, rf_feat_imp.cumulative_importance_mdi, 'b-')
ax.hlines(y = 0.95, xmin=0, xmax=len(x_values),
          color = 'g', linestyles = 'dashed')
ax.set(title='Cumulative Importances',
       xlabel='Variable',
       ylabel='Importance')
```

Running the code results in the following plot:

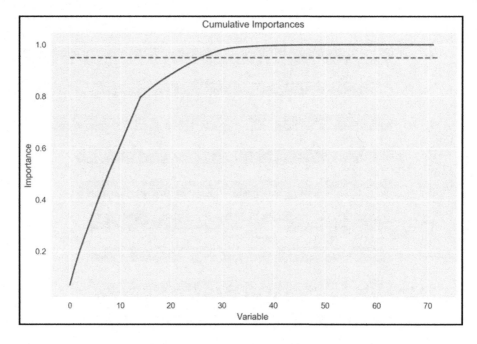

The top 10 features account for 56.61% of the total importance. The top 26 features account for 95% of the total importance.

7. Calculate and plot permutation importance:

```
perm = PermutationImportance(rf_classifier, n_iter = 25,
                             random_state=42)
perm.fit(X_train_preprocessed, y_train)
rf_feat_imp['permutation'] = perm.feature_importances_
```

Plot the results using the custom function:

```
plot_most_important_features(rf_feat_imp.permutation,
                             method='Permutation')
```

Running the code results in the following plot:

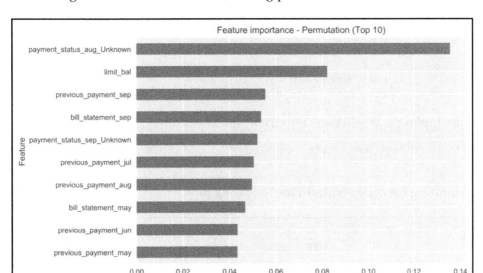

We can see that the set of the most important features re-shuffled, in comparison to the default ones. Limit balance is still very important; however, the most important now is `payment_status_aug_Unknown`, which is an undefined label (not assigned a clear meaning in the original paper) in the `payment_status_aug` categorical feature. A lot of `bill_statement` features were also replaced with `previous_payment` variables.

8. Define a function for calculating the drop column feature importance:

```
def drop_col_feat_imp(model, X_train, y_train, random_state = 42):
    model_clone = clone(model)
    model_clone.random_state = random_state
    model_clone.fit(X, y)
    benchmark_score = model_clone.score(X, y)
    importances = []
    for col in X.columns:
        model_clone = clone(model)
        model_clone.random_state = random_state
        model_clone.fit(X.drop(col, axis = 1), y)
        drop_col_score = model_clone.score(X.drop(col, axis = 1),
                                            y)
        importances.append(benchmark_score - drop_col_score)

    return importances
```

9. Calculate and plot the drop column feature importance:

```
rf_feat_imp['drop_column'] = drop_col_feat_imp(
    rf_classifier,
    X_train_preprocessed,
    y_train,
    random_state = 42
)
```

First, plot the top 10 most important features:

```
plot_most_important_features(rf_feat_imp.drop_column,
                                method='Drop column')
```

Running the code results in the following plot:

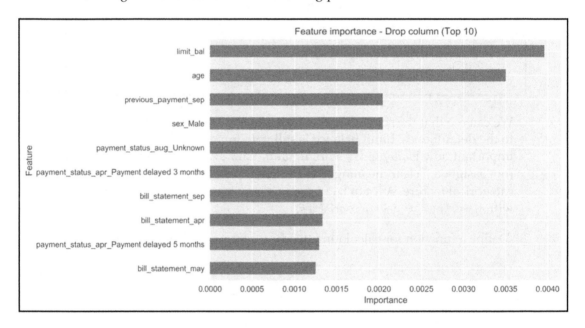

The `limit_balance` and `age` numerical features are, again, the most important. Another feature that appeared in the top selection is a Boolean variable, representing gender (male).

Then, plot the 10 least important features:

```
plot_most_important_features(rf_feat_imp.drop_column,
                                method='Drop column',
                                bottom=True)
```

Running the code results in the following plot:

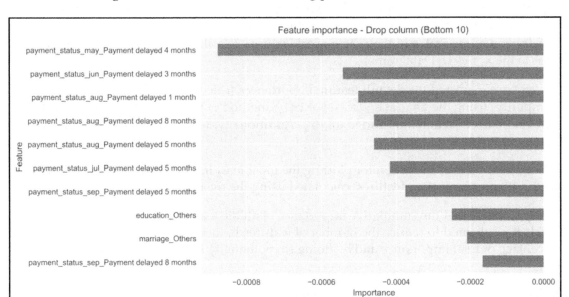

In the case of drop column feature importance, negative importance indicates that removing a given feature from the model actually improves the performance (in terms of the default score metric). We can use these results to remove features that have negative importance and thus potentially improve the model's performance and/or reduce the training time.

# How it works...

In the first step, we imported the required libraries. Then, we extracted the classifier and the `ColumnTransformer` preprocessor from the pipeline. In this recipe, we worked with a vanilla Random Forest classifier, without any hyperparameter tuning. The reason for this is that it gives a decent performance and, additionally, the computation time is much lower in comparison to the tuned one (with a higher number of estimators, and so on).

Please see the accompanying Notebook in the book's GitHub repository to see how to extract the best pipeline from a fitted grid search, or how to assign the best hyperparameter values manually.

In *Step 3*, we extracted the column names from the `ColumnTransformer` preprocessor. It is important to concatenate them (for that, we used `np.r_`) in the correct order, that is, in the same order in which they were specified in the `ColumnTransformer`. In our case, we first transformed numerical, and then categorical features. We also applied the preprocessing steps to the `X_train` DataFrame.

In *Step 4*, we extracted the default feature importances (calculated using the mean decrease in impurity) using the `feature_importances_` method of the fitted classifier. The values were normalized so that they added up to 1. Additionally, we calculated the cumulative feature importance.

In *Step 5*, we defined a function for plotting the most/least important features and plotted the top 10 most important features, calculated using the mean decrease in impurity (MDI).

In *Step 6*, we plotted the cumulative importance of all the features. Using this plot, we could decide if we wanted to reduce the number of features in the model to account for a certain percentage of total importance and by doing so, potentially decrease the model's training time.

In the next step, we calculated the permutation feature importance using `PermutationImportance` from the `eli5` library.

At the time of writing this chapter, there is a plan to add a permutation importance functionality to the `inspection` module of `scikit-learn`. However, as it is in the development version, we do not cover it here. Additionally, an implementation of permutation importance can be found in the `rfpimp` library.

We call `PermutationImportance` with the default value of the `cv` argument (`'prefit'`), which is the most useful one for calculating the importance of an existing estimator, and it does not require fitting the model again. Using `cv='prefit'`, we can pass either the training data or the validation set (in case we want to know the importances for generalization) to the `fit` method of `PermutationImportance`. We set the `n_iter` argument to 25, so the algorithm re-shuffles each feature 25 times, and the resulting score is the average of the re-shuffles. We can also set a different scoring metric than the default `score` method of the estimator (please see the documentation for more information).

In *Step 8*, we defined a function for calculating the drop column feature importance. We used the `clone` function of `scikit-learn` to create a copy of the model with the exact same specification as the baseline one. We then iteratively trained the model on a dataset without one feature, and compared the performance using the default `score` method. A possible extension would be to use a custom scoring metric instead (such as recall, or any other metric suitable for imbalanced data).

In the last step, we applied the drop column feature importance function and plotted the results, both the most and the least important features.

# There's more...

There are many other popular approaches to evaluating feature importance. We list some of them here:

- `treeinterpreter`—The idea is to use the underlying trees in Random Forest to explain how each feature contributes to the end result. This is an observation-level metric— the explanations are given for the selected rows, in the previous case, that would correspond to a specific customer of the bank.
- **Local Interpretable Model-agnostic Explanations (LIME)**—Another observation-level technique, used for explaining the predictions of any model in an interpretable and faithful manner. To obtain the explanations, LIME locally approximates the selected model with an interpretable one (such as linear models with regularization or decision trees). The interpretable models are trained on small perturbations (with additional noise) of the original observation.
- **Partial dependence plots (PDP)**—These plots isolate the changes in predictions only to come from a certain feature.
- **SHapley Additive exPlanations (SHAP)**—A framework for explaining predictions of any machine learning model (in other words, it is model-agnostic) using a combination of game theory and local explanations.

For more information on the presented model explanation methods, please see the additional resources in the *See also* section.

# See also

Additional resources are available here:

- ELI5's documentation: `https://eli5.readthedocs.io/en/latest/index.html`
- Lundberg, S. M., & Lee, S. I. (2017). A unified approach to interpreting model predictions. In *Advances in Neural Information Processing Systems* (pp. 4765-4774).
- Ribeiro, Marco Tulio, Singh, Sameer, and Guestrin, Carlos. "Why should I trust you?: Explaining the predictions of any classifier." Proceedings of the *22nd ACM SIGKDD International Conference on Knowledge Discovery and Data Mining.* ACM, 2016.
- Saabas, Ando. Interpreting random forests. `http://blog.datadive.net/interpreting-random-forests/`
- Strobl, C., Boulesteix, A. L., Kneib, T., Augustin, T., & Zeileis, A. (2008). Conditional variable importance for random forests. *BMC Bioinformatics*, 9(1), 307.
- The `treeinterpreter` library: `https://github.com/andosa/treeinterpreter`

# Investigating different approaches to handling imbalanced data

A very common issue when working with classification tasks is that of class imbalance: when one class is highly outnumbered in comparison to the second one (this can also be extended to multi-class). In general, we are talking about imbalance when the ratio of the two classes is not 1:1. In some cases, a delicate imbalance is not that big of a problem, but there are industries/problems in which we can encounter ratios of 100:1, 1000:1, or even worse.

In this recipe, we show an example of a credit card fraud problem, where the fraudulent class is only 0.17% of the entire sample. In such cases, gathering more data (especially of the fraudulent class) might simply not be feasible, and we need to resort to some techniques that can help us in understanding and avoiding the **accuracy paradox**.

 Accuracy paradox refers to a case in which inspecting accuracy as the evaluation metric creates the impression of having a very good classifier (a score of 90%, or even 99.9%), while in reality, it simply reflects the distribution of the classes. That is why, in cases of class imbalance, it is highly advisable to use evaluation metrics that account for that, such as precision/recall, F1 Score, or Cohen's kappa.

In this recipe, we consider a small selection of methods commonly used in tackling classification challenges with imbalanced classes. For a more detailed description of the techniques, please refer to the *There's more...* section.

# How to do it...

Execute the following steps to investigate different approaches to handling class imbalance.

1. Import the libraries:

```
import pandas as pd
import seaborn as sns
from imblearn.over_sampling import RandomOverSampler, SMOTE, ADASYN
from imblearn.under_sampling import RandomUnderSampler
from sklearn.model_selection import train_test_split
from sklearn.ensemble import RandomForestClassifier
from collections import Counter
from chapter_9_utils import performance_evaluation_report
```

2. Load and prepare the data:

```
df = pd.read_csv('credit_card_fraud.csv')

X = df.copy()
y = X.pop('Class')

RANDOM_STATE = 42

X_train, X_test, y_train, y_test = train_test_split(X, y,
                                                    test_size=0.2,
                                                    stratify=y)
```

3. Train the baseline model:

```
rf = RandomForestClassifier(random_state=RANDOM_STATE)
rf.fit(X_train, y_train)
```

We do not show the code here, but after fitting each model, we save the performance evaluation metrics (from the test set), calculated using the `performance_evaluation_report` function. We then use these metrics to create a summary table in the *There's more...* section.

4.  Undersample the data, and train a Random Forest classifier:

```
rus = RandomUnderSampler(random_state=RANDOM_STATE)
X_rus, y_rus = rus.fit_resample(X_train, y_train)
rf.fit(X_rus, y_rus)
```

After the undersampling, the new class proportions (in the training set) are:

```
{0: 394, 1: 394}
```

5.  Oversample the data, and train a Random Forest classifier:

```
ros = RandomOverSampler(random_state=RANDOM_STATE)
X_ros, y_ros = ros.fit_resample(X_train, y_train)
rf.fit(X_ros, y_ros)
```

After the oversampling, the new class proportions (in the training set) are:

```
{0: 227451, 1: 227451}
```

6.  Oversample using SMOTE:

```
X_smote, y_smote =
SMOTE(random_state=RANDOM_STATE).fit_resample(X_train, y_train)
rf.fit(X_smote, y_smote)
```

After using SMOTE, the new class proportions (in the training set) are:

```
{0: 227451, 1: 227451}
```

7.  Oversample using ADASYN:

```
X_adasyn, y_adasyn =
ADASYN(random_state=RANDOM_STATE).fit_resample(X_train, y_train)
rf.fit(X_adasyn, y_adasyn)
```

After using ADASYN, the new class proportions (in the training set) are:

```
{0: 227451, 1: 227346}
```

8. Use sample weights in the Random Forest classifier:

```
rf_cw = RandomForestClassifier(random_state=RANDOM_STATE,
                               class_weight='balanced')
rf_cw.fit(X_train, y_train)
```

We present the comparison of the models' performance in the *There's more...* section.

# How it works...

In *Step 1*, we loaded the required libraries. Then, we loaded the CSV data, downloaded from Kaggle (available at `https://www.kaggle.com/mlg-ulb/creditcardfraud`) into Python, using the `pd.read_csv` function.

The dataset we selected for this exercise contains information about transactions made by credit cards in September 2013 by European cardholders. The transactions happened within a period of 2 days. All the numerical variables with a name starting with `V` are the principal components, obtained by running the PCA on the original dataset (original features are not included, due to confidentiality). The only two features with clear interpretation are `Time` (seconds elapsed between each transaction and the first transaction in the dataset) and `Amount` (transaction amount).

We additionally separated the target from the features using the `pop` method, created an 80-20 train-test split with stratification (this is especially important when dealing with imbalanced data), and—lastly—verified that the positive (fraudulent) observations were indeed only 0.17% of the entire sample.

In this recipe, we only focused on working with imbalanced data. That is why we did not cover any EDA, feature engineering, dropping unnecessary features, and so on. Also, all the features were numerical, which reduced the complexity of preprocessing (no categorical encoding).

In *Step 3*, we fitted a vanilla Random Forest model, which we will use as a point of reference when comparing the outcomes of the different approaches (for a table summarizing the performance, please refer to the *There's more...* section).

In *Step 4*, we used the `RandomUnderSampler` class from the `imblearn` library to randomly undersample the majority class in order to match the size of the minority sample. Classes from `imblearn` follow the `scikit-learn`'s API style; that is why we had to first define the class with the arguments (we only set the `random_state`). Then we applied the `fit_resample` method to obtain the undersampled data. We reused the Random Forest object to train the model on the undersampled data and stored the results for later comparison.

*Step 5* is analogical to *Step 4*, with the difference of using the `RandomOverSampler` to randomly oversample the minority class in order to match the size of the majority class.

In *Step 6* and *Step 7*, we applied the SMOTE and ADASYN variants of oversampling. As the `imblearn` API makes it very easy to apply different sampling methods, we do not go deeper into the description of the process. It is interesting to notice that using SMOTE resulted in a 1:1 ratio between classes, while ADASYN actually returned more observations from the minority (fraudulent) class than the size of the majority class.

In all the mentioned resampling methods, we can actually specify the desired ratio between classes by passing a float to the `sampling_strategy` argument. The number represents the desired ratio of the number of observations in the minority class over the number of observations in the majority class.

In the last step, we used the `class_weight` hyperparameter of the `RandomForestClassifier`. By passing `'balanced'`, the algorithm automatically assigns weights inversely proportional to class frequencies in the training data.

There are different possible approaches to using the `class_weight` hyperparameter. We can pass `'balanced_subsample'`, which results in a similar weights assignment as in `'balanced'`, however, the weights are computed based on the bootstrap sample for every tree. We can additionally pass a dictionary containing the desired weights. One way of determining the weights can be the `compute_class_weight` function from `sklearn.utils.class_weight`.

# There's more...

We begin with a description of the techniques used in this recipe:

**Undersampling**: A very simple method to deal with class imbalance is to undersample the majority class—draw random samples from the majority class to obtain a 1:1, or any other desired ratio between the target classes. Using this method can lead to some issues, such as lower accuracy of the model trained on undersampled data (due to information loss, caused by discarding the majority of the training set). Another possible implication is the increased number of false positives, as the distribution of the training and test sets is not the same after the resampling. This results in a biased classifier.

**Oversampling**: In this approach, we sample multiple times with replacement from the minority class, until the desired ratio is achieved. It often outperforms undersampling, as there is no information loss due to discarding data. However, it comes with the danger of overfitting, caused by replication of observations from the minority class.

**Synthetic Minority Over-sampling Technique (SMOTE)**: SMOTE is a more advanced oversampling algorithm that creates new, synthetic observations from the minority class. This way, it overcomes the previously mentioned problem of overfitting.

To create the synthetic samples, the algorithm looks at the observations from the minority class, identifies their $k$-nearest neighbors (using the k-NN algorithm with a distance metric such as Euclidean), and creates new, synthetic observations on the lines connecting (interpolating) the observation to the nearest neighbors.

There are many variants of the algorithm available in the `imblearn` library, such as **Synthetic Minority Over-sampling Technique for Nominal and Continuous (SMOTE-NC)**, suitable for a dataset containing both numerical and categorical features.

Aside from reducing the problem of overfitting, SMOTE causes no loss of information, as there is no discarding of majority class observations. However, SMOTE can accidentally introduce more noise to the data (and cause overlapping of classes). This is because it does not take into account the observations from the majority class while creating the new synthetic observations. Also, the algorithm is not very effective for high-dimensional data (due to the curse of dimensionality).

**Adaptive Synthetic Sampling (ADASYN)**: This algorithm is a modification of the SMOTE algorithm. It differs in the way it selects the number of synthetic observations to create, and how to do it. In ADASYN, the number of observations to be created for a certain point is determined by a density distribution (instead of a uniform weight for all points, as in SMOTE). This is how ADASYN's adaptive nature enables it to generate more samples for observations that come from hard-to-learn neighborhoods. There are two additional elements worth mentioning:

- The synthetic points are not limited to linear interpolation between two points, but can also lie on a plane created by three or more observations.
- After creating the synthetic observations, the algorithm adds a small random noise to increase the variance (that is, make them more scattered), thus making the samples more realistic.

Potential drawbacks of ADASYN include a possible decrease in precision of the algorithm, caused by the adaptability and struggling with a case when minority observations are sparsely distributed (a neighborhood can contain only 1, or very few points).

**Class weights in ML models**: A lot of machine learning models (especially the ones in `scikit-learn`, but not exclusively those) have a hyperparameter called `class_weights`. We can use it to pass specific weights for the classes, thus putting more weight on the minority class. In the background, the class weights are incorporated into calculating the loss function, which in practice means that misclassifying minority observations increases the value of the loss function significantly more than in the case of the observations from the majority class.

Additionally, the `imblearn` library also features some modified versions of popular classifiers. We present an example of the modified Random Forest—the `BalancedRandomForestClassifier`. The API is virtually the same as in the `scikit-learn` implementation (including the tunable hyperparameters). The difference is that in the balanced Random Forest the algorithm randomly undersamples each bootstrapped sample to balance the classes.

Execute the following steps to estimate the balanced Random Forest classifier.

1.  Import the library:

    ```
    from imblearn.ensemble import BalancedRandomForestClassifier
    ```

2.  Train the balanced Random Forest classifiers:

    ```
    balanced_rf = BalancedRandomForestClassifier(
        random_state=RANDOM_STATE
    )

    balanced_rf.fit(X_train, y_train)

    balanced_rf_cw = BalancedRandomForestClassifier(
        random_state=RANDOM_STATE,
        class_weight='balanced'
    )

    balanced_rf_cw.fit(X_train, y_train)
    ```

3.  Group the performance results into a DataFrame:

    ```
    performance_results = {'random_forest': rf_perf,
                           'undersampled rf': rf_rus_perf,
                           'oversampled_rf': rf_ros_perf,
                           'smote': rf_smote_perf,
                           'adasyn': rf_adasyn_perf,
                           'random_forest_cw': rf_cw_perf,
                           'balanced_random_forest': balanced_rf_perf,
                           'balanced_random_forest_cw':
                           balanced_rf_cw_perf}
                           pd.DataFrame(performance_results).T
    ```

Running the code results in a table, summarizing the performance of the models (evaluated on the test set):

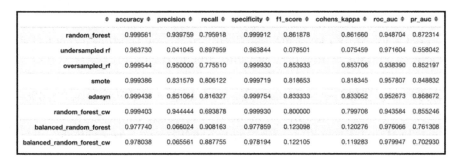

| | accuracy | precision | recall | specificity | f1_score | cohens_kappa | roc_auc | pr_auc |
|---|---|---|---|---|---|---|---|---|
| random_forest | 0.999561 | 0.939759 | 0.795918 | 0.999912 | 0.861878 | 0.861660 | 0.948704 | 0.872314 |
| undersampled rf | 0.963730 | 0.041045 | 0.897959 | 0.963844 | 0.078501 | 0.075459 | 0.971604 | 0.558042 |
| oversampled_rf | 0.999544 | 0.950000 | 0.775510 | 0.999930 | 0.853933 | 0.853706 | 0.938390 | 0.852197 |
| smote | 0.999386 | 0.831579 | 0.806122 | 0.999719 | 0.818653 | 0.818345 | 0.957807 | 0.848832 |
| adasyn | 0.999438 | 0.851064 | 0.816327 | 0.999754 | 0.833333 | 0.833052 | 0.952673 | 0.868672 |
| random_forest_cw | 0.999403 | 0.944444 | 0.693878 | 0.999930 | 0.800000 | 0.799708 | 0.943584 | 0.855246 |
| balanced_random_forest | 0.977740 | 0.066024 | 0.908163 | 0.977859 | 0.123098 | 0.120276 | 0.976066 | 0.761308 |
| balanced_random_forest_cw | 0.978038 | 0.065561 | 0.887755 | 0.978194 | 0.122105 | 0.119283 | 0.979947 | 0.702930 |

As we are dealing with a highly imbalanced problem (the positive class accounts for 0.17% of all the observations), we compare the performance of the models using recall—the number of correctly predicted frauds over all the frauds in the test sample. The best performing model is the balanced Random Forest classifier, while the worst one is the Random Forest with class weights. It is also important to mention that no hyperparameter tuning was performed, which could potentially improve the performance.

Also, we can observe the case of the accuracy paradox, where many models have an accuracy of ~99.99%, but they still fail to detect fraudulent cases, which are the most important ones.

Some general notes on tackling problems with imbalanced classes:

- Do not apply under-/oversampling on the test set.
- For evaluating problems with imbalanced data, use metrics that account for this, such as precision/recall/F1 score/Cohen's kappa/PR-AUC.
- Use SMOTE-NC (a modified version of SMOTE) when dealing with a dataset containing categorical features, as the original SMOTE can create illogical values for one-hot encoded variables.
- Use stratification when creating folds for cross-validation.
- Introduce under-/oversampling during cross-validation, not before. Doing so before leads to overestimating the model's performance!
- Experiment with selecting a different probability threshold than the default 50% to potentially tune the performance.

# See also

Additional resources are available here:

- Chawla, N. V., Bowyer, K. W., Hall, L. O., and Kegelmeyer, W. P. (2002). SMOTE: synthetic minority oversampling technique. *Journal of artificial intelligence research*, 16: 321–357.
- Chen, Chao, Andy Liaw, and Leo Breiman. "Using random forest to learn imbalanced data." University of California, Berkeley 110 (2004): 1-12.
- Wilson, D. L. (1972). Asymptotic properties of nearest neighbor rules using edited data. *IEEE Transactions on Systems, Man, and Cybernetics*, (3): 408–421.
- Pozzolo, et al., Calibrating Probability with Undersampling for Unbalanced Classification (2015), *2015 IEEE Symposium Series on Computational Intelligence*.

# Bayesian hyperparameter optimization

In the *Tuning hyperparameters using grid search and cross-validation* recipe in `Chapter 8`, *Identifying Credit Default with Machine Learning*, we described how to use grid search and randomized search to find the (possibly) best set of hyperparameters for our model. In this recipe, we introduce another approach to finding the optimal set of hyperparameters, this time based on the Bayesian methodology. The main motivation for the Bayesian approach is that both grid search and randomized search make uninformed choices, either through exhaustive search over all combinations or through a random sample. This way, they spend a lot of time evaluating bad (far from optimal) combinations, thus basically wasting time. That is why the Bayesian approach makes informed choices of the next set of hyperparameters to evaluate, this way reducing the time spent on finding the optimal set. One could say that the Bayesian methods try to limit the time spent evaluating the objective function by spending more time on selecting the hyperparameters to optimize, which in the end is computationally cheaper.

A formalization of the Bayesian approach is the **Sequential Model-Based Optimization** (**SMBO**), often combined with the **Tree-structured Parzen Estimator** (**TPE**) algorithm. In this recipe, we give a high-level overview of the methodology and refer to a list of papers (in the *See also* section) for a more in-depth explanation.

The true objective function is the (cross-) validation error of a trained machine learning model. It is often computationally very expensive, and can take hours (or even days) to calculate. That is why in SMBO we create a surrogate model (also called the **response surface**), which is a probability model of the objective function built on its past evaluations. It maps the input values (hyperparameters) to a probability of a score on the true objective function. The surrogate is easier/cheaper to optimize than the actual objective function. In the approach we follow (the one used by the `hyperopt` library), the surrogate model is created using TPEs, however, other possibilities include Gaussian processes or Random Forest regression.

The algorithm then selects the next set of hyperparameters to evaluate by applying a criterion (such as **Expected Improvement**) to the surrogate model. The model uses the history of past evaluations to make the best possible selection for the next iteration. Values close to the ones that performed well in the past are more likely to improve the overall performance than those that historically performed poorly.

The simplified steps of the Bayesian optimization are:

1. Create the surrogate model of the true objective function.
2. Find a set of hyperparameters that performs best on the surrogate.
3. Use that set to evaluate the true objective function.

4. Update the surrogate, using the results from evaluating the true objective.
5. Repeat *Steps 2-4*, until reaching the stop criterion (the specified maximum number of iterations or time).

From the steps, we see that the longer the algorithm runs, the closer the surrogate function approximates the true objective function. That is because with each iteration, it is updated based on the evaluation of the true objective function, and thus with each run, it is a bit "less wrong".

Here are the advantages of the Bayesian approach to hyperparameter tuning:

- Finds a set of hyperparameters that optimizes the objective function
- Decreases the time spent on searching for the optimal set of parameters, especially when the number of parameters is high and evaluating the true objective is computationally expensive

And here are possible shortcomings:

- Impossible to run the optimization in parallel, as the algorithm selects the set of hyperparameters based on past results.
- Choosing a proper distribution/scale for the hyperparameters can be tricky.
- Exploration versus exploitation bias—When the algorithm finds a local minimum, it might concentrate on hyperparameter values around the local minimum, instead of exploring potential new values located far away in the search space. Randomized search is not troubled by this issue, as it does not concentrate on any values.
- The values of hyperparameters are selected independently. For example, in Gradient Boosted Trees, it is recommended to jointly consider the learning rate and the number of estimators, in order to avoid overfitting and reduce computation time. TPE would not be able to discover this relationship. In cases where we know about such a relation, we can overcome this problem by using different choices to define the search space.

In this recipe, we use the Bayesian hyperparameter optimization to tune a LightGBM model. We chose this model as it provides a very good balance between performance and training time.

# How to do it...

Execute the following steps to run Bayesian hyperparameter optimization of a LightGBM model.

1. Import the libraries:

```
import pandas as pd
from sklearn.model_selection import train_test_split
from hyperopt import hp, fmin, tpe, STATUS_OK, Trials
from sklearn.model_selection import (cross_val_score,
                                     StratifiedKFold)
from lightgbm import LGBMClassifier
from chapter_9_utils import performance_evaluation_report
```

2. Define parameters for later use:

```
N_FOLDS = 5
MAX_EVALS = 200
```

3. Load and prepare the data:

```
df = pd.read_csv('credit_card_fraud.csv')

X = df.copy()
y = X.pop('Class')

X_train, X_test, y_train, y_test = train_test_split(X, y,
                                                    test_size=0.2,
                                                    stratify=y)
```

4. Define the objective function:

```
def objective(params, n_folds = N_FOLDS, random_state=42):
    model = LGBMClassifier(**params)
    model.set_params(random_state=random_state)
    k_fold = StratifiedKFold(n_folds, shuffle=True,
                             random_state=random_state)
    metrics = cross_val_score(model, X_train, y_train,
                              cv=k_fold, scoring='recall')
    loss = -1 * metrics.mean()
    return {'loss': loss, 'params': params, 'status': STATUS_OK}
```

5. Define the search space:

```
lgbm_param_grid = {
    'boosting_type': hp.choice('boosting_type', ['gbdt', 'dart',
                                                  'goss']),
    'max_depth': hp.choice('max_depth', [-1, 2, 3, 4, 5, 6, 7, 8,
                                          9, 10]),
    'n_estimators': hp.choice('n_estimators', [10, 50, 100,
                                               300, 750, 1000]),
    'is_unbalance': hp.choice('is_unbalance', [True, False]),
    'colsample_bytree': hp.uniform('colsample_bytree', 0.3, 1),
    'learning_rate': hp.uniform ('learning_rate', 0.05, 0.3),
}
```

6. Run the Bayesian optimization:

```
trials = Trials()
best_set = fmin(fn= objective,
                space= lgbm_param_grid,
                algo= tpe.suggest,
                max_evals = MAX_EVALS,
                trials= trials)
```

Inspecting the `best_set` prints the following summary:

```
{'boosting_type': 1,
 'colsample_bytree': 0.8861225641638096,
 'is_unbalance': 0,
 'learning_rate': 0.193440600772047,
 'max_depth': 6,
 'n_estimators': 0}
```

The hyperparameters defined using `hp.choice` in the grid are presented as encoded integers. In the following steps, we show how to recover the original values.

7. Define the dictionaries for mapping the results to hyperparameter values:

```
boosting_type = {0: 'gbdt', 1: 'dart', 2: 'goss'}
max_depth = {0: -1, 1: 2, 2: 3, 3: 4, 4: 5, 5: 6,
             6: 7, 7: 8, 8: 9, 9: 10}
n_estimators = {0: 10, 1: 50, 2: 100, 3: 300, 4: 750, 5: 1000}
is_unbalance = {0: True, 1: False}
```

8. Fit a model using the best hyperparameters:

```
best_lgbm = LGBMClassifier(
    boosting_type = boosting_type[best_set['boosting_type']],
    max_depth = max_depth[best_set['max_depth']],
    n_estimators = n_estimators[best_set['n_estimators']],
    is_unbalance = is_unbalance[best_set['is_unbalance']],
    colsample_bytree = best_set['colsample_bytree'],
    learning_rate = best_set['learning_rate']
)
best_lgbm.fit(X_train, y_train)
```

9. Evaluate the performance of the best model on the test set:

```
_ = performance_evaluation_report(best_lgbm, X_test, y_test,
                                  show_plot=True,
                                  show_pr_curve=True)
```

Running the code generates a plot the following plot:

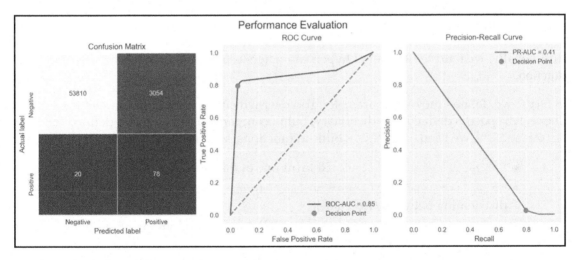

The plot contains some of the performance evaluation metrics obtained from the custom `performance_evaluation_report` function.

# How it works...

In *Step 2*, we defined a set of parameters that we use in this recipe (number of folds for cross-validation, the maximum number of iterations in the optimization procedure). Then, we imported the dataset and created the training and test sets. We used the same dataset as in the previous recipe, so please refer to it for a description.

In *Step 4*, we defined the true objective function (the one for which the Bayesian optimization will create a surrogate). The function takes the set of hyperparameters as inputs and uses stratified 5-fold cross-validation to calculate the loss value to be minimized. In the case of fraud detection, we want to detect as much fraud as possible, even if it means creating more false positives. That is why, in this case, we selected recall as the metric we optimized for. As the optimizer will minimize the function, we multiplied it by -1 to create a maximization problem. The function must return either a single value (the loss) or a dictionary, with at least two key-value pairs:

- `'loss`': The value of the true objective function.
- `'status`': An indicator that the loss value was calculated correctly. It can be either `STATUS_OK` or `STATUS_FAIL`.

Additionally, we returned the set of hyperparameters used for evaluating the objective function.

In *Step 5*, we defined the hyperparameter grid over which we wanted to conduct the search. The search space is defined as a dictionary, but in comparison to the spaces defined for `GridSearchCV`, we used `hyperopt`'s built-in functions, such as the following:

- `hp.choice(label, list)`: Returns one of the indicated options
- `hp.uniform(label, lower_value, upper_value)`: The uniform distribution between two values
- `hp.randint(label, upper_value)`: Returns a random integer in the range `[0, upper_value)`
- `hp.normal(label, mu, sigma)`: Returns a normally distributed value with mean `mu` and standard deviation `sigma`

Bear in mind that in this setup we need to define the names (`label`) of the hyperparameters twice.

We can make use of `hp.choice` to define conditional nested spaces, where the values of some hyperparameters depend on others. A possible use case is defining a space that considers multiple classifiers and their respective hyperparameters.

In *Step 6*, we ran the Bayesian optimization. First, we defined the `Trials` object, which is used for storing the history of the search. We can even use it to resume a search or expand an already finished one, that is, increase the number of iterations using the already stored history. Second, we ran the optimization by passing the objective function, the search space, the algorithm (for more details on tuning the TPE algorithm, please refer to `hyperopt`'s documentation), the maximum number of iterations, and the trials for storing the history.

In *Step 7*, we created multiple dictionaries, mapping integer values to the values from the search space we defined in *Step 5*. We did this because for hyperparameters defined using the `hp.choice` function, the results of the optimization are returned as integer-encoded values (encoded in order defined in the search space). Then, we used these dictionaries to train a LightGBM classifier with the best set of hyperparameters on the entire training set.

In the last step, we evaluated the results of the model using the custom `performance_evaluation_report` function.

# There's more...

We can also inspect the contents of the trials object to see how the algorithm worked.

1. Import the libraries:

```
from pandas.io.json import json_normalize
from hyperopt.pyll.stochastic import sample
```

2. Extract the information from `trials.results`:

```
results_df = pd.DataFrame(trials.results)
params_df = json_normalize(results_df['params'])

results_df = pd.concat([results_df.drop('params', axis=1),
                        params_df],
                        axis=1)
results_df['iteration'] = np.arange(len(results_df)) + 1
```

We had to prepare the DataFrame containing the required information per each iteration: the hyperparameters and the value of the loss function. We can extract the information from `trials.results` (this is also why we passed the `params` object to the resulting dictionary while defining the `objective`). The hyperparameters are stored in one column as a dictionary; for that reason we used `json_normalize` to create a DataFrame out of this column and later concatenate it back to the original DataFrame.

3. Sample observations from the distribution specified for the `colsample_bytree` hyperparameter:

```
colsample_bytree_dist = []

for _ in range(10000):
    x = sample(lgbm_param_grid['colsample_bytree'])
    colsample_bytree_dist.append(x)
```

We started inspecting the results by looking into the `colsample_bytree` hyperparameter. First, we used the `sample` function from `hyperopt` to randomly sample from the hyperparameter distribution, which we defined while creating the search space object ( `hp.uniform('colsample_bytree', 0.3, 1)`).

4. Plot the distributions of the `colsample_bytree` hyperparameter:

```
fig, ax = plt.subplots(1, 2, figsize = (16, 8))

sns.kdeplot(colsample_bytree_dist,
            label='Sampling Distribution',
            ax=ax[0])
sns.kdeplot(results_df['colsample_bytree'],
            label='Bayesian Optimization',
            ax=ax[0])
ax[0].set(title='Distribution of colsample_bytree',
          xlabel='Value',
          ylabel='Density')
ax[0].legend()

sns.regplot('iteration', 'colsample_bytree',
            data=results_df, ax=ax[1])
ax[1].set(title='colsample_bytree over Iterations',
          xlabel='Iteration',
          ylabel='Value')
```

Running the code results in the following plot:

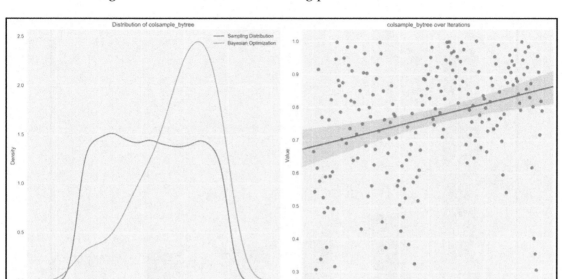

We plotted the two distributions: the one from which we sampled, and the samples used during the Bayesian optimization. Additionally, we plotted the evolution of the hyperparameter over iterations and added a regression line to indicate the direction of change. We can see that the posterior distribution of `colsample_bytree` was concentrated toward the right side, indicating the higher range of considered values. Over iterations, the values showed an increasing trend.

5. Plot the bar chart showing the realizations of `n_estimators` (a hyperparameter defined using the `hp.choice` function):

```
results_df['n_estimators'].value_counts() \
                .plot \
                .bar(title=('# of Estimators'
                            ' Distribution'))
```

Running the code generates the following plot:

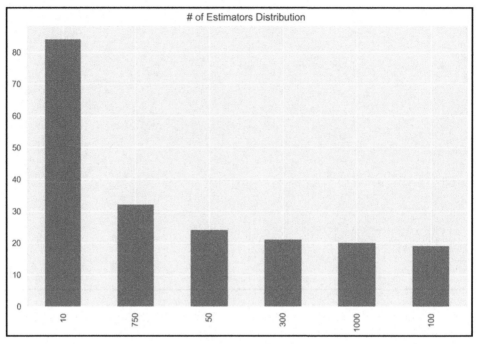

From the plot, we can observe that the algorithm most frequently chose the lowest allowed number of estimators.

6. Plot the evolution of the observed losses over the iterations:

```
fig, ax = plt.subplots()
ax.plot(results_df.iteration, results_df.loss, 'o')
ax.set(title='TPE Sequence of Losses',
       xlabel='Iteration',
       ylabel='Loss')
```

Running the code generates the following plot:

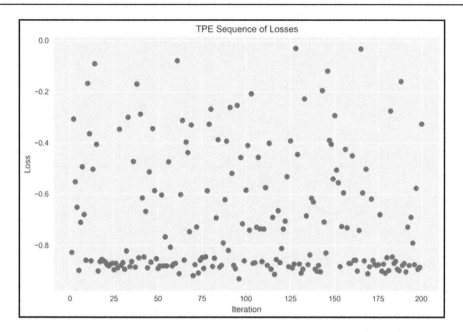

The loss represents the negative of the average recall score (5-fold cross-validation on the training set). The lowest loss (maximum recall) of -0.93 occurred in the 96th iteration.

# See also

Additional resources are available here:

- Bergstra, J. S., Bardenet, R., Bengio, Y., and Kégl, B. (2011). *Algorithms for hyper-parameter optimization*. In *Advances in neural information processing systems* (pp. 2546-2554).
- Bergstra, J., Yamins, D., and Cox, D. D. (2013, June). *Hyperopt: A Python library for optimizing the hyperparameters of machine learning algorithms*. In *Proceedings of the 12th Python in science conference* (pp. 13-20).
- Bergstra, J., Yamins, D., Cox, D. D. (2013) *Making a Science of Model Search: Hyperparameter Optimization in Hundreds of Dimensions for Vision Architectures*. Proc. of the *30th International Conference on Machine Learning* (ICML 2013).
- Shahriari, B., Swersky, K., Wang, Z., Adams, R. P., and De Freitas, N. (2015). *Taking the human out of the loop: A review of Bayesian optimization*. Proceedings of the *IEEE*, 104(1), 148-175.

# 10
# Deep Learning in Finance

In recent years, we have seen many spectacular successes achieved by means of deep learning techniques. Deep neural networks were successfully applied to tasks in which traditional machine learning algorithms could not succeed – large-scale image classification, autonomous driving, and superhuman performance when playing traditional games such as Go or classic video games. Almost yearly, we can observe the introduction of a new type of network that achieves **state-of-the-art** (**SOTA**) results and breaks some kind of performance record.

With the constant improvement in commercially available **Graphics Processing Units** (**GPU**), the emergence of freely available processing power involving CPUs/GPUs (Google Colab, Kaggle, and so on) and the rapid development of different frameworks, deep learning continues to gain more and more attention among researchers and practitioners who want to apply the techniques to their business cases.

In this chapter, we are going to show two possible use cases of deep learning in the financial domain – predicting credit card default and forecasting time series. In the first one, we present how to approach a classification task on tabular data using deep learning. Then, we focus on introducing a few possible neural network architectures for time series forecasting. Deep learning proved to deliver great results with sequential data such as speech, audio, and video. That is why it naturally fits into working with sequential data such as time series—both univariate and multivariate. Financial time series are known to be erratic and complex, hence the reason why it is such a challenge to model them. Deep learning approaches are especially apt for the task, as they make no assumptions about the distribution of the underlying data and can be quite robust to noise.

We train the neural networks using PyTorch, which is a deep learning framework developed by Facebook. There are a few reasons why we selected this framework over others (such as TensorFlow). The first one is that PyTorch is very *pythonic,* so it is relatively easy to quickly understand the entire workflow without the need to go very deep into framework-specific knowledge and syntax. PyTorch lies somewhere in between Keras and TensorFlow in terms of coding complexity – there is definitely more flexibility than in Keras, but we are also not required to work on such a low level of programming as in pure TensorFlow. Furthermore, PyTorch is compatible with many Python libraries, such as `numpy` and `pdb` (for debugging). Some of the general characteristics of PyTorch include data parallelism, support for dynamic computational graphs and Open Neural Network Exchange (ONNX). Lastly, the community around PyTorch is very active and there are many wrappers around PyTorch, which provide a lot of functionalities out of the box, such as the popular `fastai`.

 Please bear in mind that all the examples of using deep learning for time series forecasting presented in this chapter are oversimplified – using vanilla neural network architectures is not enough to accurately predict the stock prices. The goal of this chapter is to show how such techniques can be used to predict future observations of time series.

In this chapter, we present the following recipes:

- Deep learning for tabular data
- Multilayer perceptrons for time series forecasting
- Convolutional neural networks for time series forecasting
- Recurrent neural networks for time series forecasting

At the very beginning of each notebook (available on the book's GitHub repository), we run a few cells that import and set up plotting with `matplotlib`. We will not mention this later on, as this would be repetitive, so at any time, assume that `matplotlib` is imported.

In the first cell, we first set up the backend of `matplotlib` to inline:

```
%matplotlib inline
%config InlineBackend.figure_format = 'retina'
```

By doing so, each plotted figure will appear below the cell that generated it and the plot will also be visible in the Notebook should it be exported to another format (such as PDF or HTML). The second line is used for MacBooks and displays the plot in higher resolution for Retina displays.

The second cell appears as follows:

```
import matplotlib.pyplot as plt
import warnings

plt.style.use('seaborn')
plt.rcParams['figure.figsize'] = [16, 9]
plt.rcParams['figure.dpi'] = 300
warnings.simplefilter(action='ignore', category=FutureWarning)
```

In this cell, we import `matplotlib` and `warnings`, set up the style of the plots to `'seaborn'` (this is a personal preference), as well as default plot settings, such as figure size and resolution. We also disable (ignore) some warnings. In some chapters, we might modify these settings for better readability of the figures (especially in black and white).

# Deep learning for tabular data

Deep learning is not often associated with tabular data, as this kind of data comes with some possible issues:

- How to represent features in a way that can be *understood* by the neural networks? In tabular data, we often deal with numerical and categorical features, so we need to correctly represent both types of inputs.
- How to use feature interactions – both between the features themselves and the target?
- How to effectively sample the data? Tabular datasets tend to be smaller than typical datasets used for solving computer vision or NLP problems. There is no easy way to apply augmentation, such as random cropping or rotation in the case of images. Also, there is no general large dataset with some universal properties, based on which we could apply **transfer learning**.
- How to interpret the neural network's decisions?

That is why practitioners tend to use traditional machine learning approaches (often based on some kind of gradient boosted trees) to approach such tasks. In this recipe, we present how to successfully use deep learning for tabular data. To do so, we use the popular `fastai` library, which is built on top of PyTorch.

Some of the benefits of working with the `fastai` library:

- It provides a selection of APIs that greatly simplify working with **Artificial Neural Networks (ANNs)**—from loading and batching the data to training the model.
- It incorporates some best approaches to using deep learning for various tasks such as image classification, NLP, and tabular data (both classification and regression problems).
- It handles the data preprocessing automatically – we just need to define which operations we want to apply.

Another advantage of using a deep learning approach is that it requires much less feature engineering and domain knowledge.

What makes `fastai` stand out is the use of **Entity Embedding** (embedding layers) for categorical data. By using it, the model can learn some potentially meaningful relationships between the observations of categorical features. You can think about the embeddings as latent features. For each categorical column, there is a trainable embedding matrix and each unique value has a designated vector mapped to it. Thankfully, `fastai` does everything for us.

In this recipe, we apply deep learning to a classification problem based on the credit card default dataset. We have already used this dataset in `Chapter 8`, *Identifying Credit Card Default with Machine Learning*.

# How to do it...

Execute the following steps to fit a neural network to a tabular dataset using `fastai`.

1. Import the libraries:

```
from fastai import *
from fastai.tabular import *
import pandas as pd
from chapter_10_utils import performance_evaluation_report
```

2. Load the dataset from a CSV file:

```
df = pd.read_csv('credit_card_default.csv', index_col=0,
                 na_values='')
```

3. Identify the dependent variable (target) and numerical/categorical features:

```
DER_VAR = 'default_payment_next_month'

num_features = list(df.select_dtypes('number').columns)
num_features.remove(DEP_VAR)
cat_features = list(df.select_dtypes('object').columns)

preprocessing = [FillMissing, Categorify, Normalize]
```

4. Create `TabularDataBunch` from the DataFrame:

```
data = (TabularList.from_df(df,
                        cat_names=cat_features,
                        cont_names=num_features,
                        procs=preprocessing)
                .split_by_rand_pct(valid_pct=0.2, seed=42)
                .label_from_df(cols=DEP_VAR)
                .databunch())
```

We can additionally inspect a few rows from the `DataBunch` by running the following command:

```
data.show_batch(rows=5)
```

5. Define the `Learner` object:

```
learn = tabular_learner(data, layers=[1000,500],
                    ps=[0.001,0.01],
                    emb_drop=0.04,
                    metrics=[Recall(),
                            FBeta(beta=1),
                            FBeta(beta=5)])
```

6. Inspect the model's architecture:

```
learn.model
```

Running the code results in the following output:

```
TabularModel(
  (embeds): ModuleList(
    (0): Embedding(3, 3)
    (1): Embedding(5, 4)
    (2): Embedding(4, 3)
    (3): Embedding(11, 6)
    (4): Embedding(11, 6)
    (5): Embedding(11, 6)
    (6): Embedding(11, 6)
    (7): Embedding(10, 6)
    (8): Embedding(10, 6)
    (9): Embedding(3, 3)
  )
  (emb_drop): Dropout(p=0.04, inplace=False)
  (bn_cont): BatchNorm1d(14, eps=1e-05, momentum=0.1, affine=True, track_running_stats=True)
  (layers): Sequential(
    (0): Linear(in_features=63, out_features=1000, bias=True)
    (1): ReLU(inplace=True)
    (2): BatchNorm1d(1000, eps=1e-05, momentum=0.1, affine=True, track_running_stats=True)
    (3): Dropout(p=0.001, inplace=False)
    (4): Linear(in_features=1000, out_features=500, bias=True)
    (5): ReLU(inplace=True)
    (6): BatchNorm1d(500, eps=1e-05, momentum=0.1, affine=True, track_running_stats=True)
    (7): Dropout(p=0.01, inplace=False)
    (8): Linear(in_features=500, out_features=2, bias=True)
  )
)
```

`Embedding(11, 6)` means that a categorical embedding was created with 11 input values and 6 output latent features.

7. Find the suggested learning rate:

```
learn.lr_find()
learn.recorder.plot(suggestion=True)
```

Running the code results in the following output:

```
Min numerical gradient: 9.12E-07
Min loss divided by 10: 3.31E-03
```

It also produces the following plot:

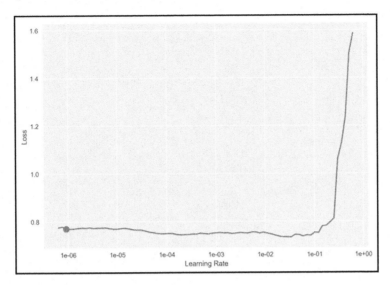

The dot suggests a possible value of the learning rate. In this case, we will use `1e-06`.

8. Train the neural network:

```
learn.fit(epochs=25, lr=1e-6, wd=0.2)
```

We present the results of the first five epochs here:

| epoch ⬍ | train_loss ⬍ | valid_loss ⬍ | recall ⬍ | f_beta ⬍ | f_beta ⬍ | time ⬍ |
|---|---|---|---|---|---|---|
| 0 | 0.715293 | 0.711141 | 0.750190 | 0.397658 | 0.702298 | 00:12 |
| 1 | 0.692178 | 0.682831 | 0.716679 | 0.404296 | 0.676473 | 00:11 |
| 2 | 0.695443 | 0.677552 | 0.724295 | 0.414831 | 0.684988 | 00:10 |
| 3 | 0.687314 | 0.657006 | 0.635948 | 0.407118 | 0.609592 | 00:11 |
| 4 | 0.680303 | 0.661530 | 0.678599 | 0.416161 | 0.647203 | 00:10 |
| 5 | 0.677046 | 0.653647 | 0.645088 | 0.417859 | 0.619187 | 00:10 |

In the first five epochs, the losses are still erratic and increase/decrease. The same goes for the evaluation metrics.

9. Plot the losses:

```
learn.recorder.plot_losses()
```

Running the code results in the following plot:

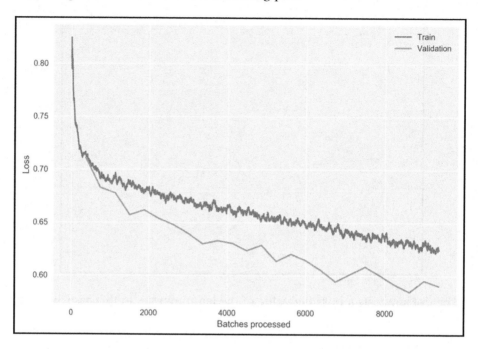

We see that both training and validation losses are still decreasing, so we might want to train the network for more epochs.

10. Extract the predictions for the validation set:

```
preds_valid, _ = learn.get_preds(ds_type=DatasetType.Valid)
pred_valid = preds_valid.argmax(dim=-1)
```

11. Inspect the performance (confusion matrix) on the validation set:

```
interp = ClassificationInterpretation.from_learner(learn)
interp.plot_confusion_matrix()
```

Running the code results in the following plot:

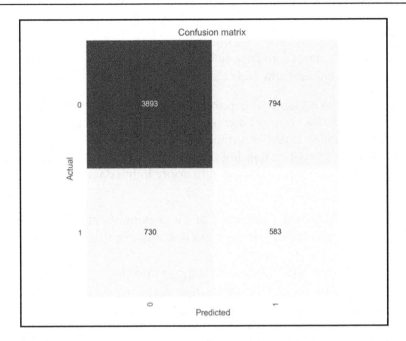

The confusion matrix represents the performance on the validation set – we can see that the total is 6,000 observations, which is 20% of the entire dataset.

12. Inspect the performance evaluation metrics:

```
performance_evaluation_report(learn)
```

Running the code results in the following output:

```
{'accuracy': 0.746,
 'precision': 0.4233841684822077,
 'recall': 0.44402132520944404,
 'specificity': 0.8305952634947728,
 'f1_score': 0.433457249070632,
 'cohens_kappa': 0.2698817102973029,
 'roc_auc': 0.7060126931437297,
 'pr_auc': 0.40368381260070746}
```

From the results, we can see that while the overall accuracy is around 75%, the model was able to correctly detect ~44% of the positive cases (customers who defaulted).

# How it works...

In Step 2, we loaded the dataset into Python using the `read_csv` function. We only indicated which column contains the index and what symbol represents the missing values.

In Step 3, we identified the dependent variable (the target), as well as both numerical and categorical features. To do so, we used the `select_dtypes` methods and indicated what data type we wanted to extract. We stored the features in lists. We also had to remove the dependent variable from the list containing the numerical features. Lastly, we created a list containing all the transformations we wanted to apply to the data. We selected the following:

- `FillMissing`: Missing values will be filled using the median of the feature's values. In the case of categorical variables, missing values become a separate category.
- `Categorify`: Converts categorical features into the categories.
- `Normalise`: Features' values are transformed such that they have zero mean and unit variance. This makes training neural networks easier.

It is important to note that the same transformations will be applied to both the training and validation set. Also, to prevent data leakage, the transformations are based solely on the training set.

In Step 4, we created the `TabularDataBunch`, which handles all the preprocessing, splitting, and batching of the input data. To do so, we chained multiple methods of `TabularList`. First, we loaded the data from a `pandas` DataFrame using the `from_df` method. While doing so, we passed the source DataFrame, numerical/categorical features, and the preprocessing steps we wanted to carry out. Second, we split the data into training and validation sets. For this case, we used the `split_by_rand_pct` method, indicated the percentage of all observations intended for the validation set, and set the seed (for reproducibility). For cases with severe class imbalance, please refer to tips in the *There's more* section. Third, we indicated the label using the `label_from_df` method. Lastly, we created the DataBunch using the `databunch` method. By default, it will create batches containing 64 observations.

In Step 5, we defined the learner using `tabular_learner`. This is the place where we defined the network's architecture. We decided to use a network with two hidden layers, with 1,000 and 500 neurons, respectively. Choosing the network's architecture can often be considered an art and may require a significant amount of trial and error. Another popular approach is to use the architecture that worked before for someone else.

As in the case of machine learning, it is crucial to prevent overfitting with neural networks. We want the networks to be able to generalize to new data. Some of the popular techniques used for fighting overfitting include the following:

- **Weight decay**: Each time the weights are updated, they are multiplied by a factor smaller than 1 (a rule of thumb is to use values between 0.01 and 0.1).
- **Dropout**: While training the NN, some activations (a fraction indicated by the `ps` hyperparameter) are randomly dropped for each mini-batch. Dropout can also be used for the concatenated vector of embeddings of categorical features (controlled via the `emb_drop` hyperparameter).
- **Batch normalization**: This technique reduces overfitting by making sure that a small number of outlying inputs cannot have too much impact on the trained network.

While defining the learner, we specified the percentage of neurons to be dropped out. Additionally, we provided a selection of metrics we wanted to inspect. We chose recall, F1-score (`FBeta(beta=1)`), and the F-beta score (`FBeta(beta=5)`).

While the F1-Score is the harmonic average of precision and recall, the F-beta score is a weighted harmonic average of the same metrics. The beta parameter determines the weight of recall in the total score. Values of beta lower than 1 place more importance on precision, while beta > 1 gives more weight to recall. The best value of the F-beta score is 1, and the worst is 0.

In Step 6, we inspected the model's architecture. In the output, we first saw the categorical embeddings and the corresponding dropout. Then, in the (`layers`) section, we saw the input layer (63 input, 1,000 output features), followed by the ReLU (Rectified Linear Unit) activation function, batch normalization, and dropout. The same steps were repeated for the second hidden layer and then the last linear layer produced the class probabilities.

In Step 7, we tried to determine the "good" learning rate. `fastai` provides a convenience method, `lr_find`, which facilitates the process. It begins to train the network while increasing the learning rate – it starts from a very low one and increases to a very large one. Then, we ran `learn.recorder.plot(suggestion=True)` to plot the losses against the learning rates, together with the suggested value. We should aim for a value that is before the minimum, but where the loss still improves (decreases).

In Step 8, we trained the neural network using the `fit` method of the learner. We briefly describe the training algorithm. The entire training set is divided into **batches** (default size of 64). For each batch, the network is used to make predictions, which are compared to the target values and used to calculate the error. Then, the error is used to update the weights in the network. An **epoch** is a complete run through all the batches, in other words, using the entire dataset for training.

Without going into too much detail, by default, `fastai` uses the **cross-entropy loss function** (for classification tasks) and **Adam** (Adaptive Moment Estimation) as the optimizer. The reported training and validation losses come from the loss function and the evaluation metrics (such as recall) are not used in the training procedure.

In our case, we trained the network for 25 epochs. We additionally specified the learning rate and weight decay. Then, we plotted the training and validation loss over batches.

In Step 10, we used the `get_preds` method to obtain the validation set predictions (`preds_valid`). To obtain the predictions from `preds_valid`, we had to use the `argmax` method.

To extract the predictions for the validation set, we passed `DatasetType.Valid` as the `ds_type` argument in the `get_preds` method. Using this approach, we can also extract the predictions for the training set (`DatasetType.Train`) and test set (by passing `DatasetType.Test` if it was specified previously).

In Step 11, we used the `ClassificationInterpretation` class to extract performance evaluation metrics from the trained network. We plotted the confusion matrix using the `plot_confusion_matrix` method. With the created object, we can also look at the observations with the highest loss – the `plot_tab_top_losses` method.

In the last step, we used the slightly modified `performance_evaluation_report` function (the convenience function defined in `Chapter 8`, *Identifying Credit Default with Machine Learning*) to recover evaluation metrics such as precision and recall.

# There's more...

Some noteworthy features of `fastai` for tabular datasets include:

- Using callbacks while training neural networks. Callbacks are used for inserting some custom code/logic into the training loop at different times (`begin_epoch`, `after_step`, `begin_fit`, and so on). They are stored in the `callbacks` module and can be added as a list via the `callback_fns` argument of `tabular_learner`. Some of the interesting callbacks include `ShowGraph` (this plots the losses while training the model), `OverSamplingCallback` (used for oversampling data in case of class imbalance), and `SaveModelCallback` (used for resuming the training following an interruption).

- Using custom indices for training and validation sets. This feature comes in handy when we are dealing with class imbalance and want to make sure that both the training and validation sets contain a similar ratio of classes. We can use the `split_by_idxs` method in combination with `scikit-learn`'s `StratifiedKFold`. Execute the following code to create `TabularDataBunch` with a custom training/validation split:

```
from sklearn.model_selection import StratifiedKFold

X = df.copy()
y = X.pop(DEP_VAR)

train_ind, test_ind = next(StratifiedKFold(n_splits=5).split(X, y))

data = (TabularList.from_df(df,
                           cat_names=cat_features,
                           cont_names=num_features,
                           procs=preprocessing)
               .split_by_idxs(train_idx=list(train_ind),
                              valid_idx=list(test_ind))
               .label_from_df(cols=DEP_VAR)
               .databunch())
```

- Adding a test set to the DataBunch via the `add_test` method. The test set should also be a `TabularList` with the same categorical/continuous feature names and preprocessing steps. The method should be called before the `databunch` method.

- Specifying the path argument in the `from_df` method of `TabularList` indicates where the model should potentially be stored.

- `fastai` provides a convenience function, `add_datepart`, which extracts a variety of features from columns containing dates (such as the purchase date). Some of the extracted features may include the day of the week, the day of the month, and a Boolean for the start/end of the month/quarter/year.
- We can use the `predict` method of a trained `Learner` to predict the class directly from a row of the source DataFrame.
- Instead of the `fit` method, we can also use the `fit_one_cycle` method. This employs the **super-convergence policy**. The idea is to train the network with a varying learning rate. It starts at low values, increases to the specified maximum, and goes back to low values again. This approach is considered to work better than choosing a single learning rate.

# See also

Additional resources are available here:

- Guo, C., and Berkhahn, F. (2016). *Entity embeddings of categorical variables.* arXiv preprint arXiv:1604.06737.
- Smith, L. N. (2018). *A disciplined approach to neural network hyperparameters: Part 1 – learning rate, batch size, momentum, and weight decay.* arXiv preprint arXiv:1803.09820. - `https://arxiv.org/pdf/1803.09820.pdf`
- Smith, L. N., and Topin, N. (2019, May). *Super-convergence: Very fast training of neural networks using large learning rates.* In *Artificial intelligence and machine learning for multi-domain operations applications* (Vol. 11006, p. 1100612). International Society for Optics and Photonics: `https://arxiv.org/pdf/1708.07120.pdf`
- Srivastava, N., Hinton, G., Krizhevsky, A., Sutskever, I., and Salakhutdinov, R. (2014). *Dropout: a simple way to prevent neural networks from overfitting. The journal of machine learning research*, 15(1), 1929-1958: `http://www.jmlr.org/papers/volume15/srivastava14a/srivastava14a.pdf`
- Krogh, A., and Hertz, J. A. (1992). *A simple weight decay can improve generalization.* In *Advances in neural information processing systems* (pp. 950-957): `https://papers.nips.cc/paper/563-a-simple-weight-decay-can-improve-generalization.pdf`
- Ioffe, S., and Szegedy, C. (2015). *Batch normalization: Accelerating deep network training by reducing internal covariate shift.* arXiv preprint arXiv:1502.03167: `https://arxiv.org/pdf/1502.03167.pdf`

# Multilayer perceptrons for time series forecasting

**Multilayer perceptrons (MLP)** are one of the basic architectures of neural networks. At a very high level, they consist of three components:

- The **input layer**: A vector of features.
- The **hidden layers**: Each hidden layer consists of $N$ neurons.
- The **output layer**: Output of the network; depends on the task (regression/classification).

The input of each hidden layer is first transformed linearly (multiplication by weights and adding the bias term) and then non-linearly (by applying activation functions such as ReLU). Thanks to the non-linear activation, the network is able to model complex, non-linear relationships between the features and the target.

A multilayer perceptron contains multiple hidden layers (also called **dense layers** or **fully connected layers**) stacked against each other. The following diagram presents a network with a single hidden layer and an MLP with two layers:

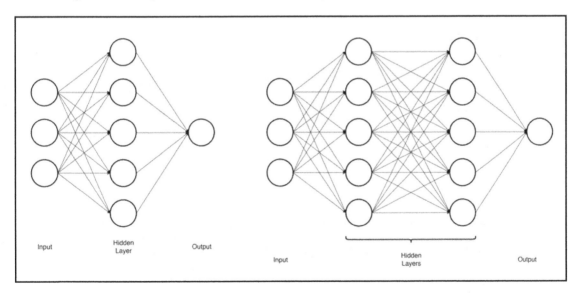

A potential benefit of using deep learning approaches to modeling time series is that they do not make assumptions about the underlying data. As opposed to ARIMA class models introduced in Chapter 3, *Time Series Modeling*, there is no need for the series to be stationary.

In this recipe, we show how to estimate a multilayer perceptron for financial time series forecasting using PyTorch.

# How to do it...

Execute the following steps to train a multilayer perceptron in PyTorch.

1. Import the libraries:

```
import yfinance as yf
import numpy as np

import torch
import torch.optim as optim
import torch.nn as nn
import torch.nn.functional as F
from torch.utils.data import (Dataset, TensorDataset,
                              DataLoader, Subset)

from sklearn.metrics import mean_squared_error

device = 'cuda' if torch.cuda.is_available() else 'cpu'
```

2. Define the parameters:

```
# data
TICKER = 'ANF'
START_DATE = '2010-01-02'
END_DATE = '2019-12-31'
N_LAGS = 3

# neural network
VALID_SIZE = 12
BATCH_SIZE = 5
N_EPOCHS = 1000
```

3. Download the stock prices of Abercrombie and Fitch and process the data:

```
df = yf.download(TICKER,
                 start=START_DATE,
                 end=END_DATE,
                 progress=False)

df = df.resample("M").last()
prices = df['Adj Close'].values
```

4. Define a function for transforming time series into a dataset for the MLP:

```
def create_input_data(series, n_lags=1):
    X, y = [], []
    for step in range(len(series) - n_lags):
        end_step = step + n_lags
        X.append(series[step:end_step])
        y.append(series[end_step])
    return np.array(X), np.array(y)
```

5. Transform the considered time series into input for the MLP:

```
X, y = create_input_data(prices, N_LAGS)

X_tensor = torch.from_numpy(X).float()
y_tensor = torch.from_numpy(y).float().unsqueeze(dim=1)
```

6. Create training and validation sets:

```
valid_ind = len(X) - VALID_SIZE

dataset = TensorDataset(X_tensor, y_tensor)

train_dataset = Subset(dataset, list(range(valid_ind)))
valid_dataset = Subset(dataset, list(range(valid_ind, len(X))))

train_loader = DataLoader(dataset=train_dataset,
                          batch_size=BATCH_SIZE)
valid_loader = DataLoader(dataset=valid_dataset,
                          batch_size=BATCH_SIZE)
```

Inspect the features from the first batch:

```
next(iter(train_loader))[0]
```

Running the code results in the following output:

```
tensor([[23.1900, 26.9100, 33.7300],
        [26.9100, 33.7300, 32.3100],
        [33.7300, 32.3100, 26.6100],
        [32.3100, 26.6100, 22.7900],
        [26.6100, 22.7900, 27.4300]])
```

To inspect the target, we should use `next(iter(train_loader))[1]`.

7. Use a naïve forecast as a benchmark and evaluate the performance:

```
naive_pred = prices[len(prices) - VALID_SIZE - 1:-1]
y_valid = prices[len(prices) - VALID_SIZE:]

naive_mse = mean_squared_error(y_valid, naive_pred)
naive_rmse = np.sqrt(naive_mse)
print(f"Naive forecast - MSE: {naive_mse:.2f}, RMSE:
{naive_rmse:.2f}")
```

Running the code prints the following line:

```
Naive forecast - MSE: 17.87, RMSE: 4.23
```

8. Define the network's architecture:

```
class MLP(nn.Module):
    def __init__(self, input_size):
        super(MLP, self).__init__()
        self.linear1 = nn.Linear(input_size, 8)
        self.linear2 = nn.Linear(8, 4)
        self.linear3 = nn.Linear(4, 1)
        self.dropout = nn.Dropout(p=0.2)
    def forward(self, x):
        x = self.linear1(x)
        x = F.relu(x)
        x = self.dropout(x)
        x = self.linear2(x)
        x = F.relu(x)
        x = self.dropout(x)
        x = self.linear3(x)
        return x
```

9. Instantiate the model, the loss function, and the optimizer:

```
# set seed for reproducibility
torch.manual_seed(42)

model = MLP(N_LAGS).to(device)
loss_fn = nn.MSELoss()
optimizer = optim.Adam(model.parameters(), lr=0.001)
```

Inspecting the `model` object results in the following:

```
MLP(
  (linear1): Linear(in_features=3, out_features=8, bias=True)
  (linear2): Linear(in_features=8, out_features=4, bias=True)
```

```
(linear3): Linear(in_features=4, out_features=1, bias=True)
(dropout): Dropout(p=0.2, inplace=False)
)
```

10. **Train the network:**

```
PRINT_EVERY = 50
train_losses, valid_losses = [], []

for epoch in range(N_EPOCHS):
    running_loss_train = 0
    running_loss_valid = 0

    model.train()
    for x_batch, y_batch in train_loader:
        optimizer.zero_grad()
        x_batch = x_batch.to(device)
        y_batch = y_batch.to(device)
        y_hat = model(x_batch)
        loss = loss_fn(y_batch, y_hat)
        loss.backward()
        optimizer.step()
        running_loss_train += loss.item() * x_batch.size(0)
    epoch_loss_train = running_loss_train /
len(train_loader.dataset)
    train_losses.append(epoch_loss_train)

    with torch.no_grad():
        model.eval()
        for x_val, y_val in valid_loader:
            x_val = x_val.to(device)
            y_val = y_val.to(device)
            y_hat = model(x_val)
            loss = loss_fn(y_val, y_hat)
            running_loss_valid += loss.item() * x_val.size(0)
        epoch_loss_valid = running_loss_valid /
len(valid_loader.dataset)
        if epoch > 0 and epoch_loss_valid < min(valid_losses):
            best_epoch = epoch
            torch.save(model.state_dict(), './mlp_checkpoint.pth')
        valid_losses.append(epoch_loss_valid)

    if epoch % PRINT_EVERY == 0:
        print(f"<{epoch}> - Train. loss: {epoch_loss_train:.2f} \t
Valid. loss: {epoch_loss_valid:.2f}")
print(f'Lowest loss recorded in epoch: {best_epoch}')
```

Running the code results in the following output:

```
Lowest loss recorded in epoch: 961
```

11. Plot the losses over epochs:

```
train_losses = np.array(train_losses)
valid_losses = np.array(valid_losses)

fig, ax = plt.subplots()

ax.plot(train_losses, color='blue', label='Training loss')
ax.plot(valid_losses, color='red', label='Validation loss')

ax.set(title="Loss over epochs",
       xlabel='Epoch',
       ylabel='Loss')
ax.legend()
```

Running the code results in the following plot:

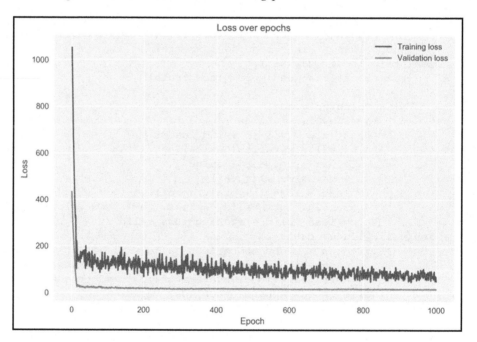

In the plot, we can see that after the initial drop (caused by randomly initialized weights), the training loss visibly decreases over epochs, while it is hard to unanimously say the same about the validation loss, as it is much smaller.

12. Load the best model (with the lowest validation loss):

```
state_dict = torch.load('mlp_checkpoint.pth')
model.load_state_dict(state_dict)
```

13. Obtain the predictions:

```
y_pred, y_valid= [], []

with torch.no_grad():

    model.eval()
    for x_val, y_val in valid_loader:
        x_val = x_val.to(device)
        y_pred.append(model(x_val))
        y_valid.append(y_val)
y_pred = torch.cat(y_pred).numpy().flatten()
y_valid = torch.cat(y_valid).numpy().flatten()
```

14. Evaluate the predictions:

```
mlp_mse = mean_squared_error(y_test, y_pred)
mlp_rmse = np.sqrt(mlp_mse)
print(f"MLP's forecast - MSE: {mlp_mse:.2f}, RMSE: {mlp_rmse:.2f}")

fig, ax = plt.subplots()

ax.plot(y_test, color='blue', label='true')
ax.plot(y_pred, color='red', label='prediction')

ax.set(title="Multilayer Perceptron's Forecasts",
        xlabel='Time',
        ylabel='Price ($)')
ax.legend()
```

Running the code generates the following plot:

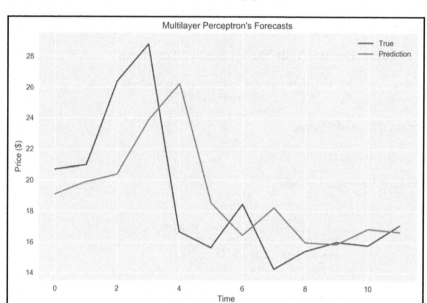

We see that the network is not able to pick up the patterns in time, hence, the predicted line is shifted to the right of the actual one.

And the evaluation is as follows:

```
MLP's forecast – MSE: 15.47, RMSE: 3.93
```

Using the multilayer perceptron, we obtained results better than with the naïve forecast.

# How it works...

In the first step, we imported the required libraries. We also created a flag variable called `device`, which indicates whether the network will be trained using the CPU or the GPU. We structured the code in a way that GPU will be used if it is available, and CPU otherwise. Structuring the code this way has the benefit of flexibility in terms of hardware used. Bear in mind that both the data and the model should be stored on the same device!

Then, we defined a variety of parameters for both downloading the data and setting up the neural network model.

In *Step 3*, we downloaded the stock prices of Abercrombie and Fitch (a clothing/lifestyle company) for the years 2010-2019 and resampled the close prices to monthly frequency by taking the last value per month.

In *Step 4*, we defined a helper function, `create_input_data`, used for transforming a time series into a dataset acceptable to the multilayer perceptron. We parametrized the function with `n_lags`, which indicated the number of lagged observations to take as features. For example, for `n_lags = 1`, we use time *t*'s stock price to forecast time *t+1*'s value. The function returns two `numpy` arrays – the features and the target.

In general, it is good practice to rescale (and potentially standardize) the input features, so that their values lie in the interval of [0, 1] or [-1, 1], depending on the activation functions used. By doing so, we make it easier for the optimization procedure to converge, hence, the training is faster. Alternatively, we could have transformed the prices to returns.

In *Step 5*, we used the `create_input_data` function to obtain the model's inputs from the times series of stock prices. We used three lagged values as features.

In a way, the neural network will try to solve a problem similar to autoregression (the AR model), in which we use past realizations of a variable to predict future values. That is why such models are also referred to as **Neural NETwork AutoRegression (NNETAR)** models: `https://otexts.com/fpp2/nnetar.html`

We also converted the `numpy` arrays into `torch` tensors using `torch.from_numpy`. Additionally, we indicated them to be float tensors using the `float` method. For the target variable, we had to use the `unsqueeze` method to convert a `1 x n` tensor into an `n x 1` tensor.

To inspect the type of a `torch` tensor, we can use the `type()` function or the `type()` method of a `torch` tensor. The benefit of the latter is that it additionally informs us where (CPU or GPU) the tensor is located. For example, if the tensors we created were stored on the GPU, using the `type()` method would result in `torch.cuda.FloatTensor`.

In *Step 6*, we created a dataset using `TensorDataset`. Then, we used `Subset` to split the dataset into the training and validation sets. To do so, we provided a list of indices for both sets. As this is a time series problem, we decided to train the network using data from the years 2010-2018 and use the year 2019 as the validation set. In cases where the order of the data does not matter, we can use `random_split` to create a random training/validation split. Lastly, we created the `DataLoader` objects by passing the previously created datasets and the desired batch size (in this case 5, as we are working with a small dataset). For this particular problem, we were satisfied with the default setting of `shuffle=False`. We will iterate over the `DataLoader` objects for training and evaluating the network. We can use `next(iter(train_loader))[0]` to inspect the first batch of features. The training set contains 105 observations, while the validation set only contains 12 observations (corresponding to monthly observations in the last year).

We have described the terms such as *batch* and *epoch* in the previous recipe. However, this is a good place to mention that the batch size influences the *type* of gradient descent that will be used for training the network. A batch size equal or greater to the training sample size means that we will use **batch gradient descent** – the weights will be updated only once after each epoch. Using a smaller batch size indicates that we are using an approach called **mini-batch gradient descent**, where the weights are updated multiple times per epoch. Lastly, an extreme case of the batch size equal to 1 indicates the **stochastic gradient descent (SGD)**. Beware that there is also an optimizer in PyTorch (and not only) under the same name: `optim.SGD()`. If we use the entire batch of data to train the network, we still carry out the batch gradient descent, even though the optimizer is called differently.

In *Step 7*, we calculated the naïve forecast – we used the last known observation as the forecast for the next period. We consider the MLP skillful when it is able to outperform the benchmark (which, in some cases, can be quite difficult). We evaluated the benchmark using the mean squared error (MSE) and the root mean squared error (RMSE). The benefit of the latter is that it is given in the same units as the measured value – in this case – Abercrombie's stock price.

In step 8, we defined the network's architecture. There are two approaches to defining networks in PyTorch and, in this section, we present the one based on defining a class, which inherits from `nn.Module`. By inheriting, we mean that it will automatically possess a series of required methods and we only need to define a few selected ones (we can also overwrite the default methods if there is such a need). We defined two methods. The first one is the `__init__` method, in which we stored all the operations that we wanted to carry out (in this method, they do not need to be in the order of execution). As a rule, we should store all the trainable operations here (such as fully connected layers called `Linear` in PyTorch), but we can also store the dropout layer with the assigned probability. Additionally, this is also the method which can accept parameters that we provide while creating the instance of the class, such as the input size in the case of the defined MLP. Secondly, we defined the `forward` method. The method uses `x`, which symbolizes the tensor of features, and sequentially passes it through all the operations in the correct order. In this method, we can use the activation functions such as ReLU, *tanh*, and sigmoid. We defined a network with two hidden layers (eight and four neurons, respectively). We experimented with a few different specifications and selected this one as it performed best. The best practice would be to either experiment, select an architecture that worked for someone else, or even use transfer learning if applicable.

In *Step 9*, we instantiated the model (after setting up the seed for reproducibility). While doing so, we indicated that we are working with three features and also passed the model to an appropriate device using the `to` method (CPU in those cases when no GPU is available). In this step, we also defined the loss function (mean squared error as we are dealing with a regression problem) and the optimizer. For our network, we selected the Adam optimizer. We also had to specify which parameters we wanted to update and the value of the learning rate, which ideally should be tuned.

In *Step 10*, we trained the network. Training of neural networks in PyTorch happens within a nested loop. The outer loop runs over epochs (we indicated 1,000, but this should be tuned or we could use early stopping when the loss ceases to decrease). We started each epoch by indicating that we are in the training phase by running `model.train()`. This is important for layers such as `nn.Dropout`, which have different behavior in the training/evaluation phases. Namely, during training, the dropout layer randomly drops a percentage of neurons. This does not happen in the evaluation phase. During the evaluation phase, we scale all the outputs from the hidden layers by a factor of $p$ (probability of a neuron being dropped) to account for the missing neurons during the training. Another example of an affected layer is batch normalization (`nn.BatchNorm1d`, and so on).

Then, we iterated over the `DataLoader` object containing training data. By doing so, each time, we received a single batch from the training dataset. In each iteration, we zeroed the gradients by running `optimizer.zero_grad()`. By default, PyTorch accumulates gradients. That is why we had to zero the gradients at the beginning of each iteration, but after using them for updating the weights (the `step` method of the optimizer). Afterward, we sent the features and target to the appropriate device (CPU/GPU). We obtained the network's predictions by running `model(x_batch)`. We plugged in the predictions and the target values into the loss function and used the `backward` method of the loss function to calculate the gradients used for the backpropagation. We do not go into the details of the backpropagation algorithm; for more information please refer to the *See also* section. Next, we ran `optimizer.step()` to carry out one step of the optimization routine using the specified learning rate. We also stored the running loss of the training phase. To do so, we used `running_loss_train += loss.item() * x_batch.size(0)`. The default behavior of the loss object is to calculate the batch average. However, it can happen that the batches are of unequal size – it often happens with the last batch. That is why we multiplied the loss by the batch size to transform the value into the overall sum of the losses and later divided it by the number of observations in the training dataset (after iterating through all the batches). This concluded the single iteration of a training step. For each epoch, we stored the average loss of the batches as the training loss. We can access the network's weights and parameters by using the `state_dict()` method of `model`.

After the training step, we also evaluated the network's performance on the validation set, so as to monitor underfitting versus overfitting. As we did not want to update any weights in this step, we temporarily turned off the Autograd engine by using `torch.no_grad()`. Autograd is PyTorch's automatic differentiation package. Turning it off means we cannot run the backpropagation algorithm (we do not need it for validation), but, at the same time, it reduces memory usage and speeds up the computations. The evaluation loop is a simplified version of the training one. We iterated over the validation `DataLoader`, used the model to obtain predictions, and calculated the value of the loss function. We stored the validation losses in the same way as we did with the training ones. Additionally, we added an option for saving the best-performing model. After each validation phase, we checked whether the epoch's validation loss was lower than the current lowest loss and if so, we saved the model using `torch.save`. We passed the model's `state_dict` (`OrderedDict` containing the trainable parameters of the network) and the path for storing the information (traditionally with `.pt` or `.pth` extension). This way of saving/loading PyTorch's models is favorable when we only care about inference (making predictions). For saving models with the ability to resume training from the last epoch, please refer to the official documentation (link provided in the *See also* section).

In *Step 11*, we plotted the training and validation loss over time.

In Step 12, we loaded the state dictionary of the network with the lowest validation loss. To do so, we first used `torch.load` to load the saved state dictionary and then passed it to a defined model using the model's `load_state_dict` method. Again, the approach would be slightly more complicated if we wanted to resume training. In our use case, however, we only used the loaded model for inference.

In *Step 13*, we used a simplified loop over the validation set (with Autograd turned off and model in the evaluation phase) to obtain the predictions and compare them to the actual observations. We used the `torch.cat` function to concatenate a list of tensors, the `numpy` method to easily convert the tensors into `numpy` arrays, and lastly, the `flatten` method to obtain 1D arrays.

 The `numpy` method of a `torch` tensor only works if the tensors are located on the CPU. If they are not, we can easily move them using the `cpu` method. To make the digression complete, we can use the `cuda` method to move the tensors to the GPU.

In the last step, we calculated the MSE and RMSE of the MPL's forecasts and plotted the actual versus predicted values.

We also list a few potential steps to tune the network further to achieve better performance:

- Experiment with a different batch size/number of epochs/learning rate
- Experiment with the number of hidden layers/neurons/activation functions
- Compare the performance with and without shuffling of the observations in the batches
- Change the number of lagged values used as features
- Scale/standardize/normalize the data

# There's more...

In this section, we wanted to mention a few additional, yet interesting things connected to MLP.

**Multivariate setting**: We can use the multilayer perceptron in the multivariate setting. Two types of possible cases are:

- **Multiple input series**: Multiple time series are used to predict the future value(s) of a single time series.
- **Multiple parallel series**: Multiple time series are used to predict future value(s) of multiple time series simultaneously.

**A sequential approach to defining the network's architecture:** We can also define the network's architecture using `nn.Sequential`, which might be similar to anyone who worked with Keras before. The idea is that the input tensor is sequentially passed through the specified layers.

In the following, we define the same network as we have already used before in this recipe:

```
model = nn.Sequential(
    nn.Linear(3, 8),
    nn.ReLU(),
    nn.Dropout(0.2),
    nn.Linear(8, 4),
    nn.ReLU(),
    nn.Dropout(0.2),
    nn.Linear(4, 1)
)

model
```

Running the code prints the following architecture:

```
Sequential(
    (0): Linear(in_features=3, out_features=8, bias=True)
    (1): ReLU()
    (2): Dropout(p=0.2, inplace=False)
    (3): Linear(in_features=8, out_features=4, bias=True)
    (4): ReLU()
    (5): Dropout(p=0.2, inplace=False)
    (6): Linear(in_features=4, out_features=1, bias=True)
)
```

The sequence of layers is marked with ordered integers. Alternatively, we can pass an `OrderedDict` to `nn.Sequential` and provide custom names for the layers – in the dictionary, the keys must be unique, so we should provide a unique name for each operation.

**Estimating neural networks using scikit-learn:** It is also possible to train multilayer perceptrons using `scikit-learn`, thanks to `MLPClassifier` and `MLPRegressor`. They are not as complex and customizable as the ones trained using PyTorch (or any other deep learning framework); however, they are a good point to start and also easy to implement as they follow the familiar `scikit-learn` API. Here, we show the code defining a simple network resembling the one we used in this recipe. Please refer to chapter 10's Notebook in the accompanying GitHub repository for a short example of how to train such a network.

We can define the MLP model as follows:

```
mlp = MLPRegressor(hidden_layer_sizes=(8, 4,),
                   learning_rate='constant',
                   batch_size=5,
                   max_iter=1000)
```

**Multi-period forecast:** Lastly, we can also use the multilayer perceptron to forecast more than one timestep ahead. To do so, we need to appropriately prepare the input data and slightly modify the network's architecture to account for more than one output. We do not present the entire code here, just the modified parts. For the entire code, including the training of the network, please refer to the accompanying Notebook on GitHub.

The following code presents the modified function for transforming the time series into a dataset accepted by the MLP:

```
def create_input_data(series, n_lags=1, n_leads=1):
    X, y = [], []
    for step in range(len(series) - n_lags - n_leads + 1):
        end_step = step + n_lags
        forward_end = end_step + n_leads
        X.append(series[step:end_step])
        y.append(series[end_step:forward_end])
    return np.array(X), np.array(y)
```

We also present the modified network's architecture:

```
class MLP(nn.Module):

    def __init__(self, input_size, output_size):
        super(MLP, self).__init__()
        self.linear1 = nn.Linear(input_size, 16)
        self.linear2 = nn.Linear(16, 8)
        self.linear3 = nn.Linear(8, output_size)
        self.dropout = nn.Dropout(p=0.2)

    def forward(self, x):
        x = self.linear1(x)
        x = F.relu(x)
        x = self.dropout(x)
        x = self.linear2(x)
        x = F.relu(x)
        x = self.dropout(x)
        x = self.linear3(x)
        return x
```

Lastly, we present the plotted forecasts:

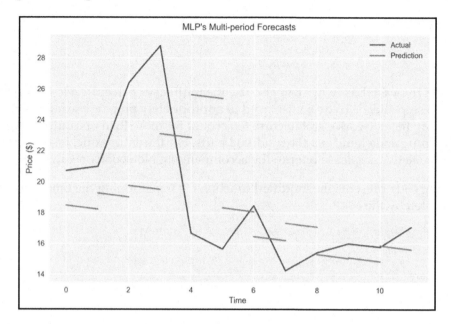

For each time point, we forecast two points – time *t+1* and *t+2*. The network's second prediction is always very close to the first one; hence, it does not accurately capture the dynamics of the stock prices.

# See also

Additional resources are available here:

- Ian Goodfellow, Yoshua Bengio, and Aaron Courville: *Deep learning. The MIT Press, 2016:* https://www.deeplearningbook.org/
- https://discuss.pytorch.org/
- https://github.com/hfawaz/dl-4-tsc/
- https://pytorch.org/tutorials/beginner/saving_loading_models.html

# Convolutional neural networks for time series forecasting

**Convolutional neural networks** (**CNN**) were developed and remained very popular in the image classification domain. However, they can also be applied to 1-dimensional problems, such as predicting the next value in the sequence, be it a time series or the next word in a sentence.

In the following diagram, we present a simplified schema of a 1D CNN:

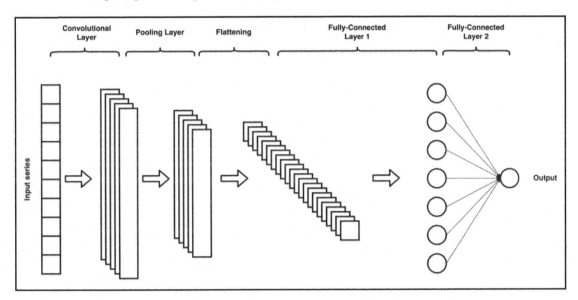

Based on the preceding diagram, we briefly describe the elements of a typical CNN architecture:

- **Convolutional layer**: The goal of this layer is to apply convolutional filtering to extract potential features.
- **Pooling layer**: This layer reduces the size of the image or series while preserving the important characteristics identified by the convolutional layer.
- **Fully connected layer**: Usually, there are a few fully connected layers at the end of the network to map the features extracted by the network to classes or values.

The convolutional layers read the input (such as a 1D time series) and drag a kernel (of a specified, tunable length) over the series. The kernel represents the features we want to locate in the series and has the same width as the time series, so it can only move in one direction (from the beginning of the time series toward its end). For each step, the input is multiplied by the values of the kernel and then a non-linear activation function is applied to the result. This way, the original input series is transformed into an interpretation of the input called the filter map. The next step of the CNN architecture is to apply a pooling layer (maximum or average), which reduces the size of the series, but-at the same time-preserves the identified characteristics.

Convolutional and pooling layers can be stacked on top of each other to provide multiple layers of abstraction (see popular CNN architectures such as **AlexNet**, **VGG-16**, **Inception**, and **ResNet50**). Alternatively, the results of the pooling layer can be passed to a fully connected (dense) layer.

Some of the benefits of using 1D CNN for time series forecasting include:

- 1D CNNs can be very effective for discovering features in fixed-length segments of the entire dataset (for example, predicting the next value based on past $n$ observations), mostly for cases in which it is not important where the feature is located within the segment.
- CNNs are able to extract informative features that are independent of the time component (translation invariant). The network can identify a pattern at one position in the series (for example, the beginning) and then locate it at another position (for example, at the end of the sequence) and use it to make a prediction of the target.
- The process of feature learning, in which the model learns the internal representation of the one (or higher) dimensional input, removes the need for domain knowledge for manual feature creation.
- 1D networks allow for larger filter sizes – in a 1D setting, a filter of size 4 contains 4 feature vectors, while in a 2D setting, the same filter contains 16 feature vectors, which is a much broader selection.
- CNNs are considered to be noise-resistant.
- 1D CNNs are computationally cheaper than RNNs and sometimes perform better.

In this recipe, we will learn how to train a CNN for one-step-ahead forecasting of stock prices.

# How to do it...

Execute the following steps to train a 1D CNN in PyTorch.

1. Import the libraries:

```
import yfinance as yf
import numpy as np
import os
import random

import torch
import torch.optim as optim
import torch.nn as nn
from torch.utils.data import (Dataset, TensorDataset,
                              DataLoader, Subset)
from collections import OrderedDict
from chapter_10_utils import create_input_data, custom_set_seed

from sklearn.metrics import mean_squared_error

device = 'cuda' if torch.cuda.is_available() else 'cpu'
```

2. Define the parameters:

```
# data
TICKER = 'INTL'
START_DATE = '2015-01-02'
END_DATE = '2019-12-31'
VALID_START = '2019-07-01'
N_LAGS = 12

# neural network
BATCH_SIZE = 5
N_EPOCHS = 2000
```

3. Download and prepare the data:

```
df = yf.download(TICKER,
                 start=START_DATE,
                 end=END_DATE,
                 progress=False)

df = df.resample('W-MON').last()
valid_size = df.loc[VALID_START:END_DATE].shape[0]
prices = df['Adj Close'].values
```

4. Transform the time series into input for the CNN:

```
X, y = create_input_data(prices, N_LAGS)
```

5. Obtain the naïve forecast:

```
naive_pred = prices[len(prices) - valid_size - 1:-1]
y_valid = prices[len(prices) - valid_size:]

naive_mse = mean_squared_error(y_valid, naive_pred)
naive_rmse = np.sqrt(naive_mse)
print(f"Naive forecast - MSE: {naive_mse:.2f}, RMSE:
{naive_rmse:.2f}")
```

Running the code produces the following output:

```
Naive forecast - MSE: 4.16, RMSE: 2.04
```

6. Prepare the `DataLoader` objects:

```
# set seed for reproducibility
custom_set_seed(42)

valid_ind = len(X) - valid_size

X_tensor = torch.from_numpy(X).float()
y_tensor = torch.from_numpy(y).float().unsqueeze(dim=1)

dataset = TensorDataset(X_tensor, y_tensor)

train_dataset = Subset(dataset, list(range(valid_ind)))
valid_dataset = Subset(dataset, list(range(valid_ind, len(X))))

train_loader = DataLoader(dataset=train_dataset,
                          batch_size=BATCH_SIZE)
valid_loader = DataLoader(dataset=valid_dataset,
                          batch_size=BATCH_SIZE)
```

7. Define the CNN's architecture:

```python
class Flatten(nn.Module):
    def forward(self, x):
        return x.view(x.size()[0], -1)

model = nn.Sequential(OrderedDict([
    ('conv_1', nn.Conv1d(1, 32, 3, padding=1)),
    ('max_pool_1', nn.MaxPool1d(2)),
    ('relu_1', nn.ReLU()),
    ('flatten', Flatten()),
    ('fc_1', nn.Linear(192, 50)),
    ('relu_2', nn.ReLU()),
    ('dropout_1', nn.Dropout(0.4)),
    ('fc_2', nn.Linear(50, 1))
]))

print(model)
```

Running the code produces the following output:

```
Sequential(
  (conv_1): Conv1d(1, 32, kernel_size=(3,), stride=(1,),
padding=(1,))
  (max_pool_1): MaxPool1d(kernel_size=2, stride=2, padding=0,
dilation=1, ceil_mode=False)
  (relu_1): ReLU()
  (flatten): Flatten()
  (fc_1): Linear(in_features=192, out_features=50, bias=True)
  (relu_2): ReLU()
  (dropout_1): Dropout(p=0.4, inplace=False)
  (fc_2): Linear(in_features=50, out_features=1, bias=True)
)
```

8. Instantiate the model, the loss function, and the optimizer:

```python
model = model.to(device)
loss_fn = nn.MSELoss()
optimizer = optim.Adam(model.parameters(), lr=0.001)
```

9. Train the network:

```python
PRINT_EVERY = 50
train_losses, valid_losses = [], []

for epoch in range(N_EPOCHS):
    running_loss_train = 0
    running_loss_valid = 0
```

```
        model.train()
        for x_batch, y_batch in train_loader:
            optimizer.zero_grad()
            x_batch = x_batch.to(device)
            x_batch = x_batch.view(x_batch.shape[0], 1, N_LAGS)
            y_batch = y_batch.to(device)
            y_batch = y_batch.view(y_batch.shape[0], 1, 1)
            y_hat = model(x_batch).view(y_batch.shape[0], 1, 1)
            loss = torch.sqrt(loss_fn(y_batch, y_hat))
            loss.backward()
            optimizer.step()
            running_loss_train += loss.item() * x_batch.size(0)
        epoch_loss_train = running_loss_train /
len(train_loader.dataset)
        train_losses.append(epoch_loss_train)

        with torch.no_grad():
            model.eval()
            for x_val, y_val in valid_loader:
                x_val = x_val.to(device)
                x_val = x_val.view(x_val.shape[0], 1, N_LAGS)
                y_val = y_val.to(device)
                y_val = y_val.view(y_val.shape[0], 1, 1)
                y_hat = model(x_val).view(y_val.shape[0], 1, 1)
                loss = torch.sqrt(loss_fn(y_val, y_hat))
                running_loss_valid += loss.item() * x_val.size(0)
            epoch_loss_valid = running_loss_valid /
len(valid_loader.dataset)
            if epoch > 0 and epoch_loss_valid < min(valid_losses):
                best_epoch = epoch
                torch.save(model.state_dict(), './cnn_checkpoint.pth')
            valid_losses.append(epoch_loss_valid)

    if epoch % PRINT_EVERY == 0:
        print(f"<{epoch}> - Train. loss: {epoch_loss_train:.6f} \t
Valid. loss: {epoch_loss_valid:.6f}")
print(f'Lowest loss recorded in epoch: {best_epoch}')
```

10. Plot the losses over epochs:

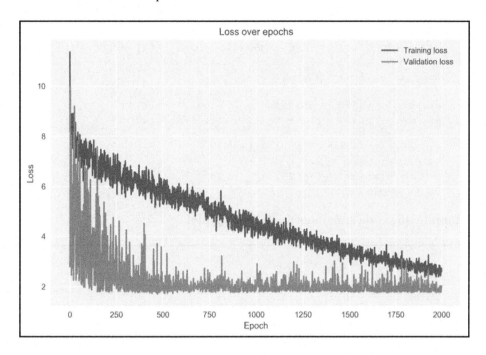

As the code is identical to the one in step 11 of the previous recipe, *Multilayer perceptrons for time series forecasting,* we are only presenting the resulting plot.

11. Load the best model (with the lowest validation loss):

```
state_dict = torch.load('cnn_checkpoint.pth')
model.load_state_dict(state_dict)
```

12. Obtain the predictions:

```
y_pred, y_valid = [], []

with torch.no_grad():
    model.eval()
    for x_val, y_val in valid_loader:
        x_val = x_val.to(device)
        x_val = x_val.view(x_val.shape[0], 1, N_LAGS)
        y_pred.append(model(x_val))
        y_valid.append(y_val)
y_pred = torch.cat(y_pred).numpy().flatten()
y_valid = torch.cat(y_valid).numpy().flatten()
```

13. Evaluate the predictions:

```
cnn_mse = mean_squared_error(y_valid, y_pred)
cnn_rmse = np.sqrt(cnn_mse)
print(f"CNN's forecast - MSE: {cnn_mse:.2f}, RMSE: {cnn_rmse:.2f}")

fig, ax = plt.subplots()

ax.plot(y_valid, color='blue', label='Actual')
ax.plot(y_pred, color='red', label='Prediction')

ax.set(title="CNN's Forecasts",
       xlabel='Time',
       ylabel='Price ($)')
ax.legend()
```

Running the code generates the following plot:

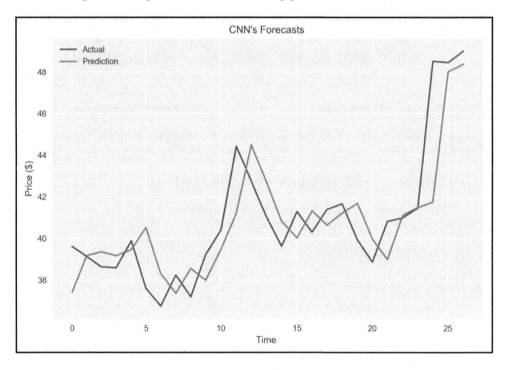

The performance is summarized as follows:

```
CNN's forecast - MSE: 3.58, RMSE: 1.89
```

The simple CNN was able to beat the naïve benchmark on the validation set.

# How it works...

In the first two steps, we imported the required libraries and defined the parameters responsible for loading the data and some of the settings of the neural network, such as the batch size and the number of epochs.

In *Step 3*, we downloaded the data. For this recipe, we resampled Intel's adjusted close prices (years 2015-2019) to weekly frequency by taking each period's last observed value. For resampling, we used the `'W-MON'` argument as the desired frequency. That is because using `'W'` would result in the data indices being created from the last day of the period. As we used the slice of the DataFrame to determine the size of the validation set, we had to make sure that the indices correspond to the first days of the weeks (otherwise, the last week would have a date somewhere in January, which would result in incorrect slicing by dates). For a complete list of allowable frequencies, please refer to the link in the *See also* section. Then, we used the custom function, `create_input_data`, introduced in the previous recipe to transform the time series into the input for the CNN. For this problem, we used 12 past observations (roughly 3 months' worth of data) to predict the next week's close price.

In *Step 5*, we calculated the naïve forecast for the next period as the last known observation. We consider a CNN skillful when it is able to outperform the benchmark. Analogous to the previous recipe, we evaluated the benchmark using the MSE and the RMSE. For the evaluation period, we took the second half of 2019, covering 27 weeks.

In *Step 6*, we prepared the training and validation `DataLoader` objects. For more details on this step, please refer to the *How it works...* section in the previous recipe. The training set contains 222 observations, while the validation set has 27 (weekly observations for the second half of 2019). Also, in this step, we used the custom function for defining the random seed to make the results as reproducible as possible.

In *Step 7*, we defined the CNN's architecture. This time, we defined the network using `nn.Sequential`, together with an `OrderedDict` object. We started with the 1D convolutional layer (`nn.Conv1d`). As input, it takes a 3D tensor, where the dimensions correspond to `[number of batches, channels, length of series]`. As the arguments of `nn.Conv1d`, we provided the number of input channels, the number of output channels, and the size of the kernel. Additionally, we specified `padding = 1`, thanks to which the convolutional layer does not reduce the size of the input series.

While defining the convolutional layers using `nn.Conv1d`, we can specify the padding argument. Padding adds extra elements at the beginning and end of the series, most commonly zeros, so that the convolutional later does not reduce the dimension of the output series. This type of padding is known as "zero" or "same" padding. In terms of images, padding adds an extra frame around the image and, by specifying this argument, we determine the width of the frame in pixels.

Then, we applied the max pooling layer with the kernel size of 2. In our network, only the pooling reduces the length of the series. The next step was to apply the activation function, in this case, ReLU.

In this particular example, running max pooling + ReLU and ReLU + max pooling results in the same output; however, the former sequence is computationally more efficient (by ~38%).

The next element of the architecture is a custom class called `Flatten`. With a network defined using `nn.Module`, we would have applied the `view` method of a tensor. However, while working with `nn.Sequential`, we need to use classes, so we defined a custom class inheriting from `nn.Module`. What follows are two fully connected layers and a dropout layer after the first dense layer.

When defining CNNs, it is common to include a batch normalization layer after the convolutional layer. We can use `nn.BatchNorm1d` for that.

As the operations on the tensors can be quite tricky to understand, we go over all the layers and specify what is the input and output of each layer using our example. The layers are as follows:

- `conv_1`—input: [5, 1, 12], output: [5, 32, 12]
- `max_pool_1`—input: [5, 32, 12], output: [5, 32, 6]
- `relu_1`—no change
- `flatten`—input: [5, 32, 6], output: [5, 192]
- `fc_1`—input: [5, 192], output: [5, 50]
- `relu_2`—no change
- `dropout_1`—no change
- `fc_2`—input: [5, 50], output: [5, 1]

Here, the first dimension (equal to 5) is the batch size.

Use PyTorch's documentation for tips regarding how to calculate the output of different layers.

In *Step 8*, we instantiated the model, selected the MSE as the loss function, and set up the the Adam optimizer.

In *Step 9*, we trained the network. The general outline of the training loop is very similar to the one used in the previous recipe, so we only describe the novelties. Refer to the *How it works...* section of the previous recipe for a more detailed description. Within the training loop, we had to reshape the features/targets coming from the `DataLoader` objects. That is because `nn.Conv1d` expects a 3-dimensional input, with the dimensions being [number of batches, channels, length of series]. Alternatively, we could have defined a custom `Dataset/DataLoader`, which would return the inputs of the correct size. For this recipe, we actually used the RMSE as the loss function. To achieve this, we took the square root of the loss function using `torch.sqrt`.

In *Step 10*, we plotted the training and validation losses. We observed that the losses, especially the validation ones, were generally decreasing, however, they exhibited very erratic behavior. There are a few potential reasons and solutions for that:

- There might not be enough data points in the validation set. We are working with a very small dataset (as evaluated by the deep learning standards), so this might very well be the case.
- The learning rate can be too high, which makes the optimization algorithm overshoot the local minima.
- No or incorrectly applied feature scaling. For simplicity, we have not transformed the input series and, by analyzing the plot of the price series (please refer to the corresponding Notebook), we see that over the years, the values covered the range of approximately $19 to $57.
- Insufficient regularization in the network.
- A random validation set, as in the case when the validation set is randomly sampled for evaluation (not our case), this might cause erratic behavior of the loss function.
- Too small a batch size, as the loss depends on the examples the model sees in each batch. We can also make the batch size larger for the validation only; for example, twice the size of the one used for training.

- The network's architecture might be too complex for the problem at hand. Even though accurately predicting stock prices might be an impossible task (at least in the long run), the selected time series is already a simplified version of the task and contains very few data points (for both training and validation).
- Lastly, we might want to experiment with the architecture and the parameters as well (please refer to the suggestions stated in the previous recipe).

Lastly, we loaded the best model (with the lowest validation loss) and evaluated the performance of the CNN using MSE and RMSE. The results indicate that the CNN achieved better performance on the validation set. However, it is worth mentioning that we should use a separate validation and test sets for such evaluation.

# There's more...

In this section, we would like to mention a few interesting and useful characteristics of CNNs.

**The stochastic aspect of training neural networks:** The inherent aspect of training neural networks is their **stochasticity** – there is a random component to it. That is why we should not judge the skill of the model based on a single evaluation. Given that the network is feasible to train multiple times, we can do so and aggregate the performance evaluation metrics. Alternatively, we can set the random seed (as we did in the recipes of this chapter), which guarantees (to a given extent) that training the same network multiple times will result in the same weights. In the previous recipe, we used `torch.manual_seed(42)` to make the results reproducible. When using more complex networks with more dependencies, it is safer to take extra precautions. That is why we defined a custom function that tries to make sure that – given it is possible – the results will be reproducible.

The function is defined as follows:

```
def custom_set_seed(seed):
    torch.manual_seed(seed)
    torch.cuda.manual_seed_all(seed)
    torch.backends.cudnn.deterministic = True
    torch.backends.cudnn.benchmark = False
    np.random.seed(seed)
    random.seed(seed)
    os.environ['PYTHONHASHSEED'] = str(seed)
```

Inside the function, we execute a series of operations, such as setting the seeds using multiple libraries and configuring some CUDA-related settings. However, there are cases when even such precautions do not help. As stated in the PyTorch documentation, there is currently no simple way to avoid non-determinism in some functions (certain forms of pooling, padding or sampling).

**Multi-headed models:** A popular approach to training more advanced CNNs is training a so-called multi-headed model. The underlying idea is to train different specifications of the convolutional parts of the network, concatenate them at the flattening stage, and feed the joined output to the fully connected layer(s).

The main benefit of using multi-headed models is the flexibility they provide, which (depending on the use case) can result in improved performance. We will illustrate them with an example. Imagine training a three-headed CNN network. Each head can apply a different number of kernels to the same input series. Additionally, the kernel size can be different. This way, each head extracts slightly different features from the input series and then uses all of them to make the ultimate prediction.

Alternatively, some heads can use a modified version of the input series. A possible example is applying some kind of smoothing to a volatile time series. Cui *et al.* (2016) present a potential architecture of a multi-headed model.

**Multivariate input:** In this recipe, we showed how to apply 1D CNN to a univariate time series. Naturally, it is possible to expand the architecture to a multivariate case, in which multiple univariate time series are used to predict the next value of a given series (it is also possible to predict the next value of multiple parallel series, but, for simplicity, we do not elaborate on that).

For a good understanding of using multivariate input for the CNNs, we start with 2D images, as this was the original application of the CNNs. A **grayscale** image can be represented as a matrix of numbers in the range of 0-255, where 0 represents black, 255 stands for white, and all the numbers in between are shades of gray. The common **RGB** representation of colored images consists of 3 components – red, green, and blue. In other words, we can represent any image using 3 matrices (of the same size), each one of them representing the intensity of a different RGB color.

That is why CNNs accept multi-channel input. A grayscale image has 1 channel, while a colored one has 3 channels. Using this approach, we can use the channels to store different time series used as features. We need to make sure that all of them are of the same size (same number of observations).

**Multi-output CNN:** Similar to the multilayer perceptron presented in the previous recipe, CNNs can also produce multi-step output. To do so, we need to appropriately define the last fully connected layer. Please refer to the *There's more* section of the previous recipe for more information.

**Combining CNNs with RNNs:** In the next recipe, we cover recurrent neural networks, which account for the time component in the time series and where the feature was located within the series. We have already mentioned that CNNs are translation invariant – they do not distinguish where the feature was located within the series, just that it was there. That is why CNNs and RNNs make a natural combination. CNNs offer the speed and feature-extracting capabilities, while RNNs cover the sensitivity of the network to the time component. A possible use case is when we consider series that are too long to be processed using RNNs (thousands of observations). We can use CNNs to downsample (shorten) the series by extracting the higher-level features and then feeding them as input to the RNN. This approach has been proven in the literature to perform better than using CNNs or RNNs alone.

# See also

Additional resources are available here:

- Cui, Z., Chen, W., and Chen, Y. (2016). *Multi-scale convolutional neural networks for time series classification.* arXiv preprint arXiv:1603.06995: https://arxiv.org/pdf/1603.06995.pdf
- Krizhevsky, A., Sutskever, I., and Hinton, G. E. (2012). *Imagenet classification with deep convolutional neural networks.* In *Advances in neural information processing systems (pp. 1097-1105):* http://papers.nips.cc/paper/4824-imagenet-classification-with-deep-convolutional-neural-networks.pdf
- LeCun, Y., Bottou, L., Bengio, Y., and Haffner, P. (1998). *Gradient-based learning applied to document recognition.* Proceedings of the IEEE, 86(11), 2278-2324: http://yann.lecun.com/exdb/publis/pdf/lecun-01a.pdf
- https://pandas.pydata.org/pandas-docs/stable/user_guide/timeseries.html#dateoffset-objects

# Recurrent neural networks for time series forecasting

**Recurrent Neural Networks (RNNs)** are a special type of neural network designed to work with sequential data. They are popular for time series forecasting as well as for solving NLP problems such as machine translation, text generation, and speech recognition. There are numerous extensions of the RNNs, such as **Long-Short Term Memory (LSTM)** networks and **Gated Recurrent Unit (GRU)** networks, which are currently part of some of the state-of-the-art architectures. However, it is good to be familiar with the original vanilla RNN. The following diagram presents the typical RNN schema:

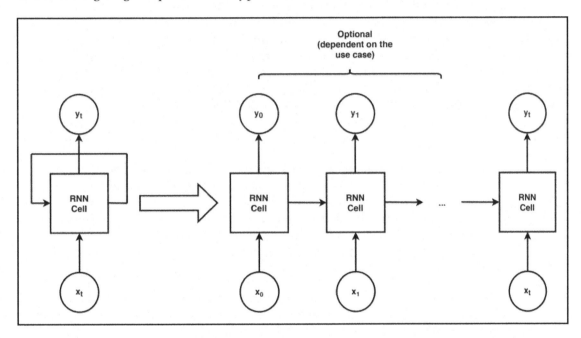

One of the main differences between the feedforward networks and RNNs is that the former take a fixed size input at once to produce a fixed size output. On the other hand, RNNs do not take all the input data at once – they ingest the data sequentially, one at a time. At each step, the network applies a series of calculations to produce the output, also known as the hidden state. Then, the hidden state is passed over and combined with the next input to create the following output. And so the algorithm continues until reaching the end of the input sequence. The hidden states can be described as memory in RNNs as they contain the context of the past inputs of the sequence. Summing up, the RNNs take into account the past observations in the sequence to model the future ones.

Another difference is that RNNs share the weights/parameters across all the time steps, as it is the same RNN cell that is doing all the calculations for each element of the sequence. In other words, only the input and the hidden state are unique at each time step. For training (reducing the loss) they use a variation of the backpropagation algorithm called **Backpropagation Through Time** (BPTT). The gradient of error at each time step is also dependent on the previous steps, so they need to be taken into account while updating the weights. In BPTT, the structure of the network is unrolled (as in the preceding diagram) by creating copies of neurons that have recurrent connections. By doing so, we can turn the cyclic graph of an RNN into an acyclic graph (such as the one of MLPs) and use the backpropagation algorithm.

Theoretically, RNNs have infinite memory. However, there are issues resulting from the backpropagation algorithm that make learning long-term dependencies pretty much impossible. As the gradient is also dependent on the previous steps, we can experience either the exploding or vanishing gradient. The **Exploding Gradient** occurs when the values of the gradient grow very large due to accumulation during the update. When this happens, the minimum of the optimization function is never reached and the model is unstable. This issue can be solved by applying gradient clipping (capping the value of the gradient to a predefined threshold). The **Vanishing Gradient** occurs when the values of the gradient become close to zero (also due to accumulation), which results in no (or very small) updates to the weights of the initial layers (as in the RNN's unrolled structure).

 The derivatives of the hyperbolic tangent (*tanh*) and sigmoid activation functions approach a flat line of 0 at both ends (called saturation regions). When this happens and the values of the gradient are close to (or equal) zero, they drive the gradients in the "further" layers toward zero as well, thus stopping the learning of the initial layers. This problem is not exclusive to RNNs, but it is frequently observed when dealing with long sequences.

That is why RNNs have trouble learning long-term dependencies from the input series. Some of the solutions include using ReLU activation functions (instead of *tanh* or sigmoid), or using more advanced networks such as LSTMs or GRUs.

# How to do it...

Execute the following steps to train an RNN for a time series prediction problem.

1. Import the libraries:

```
import yfinance as yf
import numpy as np
```

```
import torch
import torch.optim as optim
import torch.nn as nn
from torch.utils.data import (Dataset, TensorDataset,
                              DataLoader, Subset)
from chapter_10_utils import create_input_data, custom_set_seed

from sklearn.metrics import mean_squared_error
from sklearn.preprocessing import MinMaxScaler

device = 'cuda' if torch.cuda.is_available() else 'cpu'
```

2. Define the parameters:

```
# data
TICKER = 'INTL'
START_DATE = '2010-01-02'
END_DATE = '2019-12-31'
VALID_START = '2019-07-01'
N_LAGS = 12

# neural network
BATCH_SIZE = 16
N_EPOCHS = 100
```

3. Download and prepare the data:

```
df = yf.download(TICKER,
                 start=START_DATE,
                 end=END_DATE,
                 progress=False)

df = df.resample("W-MON").last()
valid_size = df.loc[VALID_START:END_DATE].shape[0]
prices = df['Adj Close'].values.reshape(-1, 1)
```

4. Scale the time series of prices:

```
valid_ind = len(prices) - valid_size

minmax = MinMaxScaler(feature_range=(0, 1))

prices_train = prices[:valid_ind]
prices_valid = prices[valid_ind:]

minmax.fit(prices_train)

prices_train = minmax.transform(prices_train)
```

```
prices_valid = minmax.transform(prices_valid)

prices_scaled = np.concatenate((prices_train,
                                prices_valid)).flatten()
```

5. Transform the time series into input for the RNN:

```
X, y = create_input_data(prices_scaled, N_LAGS)
```

6. Obtain the naïve forecast:

```
naive_pred = prices[len(prices)-valid_size-1:-1]
y_valid = prices[len(prices)-valid_size:]

naive_mse = mean_squared_error(y_valid, naive_pred)
naive_rmse = np.sqrt(naive_mse)
print(f"Naive forecast - MSE: {naive_mse:.4f}, RMSE:
{naive_rmse:.4f}")
```

The naïve forecast results in the following performance:

```
Naive forecast - MSE: 4.1568, RMSE: 2.0388
```

7. Prepare the `DataLoader` objects:

```
# set seed for reproducibility
custom_set_seed(42)

valid_ind = len(X) - valid_size

X_tensor = torch.from_numpy(X).float().reshape(X.shape[0],
                                               X.shape[1],
                                               1)
y_tensor = torch.from_numpy(y).float().reshape(X.shape[0], 1)

dataset = TensorDataset(X_tensor, y_tensor)

train_dataset = Subset(dataset, list(range(valid_ind)))
valid_dataset = Subset(dataset, list(range(valid_ind, len(X))))

train_loader = DataLoader(dataset=train_dataset,
                          batch_size=BATCH_SIZE,
                          shuffle=True)
valid_loader = DataLoader(dataset=valid_dataset,
                          batch_size=BATCH_SIZE)
```

8. Define the model:

```
class RNN(nn.Module):
    def __init__(self, input_size, hidden_size, n_layers,
output_size):
        super(RNN, self).__init__()
        self.rnn = nn.RNN(input_size, hidden_size,
                          n_layers, batch_first=True,
                          nonlinearity='relu')
        self.fc = nn.Linear(hidden_size, output_size)
    def forward(self, x):
        output, _ = self.rnn(x)
        output = self.fc(output[:,-1,:])
        return output
```

9. Instantiate the model, the loss function, and the optimizer:

```
model = RNN(input_size=1, hidden_size=6,
            n_layers=1, output_size=1).to(device)
loss_fn = nn.MSELoss()
optimizer = optim.Adam(model.parameters(), lr=0.001)
```

10. Train the network:

```
PRINT_EVERY = 10
train_losses, valid_losses = [], []

for epoch in range(N_EPOCHS):
    running_loss_train = 0
    running_loss_valid = 0

    model.train()
    for x_batch, y_batch in train_loader:
        optimizer.zero_grad()
        x_batch = x_batch.to(device)
        y_batch = y_batch.to(device)
        y_hat = model(x_batch)
        loss = torch.sqrt(loss_fn(y_batch, y_hat))
        loss.backward()
        optimizer.step()
        running_loss_train += loss.item() * x_batch.size(0)
    epoch_loss_train = running_loss_train /
len(train_loader.dataset)
    train_losses.append(epoch_loss_train)

    with torch.no_grad():
        model.eval()
        for x_val, y_val in valid_loader:
```

```
                    x_val = x_val.to(device)
                    y_val = y_val.to(device)
                    y_hat = model(x_val)
                    loss = torch.sqrt(loss_fn(y_val, y_hat))
                    running_loss_valid += loss.item() * x_val.size(0)
                epoch_loss_valid = running_loss_valid /
        len(valid_loader.dataset)
                if epoch > 0 and epoch_loss_valid < min(valid_losses):
                    best_epoch = epoch
                    torch.save(model.state_dict(), './rnn_checkpoint.pth')
                valid_losses.append(epoch_loss_valid)

        if epoch % PRINT_EVERY == 0:
            print(f"<{epoch}> - Train. loss: {epoch_loss_train:.4f} \t
        Valid. loss: {epoch_loss_valid:.4f}")
        print(f'Lowest loss recorded in epoch: {best_epoch}')
```

11. Plot the losses over epochs. This step is identical to the corresponding steps in the previous recipes, so we do not include the code for brevity. Running the code results in the following plot:

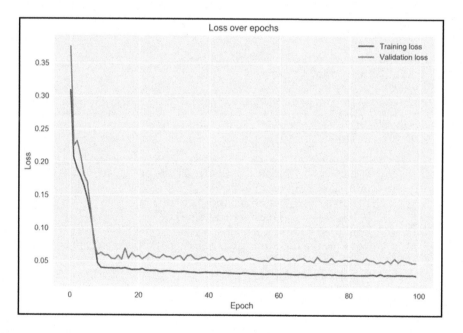

12. Load the best model (with the lowest validation loss):

```
state_dict = torch.load('rnn_checkpoint.pth')
model.load_state_dict(state_dict)
```

13. Obtain the predictions:

```
y_pred = []

with torch.no_grad():
    model.eval()
    for x_val, y_val in valid_loader:
        x_val = x_val.to(device)
        y_hat = model(x_val)
        y_pred.append(y_hat)
    y_pred = torch.cat(y_pred).numpy()
    y_pred = minmax.inverse_transform(y_pred).flatten()
```

14. Evaluate the predictions. This step is identical to the corresponding steps in the previous recipes, so we do not include the code for brevity. Running the code results in the following plot:

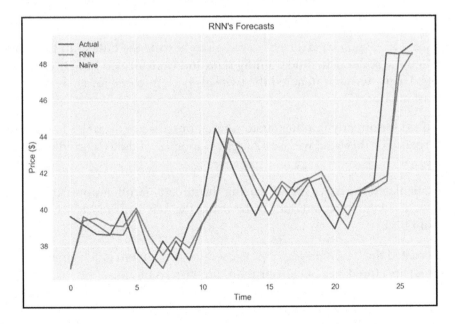

The RNN achieved the following performance on the validation set:

```
RNN's forecast — MSE: 4.0315, RMSE: 2.0079
```

We managed to beat the benchmark in terms of the considered performance evaluation metrics. However, the most probable case is that the model simply overfits to the data. For better diagnostics, we should use another, larger set purely for testing.

# How it works...

As this is the third recipe on training neural networks using PyTorch, many of the concepts are already familiar. That is why we focus on the new ones and refer to the previous two recipes for more details.

After loading the libraries, we defined a number of parameters for the data and training of the RNN. In *Step 3*, we downloaded stock prices of Intel from the years 2010-2019. We resampled to the weekly frequency by taking each week's last adjusted close price. For the validation set, we use the second half of 2019. We used index slicing with the selected dates to calculate the size of the validation set (27 weeks).

In *Step 4*, we used `MinMaxScaler` of `scikit-learn` to scale the data to fit the range of `[0,1]`. We fitted the scaler using the training data and transformed both training and validation sets. Lastly, we concatenated the two sets back into one array, as we will use it to create the input dataset.

In *Step 5*, we used the already familiar custom function, `create_input_data`, to create the inputs and targets. For this task, we use 12 lags (~3 months of data) to predict the next week's close price.

In *Step 6*, we calculated the naïve forecast using the already familiar approach. For the calculations, we used the unscaled data, as by using the naïve approach, we are not introducing any bias.

In *Step 7*, we created the `DataLoader` objects used for convenient batch generation. The inputs (features) are stored as a 3D tensor with dimensions of `[number of observations, length of the series, number of features]`. As we are using a univariate time series for forecasting future values, the number of features is 1. We allowed the training set to be shuffled, even though we are dealing with a time series task. The reason for this is that the sequence order we want to learn using the RNN is already captured within the lagged features. The training set contains 483 sequences of length 12.

In *Step 8*, we defined the RNN model. The approach is very similar to what we did in the previous recipes (defining a class inheriting from `nn.Module`). This time, we specified more arguments for the class:

- `input_size`: The expected number of features
- `hidden_size`: The number of neurons in the hidden state (and the RNN's output)
- `n_layers`: The number of RNN layers stacked on top of one another (default of 1)
- `output_size`: The size of the output; for our many-to-one case, it is 1

While defining the RNN part of the network, we indicated `batch_first=True`. This tells the network that the first argument of the input will be the batch size (the next ones will be the length of the series and the number of features). We also wanted to use the ReLU activation function instead of the default *tanh* (as a potential solution to the vanishing gradient problem; however, this should not be the case with such a short series). In our architecture, we passed the last time step's values of the RNN's output (we do not use the additional output, which is the hidden state) to a fully connected layer, which outputs the predicted value for the next element of the sequence.

While defining the architecture, we used the `nn.RNN` module instead of `nn.RNNCell`. The reason for this is that the former leads to easier modifications such as stacking multiple RNN cells. The same principles apply to LSTMs and GRUs.

We can manually initialize the hidden state in the class using `torch.zeros`. However, doing nothing results in automatic initialization with zeros.

Another possible solution to the vanishing gradient problem is **Truncated Backpropagation Through Time**. Without going into too much detail, we can detach the hidden state (using the `detach` method) while passing it to the RNN layer.

In *Step 9*, we instantiated the model (with 6 neurons in the hidden state, 1 RNN layer, 1 feature), optimizer, and the loss function (MSE; however, we actually used the RMSE as in the previous recipe). In *Step 10*, we trained the network.

The rest of the steps are analogous to the steps in the previous recipes. The only difference that must be mentioned is that the predictions obtained using the model are on a different scale than the stock prices. To convert them back to the original scale, we had to use the `inverse_transform` method of the previously defined `MinMaxScaler`.

# There's more...

In this section, we wanted to briefly mention some characteristics and extensions of the RNNs.

RNNs can be used for a variety of tasks. Here, we present the groups of models defined by the type of mapping they offer (together with an example of a use case):

- **one to one**: binary image classification
- **one to many**: creating a caption for an image
- **many to one**: classifying the sentiment of a sentence
- **many to many**: machine translation

Over the years, researches have come up with many new extensions/variants of the vanilla RNN model, each one overcoming some of the shortcomings of the original.

**Bidirectional RNNs** account for the fact that the time $t$ output might not only depend on the past observations in the sequence, but also on the future ones. Identifying a missing word in a sentence could serve as an example. To properly understand the context, we might want to look at both sides of the missing word.

**Long Short-Term Memory** (LSTM) networks were already mentioned as one of the possible solutions to the vanishing gradient problem. LSTMs' core is based on the cell state and various gates. We can think of the cell state as the memory of the network, which can transfer information even from the initial layers of a sequence to the final ones. Additionally, there are several gates that add and remove information from the cell state as it gets passed along the layers. The goal of the gates is to learn which kind of information is important to retain and what can be forgotten.

LSTMs contain the following gates:

- Forget gate: By using the sigmoid function, it decides what information should be kept (values of the sigmoid closer to 1) or forgotten (values closer to 0). The function is applied to the current input and the previous hidden state.
- Input gate: Decides which information from the past hidden state and the current input to save into the state cell.
- Output gate: Decides what the LSTM cell will output as the next hidden state. It uses the current input and the previous hidden state to filter the cell state in order to create the next hidden state. It can filter out short- and/or long-term memories from the cell state.

The forget and input gates govern what is removed and what is added to the cell state. Each LSTM cell outputs the hidden state and the cell state.

**Gated Recurrent Unit** (GRU) is a variation of the LSTM network. In comparison to the LSTMs, GRUs have two gates. The first one is the update gate, which is a combination of LSTM's forget and input gates. This gate determines how much information about the past to retain in the hidden state. The second gate is the reset gate, which decides how much information to forget. In the extreme case of setting all the values of the reset gate to ones and the values of the update gate to zeros, we would obtain the vanilla RNN. Another distinction between the two architectures is the fact that GRUs do not have the cell state; all the information is stored and passed through the cells using the hidden state.

Summing up, GRUs are simpler than the LSTMs, have fewer trainable parameters, and thus are faster to train. That does not mean that they offer worse performance.

Thanks to PyTorch, it is very easy to define the LSTM/GRU models. We must only replace the `nn.RNN` module in the class definition from this recipe with `nn.LSTM` or `nn.GRU`, as all of them share the same parameters (with the exception of `nonlinearity`, which can only be defined in the case of RNNs).

An additional concept that can come in handy when training RNNs is **teacher forcing**, commonly used in language models. At a very high level, while training at time *t*, the network receives the actual (or expected) time *t-1* output as input instead of the output predicted by the network (which can potentially be incorrect).

# See also

Additional resources are available here:

- Chen, G. (2016). *A gentle tutorial of recurrent neural network with error backpropagation.* arXiv preprint arXiv:1610.02583: `https://arxiv.org/pdf/1610.02583.pdf`
- Cho, K., Van Merriënboer, B., Gulcehre, C., Bahdanau, D., Bougares, F., Schwenk, H., and Bengio, Y. (2014). *Learning phrase representations using RNN encoder-decoder for statistical machine translation.* arXiv preprint arXiv:1406.1078: `https://arxiv.org/pdf/1406.1078v3.pdf`

- Chung, J., Gulcehre, C., Cho, K., and Bengio, Y. (2014). *Empirical evaluation of gated recurrent neural networks on sequence modeling.* arXiv preprint arXiv:1412.3555: https://arxiv.org/pdf/1412.3555.pdf

- Hochreiter, S., and Schmidhuber, J. (1997). *Long short-term memory. Neural computation,* 9(8), 1735-1780: http://www.bioinf.jku.at/publications/older/2604.pdf

- Pascanu, R., Mikolov, T., and Bengio, Y. (2013, February). *On the difficulty of training recurrent neural networks.* In *International conference on machine learning* (pp. 1310-1318): https://arxiv.org/pdf/1211.5063v2.pdf

- http://karpathy.github.io/2015/05/21/rnn-effectiveness/

- http://colah.github.io/posts/2015-08-Understanding-LSTMs/

# Other Books You May Enjoy

If you enjoyed this book, you may be interested in these other books by Packt:

**Hands-On Python for Finance**

Krish Naik

ISBN: 978-1-78934-637-4

- Clean financial data with data preprocessing
- Visualize financial data using histograms, color plots, and graphs
- Perform time series analysis with pandas for forecasting
- Estimate covariance and the correlation between securities and stocks
- Optimize your portfolio to understand risks when there is a possibility of higher returns
- Calculate expected returns of a stock to measure the performance of a portfolio manager
- Create a prediction model using recurrent neural networks (RNN) with Keras and TensorFlow

## Mastering Python for Finance - Second Edition
James Ma Weiming

ISBN: 978-1-78934-646-6

- Solve linear and nonlinear models representing various financial problems
- Perform principal component analysis on the DOW index and its components
- Analyze, predict, and forecast stationary and non-stationary time series processes
- Create an event-driven backtesting tool and measure your strategies
- Build a high-frequency algorithmic trading platform with Python
- Replicate the CBOT VIX index with SPX options for studying VIX-based strategies
- Perform regression-based and classification-based machine learning tasks for prediction
- Use TensorFlow and Keras in deep learning neural network architecture

# Leave a review - let other readers know what you think

Please share your thoughts on this book with others by leaving a review on the site that you bought it from. If you purchased the book from Amazon, please leave us an honest review on this book's Amazon page. This is vital so that other potential readers can see and use your unbiased opinion to make purchasing decisions, we can understand what our customers think about our products, and our authors can see your feedback on the title that they have worked with Packt to create. It will only take a few minutes of your time, but is valuable to other potential customers, our authors, and Packt. Thank you!

# Index